WARSHIP
LOSSES
OF WORLD WAR TWO

Brief Biography

David Brown served as a naval aviator before joining the Naval Historical Branch in 1969. Head of the Branch since 1977, his published works include books on aviation and general 20th century naval history.

Parameters

The purpose of this book is to list and account for the loss, whether by enemy action or accident, of all ocean-going purpose-built warships of all navies, combatant and neutral, between August 1939 and September 1945. The only conscious excursions from this principle are the inclusion of merchant ships employed as auxiliary cruisers (for example, the British Armed Merchant Cruisers and the German disguised raiders) and the exclusion of armed trawlers, even though many of these were purpose-built small fighting ships.

'Loss' has been extended to include ships which were sunk in shallow water, salvaged and returned to service, and also to those which were not sunk but were 'damaged beyond economical repair' and were therefore lost to the service of their respective navies. Scuttling and capture in harbour resulted in ships changing hands and subsequent loss, usually under a different name – both occasions are listed.

The intention is that a companion volume on submarine losses will be completed in due course. This has been delayed beyond expectation by the scale of work involved, in particular in the re-analysis of German U-boat losses, over 25 per cent of which have so far proved to be incorrectly attributed.

WARSHIP LOSSES

OF WORLD WAR TWO

DAVID BROWN

NAVAL INSTITUTE PRESS
Annapolis, Maryland

First published in Great Britain in 1990 by Arms and Armour Press, Wellington House, 125 Strand, London WC2R 0BB.

First paperback edition 1995

Library of Congress Catalog Card Number 94-73841
ISBN 1-55750-914-X

Published and distributed in the United States of America and Canada by the Naval Institute Press, 118 Maryland Avenue, Annapolis, Maryland 21402-5035.

This edition is authorized for sale only in the United States, its territories and possessions, and Canada.

Cover illustration: HMS *Bickerton* seen minutes after she was hit by a 'Gnat' homing torpedo fired by the German submarine *U.354* off the North Cape early on 22 August 1944. (via the late Captain D. G. F. W. Macintyre)

Designed and edited by DAG Publications Ltd. Designed by David Gibbons; edited by David Dorrell; typeset by RGM Typesetting, Southport, Lancs; camerawork by M&E Reproductions, North Fambridge, Essex.

Printed and bound in Great Britain.

Contents

Introduction

More warships were sunk during the Second World War than had been lost in all the great battles and minor actions during the four centuries when the world's navies depended on forests for construction and the wind for propulsion. However, in the days of sail few ships were actually sunk. This was not because, as early opponents of the iron ship alleged, wood floats and wooden ships stay afloat – they do not, if sufficiently damaged. What had been lacking were ship-sinking weapons: by 1939, they were available in abundance and six years of war were to hone their lethality.

The gun had been adopted as the only stand-off naval weapon as early as the fifteenth century, displacing the mechanical 'engines' which had preceded it and eclipsing the oar-driven ram. By the end of the sixteenth century the gun had been developed as an effective means of dismasting ships and killing their crews; but there it rested, for although the number of guns, firing heavier projectiles, steadily increased, the solid shot which they fired could not cause the underwater damage needed to let in sufficient water to sink ships. Heavy casualties and dismasting usually resulted in surrender before an accumulation of hull damage caused the structure to fail catastrophically. Realism also saved ships – a small ship faced by a heavier weight of metal would often surrender after only token resistance 'for the honour of the flag'.

Almost as important as the inability to sink ships was the positive wish to capture them, to augment one's own fleet while reducing the other side's. The British system of Prize Money – large sums of money shared between participants in a capture – certainly encouraged individuals to even greater effort, particularly as they knew that they had 'insurance cover' should they be unfortunate enough to sink their opponent, 'head money' being paid on the basis of the size of the enemy's crew.

In open sea engagements between ships of the line, the most common form of outright destruction was fire and explosion, invariably accompanied by heavy casualties: the loss of *L'Orient* at the Battle of the Nile in 1798 cost over 1,000 lives. Even this was eclipsed three years later when two Spanish First-Rates blew up during an action off Cadiz, with the loss of 2,600 men.

The circumstances of blockade warfare, with the stronger navies pinning their enemies against their own coasts and harbours, brought a different form of total loss, that of grounding or wreck through stress of weather or inadequacy of charts. Between 1793 and 1801, during the French Revolutionary War, 295 French, Spanish, Dutch and Danish ships of the line and frigates were 'lost' in action, but only eleven of these sank or blew up and ten more were chased ashore; smaller vessels suffered even fewer outright losses, just twelve being destroyed out of 275 involved.

The Royal Navy suffered a greater number of ships totally lost, but out of 64 major warships and 63 minor vessels only one small sloop was sunk in action (and she took her bigger assailant with her in the final explosion). More than half of the other 126 foundered or were wrecked in the continuous and demanding year-round exercise of naval supremacy, in mid-ocean, in the narrow seas and on blockade patrols close off the enemy coasts; a few were lost to accidental fire and explosion. Fifty-eight ships – eighteen ships of the line and frigates and 40 sloops and brigs – were taken by the enemy and of these nineteen were retaken before the end of the French wars, in 1814.

The Arrival of Naval Technology

A century elapsed between the end of this world war and the outbreak of the next – inaccurately named 'The First'. During that century new navies came into being, either through the birth of new nations, such as Germany and Italy, or the revitalization of the old empires, such as Japan and Austria-Hungary. Two of the older navies which had in their day been supreme – those of Spain and the Netherlands – declined to the point at which they could no longer influence maritime affairs, while two of the minor navies of 1814 expanded as Russia and the United States came to realize the value of sea power. The Royal Navy remained the most powerful and provided an example of the dependence of the state upon mastery of the sea, protecting trade and the overseas empire from a network of bases which, by the end of the long world peace, dominated every major ocean turning point and cross-roads. France, too, retained a powerful fleet to support her overseas colonies, as well as to defend her shores in a European war: she may have continued to regard Britain as the ancient enemy to watch (and the suspicion was mutual) but from 1827, when the two fought in the same action, it was always on the same side.

No preceding century saw such technological change, in methods of propulsion, constructional materials and techniques, and in weapons. Steam power began to supplement sail on a significant scale in the 1830s and was general (and reliable) by the late 1850s, when the major navies realized that wooden hulls would have to give way to iron. It had long been accepted that construction would be much simplified and that more durable and much larger vessels could be built if traditional plank and beam were replaced by industrial plate and girder, but the latter had to await mass-production fabrication capability and then had to prove itself against the diehard supporters of the wooden ship.

The incendiary effects on wooden ships of explosive shells fired by coastal batteries had long been known, but at the Battle of Sinope, in 1853, the Russian Navy made a significant advance by firing shells from ships' guns, instead of solid shot, to destroy a Turkish squadron. In the misnamed (again) Crimean War which ensued the Russians could not face the Anglo-French fleet at sea and withdrew their ships into fortified dockyards. The allies suffered considerable damage in their early attempts to bombard these from the sea and it was this experience that led directly to the development of armoured 'ironclad' ships capable of standing up to shell-fire.

For their part, unable to contend at sea with France and Britain, the Russians devised a new weapon to push the blockaders beyond gun range of the forts.

Moored underwater mines were first laid in the Gulf of Finland, where they were viewed with cautious curiosity by the blockading fleet; although they were ineffective and failed to drive off the inshore patrols, the significance of a practical weapon which could sink ships by causing severe underwater damage was not lost upon the maritime world.

Confirmation of the potential of the mine came in 1862, during the American Civil War, when it claimed its first victim. The same conflict also saw the first successful attempt to overcome the inherent disadvantage of the mine – its immobility. The Confederate 'submersible' was only barely mobile and, carrying an explosive charge on a fixed spar, it was virtually a suicide weapon, but it did manage to reach and sink a blockading frigate. The *Hunley* is commonly regarded as a step in submarine development, but it was in reality the first working torpedo.

Technology and industrial capability – specifically improvements in metallurgy and fine machining – had by now made sufficient advances to permit the construction of an independent, self-propelled torpedo. Robert Whitehead's first primitive but practical 'fish' was demonstrated in 1866 and was gradually taken up and developed by all the major navies.

The introduction of effective underwater weapons gave rise in the 1880s in France to a new school of strategic thought which advocated the cheap and fast torpedo-boat as the ideal counter to the expensive armoured battleship. Incapable of long-range operations in open waters, in coastal waters the torpedo-boat could repel amphibious assaults or break a blockade, to clear the way for fast cruisers which were intended to embark on the traditional raiding campaign against the enemy's trade; used offensively in its own right, the torpedo-boat could cripple the enemy in his harbours.

France's traditional enemy, the Royal Navy – subject during the second half of the nineteenth century to periodical 'French Scares' – had little to fear from the cruiser threat. British strength and dispositions, linked by a network of telegraphic communications which spread across the world during the 1870s and 1880s, ensured that not only could its own trade be adequately defended but that any potential enemy's trade would rapidly be brought to a standstill. The torpedo-boat threat was not so readily dealt with, but in 1893, after several promising solutions had proved to lead to blind alleys, the innovative genius of Admiral John Fisher thought up the 'torpedo-boat destroyer'. With a speed at least as high as its prey's but with a heavier gun armament, as well as torpedoes with which it could attack the enemy battle fleet, the destroyer's larger size gave it superior sea-keeping characteristics, although another decade was to elapse before the 'destroyer' became an ocean-going ship.

The gun developed almost out of recognition during the last forty years of the 19th century, growing in size and destructive effect. The short cast-iron muzzle-loading tube mounted on a wheeled truck restrained by ropes was developed into a 40-foot built-up barrel with a rifled bore and elaborate breech-loading mechanism, whose considerable recoil was contained by a hydraulic system. The largest guns, mounted in battleships, were carried in armoured gunhouses, to protect the crews and ammunition, and these became more elaborate, with the below-decks handling arrangements and machinery being incorporated into a rotating armoured structure which extended deep into the hull. The projectiles had evolved from round shot into finely machined hollow cylinders, filled with high explosive and propelled by nitro-cellulose charges which gave greater and more consistent ranges than had been possible with gunpowder. Gun range had increased from hundreds to thousands of yards – only the lack of accurate ranging and sighting equipment prevented accurate firing at tens of thousands of yards.

Twentieth Century War

The new weapons and warship types were first used on a major scale by one of the 'new' navies. The renaissance of the Imperial Japanese Navy dated back only to 1869, but it expanded rapidly, coached by the Royal Navy, which provided instructors and advisers. Although the basic principles of maritime operations were founded on British strategic experience and technical development, the Japanese were not averse to borrowing the ideas of the French 'Jeune École', particularly in the employment of torpedo-boats, and to these they added their own natural bent for tactical innovation. Thus, in 1894, the Japanese Fleet was able to defeat a superior Chinese fleet in the Yellow Sea, using long-range gunnery, following this up with a blockade of the enemy's main base; as the Chinese would not come out to fight, torpedo-boats were sent in to deliver successful night attacks.

This strategy was modified for the short but violent Russo-Japanese War which was fought in the Far East between February 1904 and September 1905. The Imperial Japanese Navy, barely equal in force to the Russian 'Pacific Squadron', began with a night surprise attack on the fortified Russian base at Port Arthur, but this only temporarily reduced the odds, for the destroyers' torpedoes failed to sink any of the three battleships hit. The Japanese then conducted an aggressive close blockade of Port Arthur, to contain the Russian main force and protect the passage of the Japanese Army to Manchuria via Korea.

The Russian squadron responded with tactical minelaying in the Yellow Sea and 'cruiser warfare' in the Sea of Japan, to the east of Korea. The Japanese blockading forces sustained significant losses to the mines but never relaxed their grip. The double-edged nature of the mine, which did not discriminate between friend and foe, was also shown when the talented Russian admiral was lost with his flagship in one of his own minefields.

The Russian Port Arthur squadron made one half-hearted attempt to escape to Vladivostok in August 1904 but was turned back. The Vladivostok cruiser squadron, which had enjoyed some success in attacks on Japanese merchant shipping and Army transports, sailed in support of the break-out only to be driven back by the more powerful Japanese cruiser force. With these actions the Japanese gained a total maritime supremacy which was not to be challenged for a further nine months.

The challenge came in May 1905 when the Russian European fleet, despatched in October 1904, attempted to fight its way through to Vladivostok. Its presence was strategically irrelevant, for Port Arthur had fallen five months earlier, the blockaded battleships had been eliminated by Japanese Army artillery, and the Russian admiral had no advantages – material, morale or tactical over his opposite number. The Battle of Tsu-Shima, fought in the straits between Japan and Korea on 27 and 28 May 1905, was only the second overwhelmingly decisive strategic action ever fought by opposing armoured battleship fleets – it was also the last. Japanese gunfire and destroyer torpedo attacks sank six battleships, a coast defence ship, five cruisers and five destroyers, for the loss of three torpedo-boats. Three ships escaped the catastrophe and reached Vladivostok.

A century had elapsed between the Battles of Trafalgar and Tsu-Shima. Nelson's victory had marked the apotheosis of sailing warfare, in which success was ultimately measured by the number and size of ships of the line which changed hands – just one ship had sunk on 21 October 1805, a victim of fire and explosion, and seventeen had been taken. Admiral Togo's shells and torpedoes were intended to destroy enemy ships: Tsu-Shima confirmed that the nature of naval battles had been irreversibly changed. There was one dying echo of the old era – for the last time in the history of naval warfare, ships of the line of a beaten fleet surrendered on the high seas.

The nine years which followed Tsu-Shima witnessed evolution accelerated by the hot-house atmosphere of a European naval arms race. First, the Royal Navy, spurred by Admiral Fisher, introduced a new type of capital ship – the 'dreadnought' – which rendered all its predecessors obsolete by virtue of its concentration of heavy guns, high speed and scale of protection. Improvements in the control of gunfire extended the probability of scoring hits on moving targets at ranges out to the visible horizon. In the hands of the French, German and British navies, the submarine achieved a degree of maturity which permitted its use beyond coastal waters, against warships or merchant ships. The potential of the third major invention was only barely glimpsed prior to the outbreak of war in August 1914, but the visionaries were not alone in prophesying an important future for aircraft.

The new world war began much as the last had ended, with the Royal Navy unchallengeable in its full strength and obliged to assert its supremacy by blockade until its opponent should come out to do battle. Mines and submarines prohibited surface ships from maintaining a close watch on even the few bases which the German Navy possessed on its North Sea coastline, and the Allied strategy soon became one of watching and waiting. A system of patrols by cruisers and smaller vessels was established to close the northern and southern exits from the North Sea to enemy raiding cruisers and blockade-runners, while the full battleship strength of the Grand Fleet was poised at Scapa Flow, ready to descend on any German fleet sortie.

Minefields were laid in the North Sea by both sides to protect coasts and harbours and to provide a barrier behind which friendly ships could go about their occasions, or to attempt to deny surface ships and submarines access to certain sea areas; the Baltic approaches were rendered impassable to the Allies, while the Northern and Dover Barrages were intended to restrict German access to the open Atlantic. Offensively, mines were laid by fast surface ships and, increasingly, by submarines, to interdict known movements or simply to obstruct the enemy's safe routes; usually discovered only as the result of an unexpected loss, clearance of these fields required a considerable effort on the part of the defenders. It was inevitable that there should be numerous victims of such a form of warfare, with merchant ships and warships becoming casualties of mines, 'friendly' as well as 'hostile', through errors of navigation or ignorance of new-laid fields.

Deadly as the mine was, it could nevertheless be countered in home waters by intensive sweeping and accurate marking of safe channels. Minesweeping, which had been regarded as a task for converted trawlers, whose crews were accustomed to dragging up submerged objects, became more sophisticated, with specialized sweep gear being used by large classes of purpose-built vessels of increasing size. Sweeping speeds increased, but insufficiently to provide protection; for the fleet, faster ships were fitted with a novel self-defence measure – wires which were attached to the forefoot of the ship and drawn outwards by floats (paravanes) to cut a narrow swathe through a minefield. Moored buoyant mines, actuated by direct contact with ships, were used by all combatants, but towards the end of the war the Royal Navy introduced a ground mine, laid in shallow water, which was exploded by the magnetic field of a ship passing within range of its sensor.

Submarines soon became the most feared weapon in the German Navy's armoury, although they were frequently assisted by the lack of basic commonsense displayed by some Royal Navy commanders, even after the first U-boat success, on 5 September 1914, off the Scottish coast. Only seventeen days later, three large armoured cruisers were sunk in the space of an hour by a single U-boat, and in October another cruiser and the Royal Navy's first seaplane-carrier (a converted cruiser) were lost to torpedoes. Speed and random zig-zag patterns were the only effective counters to surprise attack up to the end of the war; the first warning of the presence of a submarine was usually the sighting of a submarine wake too close to avoid. Once its presence had been revealed or detected, however, the U-boat seldom had opportunity for a second attack, for it lacked the submerged speed to outmanoeuvre any alerted and undamaged surface vessel.

Whatever the significance of the new weapons, the gun remained the arbiter in virtually every clash at sea. Ill-protected British ships suffered reverses in duels with apparently lightly armed but more accurate opponents, suffering loss and damage when cordite propellant caught fire*. But both sides recognized that in a running fight between near-equals, a huge expenditure of ammunition was usually needed to sink ships.

This was borne out in the first capital ship action of the war, on 24 January 1915, in the North Sea. It was not sought by the German Navy, whose battlecruisers had sortied to attack the British fishing fleet and patrols off the Dogger Bank, and the squadron was surprised by the British Battlecruiser Force. The engagement became a long-range gunnery duel and indifferent British communications permitted the German ships to escape with the loss of a single large armoured cruiser and a number of useful lessons about damage control and magazine safety arrangements.

After this first skirmish, the two fleets did not meet again until 31 May 1916, when British naval intelligence, reading the German cyphers, contributed to bringing the enemy to action. The Battle of Jutland was simultaneously the largest and last capital ship engagement fought for 'pure' naval supremacy, without any local influences such as the defence of a convoy or an amphibious beach-head. Jutland was fought in three main phases: the battlecruiser actions,

---

*Cordite fires also led to the accidental loss in harbour of three major British units.

in which the British ships suffered catastrophically, losing three battlecruisers and two armoured cruisers to superior German gunnery and their own inherent defects, material and tactical; the battleship action, in which the much superior British gunnery was prevented from inflicting a crushing defeat by undue caution in the face of a threatened destroyer torpedo attack; and, during the night of 31 May/1 June, the confused withdrawal action, during which Royal Navy destroyers' torpedo attacks inflicted a few casualties on the retreating enemy but the battle line lost touch with the battered German fleet. The latter claimed a victory but never again came out in force sufficient to challenge the Grand Fleet.

Personnel losses in the open sea battles were very high. Off Coronel and the Falklands in 1914, more than 3,500 German and British sailors had perished aboard the six cruisers sunk, only one of which had blown up. At Jutland, the five British major ships which were lost blew up under shellfire which either penetrated their magazines directly or caused fires which reached them via the inadequately protected ammunition supply route. Of the 5,096 officers and men of their ships' companies, only 27, all from the battlecruisers, survived. Nine other ships – a third armoured cruiser and eight destroyers – were sunk, with the loss of 1,001 men. All but one of these ships were disabled by gunfire (two were finished off by torpedoes when dead in the water), the ninth being the victim of two collisions.

Outside the North Sea, the most important offensive Allied naval campaign took place in the waters around the Gallipoli peninsula, in 1915 and 1916. Supporting an amphibious landing which came to a premature halt almost within sight of the beaches, French and British pre-dreadnought battleships suffered heavy casualties, not to Turkish coast defence batteries but to mines and torpedoes, six ships being lost in two months in the spring of 1915. This new feature, of naval losses associated with a slow-moving land campaign, was to be repeated in the 1939–45 war.

Shipboard naval aviation scored its first significant offensive success in this campaign: in August 1915 a Royal Navy floatplane, operating from a seaplane-carrier, delivered the first successful airborne torpedo attack. A month later, the first air bombing success was obtained by an Austrian Navy flying-boat, the victim being a French submarine.

In the Adriatic, the Italian and Austro-Hungarian navies fought a 'private war' which was unusual in that both sides espoused a Fleet-in-being strategy and therefore resorted to unconventional tactics to inflict attrition. The Austrians enjoyed the earliest successes, in 1916, destroying a pre-dreadnought and then a dreadnought in harbour by sabotage. Towards the end of 1917 the Italian Navy used motor torpedo-boats – small, high-speed craft which were also in Royal Navy service – to sink an Austrian pre-dreadnought off Trieste. Six months later, off Pola, the MTBs sank the dreadnought *Szent István*, the only modern battleship to be sunk by torpedo during the war. Finally, on 1 November 1918, Italian swimmers succeeded in entering Pola harbour and fixing charges which sank another dreadnought – a feat which was to be repeated 23 years later, against an erstwhile ally.

Lessons and Limitations
Wartime experience of the damage inflicted by shell, torpedo and mine was analyzed by the navies of the major powers (except the newly born Soviet Union)

and incorporated in new designs. In practice, most were still-born, for in 1922 Great Britain, the United States, Japan and Italy signed the 'Washington Treaty of Naval Limitations', the first effective arms-limitation treaty intended to check the growth of strategic weapons. Total tonnage restrictions were imposed, the displacement of individual capital ships and cruisers was limited, as was the calibre of their main armament, and, in the case of capital ships, a ceiling was placed on the weight of armour protection.

Wholesale scrapping of ships and the abandonment of programmes followed the ratification of the Treaty. Britain had to discard 22 dreadnoughts and battlecruisers, as well as 635 lesser warships, and although Japan and the United States together only scrapped seven completed battleships, their extensive building programmes had to be virtually abandoned. Four of the hulls were, however, retained (two by each country) and completed as aircraft-carriers, while the Royal Navy converted three light battlecruisers to carriers.

Aviation was to play an ever-increasing part in naval design and operations. The 1914-18 war had seen it used for long-range reconnaissance in support of the fleet, for spotting for the ships' guns against shore targets, and by the end of the war the Royal Navy was working up a carrier-based torpedo-attack capability. Three years later, in 1921, in the course of bombing trials against ex-German warships, Colonel William Mitchell of the US Army Air Corps appeared to 'prove' conclusively, by sinking the dreadnought *Ostfriesland*, that the armoured battleship was vulnerable to air attack. In practice, Mitchell, for the sake of publicity for his own Service, bombed the immobilized ship from very low level, far below the height prescribed for the trial, using 2,000lb bombs. The US Navy's anger was not, as Mitchell subsequently alleged, at the supposed exposure of the weakness of their favourite warship type but at the wanton destruction of a ship that would have been of more value afloat, for a thorough study of the weapons' effects.

The wild claims made on behalf of land-based aviation during the 1920s and 1930s found willing listeners in the governments of the Western democracies, who, unwilling to spend a great deal on defence in hard times, were prepared to believe that bomber aircraft offered an economical common solution to most military problems. In practice, air power was barely out of its infancy and the claims of its enthusiasts were based on its potential and not on any realistic demonstration of contemporary capability. Lack of suitable aircraft, ordnance and tactics, together with inadequate training, ensured that when the first trial occurred, the pathetic fallacy of the doctrine of universal air power was exposed – to be effective, air forces needed to be able to score lethal hits.

The US Navy developed an alternative to the massed formations of bombers favoured by the air forces. Attacking at medium level, the latter depended upon a 'carpet' of bombs, dropped nearly simultaneously, for their effect: against any small target, accuracy was governed more by mathematical chance than skill, but against moving targets this was further reduced by the time of flight of the bombs, between release and impact. With relatively small numbers of aircraft available for any one attack, and unable to carry more than a single medium bomb apiece, the US Navy required a high degree of accuracy from individual aircraft. Releasing the bomb in a steep dive, at fairly low level, allowed it only a brief flight, giving the target less time to take evasive action, while the gun defences could be overwhelmed by a group of aircraft attacking in rapid succession. The Japanese Navy quickly realized the value of the dive-bomber, as did the German Air Force, almost alone among air forces in realizing the real needs of tactical aviation.

In Britain the Royal Air Force monopolized official policies on all aspects of aviation and, as the only adviser, it even had a voice in naval defence against air attack. Anti-aircraft weapons and fire-control were optimized against RAF tactics and passive protection – armour and sub-division – were on a scale which would defeat bombs of the sizes which the airmen believed would be employed: in 1939 the Royal Navy's ships were ideally equipped to fight-off the RAF. The RAF-controlled Fleet Air Arm concentrated on the torpedo-bomber as its principal ship-killing weapon, developing effective tactics which were limited by the small number of aircraft which could take part in any single attack. Not until the late 1930s did the Royal Navy demand a purpose-built dive-bombing capability and this was provided only after considerable resistance from the Air Force, which continued to be unconvinced by the merits of this form of attack. British (naval) dive-bombers scored the first major anti-warship aircraft 'kill' of the war as early as April 1940, but even this failed to alter Air Ministry policy and for the first four years of the war the RAF was the least successful of the large air forces in this role.

Ships designed to conform to the Washington Treaty restrictions began to appear in the late 1920s, all the signatories producing new heavy cruisers in the 8in gun/10,000-ton category. These reflected the individual nations' requirements, with the extremes represented by lightly protected British and French ships intended for cruising in distant colonial waters as well as working with the fleet, while the Japanese used considerable ingenuity to build relatively well-armoured and heavily armed ships to compensate for what they believed to be an inadequate allowance of capital ships. Light cruisers, armed with guns of about 6in calibre, could be built up to the same tonnage and, subject to the amount of money available, could be given better protection than the heavy ships. Neither the United States nor Japan took advantage of this, however, and prior to 1938 the only ships of modern design in this category were built by the European navies.

The Japanese had a substantial number of light cruisers of older design which they used as destroyer flotilla leaders. Since Tsu-Shima, considerable attention had been devoted to the development of torpedo tactics and it was in this area that the Japanese Navy was best able to devise a 'force equalizer' which would allow it to take on the numerically superior United States and Royal Navies. From 1930 large (2,000 tons) destroyers, armed with up to six 5in (127mm) guns and, more important, the fast long-range 24in (610mm) torpedo, were built in considerable numbers, no fewer than 68 being completed before Japan entered the war. Cruisers and destroyers exercised together, practising every imaginable tactical situation and the best responses, using gunfire and torpedoes, by day and night; this intensive realistic training appears to have gone unrecognized by the western navies, who were overwhelmed when first they encountered the much-underrated Japanese Navy.

The size and gun armament of the Japanese destroyers was, however, recognized. The French had initiated the construction in the 1920s of large (2,400 tons), very fast 'contre-torpilleurs' intended to combat the large numbers of

Italian torpedo-boats (or light destroyers) and also capable of commerce raiding in the Mediterranean. The Italians matched these with a series of classes of equally fast light cruisers while, like the Royal Navy, they continued to build medium-sized destroyers – typically of up to 1,500 tons and armed with four 4.7in (120mm) guns and six to eight torpedo-tubes – intended to screen the battlefleet or to act as independent striking forces. By 1930 the rivalry between France and Italy was such that they chose to not to adhere to a fresh naval arms limitation agreement – the London Treaty – and went their own way, limited only by their economic means and industrial capacity.

In 1934 the Japanese gave formal notice that they would not renew their adherence to the Washington Treaty restrictions when the latter expired in 1936, but the United States and Great Britain continued to build ships to the existing limits on individual tonnage and armament. In Germany Hitler denounced the Versailles Treaty, committing the country to rearmament, and Britain, attempting to prevent a fresh naval arms race, signed in 1935 a bilateral agreement which laid down the size and tonnage of the future German fleet, the individual limits following the lines of those laid down at Washington.

No new capital ships were laid down between 1923 and 1932, when the French began construction of a battlecruiser whose displacement was well within the 35,000-ton Washington limit and announced plans to build a second ship of this type. These were matched by a pair of German ships of similar displacement and two 35,000-ton Italian battleships, all laid down in 1934. The other navies restricted themselves to modernizing existing shps until 1937, when Britain and the USA began the construction of 35,000-ton vessels and Japan, freed of any moral obligations, laid down a 64,000-ton ship armed with 18.1in (460mm) guns. By now the feared arms race had begun in earnest, for in the same year the French and Germans started work on 35,000-tonners.

Weapons and Defences

All the naval architects did their best to reduce the vulnerability of their creations to shell, torpedo, mine and bomb. All, with the exception of the Japanese, were severely handicapped by the artificial tonnage limitation, which was in each case exceeded to a greater or lesser extent. In working out a compromise between speed, offensive firepower and defensive resilience, the designers could scarcely avoid leaving weaknesses in one or other of the most important areas. In action, however, none of these Achilles' heels was the direct cause of the loss of a ship; rather the victim was sunk by an accumulation of hits on a scale which she could not be expected to survive.

The modernized older capital ships were more prone to loss through a single 'lucky hit', such as the 15in (380mm) shell which caused the *Hood* to blow up, but most showed that they were able to withstand heavy punishment. Additional protection against shells descending at high angles served the same purpose against medium bombs, and thicker torpedo bulkheads contained underwater damage, whether caused by torpedo, mine or near-miss bomb.

Lesser ships could not be protected against damage on any corresponding scale, by armour or sub-division. A single torpedo hit was almost invariably incapacitating – the ship might be able to remain afloat and continue under her own power, but her fighting efficiency was usually much reduced. Bomb hits penetrating into the hull of a lightly protected (or unprotected) ship usually caused fires as well as structural damage; while the shock effect of near-misses could inflict damage as severe as that caused by mining, even on ships as large as a cruiser.

Size was a major factor in survival – an 8,000-ton cruiser could cope with the influx of 200 tons of water more readily than could a 1,500-ton destroyer; but aircraft-carriers of all sizes proved to be vulnerable, due largely to the quantities of volatile aviation fuel embarked, but also because of the weight of attack they frequently attracted. The British armoured carriers justified their designer's attention to protection against bombing and the consequent fires, but were indifferently protected against underwater damage.

The torpedo had proved to be an effective ship-killer but after the 1914-18 war most navies had concentrated on improving the reliability of its propulsion, gyroscopic guidance and warhead fusing. Few revolutionary developments had been made; the British and German navies introduced magnetic firing circuits, to explode the warhead under heavy ships, but both had serious problems at one time or another and they generally relied upon unremarkable but effective contact fuses. From September 1943, however, German submarines began to use an acoustic homing torpedo against Allied warships. The development had been expected (the US Navy already had an acoustic anti-submarine torpedo in service) and tactical and technical counter-measures were rapidly introduced, but the 'Gnat' torpedo took a steady toll of ships to the end of the war, but only at the cost of prodigious expenditure of the weapon.

The one spectacular advance in torpedo performance was made, unsurprisingly, by the Imperial Japanese Navy, which viewed the weapon as the great equalizer in a fleet action. The Type 93 'Long Lance' oxygen-enriched torpedo was big, very fast and had a range as great as that of a 16in gun. Constant training and drills added tactical flexibility and initiative to a superlative weapon and the combination proved irresistible again and again in 1942 when pitted against unsuspecting opposition. Thereafter, the Allies' technical advantage in radar deprived the Japanese of positional surprise, and while the US Navy's tactics improved Japanese expertise declined as the pre-war generation of destroyer officers became casualties.

A high degree of individual and group expertise was also needed for aerial torpedo attack, whose tactics invariably called for release at very short range and low level. The weapons were, in general, sound rather than spectacular, although the US Navy squadrons were initially armed with the worst torpedo to be used by any force. Usually too light to carry a warhead capable of sinking a major warship with a single hit, the 17.7in-18in (450mm-457mm) torpedo was nevertheless capable of inflicting crippling damage (as on the *Bismarck*) or, when hitting in large numbers, of overwhelming a modern capital ship's underwater protection (eg, *Prince of Wales* and *Musashi*). The light weight also made the aerial torpedo suitable for launching from smaller types of motor torpedo-boat.

Few air forces began the war with bombs specifically designed to attack ships (a reflection of the general-purpose view of air power). Against unarmoured ships, medium-capacity bombs proved to be effective while semi-armour-piercing bombs could deal satisfactorily with light protection, but heavy armour-piercing weapons, in the 1,000-1,600lb (450-730kg) category were needed to defeat even moderate thicknesses (3in/75mm) of armour. The German air force demonstrated on numerous occasions what could be achieved with the appropriate weapons, usually delivered in a diving attack and, as defences against this form of attack improved, was the first to introduce successful guided weapons – the rocket-propelled glider-bomb and the unpowered ballistic guided bomb – in the autumn of 1943.

Near-miss bombs caused substantial damage to many ships and sank several. The effect, similar to that of mining, was multiplied in shallow waters and the Royal Navy suffered particularly severely from this form of inaccurate attack during the early years of the war.

As in 1914-18, minefields were used for defensive and offensive purposes. For the former, moored buoyant (spherical) mines were invariably employed, laid in vast numbers by surface ships; but the offensive fields gradually became much more varied in content, with buoyant mines giving way to the new magnetic and acoustic ground mines which could be laid by light craft, submarines and aircraft in relatively shallow seas.

Mine warfare became more and more complex, as technological advances in influence firing systems – magnetic, acoustic and combined pistols – had to be countered by the development of appropriate sweeping gear (the pressure mine introduced in 1944 was 'unsweepable' and had to be neutralized by tactics, not technology). The minefields, defensive and offensive, were themselves protected by anti-sweeping gadgetry, such as explosive floats for cutting sweep wires or counters on influence sensors to allow escorts and 'sweepers to pass unharmed and then detonate the mine when the heavy ships passed over, while the mines themselves incorporated lethal anti-defusing devices to protect their technical secrets.

The need for purpose-built minesweepers had been fully demonstrated during the 1914-18 war, but only four navies devoted their resources to building modern vessels in adequate numbers. The larger of these ships had intended secondary roles, which in wartime tended to become dominant: the Royal Navy's large ocean-going Fleet minesweepers were in such demand as anti-submarine escorts that a smaller, cheaper vessel had to be procured to specialize in the original role. The German Navy had ended the earlier war with an efficient 'sweeper, many of which were to be found in minor navies in 1939 as well as in the 'new' German Navy, and from this design was developed a succession of 'M'-class ships which proved to be just as useful as coastal convoy escorts. The French and Japanese navies favoured faster (20-knot) minesweeper/escorts, but while the former's 2nd Class 'avisos' were relatively lightly armed, the Japanese ships carried a pair of 4.7in guns and were employed as cruising gunboats in the East Indies, where most were lost before the mining campaign started in earnest against Japanese shipping.

That the 20th century underwater and air-dropped ordnance proved to be lethal cannot be denied, but the gun retained its traditional dominance throughout the war. No other weapon was so genuinely multi-purpose, able to engage any above-water target, afloat or ashore, and it continued to sink large numbers of ships. Ballistic performance was improved by developments in the aerodynamics and the construction of projectiles, while the lessons of the earlier war made the stowage and handling of ammunition safer. The greatest advances were, however, made in fire control which became less of an art and more of a science, requiring the most up-to-date mechanical and electrical computers then in existence to provide solutions which enabled gunnery officers to miss by ever-decreasing distances. Radar, besides giving long-range warning, was of particular value to the gunnery world, for not only did it provide accurate ranges on the enemy, but it could also be used to spot the fall of friendly shot to enable corrections to be made.

Anti-aircraft weapons had been fitted in small numbers from 1914 and considerable development work had been carried out between the wars into long-range fire control. Early wartime experience was to show that the first requirement was for a high volume of close-range gunfire and from 1940 small calibre (40mm and below) automatic weapons were fitted in large numbers by all navies. Effective against all forms of low-level air attack, the heavier automatic weapons were essential for dealing with the suicide aircraft encountered during the final ten months of the war. Heavier guns, between 3.9in (100mm) and 5in (127mm), could attain high rates of fire, with power loading and automatic fuse setting, but were more suitable for firing predicted AA barrages than for individual aiming against aircraft at close range. Only the US Navy (from late 1942) and the Royal Navy (from 1944) enjoyed the benefit of radar proximity-fused ammunition, which proved to be useful against all aircraft targets, including last-ditch defence against suicide aircraft. A typical mid-war carrier group, composed of two carriers, a battleship, four cruisers and eight destroyers, had an anti-aircraft armament of approximately 60 fighters, over 100 heavy guns and 300 automatic weapons – covering the area of a small town, the formation possessed defences which would have been the envy of a major city.

In spite of all the modern defences, active and passive, ships did get hit. Some went down like rocks, their small size being unable to cope with massive inflows of water. Ships of all sizes blew up with incredible violence as projectiles found small gaps in their protection or, more often, large holes in the designs of the victims. More often, the ship died a more or less protracted death. The crews faced the traditional sailors' problems of fire and flooding but had many advantages that their ancestors lacked. Protective clothing enabled them to get close to a fire and fight it with modern compounds and water at high pressure, supplied by pumps driven by the ship's machinery or, when that failed, emergency diesel generators or, in the last resort, from another ship, lying alongside. Internal subdivision, with watertight bulkheads, doors and hatches, could control flooding, and timber was kept to hand to shore up damaged or weakened structure. Large angles of heel could be compensated by counter-flooding, provided that the overall loss of buoyancy did not endanger the ship.

The keys to survival were, however, the training and morale of the crew – they had to know how to use the equipment to hand and believe that they could save the ship. Many derelicts were brought back to harbour to be repaired after sustaining damage which should have been fatal; as the war progressed the men of the Allied navies acquired such expertise in keeping afloat that they brought home many ships that were beyond repair. As numerous were the ships, of all navies, lost unnecessarily because their crews did not know how to save them.

1939 – 1945

The balance of naval power between the belligerent nations in 1939 was even more in favour of France and Great Britain than it had been 25 years earlier. Germany had not been able to build up a surface fleet that could offer any major challenge to either of her antagonists, and once again Britain was faced by an enemy whose maritime strategy was directed against her merchant shipping, with warship raiders at loose and submarines taking a major part from the very first day of the war. While the Press and armchair strategists once again pontificated on the likelihood of any early end to hostilities, the British Admiralty made preparations for a long war.

A familiar situation was countered by familiar measures. Convoy had proved to be as effective against German U-boats in 1917 and 1918 as it had been against French and Spanish cruisers in the preceding centuries and so it was to prove again. Strong escorts were provided for troop convoys, battleships covered the transatlantic routes against raiders and the Allies still had sufficient big ships left over to form hunting groups to round up German merchant ships as they left neutral ports and to seek out the few enemy warships in distant waters. The sinking of the pocket battleship *Graf Spee* in the River Plate provided the first important Royal Navy victory in what had become known as the 'Phoney War' – a complete misnomer for the struggle at sea.

Minefields and aircraft made close blockade by surface ships impossible, but both could be used for attacks on shipping at sea and aircraft could reach ships in their ports and defended anchorages – the first attacks made in the west by the Royal Air Force and the Luftwaffe in September 1939 were against the other side's naval forces in their bases. As in 1914, the Allies sealed the southern entrance to the North Sea and attempted to deny the enemy access via the channel between Scotland and Norway.

The Royal Navy Alone

These arrangements for containing a weaker enemy were thrown into complete disarray by the events of April, May and June 1940. After 125 years, the coastline of north-west Europe was once again in hostile hands. The German Navy was a major participant in the invasion of Norway, the occupation of which outflanked the Royal Navy's defence of the northern approaches to the North Sea; but the losses incurred by the German surface fleet were such that it could no longer have any pretensions to being more than a raiding force. The Allies' losses were nearly all to air attack, against which they were as yet ill-defended, and most occurred close inshore.

Surface warships were involved from the first day of the brief campaign in the Low Countries and France, in May 1940, and again the pattern of heavy inshore losses suffered while supporting military operations was repeated, as it was, again and again, to the end of the war. British and French ships were sunk off the Schelde, Calais, Boulogne and Dunkirk by motor-torpedo-boat, submarine, mine and, above all, dive-bombing, but they were never withdrawn, continuing to evacuate the defeated Allied armies with little protection from the impotent Allied air forces.

The fall of France in June 1940 outflanked the remaining barrier to the North Sea and provided the German Navy with substantial naval bases with immediate access to the Atlantic. The German warship losses in Norway prevented the build-up of a substantial offensive surface force in western France (although Brest was to be invaluable as a harbour of refuge in 1941) but the U-boats were quickly moved to these new bases. Britain herself was now facing blockade and was fortunate that, in spite of casualties during the previous months and the disappearance of a powerful naval ally, the Royal Navy could keep the German Navy at arm's length from her coasts.

The declaration of war by Italy in June 1940 opened a new front. France had been responsible for the western basin of the Mediterranean and her surrender had left a vacuum which had to be filled from the Royal Navy's overstretched resources. The Italian Navy was, to all appearances, well equipped and able to operate, with adequate air support, from secure bases which dominated the central Mediterranean, where the only British base was on the island of Malta, 90 miles (160km) from Sicily. The Royal Navy's Mediterranean Fleet, under a particularly talented commander, more than made up for its isolation and relative weakness by sheer aggression, seeking out and destroying the enemy wherever he could be reached, even in his main fleet base (Taranto), where a carrier strike temporarily crippled the opposing battle fleet. The Italian fleet made only one major foray in 1941, returning to base with a damaged battleship and short of three heavy cruisers and a pair of destroyers.

The German Air Force arrived in the Mediterranean in January 1941. Royal Navy casualties began to increase immediately, in defence of operations to resupply Malta and, to a more marked extent, in supporting the Army as it retreated eastward along the North African coast and withdrew, in defeated disarray, from Greece and then Crete. Despite its own serious losses, the Mediterranean Fleet continued to sink Italian warships. The main fleet would not come out, but the destroyers and torpedo-boats were required to escort Axis supply convoys between Italy and North Africa. The convoys were attacked by every means available, with Malta providing bases for RN torpedo aircraft and RAF bombers, submarines and, most destructive of all, cruiser and destroyer forces, which inflicted great execution up to the end of 1941.

The Royal Navy reached its lowest ebb in the Mediterranean in November and December 1941, losing an aircraft-carrier in the western basin, both its battleships at the eastern end and the cruiser striking force operating from Malta. The Royal Navy's losses could not have occurred at a more awkward moment and they were, for the time being, irreplaceable.

Alliance – Initial Defeat, Final Victory

On 7 December 1941 the Japanese entered the war, eliminating the US battle fleet at Pearl Harbor as a precursor to an amphibious blitzkrieg which overran the Philippines, Malaya and the Netherlands East Indies in twelve weeks. Allied naval interference with the programme was repeatedly brushed aside by a combination of Japanese naval air power and devastating surface action: few ships sent to join the final stand off Java in late February 1942 survived the main battle or the determined and relentless mopping-up.

What could not be realized in the aftermath of the fall of Java was that the Japanese Navy had fought its last successful campaign, although it still had some victories ahead. Within two months, its next amphibious thrust had been turned back by a pyrrhic US victory in the Coral Sea and a month after that the US Navy's carrier aircraft won a decisive battle off Midway Island, shutting the central Pacific line of advance for the duration. By August 1942 the US Navy was able to begin a limited, small-scale offensive in the Solomon Islands. The landings on Guadalcanal prompted a violent reaction from the Japanese, who threw in virtually their entire fleet in attempts to recover the island. Seven major battles were fought and although the US Navy eventually won the strategic victory, it lost 28 ships to the Japanese 19; the true victory lay in the fact that the Japanese could not replace their lost ships, crews and expertise, whereas the United States had the industrial base and manpower to build, man and train a completely new navy.

At the same time that the US Navy had landed the Marines on Guadalcanal, the Royal Navy fought through a convoy to save Malta and, in the next month, did the same to reach North Russia. The Soviet Union had been in the war since June 1941, but the naval war had been one-sided in the Baltic and Black Sea, where air attack and mines virtually eliminated the Red Navy as it retreated in step with the Red Armies. Only when the latter were able to go over to the offensive once more, in 1943, was German naval superiority in the two land-locked seas challenged; but even when the Russians had almost complete air supremacy, the German Navy was able to act as it wished, suffering greater losses in its own minefields than it did at the hands of the enemy.

The Allies returned to the Mediterranean in strength in November 1942, as the naval struggle for Guadalcanal was reaching its climax; few ships were lost by the invaders of North Africa during the assault phase, but the French Navy ceased to exist as an entity, for all practical purposes. The operational Vichy French ships at Oran and Casablanca suffered heavy losses fighting heroically against overwhelming odds and, a fortnight later, the fleet at Toulon was scuttled in harbour to prevent it from falling into the hands of Germany.

The North African campaign lasted until early May 1943, when Tunis fell. The Italian Navy used its destroyers, torpedo-boats and corvettes to escort reinforcements to Tunisia and, in the latter days, to run in troops, fuel and ammunition; these missions were opposed, as the Cyrenaican convoys had been, by every means available and once more the casualties sustained were heavy. From Tunisia, the Allies went on to invade Sicily, an operation which, unusually, was completed with few warship losses on either side. The invasion of the Italian mainland, at Salerno, in September 1943, brought out the newest weapon in the Luftwaffe's arsenal, a guided bomb. The effect which these successful attacks produced was overshadowed by the sudden surrender of Italy. The main battle fleet escaped to reach Sicily, although not without the loss of the newest battleship to the first guided bomb attack, and many of the more modern smaller units subsequently saw service with the Allies. The ships which could not get away were either scuttled or captured by the Germans, in Italian ports and in the Aegean. These fought on under German colours, to the end of the war in Europe; not until the beginning of 1945 did the losses in the Pacific exceed in total those in the Mediterranean.

The Battle of the Atlantic, fought principally against the submarine, was not accompanied by particularly severe warship losses. The U-boats were given an anti-escort weapon, the acoustic homing torpedo, in the autumn of 1943 but it did not prove to be as dramatically successful as had been hoped and the ascendancy which the convoy escorts and support groups had established over the submarines in the spring of that year – largely due to code-breaking successes – remained unbroken.

The US submarines in the Pacific were beginning to enter their stride as the U-boat arm went into decline. Like the Germans, the Americans concentrated on merchant shipping as being the best means of bringing down a maritime nation, but the US submarines were also used in support of fleet operations, to watch Japanese naval bases and anchorages and give warning of major enemy movements. Such patrols offered excellent opportunities for inflicting severe casualties on surface warships.

During 1943 the US Navy forced its way up the Solomon Islands chain, fighting and winning occasional battles against Japanese destroyers by using the enemy's own torpedo tactics. At the end of the year the axis of advance changed to the Central Pacific, where the Gilbert Islands were taken, followed in January 1944 by the Marshalls. Japanese air counter-attacks were ineffectual and the US Fast Carrier Task Force went over to a wide-ranging mobile offensive, striking at the advanced fleet and air bases at Truk, in the western Caroline Islands, Guam and Saipan and in the Palau Islands, before supporting an Army advance along the north coast of New Guinea.

The Japanese Mobile Fleet made no attempt to interfere with these operations but did come out in June 1944, when the Marianas Islands were invaded. The 'Battle of the Philippine Sea' was primarily an aerial battle and the loss of nearly 500 Japanese carrier aircraft and their crews rendered the sinking of two of their carriers almost incidental. This battle set the final seal on the US Navy's supremacy in the Pacific: without a viable carrier fleet, any navy in this theatre was condemned to the defensive, operating only within range of shore-based aircraft.

Shortly before the Marianas campaign began, the Allies launched their invasion of Normandy. Completely out-matched, the German Navy fought back as best as it was able, inflicting a few casualties which the armada could shrug off while the Germans lost virtually all the ships based to the west of the Straits of Dover, to direct surface and air attack or by scuttling. The biggest cause of Allied loss was the new pressure-actuated mine, laid in large numbers by the Luftwaffe; other novelties, such as 'human torpedoes' and explosive motor-boats, were less successful. The 83-day naval campaign, which lasted far longer than had been expected due to the inability of the Anglo-Canadian Army to break out through the German defences, cost the Allies 34 warships and many more small craft; as the US Navy had found off Guadalcanal, support of a victorious army was almost as expensive as the evacuation of a beaten army.

The Japanese Navy rallied for the defence of the Philippine Islands, invaded in October 1944. The battleships and cruisers provided the striking forces on this occasion, the aircraft-less carriers serving as decoys for the US fast carriers. The complicated plan attained one objective, that of drawing off the fast carriers, but then went badly awry: the four individual actions which made up the 'Battle of Leyte Gulf' gave the US Navy a decisive victory which completely annihilated the Japanese carrier fleet and eliminated the battleship and cruiser threat. The last desperate destroyer night actions also took place during the later stages of the

Leyte campaign, as both sides fought to resupply their troops in Ormoc Bay.

Suicide aircraft – Kamikazes – made their debut during these battles. The material effect was every bit as devastating as the effect on morale and the toll of loss and damage mounted as the US Navy continued to land and support troops in the successive invasions of Mindoro, Luzon, Iwo Jima and Okinawa. The sheer size and momentum of the US Navy sustained the advance, soaking up the losses, which occurred mainly among the destroyers and the escort carriers. Okinawa, where the land offensive was slowed by fanatical Japanese resistance, cost the US Navy no fewer than 35 destroyers, destroyer escorts and 'fast transports' sunk or damaged beyond repair; the Japanese lost the last surface striking force which it could muster, sunk by air attack without a final glimpse of the US Pacific Fleet.

There was thus little expectation of a cheap or easy end to the naval war, even though no effective opposition could be expected from the Japanese Navy. The remnants of the heavy squadrons were sunk in harbour by carrier air attack late in July 1945 and the waters between the islands had earlier been rendered hazardous by US Army Air Force minelaying, but the Japanese had husbanded their air forces and were training a new generation of Kamikaze pilots. The invasion of the Japanese Home Islands would have been a long and expensive affair, for the Allied navies no less than the armies. Only the timely fruition of the atomic bomb project and the dropping of the first two bombs, in the middle of an Allied carrier offensive against the Home Islands, brought the world war to a premature end.

Sources

Although the many good standard works of reference on the Second World War at sea contain the names of the ships lost by the various combatant and neutral navies, even in combination they do not provide the detail of cause, circumstance and precise agent. Besides such standard works as Stephen Roskill's four-volume 'War at Sea' Official History, Samuel E. Morison's 15-volume 'History of United States Naval Operations in WWII' and the series of books published by Ian Allan Ltd listing various countries' 1939–45 warships, the following sources were extensively employed.

BRITISH AND COMMONWEALTH NAVIES AND ALLIED NAVIES UNDER BRITISH CONTROL

'Ships of the RN: Statement of Losses during the Second World War', HMSO 1949
Admiralty War Diary (PRO ADM199/2130–1322)
Fleet and Command War Diaries (ADM199 various)
'The War at Sea' (Naval Historical Section Preliminary Narrative)
Individual Reports of Proceedings (ADM199 various)
'HM Ships Sunk or Damaged by Enemy Action 1939–45', Admiralty 1952

FRENCH NAVY

Official Histories series published by the *Service Historique de la Marine*, Vincennes 1954–60

GERMAN NAVY

'List of Foreign War Vessels Reported Lost during the War', Admiralty 1947
Naval Staff War Diaries (*KTB*)
Command *KTB*

ITALIAN NAVY

'List of Foreign War Vessels Reported Lost during the War', Admiralty 1947
Official Histories series published by the *Ufficio Storico della Marina Militare*, Rome [particularly *'Navi Perdute'*, published 1959]

IMPERIAL JAPANESE NAVY

Allied Technical Intelligence Group ('ATIG') Reports, 1945–47
'List of Foreign War Vessels Reported Lost during the War', Admiralty 1947
'Warships of the Imperial Japanese Navy 1860–1945' by Mickel, Jung and Jentschura, translated and revised by Preston and Brown (Arms & Armour Press, London 1977)
'US Submarine Attacks during WWII' by J.D. Alden (US Naval Institute Press, Annapolis 1989)

SOVIET NAVY

'Soviet Warships of the Second World War' by J. Meister (Macdonald & Janes, London 1977)
'The Soviets as Naval Opponents 1941–45' by F. Ruge (Patrick Stephens Ltd., Cambridge 1979)
    [German sources cited above]

US NAVY

'Dictionary of American Fighting Ships', US Naval Historical Center, Washington 1961–81

MINOR NAVIES

'Les Flottes de Combat', P. Vincent-Bréchignac and H. le Masson (Paris, 1942)

Part One:

Chronology of Warship Losses

AUGUST 1939

The German decision to invade Poland was taken on 15 August 1939. Fourteen U-boats sailed for the Atlantic on the 19th, the pocket-battleship *Graf Spee* left two days later and the Baltic fleet, consisting of four cruisers, four destroyer divisions and three torpedo-boat flotillas, was at sea in a holding position in the western Baltic by the evening of 22 August. 'Y'-Day was set for 26 August but the British Government's signing of a defensive alliance with Poland on the 25th led to cancellation of the original timetable. The naval units remained at sea, exercising while awaiting the decision to resume the operation.

NW EUROPE 27   German Torpedo-Boat
Tiger   0230 hours: Collision with destroyer *Max Schultz* off Bornholm – 2
                   men lost; *Max Schultz* towed to port

The Polish Government appreciated that the country's small navy, whose main combat strength consisted of just four modern destroyers and five submarines, had from the outset no real chance of influencing the outcome. The three destroyers which were ready for sea and one submarine which was not ready for operations were accordingly sailed for Britain on 30 August, to continue a war which now seemed inevitable; their departure was one of the factors which affected the German decision on the 31st to invade Poland on 1 September. The other four Polish submarines were sent on patrols in the western Baltic, three going into internment in Sweden when their fuel ran out, while the fourth escaped to Britain after an epic journey which did not end until her arrival on 14 October. The ships which remained in harbour or in Polish waters were sunk by German dive-bombers.

SEPTEMBER 1939

The war at sea began in the early hours of 1 September in the Gulf of Danzig, with bombardments of the fortified Polish naval base at Hela and the Westerplatte coast defences. German aircraft concentrated on the defences and it was not until the third day that the ships came in for heavy attack.

3   Polish Destroyer
Wicher   Sunk by air attack, Gdynia
Polish Minelayer
Gryf   Sunk by air attack, Hela

Minefields laid in international waters by the Anglo-French allies and Germany were notified to neutral nations, in accordance with international law. The neutrals themselves laid defensive fields to protect their territorial waters and one of these claimed the first mine victim of the war.

8   Dutch Minesweeper
Willem van   Mined off Terschelling
Ewijck

The first French loss was due to a catastrophic accident which caused widespread damage to the Casablanca naval base.

ATLANTIC 13   French Cruiser
La Tour   1040: Blew up and sank at Casablanca while disembarking mines
d'Auvergne   – 186 men lost. The explosion and fire which followed destroyed
(ex-**Pluton**)   three armed trawlers and damaged nine other patrol vessels and
                   auxiliary minesweepers – 21 men lost

The first British warship to be lost was a victim of mistaken doctrine. Later experience was to prove that highly specialized training and equipment were needed for the anti-submarine task and that hopeful patrolling, without up-to-date intelligence, in an area of U-boat activity was as unproductive as it was dangerous.

17	British Carrier		ATLANTIC
	Courageous	2000: Torpedoed SW of Ireland (50-10N 14-45W), by German submarine *U.29*; sank in less than 15 minutes – 518 men lost	

OCTOBER 1939

The Polish naval garrison at Hela capitulated on 1 October, after enduring a month of bombing and naval bombardment. On the same day Polish mines claimed their only significant victim.

1	German Minesweeper		NW EUROPE
	M.85	1440: Mined 3 miles* east of Heisternest, Danzig Bay (54-45N 18-45E)	

A serious psychological blow was struck on the night of 13/14 October 1939 by a daring U-boat commander who penetrated the shoals and currents among the islands surrounding Scapa Flow and sank an elderly battleship. The sinking of the *Royal Oak* was a magnificent feat of arms and navigation, but was possible only because of the inadequacy of the fixed defences and obstructions at the Royal Navy's main Fleet base in Home Waters.

14	British Battleship	
	Royal Oak	0130 and 0145: Torpedoed by German submarine *U.47*, in Scapa Flow – 786 men lost

NOVEMBER 1939

The German Air Force began a minelaying campaign off the East Coast of the United Kingdom in the first half of November 1939. Laid on the sea-bed, in relatively shallow water, the mines were actuated by the magnetic influence of steel-hulled ships. Although defensive protection and suitable sweeping methods were rapidly improvised, magnetic mines continued to inflict casualties throughout the war.

13	British Destroyer		
	Blanche	Sunk by magnetic mine in the Thames Estuary (51-29N 01-30E), while escorting HMS *Adventure* which had been mined several hours previously	
21	British Destroyer		
	Gipsy	Mined leaving Harwich; back broken and ship beached (51-57N 01-19E) – total loss	
23	British Armed Merchant Cruiser		ATLANTIC
	Rawalpindi	pm; Sunk off Iceland (63-40N 12-31W) by 11in gunfire of German battlecruisers *Scharnhorst* and *Gneisenau*; abandoned at 1616 – 11 survivors rescued by RN, 26 by German Navy	

DECEMBER 1939

Accidental losses to destroyers and torpedo craft screening heavy units have been a feature of Fleet operations in peace and war throughout the 20th century. The risk was increased during wartime, when steaming and navigation lights were extinguished.

*'Miles' throughout the text refer to nautical miles (1 nautical mile = 1·842 kilometres)

NW EUROPE 12 British Destroyer
Duchess Sunk in collision with HMS **Barham**, North Channel, 9 miles off Mull of Kintyre (55-22N 06-03W)

By a curious coincidence, the first decisive British naval victory of the war took place in the South Atlantic, as had occurred in the First World War. Appropriately, the German raider which was disposed of in December 1939 was named after the admiral commanding the cruiser squadron wiped out off the Falklands in December 1914.

ATLANTIC 13 German Pocket Battleship
Graf Spee 0618–0800: Damaged off River Plate by 8in gunfire of RN cruiser **Exeter** and 6in gunfire of cruisers **Ajax** and **Achilles**; scuttled off Montevideo 17 December to avoid renewed action

NW EUROPE 14 German Escort
F.9 Torpedoed by RN submarine **Ursula** off Heligoland (54-08N 07-55E). **Ursula** was firing at the cruiser **Leipzig** which, with the **Nürnberg**, had been damaged on the previous day by the RN submarine **Salmon** – **F.9** was unlucky to cross the torpedo tracks

JANUARY 1940

19 RN Destroyer
Grenville 1250: Mined in the southern North Sea, 23 miles (42 km) east of the Kentish Knock Light Vessel (51-39N 02-17E) – heavy loss of life

21 RN Destroyer
Exmouth 0445: Torpedoed off Tarbet Ness, Moray Firth (58-18N 02-25W), by German submarine **U.22** – lost with all hands

MED 24 Yugoslav Destroyer
Ljubljana Lost by accident at Kotor. Subsequently salvaged and under repair when Yugoslavia was invaded (see 17 April 1941)

FEBRUARY 1940

NW EUROPE 3 RN Minesweeper
Sphinx Badly damaged by air attack 15 miles (28 km) north of Kinnaird Head, Moray Firth (57-57N 02-00W), and foundered on the following day – 40 men lost

18 RN Destroyer
Daring 0255: Torpedoed 40 miles (75 km) east of Duncansby Head (58-38N 01-40W) by German submarine **U.23** – 15 survivors

A German air strike following up a reported sighting of the British destroyer minelaying flotilla heading for the Heligoland Bight found a German destroyer force heading to intercept the British ships. In the dusk, the inexperienced airmen misidentified the ships and attacked. While the bombing itself caused no damage, the violent evasive action took the German destroyers into a line of British mines laid to foul the swept channel in the German minefield.

22 German Destroyers
Leberecht Maass 1956: Mined while avoiding German air attack north-west of Borkum in field laid by RN destroyers in Heligoland Bight – 282 men lost
Max Schultz 2005: Mined with **Leberecht Maass** – 308 men lost

MARCH 1940

The second French naval loss, like the first, was caused by an accidental explosion, again at Casablanca.

24   French Destroyer   ATLANTIC
      La Railleuse   1655: Lost at Casablanca by accidental explosion in forward torpedo-tubes; ship broke in half and forward portion sank – 20 men lost

APRIL 1940

The German occupation of Denmark and invasion of Norway marked the first major turning point in the war at sea. In the opening stages the German Navy suffered its first substantial losses in European waters but later, as the German land operations ended in success, the German Navy was able to operate from bases which opened directly on the Atlantic. The destroyer and cruiser losses were, however, never made good and the main beneficiary of the acquisition of the Norwegian bases was the submarine arm.

The British Home Fleet was at sea, one contingent supporting a major minelaying operation off Narvik while, from late on 7 April, the main body cruised to the west of Bergen awaiting developments. The first loss of the campaign (an RN destroyer detached from the minelaying force) occurred as the result of a chance encounter on the day before the invasion, as the German Navy moved into position for the assault.

8   RN Destroyer   NW EUROPE
     Glowworm   0905: Sunk by 8in gunfire of German heavy cruiser *Admiral Hipper* and destroyers (5in) west of Trondheim (64-27N 06-28E)

The first German losses were at the hands of the Norwegian defences in Oslofjord, sited to fire at point-blank range. The defenders had no orders for dealing with an undeclared act of war and the decision to open fire first was taken by a relatively junior officer, on his own initiative.

9   German Heavy Cruiser
     Blücher   0235: Sunk by shore batteries' torpedoes and gunfire, Drobak, Oslofjord; very heavy casualties included civilian occupation officials

     German Torpedo-Boat
     Albatros   Damaged by shore batteries' gunfire and stranded in fog at Bolaerne, Oslofjord

The German Navy also experienced resistance from shore batteries at Bergen, where a cruiser was damaged, and at Narvik, where two elderly coast defence ships opened fire on the invaders.

9   Norwegian Coast Defence Ships
     Eidsvold   0525: Torpedoed off Narvik by German destroyer *Wilhelm Heidkamp*
     Norge   0530: Torpedoed in Narvik Harbour by German destroyer *Bernd von Arnim*. Very heavy casualties in both Norwegian ships

     Norwegian Torpedo-Boat
     Aegir   Sunk by air attack at Stavanger

     Norwegian Torpedo-Boat
     Tor   Scuttled at Frederikstad, raised and renamed *Tiger* in German service
     Norwegian Coast Defence Ship
     Harald Haarfagre   Captured at Horten; commissioned as German flak battery *Thetis*

9   Norwegian Coast Defence Ship

Tordenskjold Captured at Horton; commissioned as German flak battery **Nymphe**

Not all the Royal Norwegian Navy's ships were in a condition to resist or scuttle themselves and a number were taken intact in harbour and subsequently taken into German service.

Torpedo-Boats

Balder	Captured at Horten, renamed **Leopard**
Odin	Captured at Marvika, renamed **Panther**
Gyller	Captured at Marvika, renamed **Löwe**
Minelayer	Captured at Horten, after damaging the German light cruiser **Emden**
Olav Tryggvason	and sinking the motor-minesweeper R.17; renamed **Brummer** – scuttled in May 1945

The Home Fleet was attacked from the air continuously for three hours during the afternoon of 9 April but sustained only one loss.

9   RN Destroyer

Gurkha   pm: Sunk by air attack, west of Bergen (59-13N 04-00E)

German Light Cruiser

Karlsruhe   1900: Sunk by RN submarine **Truant** off Kristiansand; scuttled by German torpedo-boat **Greif** at 2150

A dawn attack on German destroyers and captured merchant ships in Narvik harbour marked the opening of the First Battle of Narvik. Although honours were apparently even by the end of the action, the German flotilla was low on fuel and ammunition and only three of their destroyers were undamaged.

10   German Destroyers

Wilhelm Heidkamp

Anton Schmidt   0415: Sunk by British destroyers' torpedoes and 4.7in gunfire at Narvik

RN Destroyers

Hardy   0615: Damaged by German destroyers' 5in gunfire, Ofotfjord, and beached (68-23N 17-06E)

Hunter   Damaged by German destroyers' gunfire and sank after collision in Ofotfjord with HMS **Hotspur** (68-20N 17-04E)

The light cruiser **Königsberg** was damaged on 9 April by the Bergen shore batteries and was still alongside in the harbour when she was attacked by Royal Navy Skua dive-bombers operating from the Orkney Islands. Hit by 500lb bombs, she was the first major warship ever to be sunk in wartime by air attack.

10   German Light Cruiser

Königsberg   0700: Sunk at Bergen by RN aircraft (800 and 803 Squadrons); raised but hulk capsized on 22 September 1944

The Royal Navy returned to Narvik in strength on 13 April, nine destroyers being supported by the battleship **Warspite** and aircraft from the carrier **Furious**. The Second Battle of Narvik cost the German Navy all eight of the destroyers which had survived the previous encounter, as well as a U-boat which was sunk by the **Warspite**'s Swordfish floatplane; one British destroyer was severely damaged but reached harbour and was repaired.

13   German Destroyers

Erich Koellner (Unfit for sea due to grounding on 11/12 April) 1015: Sunk at Djupviken, Ofotfjord (68-24N 16-48E) by RN destroyers **Bedouin** and **Eskimo** (torpedoes) and battleship **Warspite** (gunfire) – 31 men lost

Erich Giese   1230: Torpedoed off Narvik (68-25N 17-34E) by RN destroyers **Cossack** and **Foxhound** – 83 men lost

Diether von	(Severely damaged by gunfire on 10 April)	
Roeder	1230: Scuttled at Narvik by depth-charges – 16 men lost	
Hermann	1330: Scuttled in Herjangsfjord (68-31N 17-35E); undamaged but	
Künne	no fuel or ammunition remaining	
Georg Thiele	1500: Beached in Rombaksfjord (68-24N 17-55E) and later slid off	
	rocks and sank – 27 men lost	
Wolfgang	Scuttled in Rombaksfjord (68-25N 17-55E)	
Zenker		
Bernd von	Scuttled in Rombaksfjord (68-24N 17-55E); undamaged but fuel	
Arnim	and ammunition expended	
Hans	Abandoned in Rombaksfjord (68-25N 17-54E) with no fuel or	
Lüdemann	ammunition remaining – torpedoed by RN destroyer ***Hero***	

14 German Minelayer
Brummer   Sunk by RN submarine ***Sterlet*** in Kattegat

26 Norwegian Torpedo-Boat
Garm   Sunk at Bjordal, Sognefjord, by German air attack

30 RN Sloop
Bittern   pm: Severely damaged by air attack, Namsos (64-28N 11-30E);
                    abandoned and scuttled by HMS ***Carlisle***
RN Minesweeper
Dunoon   Mined while sweeping off Great Yarmouth (52-45N 02-23E)

Accidental losses continued after the intensive fighting began and April ended with one on each side; the loss of the 1,000-ton German torpedo-boat hardly balanced the sinking of a 2,400-ton contre-torpilleur (heavy destroyer or flotilla leader).

30 French Flotilla Leader
Maillé Brézé 1415: Accidental explosion of torpedo air vessel while at Tail o' the
                    Bank, Clyde, followed by fire; abandoned at 1515 and sank at 2000
                    – 27 men lost
German Torpedo-Boat
Leopard   Sunk in collision with naval auxiliary ***Preussen*** in the Skagerrak
                    (approximately 58N 10E)

MAY 1940

3 French Flotilla Leader
Bison   1008: Severely damaged by air attack off Namsos (65-42N 07-17E);
                    scuttled at 1207 by HMS ***Afridi*** – approximately 100 men lost

RN Destroyer
Afridi   1446: Sunk by air attack off Namsos (66-14N 05-45E), heavy losses,
                    including most of the ***Bison***'s survivors

5 Polish Destroyer
Grom   Sunk by air attack in Ofotfjord, off Narvik

The Royal Air Force scored its first anti-shipping success on 9 May. Lacking suitable aircraft and weapons, three more years were to elapse before the RAF became a potent ship-killer in the waters of northern Europe.

   The victim had a varied post-sinking career. Raised in October 1940, she was repaired and recommissioned in the following March, when she was re-numbered as ***M.534***. Later in 1941 she was converted as a motor minesweeper depot ship and in February 1943 was renamed ***Jungingen***. Finally, in September 1943, she was allocated for use as an escort; her life in her new career was brief – see 27 September 1943.

NW EUROPE 9 German Minesweeper
M.134 Sunk in Bergen Roads by air attack (No 254 Squadron, RAF)

The invasion of the Low Countries, while the Norwegian campaign was still at a critical stage, placed fresh strain upon the Allied navies, now joined by the small but efficient Royal Netherlands Navy, whose smaller units fought gallantly in support of the Netherlands Army.

10 Dutch Destroyer
Van Galen Sunk by air raid at Rotterdam

12 Dutch Gunboat
Friso Scuttled after damage sustained in air attack, Ijsselmeer

14 Dutch Gunboats
Johan Maurits
van Nassau Sunk by air attack off Callantsoog
Brinio Scuttled after damage sustained in air attack, Ijsselmeer

Dutch Destroyers scuttled at Rotterdam
Tjerk Hiddes Scrapped
Gerard Callen- Salvaged, repaired and commissioned by German Navy as **ZH.1**
burgh (see 9 June 1944)

15 RN AA Destroyer
Valentine Damaged by air attack (dive-bombers) and beached near Terneuzen, Schelde Estuary (51-20N 03-49E) while providing AA defence to Allied troops

The first Royal Navy cruiser loss of the war was caused by a soft pencil and precise navigation – the line drawn on the chart to show HMS **Effingham**'s course obscured an isolated shallow pinnacle and the ship was exactly on track.

18 RN Cruiser
Effingham 2300: Stranded on rock pinnacle in the Narvik area (67-17N 13-58E); sunk by gunfire 21 May

Norwegian Torpedo-Boat
Troll Captured by Germans at Floro (immobilized for want of crew)

The rapid advance of the German Army to the Dutch and Belgian coasts provided forward airfields for the German Air Force dive-bomber units, whose accuracy was of a higher order than any yet experienced. The German Navy also moved up its Schnellboote torpedo flotillas to operate from Dutch ports as a nocturnal supplement to the Air Force's daylight operations.

19 RN AA Destroyer
Whitley am: Damaged by air attack (dive-bombers) 2 miles (3,700m) off Nieuport and beached (51-09N 02-04E); destroyed pm by RN destroyer **Keith**

21 French Destroyer
L'Adroit 0100: Sunk by air attack off Malo-les-Bains, Dunkirk

23 French Flotilla Leaders
Jaguar 0030: Torpedoed by German motor torpedo-boats (E-Boats) **S.21** and **S.23** off 6W Buoy, Dunkirk; ran aground and abandoned, subsequently destroyed by German air attack – 13 men lost

Chacal 0830: Sunk off Alprech, Pas de Calais, by air attack and German Army artillery – 21 survivors

French Destroyer
Orage   1812: Severely damaged by air attack 4 miles (7 km) west of Boulogne, burned through the night and sank at 0330 on 24 May – 28 men lost

25   RN Destroyer
Wessex   Sunk by air attack off Calais (51-00N 01-48E)

26   RN Anti-Aircraft Cruiser
Curlew   Sunk by air attack off Skutenes, Lavang Fjord, Narvik area (67-32N 16-37E)

The order to evacuate the British Expeditionary Force through the port of Dunkirk was given in the evening of 26 May 1940 and operations lasted until dawn on 4 June, by which time more than 335,000 British, French and Belgian servicemen and civilians had been brought to England. Of 720 vessels and craft of all types and sizes employed in the evacuation, 71 were lost, among them six of the 38 Royal Navy destroyers and three of the 20 French destroyers involved; many others were so badly damaged (seven on 29 May alone) that they were out of action for months to come.

29   RN Destroyers
Wakeful   0045: Torpedoed by E-boat **S.30** 13 miles (24 km) north of Nieuport (51-22N 02-43E) – 25 of crew and one soldier survived, but 650 troops lost. Capsized wreck sunk by RN corvette **Sheldrake** by gunfire and depth-charges on 30 May
Grafton   0240: Torpedoed by German submarine **U.62** while rescuing personnel from **Wakeful**. 0430: survivors taken off by HMS **Ivanhoe** and scuttled by gunfire
Grenade   1750–55: Severely damaged alongside East Pier, Dunkirk, by air attack; abandoned on fire at 1815 and blew up several hours later

30   French Destroyer
Bourrasque 1625: Mined in French field 5 miles (9 km) north of Nieuport while evading German artillery fire – 16 men lost

31   French Destroyer
Siroco   0145; Torpedoed by E-boats **S.23** and **S.26** off West Hinder buoy (51-22N 02-26E) and sank in 2 minutes – 59 men lost (plus over 600 troops).
           (The French destroyer **Cyclone** had been torpedoed by an E-boat near the same position 20 minutes earlier)

JUNE 1940

1   French Destroyer
Foudroyant 1030: Sunk off 6W Buoy, Dunkirk, by air attack – 137 members of the crew and 83 soldiers rescued

RN Destroyers
Keith   0800: Severely damaged off Bray, Dunkirk (1-05N 02-27E), by dive-bombers and abandoned at anchor in a sinking condition; sunk by bombing at 0940 – 36 men lost (100 more lost in tug **St. Abbs**, *sunk at 0950 with* **Keith** *survivors on board*)
Basilisk   0800: Damaged off La Panne, Dunkirk (51-08N 02-35E) by dive-bombers – immobilized
           1200: Sunk in shallow water by dive-bombers and destroyed by gunfire and torpedoes from HMS **Whitehall**
Havant   0906: Hit off Dunkirk (51-08N 02-16E) by dive-bombers; rolled over and sank at 1015 – 8 men lost

NW EUROPE   RN Minesweeper
Skipjack   0845: Sunk by air attack of Malo-les-Bains, Dunkirk (51-03N 02-24E); capsized almost immediately – over 270 troops lost

RN Gunboat
Mosquito   1330: Sunk off Dunkirk Channel by dive-bombers

6   German Minesweeper
M.11   Mined off Feisten, south-west Norway, in field laid by RN submarine **Narwhal**

7   RN Armed Merchant Cruiser
Carinthia   1315: Sunk by German submarine **U.46** off north-west Ireland (53-13N 10-40W)

Although Allied troops had established a favourable situation in the Narvik area by late May, the military collapse in the Low Countries and northern France necessitated the abandonment of the Norwegian campaign. The evacuation of 27,000 men was carried out during the first week in June, almost without loss. A questionable decision to use one of the Royal Navy's few carriers to evacuate seventeen RAF fighters (of which ten were obsolete biplanes) and a lapse in her captain's tactical awareness led to the loss of the carrier and her two screening destroyers.

8   RN Aircraft-Carrier
Glorious   1600–1730: Sunk south-west of Narvik (68-45N 04-30E) by gunfire of German battlecruisers **Scharnhorst** and **Gneisenau**

RN Destroyers
Ardent   Sunk in same action; one torpedo hit obtained on **Gneisenau**
Acasta

The Italian Government, observing diplomatic niceties, informed the British and French on 10 June that it would consider its country to be in a state of war with them from 11 June 1940. Although the Royal Navy had weakened its Mediterranean Fleet, whose primary area of responsibility was the eastern basin, the French Fleet, based on Toulon and Oran (Mers el Kebir), was strong enough to contain the powerful Italian Navy.

MED   12   RN Light Cruiser
Calypso   0200: Torpedoed south of Crete (33-45N 24-32E) by Italian submarine **Bagnolini** – sank at 0330

NW EUROPE   13   RN Armed Merchant Cruiser
Scotstoun   0715: Torpedoed by German submarine **U.25** north of Ireland (57-00N 09-57W)

The German Army began the second phase of its invasion of France towards the end of the first week in June and on the 14th entered Paris. On the following day the Soviet Government, satisfied that the Baltic States could no longer expect any measure of protection from Britain or France, occupied Lithuania and seized her small navy. On the same day Latvia and Estonia were presented with ultimatums which they could not refuse.

15   Lithuanian Minesweeper
Prezident   Seized by Russians; commissioned as gunboat **Korall** in June 1941
Smetona   and possibly lost in 1944

ATLANTIC   16   RN Armed Merchant Cruiser
Andania   0025: Torpedoed by German submarine **UA** (ex-Turkish **Batiray**) 200 miles (370 km) south-east of Iceland (62-36N 15-09W)

NW EUROPE   18   German Minesweeper
M.5   Mined off Kristiansand (63-30N 06-20E) in field laid by RN submarine **Porpoise**

18	French Aviso (sloop)		NW EUROPE
	Vauquois	Mined off Brest	

French Destroyer
Cyclone   (damaged 30 May by E-boat)
              Scuttled at Brest

French Avisos
Etourdi   Scuttled at Brest
Enseigne   Scuttled at Lorient
  Henri

20   Latvian Minesweeper
Virsaitis   Seized by Russians at Libau (Liepaja) and commissioned (name unchanged) by Soviet Navy in August 1940 (see 2 December 1941)

22   French Corvette
La Bastiaise Mined off West Hartlepool while running trials

The Italian Navy destroyers and submarines based at Massawa on the Red Sea threatened Allied shipping on the route between the Indian Ocean and the Suez Canal, but only the submarines achieved any measure of success, however limited.

22	RN Destroyer		RED SEA
	Khartoum	Beached on Perim Island (12-38N 43-24E) following fire caused by burst torpedo air vessel. The accident occurred during an action in which the Italian submarine **Torricelli** was sunk	

23	Royal Indian Navy Sloop		INDIAN O
	Pathan	0100: Torpedoed by Italian submarine **Galvani** off Bombay (18-56N 72-45E) and sank early on the 24th – 5 men lost; initially attributed to a contact mine. **Galvani** was sunk 24 hours later by RN sloop **Falmouth**	

The French Government signed an armistice with Germany on 22 June and with Italy on the 24th and early on the 25th all hostilities in France came to an end, with the exception of the British and Dominion forces still engaged in evacuation work.

25	Royal Canadian Navy Destroyer		NW EUROPE
	Fraser	2215: Sunk in collision with RN cruiser **Calcutta** off the Gironde (45-44N 01-31W) while covering the final evacuation of British and Allied personnel from France	

28	Italian Destroyer		MED
	Espero	2015: Sunk west of Crete (37-18N 20-12E) by 6in gunfire of five British cruisers (**Orion, Neptune, Liverpool, Gloucester,** HMAS **Sydney**). **Espero** was on passage from Taranto to Benghazi with **Ostro** and **Zeffiro**; hit by the opening salvoes, she was slowed and covered her sister-ships' escape	

JULY 1940

Up to 25 June 1940, the French Navy, based at Toulon and Oran, had been responsible for containing the Italian Fleet in the Western Mediterranean. Thereafter, the Royal Navy was obliged to provide, from its already stretched resources, a balanced squadron – Force 'H' – based at Gibraltar, to operate between 'the Rock' and Malta and, when required, in the Atlantic. The future control of the powerful French Fleet which had concentrated at Oran was uncertain in British eyes and after the local French commander had rejected suggestions that his ships should continue to fight on alongside the Royal Navy or that they should be disarmed and immobilized, the political order was given that they should be destroyed by gunfire and carrier air attack. The execution was less than successful, for only one old dreadnought was sunk and one modern battleship severely damaged by freakish means (an aircraft torpedo sank an armed trawler alongside the **Dunkerque** which was damaged by the subsequent explosion of the trawler's depth-charges). However negligible the effects of the attacks on Oran on 3 and 6 July 1940 might have been, they left a legacy of bitterness and mistrust on the part of the French.

MED   3   French Battleship
Bretagne   1755: Sunk at Mers el Kebir, Oran, by 15in gunfire of capital ships of RN Force 'H'

     4   French Aviso
Rigault de   1407: Torpedoed by RN submarine **Pandora** 10 miles (18 km) north
Genouilly   of Algiers; broke in half and sank at 1540

The opening phase of the 'Battle of Britain' saw the German Air Force attacking shipping and ports in southern and eastern England. Remarkably little damage was inflicted during the early days, but from mid-July the increased experience of the aircrew began to result in heavier shipping casualties.

NW EUROPE   4   RN Auxiliary Anti-Aircraft Ship
Foylebank   Sunk in Portland Harbour by air attack

ATLANTIC   5   RN Destroyer
Whirlwind   1825: Torpedoed 120 miles (220 km) west of Land's End (50-17N 08-48W) by German submarine **U.34** – 57 men lost; scuttled 4 hours later by destroyer HMS **Westcott**

The old aircraft-carrier HMS **Eagle** could operate only eighteen Swordfish aircraft but her squadrons were probably the most experienced and they carried out a series of successful torpedo and minelaying operations which were noteworthy for their economy of effort.

MED   5   Italian Destroyer
Zeffiro   2035: Torpedoed at Tobruk by RN aircraft (813 Squadron, HMS **Eagle**); destroyer **Euro** also hit and flooded, one merchant vessel sunk, one damaged

NW EUROPE   9   RN Sloop
Foxglove   1130: severely damaged 8nm (15km) south of the Nab Tower, Isle of Wight, by German aircraft; towed to Portsmouth Dockyard but not repaired; used as base ship in River Foyle 1943–5

MED   10   Italian destroyer
Leone   2140: Torpedoed in Augusta Harbour by RN aircraft (813 and 824
Pancaldo   Squadrons, HMS **Eagle**). Hit while lying at a buoy and sank at 2139 (First sinking – see also 30 April 1943)

   11   RN Destroyer
Escort   0215: Torpedoed north of Algiers (36-11N 03-36E) by Italian submarine **Marconi**; sank at 1115 after crew had been transferred to HMS **Forester**

NW EUROPE   16   RN Destroyer
Imogen   2355: In collision off Duncansby Head (58-34N 02-54W) in thick fog with cruiser HMS **Glasgow**; the destroyer caught fire, was abandoned and sank later

A chance encounter off Crete cost the Italian Navy three more ships. The cruiser **Giovanni delle Bande Nere,** although damaged by gunfire, managed to outrun HMAS **Sydney** and was believed to have taken refuge at Tobruk. HMS **Eagle**'s Swordfish were ordered to attack Tobruk and although the cruiser was not present they nevertheless found and sank two destroyers.

MED   19   Italian Light Cruiser
Bartolomeo   0829–0923: Damaged north-west of Crete by 6in gunfire of
Colleoni   Australian cruiser **Sydney** and finished off, 6 miles (11 km) from

Cape Spada, by RN destroyer torpedoes (HMS *Hyperion, Ilex, Hero* and *Hasty*)   MED

20   Italian Destroyers
Nembo
Ostro   0145: Torpedoed by RN aircraft (824 Squadron, HMS *Eagle*) in Tobruk Roads; *Nembo* hit in boiler-room and *Ostro* in after magazine – both sank very quickly

20   RN Destroyer   NW EUROPE
Brazen   Damaged by air attack in Straits of Dover while escorting a convoy; later sank in tow (51-01N 01-17E)

26   German Torpedo-Boat
Luchs   Torpedoed by RN submarine *Swordfish* in North Sea (58-30N 04-30E)

German Minesweepers
M.61, M.89,   Mined 1,000 yards off the Hook of Holland
M.136

27   RN Destroyer
Codrington   Sunk by air raid at Dover; HMS *Walpole* and *Sandhurst* damaged in same attack

RN Destroyer
Wren   Sunk by air attack off Aldeburgh (52-10N 02-06E) while providing AA defence for minesweepers; HMS *Montrose* damaged in same attack and towed to Harwich

29   RN Destroyer
Delight   Damaged and set on fire by air attack off Portland; sank in Portland Harbour early on 30 July

AUGUST 1940

10   RN Armed Merchant Cruiser
Transylvania   0001: Torpedoed 40 miles (75 km) north-west of Malin Head (55-50N 08-03W) by German submarine *U.56*

15   Greek Cruiser   MED
Helle   Torpedoed, while at anchor off Tenos Island, Crete, by Italian submarine *Delfino*. Greece was not at war with Italy and crew was celebrating the Feast of the Assumption – heavy casualties included civilians

23   RN Destroyer
Hostile   0317: Mined 18 miles (33 km) south-east of Cap Bon, Tunisia (36-53N 11-19E); scuttled by HMS *Hero*

24   RN Sloop   ATLANTIC
Penzance   1840: Torpedoed west of Ireland (56-16N 27-19W) by German submarine *U.37* – heavy casualties

27   RN Armed Merchant Cruiser
Dunvegan   2310: Torpedoed 120 miles (220 km) south-west of Ireland (55-05N
   Castle   11-00W) by German submarine *U.46*; sank at 0600 on 28 August

The career of the Royal Navy's only offensive minelaying surface force, the 20th Destroyer Flotilla, was abruptly curtailed on the night of 31 August/1 September 1940. At sea off the Dutch coast to lay another field off Vlieland, the five destroyers ran into a minefield laid only hours before by German torpedo-boats.

NW EUROPE 30 RN Destroyers

[Express	2307: Mined north of Terschelling while proceeding to intercept German convoy; towed stern first to Humber and repaired]
Esk	2325: Mined off Dutch coast (53-30N 03-47E) and sank in less than 2 minutes
Ivanhoe	0051, 1 September: Damaged by mine and abandoned after air attack (53-25N 03-48E); scuttled by HMS *Kelvin* at 1700 that day

SEPTEMBER 1940

6 RN Corvette

Godetia	2300: Sunk in collision with SS *Marsa* 3 miles (5 km) off Altacarry Head, Irish coast (55-18N 05-57W)

ATLANTIC 15 RN Sloop

Dundee	0200: Torpedoed west of Ireland (56-45N 14-14W) by German submarine *U.48*

The new armoured carrier HMS *Illustrious* joined the *Eagle* in the Eastern Mediterranean in September 1940, doubling the number of Swordfish available for attacks on Italian ports.

MED 17 Italian Destroyers

Borea	0100: Bombed by RN aircraft (815 Squadron, HMS *Illustrious*) in Benghazi Harbour. Two merchant vessels also sunk
Aquilone	2050: Sunk by magnetic mine laid by RN aircraft (819 Squadron, *Illustrious*) while leaving Benghazi. Two small patrol vessels lost in same field

NW EUROPE 18 German Torpedo-Boat

T.3	Damaged by air raid at Le Havre, flooded rapidly and capsized; 9 men lost

MED 22 Italian Torpedo-Boat

Palestro	1820: Torpedoed by RN submarine *Osiris* in Otranto Straits (41-19N 18-34E) while escorting Durazzo-Bari convoy – sank in 10 minutes

Another unsuccessful attack was made by the Royal Navy on a Vichy French naval base in late September 1940. The raid on Dakar was intended to be part of a landing/occupation operation but the bombardment and air attacks failed to inflict serious damage and the amphibious operation was abandoned

ATLANTIC 23 French Flotilla Leader

L'Audacieux	1635: Damaged by 8in gunfire of Australian heavy cruiser *Australia*; set on fire and beached near Dakar. Subsequently refloated (1941) and towed to Bizerta for repairs – destroyed by US Army Air Force air raids in early 1943

OCTOBER 1940

The Italian Navy attempted to intercept an eastbound convoy from Malta on the night of 11/12 October 1940 but its torpedo-boats and destroyers ran into a covering force which included HMS *Ajax*, the first radar-equipped cruiser to join the Mediterranean Fleet.

MED 12 Italian Destroyer

Artigliere	0153: Damaged and brought to a halt east of Malta by 6in gunfire of RN cruiser *Ajax*; taken in tow by destroyer *Camicia Nera* but

cast off when further RN forces sighted after dawn. Surrendered to HMS *York* but scuttled in 36-30N 16-07E at 0905 on the 12th   MED

Italian Torpedo-Boats
Ariel	0214:
Airone	0235: Sunk 70 miles (130 km) east of Malta by gunfire of HMS *Ajax* – 125 men were rescued, approximately half of the two ships' combined complements

16   RN Minesweeper   NW EUROPE
     Dundalk   1830: Mined off Harwich (52-03N 01-48E); taken in tow by HMS *Sutton* but foundered 0245 on the 17th (51-57N 01-27E)

19   RN Destroyer
     Venetia   0841: Mined off Knob Buoy, Thames Estuary (51-33N 01-10E)

The heavy convoy traffic in the Red Sea was subjected to frequent but inaccurate Italian air attack and a more aggressive employment of the Italian East African destroyer squadron led to its first loss, an attempt by two ships to intercept a British convoy being foiled by the escort.

21   Italian Destroyer   RED SEA
     Francesco   0330: Ran aground on Harmil Island, Red Sea (16-28N 40-13E)
     Nullo   while being pursued by RN convoy escort; destroyed after dawn (0635) by torpedo from RN destroyer *Kimberley*, which was, in turn, damaged by shore batteries

22   RCN Destroyer   ATLANTIC
     Margaree   Sunk in collision with SS *Port Fairy*, 450 miles (830 km) west of Ireland (53-24N 22-50E); 140 of crew of 171 lost. (Formerly HMS *Diana*, this ship had been transferred to the RCN to replace HMCS *Fraser*, lost in collision on 28 June)

30   RN Destroyer   NW EUROPE
     Sturdy   Ran aground on island of Tiree, west coast of Scotland (56-29N 06-59W) – 3 men lost

NOVEMBER 1940

3   RN Armed Merchant Cruisers   ATLANTIC
     Laurentic   2107: Torpedoed by German submarine *U.99* north-west of Ireland (54-09N 13-44W)
     Patroclus   2222: Torpedoed by *U.99* in 53-43N 14-41W. (The survivors of this double sinking were recued by HMS *Hesperus*)

5   RN Armed Merchant Cruiser:
     Jervis Bay   2030: Sunk in the Eastern Atlantic (52-41N 32-17W) by 11in gunfire of German pocket battleship *Admiral Scheer*

6   German Torpedo-Boat   NW EUROPE
     T.6   2015: Mined off Kinnaird Head, North Sea (57-50N 00-50W), during offensive sortie off east coast of Scotland – 45 men lost

9   French Aviso   ATLANTIC
     Bougainville   1455: Sunk off Libreville by 5.5in gunfire of Free French aviso *Savorgnan de Brazza* – a very rare (and sad) encounter between ships of the same class manned by crews of the same nationality

The most successful exploit of the Royal Navy's carrier torpedo-bombers in 1940 was the attack on the main Italian Fleet base at Taranto on the night of 11/12 November. For the loss of two aircraft, one modernized battleship was sunk and another (*Caio Duilio*)

was damaged and beached, while the new battleship **Littorio** was severely damaged by three torpedo hits.

MED 11 Italian Battleship
Conte di 2314: Torpedoed by RN aircraft (HMS **Illustrious**) in Taranto
Cavour Harbour. Raised and transferred to Trieste (see 15 February 1945)

20 Italian Torpedo-Boat
Confienza 0020: Sunk 2 miles (3,700 metres) north-west of Brindisi in collision with auxiliary patrol vessel **Cecchi**, at night, in bad visibility

DECEMBER 1940

ATLANTIC 2 RN Armed Merchant Cruiser
Forfar 0250: Torpedoed west of Ireland (54-35N 18-18W) by German submarine **U.99** (see also 3 November)

MED 5 Italian Torpedo-Boat
Calipso 0945: Sunk by mine laid by RN submarine **Rorqual** 4 miles (7 km) off Misurata, Libya

NW EUROPE 14 Ex-French Torpedo-Boat (RN-manned)
Branlebas Foundered after back broken in heavy weather east of the Lizard peninsula (49-47N 04-91W); 3 survivors rescued by Free French destroyer **Mistral**

15 RN Destroyer
Cameron Damaged beyond repair in air raid on Portmouth Dockyard

17 RN Destroyer
Acheron Mined south of the Isle of Wight (50-32N 01-26W) during high-speed trials following repairs – stern had been blown off on 24 August in air raid on Portsmouth Dockyard

MED 22 RN Destroyer:
Hyperion 0156: Torpedoed 24 miles (45 km) east of Cap Bon (37-40N 11-31E) by Italian submarine **Serpente**; taken in tow but later scuttled by HMS **Janus**

23 Italian Torpedo-Boat
Fratelli 1030: Mined off Misurata (32-48N 14-50E) in same field as **Calipso**
Cairoli (see 5 December 1940)

JANUARY 1941

NW EUROPE 8 German Torpedo-Boat
Wolf Sunk by mine laid by RN Motor Launches (MLs) north of Dunkirk (51-05N 02-08E) – 13 men lost

A major British operation involving Force 'H' and the Mediterranean Fleet, escorting a convoy from Gibraltar to Alexandria, coincided with the arrival of a specialized German Air Force anti-shipping unit (Fliegerkorps X) in Sicily. While the convoy reached its destination, the cost to the Royal Navy was heavy, for besides the two ships lost the aircraft-carrier HMS **Illustrious** was severely damaged and forced to leave the Mediterranean for repairs.

MED 10 Italian Torpedo-Boat
Vega 0830: Sunk in surface action 6 miles (11 km) south of Pantelleria (36-30N 12-07E) while attempting to intercept British convoy; hit

by 5.25in shell from HMS **Bonaventure**, then 4.7in shells and one 21in torpedo from HMS **Hereward** – only 2 survivors

MED

RN Destroyer
Gallant   0835: Mined 120 miles west (220 km) of Malta (36-27N 12-11E) – 60 men lost. Bows blown off, towed to Malta by HMS **Mohawk** and beached in Grand Harbour. Declared a total loss on 20 January (but see 5 February 1942)

11   RN Cruiser
Southampton   1520: Damaged and set on fire 180 miles (330 km) east of Malta (34-54N 18-24E) by German air attack; fire in after engine-room could not be brought under control and she was scuttled during the same evening – 80 men lost

Thailand took advantage of the military weakness of the French administration in Indo-China to press territorial claims. From September 1940 there were a number of clashes along the mutual border and in mid-January 1941 the Royal Thai Navy made the mistake of challenging the small but efficient Vichy French squadron. On 17 January the Thai Navy was virtually eliminated in the Koh-Chang estuary, Cambodia (11-20N 103E) by the gunfire of the cruiser **Lamotte-Picquet** *and the avisos* **Amiral Charner, Dumont d'Urville** *and* **Tahure.**

17   *Thai Coast Defence Ships*
Domburi
Ahidea

PACIFIC

Thai Torpedo-Boats
Chonburi
Songkla
Trat

22   Italian Coast Defence Ship (ex-Armoured Cruiser)
San Giorgio   1415: Scuttled in Tobruk Harbour to prevent capture; damage sustained in previous RAF air raids had rendered her unseaworthy

MED

The capture of Tobruk gave the British Eighth Army an invaluable forward supply port but added to the burdens of the Mediterranean Fleet, whose 'Inshore Squadron' suffered heavy losses to aircraft in maintaining the flow of supplies.

31   RN Minesweeper
Huntley   Sunk 30 miles west of Mersa Matruh, Eastern Mediterranean (31-25N 26-48E), by German air attack – 18 men lost

FEBRUARY 1941

The Royal Danish Navy co-operated with the German Navy in the Kattegat and the Baltic approaches in keeping channels swept in territorial waters. Such co-operation was not entirely wholehearted and casualties were inevitably sustained, particularly among the small fishing craft impressed for the work.

14   Danish Torpedo-Boat
Dragen   Sunk in Danish waters, probably by mine

NW EUROPE

22   RN Monitor
Terror   Damaged off Tobruk by German dive-bombers and sank off Derna (32-04N 24-05E) at 0400/23rd – no men lost

MED

24   RN Destroyer
Dainty   dusk: Sunk in Tobruk Harbour by German dive-bomber – 33 casualties

MED   25   Italian Cruiser
           Armando Diaz   0245: Sunk 60 miles (110 km) east of Sfax, Tunisia (34-33N 11-45E), by one torpedo fired by HM Submarine **Upright**; magazine exploded and ship sank in 6 minutes

NW EUROPE   25   RN Escort Destroyer
           Exmoor   night: Sunk by German E-Boat **S.30** off Lowestoft (52-34N 02-05E)

MARCH 1941

MED   18   Italian Torpedo-Boat
           Andromeda   0001: Sunk off Karaborum, Valona Bay, Albania, by RN torpedo aircraft (815 Squadron, shore-based at Paramythia, N. Greece); sank quickly following hit in boiler-room

      26   RN Cruiser
           York   Severely damaged at Suda Bay by Italian Explosive Motor Boats (**MTM**-type); both engine-rooms and boiler-rooms flooded, ship beached in 27 feet of water (see 22 May 1941 for final fate)

      28   Italian Torpedo-Boat
           Generale   0940: Mined while on anti-submarine patrol off Cape Gallo, 10
           Antonio   miles (18 km) north-east of Palermo, in field laid by RN submarine
           Chinotto   **Rorqual**

The Italian Fleet, its battle-line reduced by the carrier strike on Taranto in November 1940, made few sorties in strength in the months which followed. Towards the end of March 1941 the Royal Navy obtained intelligence of a planned sweep and was thus at sea in strength in an attempt to bring about a fleet action. In the event, the one Italian modern battleship in service was damaged by a carrier aircraft's torpedo, as was a cruiser. The former made good her withdrawal but in attempting to assist the cruiser the Italian Fleet lost a division of heavy cruisers and two destroyers in a night battle.

      28   Italian Cruisers
           Pola   1930: Badly damaged and brought to a stop by RN aircraft torpedo; 900 of her crew taken off by RN destroyers before she was scuttled early on the 29th by HMS **Jervis** and **Nubian** in 35-18N 21-13E
           Zara   2230: Badly damaged by 15in gunfire of RN battleships **Warspite**, **Valiant** and **Barham**; scuttled at 0200 by RN destroyer in 35-21N 20-57E
           Fiume   2230: Sunk by 15in gunfire of RN battleships (35-21N 20-57E); sank in less than 30 minutes with very heavy loss of life

           Italian Destroyers
           Vittorio Alfieri
           Giosue   2330–2345: Sunk by 4.7in gunfire of RN destroyers **Stuart,**
           Carducci   **Greyhound, Griffin** and **Havoc**

      31   RN Anti-Aircraft Cruiser
           Bonaventure   0307: Sunk 90 miles (165 km) south of Crete (33-20N 26-35E) by Italian submarine **Ambra** – 310 men rescued; she had previously been attacked, unsuccessfully, 4 hours earlier, by submarine **Dagabur**

APRIL 1941

By the beginning of April 1941, the campaign in Italian East Africa was reaching its final stages, with the British troops approaching the main Italian naval base of Massawa. The sizeable force of Italian destroyers made a final sortie to attack shipping in the Gulf of Suez but were turned back by HMS *Eagle*'s Swordfish squadrons, disembarked to Port Sudan for what was to be a fitting finale to their offensive against the Italian Navy.

1	Italian Destroyer		RED SEA
	Leone	0700: Struck uncharted rock 15 miles (28 km) north of Awali Hutub, Red Sea (16-09N 39-55E), while on passage. Flooding and fire in machinery spaces led to abandonment – scuttled 1400 as fires could not be brought under control	

3   Italian Destroyers
Nazario Sauro   0615: Sunk west of Jeddah, Red Sea (20N 30E), by RN aircraft (813 and 824 Squadrons, shore-based at Port Sudan); capsized and sank within 30 seconds
Daniele   0745: Damaged by bomb and brought to a stop; later capsized and
Manin   sank 100 miles (180 km) north-east of Port Sudan (20-20N 30-10E)
Cesare   1400: Damaged by RN aircraft and scuttled off Scio Aiba, Arabian
Battisti   coast, later on the same day

Italian Destroyers
Pantera
Tigre   pm: Scuttled off Someina, Arabian coast, to avoid action with British forces

Italian Torpedo-Boat
Giovanni   Severely damaged in RAF air raid on Massawa; hit by several
Acerbi   bombs and reduced to a hulk

British Armed Merchant Cruisers had sustained severe losses since the winter of 1939/40 but all had been at the hands of 'regular' naval forces – heavy surface units and submarines. Not until December 1940 did an AMC encounter its intended prey, a German merchant raider. Though damaged, HMS *Carnarvon Castle* survived the engagement while the raider, *Thor*, clearly benefitted from the experience.

4	RN Armed Merchant Cruiser		ATLANTIC
	Voltaire	Sunk in N. Atlantic (14-25N 40-40W) by 5.9in gunfire of German raider *Thor* – severe personnel losses	

4   French Avisos   NW EUROPE
La Conquérante
Suippe   Sunk in air raid on Falmouth

6   RN Armed Merchant Cruiser   ATLANTIC
Comorin   Lost by fire (accident) in N. Atlantic (54-34N 21-20W); scuttled by RN destroyer *Broke*, which, with HMS *Lincoln* and SS *Glenartney*, picked up 405 of 425 on board in a gale

8   Italian Minelayer   RED SEA
Ostia   1200: Scuttled at Massawa to avoid capture

8   Italian Torpedo-Boat
Vincenzo
Giordano   1240: Scuttled in entrance to Massawa Harbour following damage
Orsini   from British Army artillery

13   RN Armed Merchant Cruiser   ATLANTIC
Rajputana   0845: Sunk in N. Atlantic (64-50N 27-25W) by German submarine *U.108*; 277 men rescued by HMS *Legion* – 40 lost

Yugoslavia was invaded by the German Army on 6 April, followed by the Hungarians on the 10th. After eleven days' resistance, the Yugoslav Army was obliged to capitulate; few units of the Navy were able to escape from the Adriatic and some useful modern ships were later commissioned in the Italian Navy.

MED 10   Yugoslav Minesweeper

    Kobac   Captured at Sebenico, commissioned as Italian *Unie* (see 30 January 1943)

In the early hours of 16 April 1941 five Axis steamers forming a convoy escorted by the Italian destroyers *Tarigo, Baleno* and *Lampo* were intercepted off No 4 Buoy, Kerkenah Bank by the RN destroyers *Jervis, Janus, Mohawk* and *Nubian.* All eight ships were lost, only one destroyer being subsequently salvaged; one British ship was sunk. Although the Axis shipping traffic between Italy and North Africa was to suffer heavily during the next two years, seldom was such complete success achieved.

16   Italian Destroyers

    Luca Tarigo   0220: Badly damaged by 4.7in gunfire but fired torpedoes. Sank at 0300

    Baleno   0225: Set on fire and stopped by 4.7in gunfire; anchored to prevent her drifting on to Kerkenah Bank but capsized and sank, with heavy loss of life, on the 17th

    Lampo   0225: Set on fire by 4.7in gunfire and beached. Refloated 11 August 1941 and repaired at Genoa; recommissioned May 1942 (see 30 April 1943)

    RN Destroyer

    Mohawk   0225: Torpedoed by Italian destroyer *Tarigo*; remained afloat, despite two hits but was scuttled by gunfire of RN destroyer *Janus* in 34-56N 11-42E – 168 men rescued

17   Yugoslav Destroyer

    Zagreb   Blown up at Kotor to avoid capture

    Yugoslav ships captured at Kotor:
    Destroyers:

    Dubrovnik   Italian *Premuda,* then German *TA.32*

    Beograd   Italian *Sebenico,* then German *TA.43*

    Ljubljana   Under repair, see 24 January 1940; Italian *Lubiana,* see 1 April 1943

    Old Cruiser

    Dalmacija, ex-German *Niobe* (1899):
                         Italian *Cattaro,* then German *Niobe* (see 22 December 1943)

    Seaplane Tender

    Zmaj   German minelayer *Drache* (see 22 December 1943)

    Yugoslav Minesweepers captured

    Galeb   Italian *Selve* (see 6 November 1942)

    Jastreb   Italian *Zirona* (see 25 November 1941)

    Labud   Italian *Oriole* (see 10 July 1943)

    Orao   Italian *Vergada* – restored to Royal Yugoslav Navy at Malta, 7 December 1943

    Sokol   (at Split) Italian *Eso* (see 19 January 1943)

The Axis offensive in Greece moved to a swift end after the fall of Yugoslavia. The overwhelming air supremacy enabled the Luftwaffe dive-bombers to concentrate unhindered upon the Greek warships concentrated in the Gulf of Athens to protect the merchant ships gathered to evacuate the Government and the Allied armies. Besides the larger warships, eight small torpedo-boats, four minelayers and all but one of the Greek Navy's auxiliaries were sunk by air attack.

20 Greek Destroyer   MED
    Psara   Sunk off Megara by German air attack – 40 men lost

22 Greek Destroyers
    Thyella
    Ydra   Sunk by German air attack off Piraeus
    Leon   Damaged off Piraeus by German air attack, bows blown off; towed
                       to Crete and beached on N. coast, near Suda Bay. Hulk destroyed
                       by further air attacks on 14 May

23 Greek Battleships
    Kilkis
    Lemnos   Sunk at Salamis by German air attack (neither ship was in service
                       as an operational unit)

24 Italian Torpedo-Boat
    Simone   Mined off Cape Bon (37-08N 11-10E) outside buoyed limits of
      Schiaffino   Italian-laid field

27 Greek Destroyer
    Vasilevs   (Damaged on the 13th). Captured in floating dock at Salamis; dock
      Georgios I   damaged by German air attack on the 20th. Salvaged and repaired
                       as German **Hermes (ZG.3)** – see 30 March 1943

    RN Destroyer
    Diamond and
    RN Escort Destroyer
    Wryneck   1315: Sunk by German air attack south of Nauplia (36-30N 23-34E).
                       The two ships had rescued 700 troops from the Dutch liner **Slamat**
                       a few hours earlier – only 50 survivors were found from the three
                       ships, none of them from HMS **Diamond**

MAY 1941

2   RN Destroyer
    Jersey   Mined in the entrance to Grand Harbour, Malta (35-54N 14-30E)

3   Italian Torpedo-Boat
    Canopo   2320: Set on fire by RAF air raid on Tripoli; lost by ensuing
                       explosion

4   Italian Torpedo-Boat
    Giuseppe La   0530: Mined off Kerkenah Bank (34-55N 11-50E) while escorting a
      Farina   convoy to Libya: broke in half and sank in less than 2 minutes

    RN Minesweeper
    Fermoy   Destroyed in dry-dock at Malta by air raid

7   RN Minesweeper
    Stoke   Sunk by German air attack on Tobruk Harbour

8   German Raider   INDIAN O.
    Pinguin   1215: Sunk in Indian Ocean (03-10N 57-10E) by 8in gunfire of RN
                       cruiser **Cornwall**; ship blew up with loss of 292 German crew and
                       155 British prisoners

12 RN River Gunboat   MED
    Ladybird   pm: Sunk by German air attack off Libyan coast

ATLANTIC 13 RN Armed Merchant Cruiser
Salopian 0630: Sunk in N. Atlantic (56-43N 38-57W) by German submarine **U.98**

MED 20 RN Minesweeper
Widnes 0930: Sunk in shallow water at Suda Bay by German air attack. Salvaged, repaired and commissioned as German **Uj.2109** (see 17 October 1943)

Italian Torpedo-Boat
Curtatone 1350: Mined and sunk in Greek minefield 2,500 yards off Piraeus

21 Italian Destroyer
Carlo Mirabello 0600: Mined 2 miles south of Cape Ducato, Ionian Is, while proceeding to assistance of Italian auxiliary gunboat **Matteuci**, which had also been mined in this field, laid by RN minelayer **Abdiel**; destroyer's bow blown off – sank at 1145

The German airborne invasion of Crete was one of the more spectacularly successful military operations of the war. The German Air Force's performance against the British warships attempting to support and, subsequently, evacuate the defenders of the island was of an equally high standard. In addition to the ships listed below as sunk, two battleships, an aircraft-carrier, five cruisers and four destroyers were damaged between 21 May and 1 June 1941.

21 RN Destroyer
Juno 1250: Sunk by German air attack off Crete (34-35N 26-34E); sank in less than 2 minutes

22 RN Destroyer
Greyhound 1351: Sunk by German air attack off Crete (36-00N 23-10E)

RN Cruisers
Gloucester 1550: Sunk by German air attack off Crete (35-50N 23-00E)
Fiji 2015: Capsized and sank (34-35N 23-10E) after sustaining several hits during air attacks from 1845

RN Cruiser
York Scuttled at Suda Bay; already damaged and immobilized by Italian forces (see 26 March 1941) and subsequently by German air raids

23 RN Destroyers
Kelly
Kashmir 0755: Sunk by German air attack 13 miles (24 km) south of Gavdo, Crete (34-40N 24-10E); HMS **Kipling** rescued 279 survivors

While the Royal Navy was suffering heavy losses off Crete, the attention of the Home Fleet and Force 'H' was focused on the search for the German battleship **Bismarck** which, accompanied by the cruiser **Prinz Eugen**, had broken into the North Atlantic for a raiding cruise. The first encounter with the German ships proved to be disastrous for the Royal Navy, for it cost a prestigious capital ship.

ATLANTIC 24 RN Battlecruiser
Hood 0600: Sunk in Denmark Strait (63-25N 31-55W) by 15in gunfire of German battleship **Bismarck** – 3 survivors

MED 25 French Aviso
Meulière Stranded off Ajaccio, Corsica, and became total loss

RN Sloop
Grimsby 1600: Sunk by German air attack 40 miles (74 km) north of Tobruk (32-30N 24-40E)

Although the **Bismarck** managed to shake off her pursuers for over a day, she was at last relocated and damaged by carrier aircraft torpedoes, giving the Home Fleet's battleships the opportunity to come up and batter the German ship into a wreck which had to be despatched by torpedoes.

27	German Battleship		ATLANTIC
	Bismarck	1040: Sunk in N. Atlantic (48-09N 16-07W) by 16in gunfire of RN battleship **Rodney** and 14in gunfire of RN battleship **King George V** and torpedoes of RN cruiser **Dorsetshire**; 110 men rescued by RN ships	

28	RN Destroyer		
	Mashona	0925: Damaged 100 miles (185 km) west of Ireland (52-58N 11-36W) while returning from the **Bismarck** hunt, by German air attack; capsized at about 1200 – 46 men lost	

29	RN Destroyer		MED
	Imperial	0350: Damaged by near-miss bomb off Crete (35-23N 25-40E); damage to steering gear could not be repaired and she was scuttled by HMS **Hotspur**	
	RN Destroyer		
	Hereward	0625: Sunk 5 miles (9 km) south of Crete (35-20N 26-20E) by German air attack (RN cruisers **Orion** and **Dido** and destroyer **Decoy** were severely damaged during this operation to evacuate Commonwealth troops from Heraklion)	

31	Italian Torpedo-Boat		
	Pleiadi	noon: Struck by Italian Cant Z.506 aircraft off Tobruk. Superstructure destroyed and hull damaged by fire; beached at Tobruk (see 13 October 1941)	

JUNE 1941

1	RN Anti-Aircraft Cruiser		
	Calcutta	0920: Sunk 100 miles (185 km) north-west of Alexandria (31-55N 28-05E) by German air attack	

10	RN Coastal Escort (ex-Corvette)		NW EUROPE
	Pintail	Mined off the Humber (53-30N 00-53E)	

16	French Flotilla Leader		MED
	Chevalier Paul	0300: Torpedoed by RN aircraft (815 Squadron, shore-based in Cyprus) off Turkish coast (35-18N 35-18E)	

The German Army launched the invasion of the Soviet Union on 22 June 1941. Although the colossal Russian losses in men, military aircraft and material have been widely publicized, it is not always appreciated that the Red Fleet, operating in its intended role in close support of the Army, also sustained heavy casualties, primarily in the Baltic but also in the Black Sea and Arctic.

23	Russian Destroyer		NW EUROPE
	Gnevny	Mined off the Oleg Bank, Baltic	

24	RN Sloop		MED
	Auckland	Dive-bombed 20 miles (37 km) east-north-east of Tobruk (32-15N 24-30E) by German aircraft; 162 survivors rescued by HMAS **Parramatta**	

24	Russian Destroyer		NW EUROPE
	Lenin	Under repair at Libau (Liepaja). Scuttled to avoid capture	

NW EUROPE		Russian Minesweeper	
		Shkiv	Mined off Mukhuveina, Baltic
BLACK SEA	26	Russian Flotilla Leader	
		Moskva	Mined off Constanta, Romania
MED	29	RAN Destroyer	
		Waterhen	2005: Damaged by German air attack off Tobruk; taken in tow by HMS **Defender** but capsized at 0150 on 30th and sank in 32-15N 25-20E
	30	RN River Gunboat	
		Cricket	1400: severely damaged east of Mersa Matruh by German dive-bombers and boiler room flooded; towed to Alexandria; not repaired, but used as AA platform

JULY 1941

BLACK SEA	1	Russian Destroyer	
		Bystry	Mined off Sevastopol
	7	Russian Minesweeper	
		T.216	Mined in Gulf of Finland (59-10N 22-37E)
MED	11	RN Destroyer	
		Defender	Damaged by German air attack off Libyan coast; taken in tow by HMAS **Vendetta** but sank at 1115 off Sidi Barrani (31-45N 25-31E)
NW EUROPE	18	Russian Destroyer	
		Statny	Mined off Oesel Island, Gulf of Riga
	19	Russian Destroyer	
		Serdity	Sunk by German air attack off Oesel Is
	20	Russian Destroyer	
		Stremitelny	Sunk in Kola Inlet by German air attack
MED	23	RN Destroyer	
		Fearless	0945: Torpedoed south of Sardinia by Italian aircraft while escorting 'Substance' convoy to Malta; stopped and on fire aft. Scuttled by HMS **Forester** (37-40N 08-20E) – 27 men lost
NW EUROPE	27	Russian Destroyer	
		Smely	Mined in Gulf of Riga
	nk	German Minesweeper	
		M.23	Mined off Pernau, Baltic; salvaged 1942 and returned to service

AUGUST 1941

	3	Russian Minesweeper	
		Shtag	Mined off Soelavein Straits
		Russian Minesweeper	
		Zaryad	Mined off Ristna Lighthouse, Gulf of Finland
	8	Russian Destroyer	
		Karl Marx	Sunk in Loksa Bight by German air attack
	10	Russian Escort (ex-NKVD Patrol Vessel)	
		Zhemchug (SKR.27, ex PS.1)	2212: Torpedoed in entrance to White Sea, south-east of Cape Kanin, by German submarine **U.451**
	11	Russian Minesweeper	
		Krambol	Mined east of Cape Juminda, Gulf of Finland (59-47N 25-17E)

12   RN Corvette   ATLANTIC
     Picotee   0310: Torpedoed south of Iceland (62-00N 16-00W) by German
                        submarine **U.568**

15   Russian Minesweeper   NW EUROPE
     Bui   Mined off Cape Juminda, Gulf of Finland

19   RN Escort Destroyer (Norwegian-manned)   ATLANTIC
     Bath   0205: Torpedoed south-west of Ireland (49-00N 17-00W) by
                        German submarine **U.204**, while escorting convoy OG 71

23   RN Corvette
     Zinnia   0525: Torpedoed west of Portugal (40-43N 11-39W) by German
                        submarine **U.564**, while escorting convoy OG 71

British and Russian forces occupied parts of Iran from 25 August 1941, to assure the
supply route to the Soviet Union and also to remove the growing number of Axis
'technicians' and 'tourists' who had recently been arriving in the country. Two Italian-
built sloops resisted the occupation of Iran's main ports but the remainder of the Iranian
Navy was taken intact.

24   Iranian Sloops   PERSIAN GULF
     Babr   Sunk at Korramshah by 4in gunfire of RAN sloop **Yarra**
     Palang   Sunk at Abadan by 4in gunfire of RN sloop **Shoreham**

The German Army reached the Gulf of Finland to the east of Reval (Tallinn) on 7 August
1941, cutting off the Russian forces in western Estonia. In mid-August the Russian Navy
began the evacuation of Reval, providing strong escorts for the convoys of transports.
Tactical offensive minelaying by the Finnish Navy created a trap off Cape Juminda, 30
miles (55 km) to the east of Reval: on 24 and 28 August the Russian convoys came under
heavy air attack but all their losses were sustained in the minefields.

24   Russian Destroyer   NW EUROPE
     Engels   Mined off Cape Juminda

     Russian Minesweepers
     Knekht   Mined east of Cape Juminda (59-47N 25-20E)
     Bugel   Mined east of Cape Juminda (59-47N 25-17E)

28   Russian ships mined off Cape Juminda:

     Destroyers
     Kalinin
     Artem
     Skory

     Torpedo-Boats
     Tsiklon
     Snieg

28   Russian Destroyer
     Yakov   Mined off Moon Island, Gulf of Riga
       Sverdlov
     Russian Destroyer
     Volodarski   Mined off Seiskari

SEPTEMBER 1941

6   German Minelayer
     Bremse   near dawn: Sunk off Porsanger Fjord by 6in gunfire and ramming
                        by RN cruiser **Nigeria**, while escorting a coastal convoy

BLACK SEA	12	Russian Minesweeper
		Minrep Mined off Feodosia, Black Sea
NW EUROPE		Finnish Coast Defence Ship
		Ilmarinen Mined off Hangö while in action with Russian MTBs

On 17 September 1941 the Royal Swedish Navy suffered a serious loss when a fire caused by a magazine explosion in the destroyer **Klas Uggla**, at the Hårsfjarden naval base in the Stockholm archipelago, spread and destroyed two other ships. Swedish suspicions of British sabotage persist.

NW EUROPE	17	**Klas Uggla**
		Klas Horn Severely damaged by explosion and fire. Forward and midships section of **Klas Horn** married to stern of **Klas Uggla** to produce a composite ship which took the name of the former
		Göteborg Damaged beyond repair by explosion and fire
ATLANTIC	20	RCN Corvette
		Levis 0115: Torpedoed south of Iceland (60-07N 38-37W) by German submarine **U.74**, while escorting convoy SC 44
	21	Russian Destroyer
		Frunze Sunk east of Tendra Is, Baltic, by German air attack

Russian ships sunk at Kronstadt by German air attacks:

	21	Destroyer
		Steregushchy Subsequently raised and repaired
		Torpedo-Boat
		Vikhr Subsequently raised and repaired
	23	Battleship
		Marat Sank in shallow water (some of her 12in guns remained in operation throughout the siege of Leningrad)
		Flotilla Leader
		Minsk Subsequently raised and recommissioned in November 1942
	25	German Minelayer
		Königin Luise Mined off Helsinki (60-00N 25-09E)
ATLANTIC	27	RN Auxiliary Anti-Aircraft Ship
		Springbank 0210: Torpedoed west of Ireland by German submarine **U.201**, while escorting convoy HG 73; sank at 1915 in 49-50N 21-40W
NW EUROPE	30	Russian Destroyer
		Sovershenny Mined off Kronstadt and beached; destroyed by German artillery in April 1942

OCTOBER 1941

ATLANTIC	4	Argentine Destroyer
		Corrientes Sunk in collision with cruiser **Almirante Brown** off Tierra del Fuego
MED	13	Italian Torpedo-Boat
		Pleiadi Damaged by RAF air raid at Tripoli while being salvaged (see 31 May 1941); written off as total loss

14 RN Corvette ATLANTIC
Fleur de Lys 0240: Torpedoed in western approaches to Straits of Gibraltar (36-00N 06-30W) by German submarine *U.208*; broke in half and sank quickly – 3 survivors rescued

16 RN Corvette
Gladiolus Missing from 1930, while escorting convoy SC 48 in N. Atlantic (in about 57N 25W): possibly sunk by *U.558*, although latter's report does not entirely correspond with RN account

18 RN Escort Destroyer
Broadwater 0400: Torpedoed in N. Atlantic (57-01N 19-08W) while escorting convoy SC 48, by German submarine *U.101*; sank at 1340

20 Italian Torpedo-Boat
Altair 1930: Mined while escorting a convoy off Gaidaro, Gulf of Athens; MED taken in tow by torpedo-boat *Lupo* but sank at 0250 on the 21st

21 Italian Torpedo-Boat
Aldebaran 0300: Mined while going to assistance of *Altair* and sank at 0940 on the 21st. Field laid by RN submarine *Rorqual* on 8 October 1941
RN River Gunboat
Gnat 0445: torpedoed north of Bardia (32-08N 25-22E) by German submarine *U.79*; towed to Alexandria and beached; not repaired

23 RN Destroyer ATLANTIC
Cossack 2337: Torpedoed west of Portugal (35-12N 08-17W) while escorting convoy HG.75 by German submarine *U.563*; strenuous efforts to save the ship failed and she sank at 1043 on the 27th

German Minesweeper NW EUROPE
M.6 Mined off Lorient

24 Russian Minesweeper
Patron Mined off Hangö

25 RN Minelayer MED
Latona 2015: Damaged and set on fire 30 miles (55 km) north of Bardia (32-15N 24-14E) by German air attack; fire reached after magazine and ship blew up and sank at 2220 – 37 men lost

Although the United States was not a belligerent, the US Navy had been escorting trans-Atlantic convoys in the western sector of the North Atlantic since mid-September 1941. Casualties were inevitable and the first successful U-boat attack on a US warship had occurred on 17 October, when the destroyer *Kearny* had been damaged by a torpedo. The first loss of a US Navy ship in the Second World War occurred a fortnight later.

31 USN Destroyer ATLANTIC
Reuben James 0540: Sunk in N. Atlantic 600 miles (1,100 km) west of Ireland (51-59N 27-05W) by German submarine *U.526* – 115 men lost

NOVEMBER 1941

3 German Minesweepers NW EUROPE
M.511
M.529 Mined off Kolberg (54-15N 15-33E – Polish 'Kolobrzegh')
4 Russian Destroyer
Smetlivy Mined off Hangö

A convoy bound for Tripoli was intercepted 150 miles ENE of Malta early on 9 November 1941 by RN Force 'K' (cruisers HMS *Aurora* and *Penelope*, destroyers *Lance* and *Lively*). Two tankers and five cargo vessels were sunk by torpedoes and gunfire; two Italian destroyers were sunk and two (*Euro* and *Maestrale*) damaged.

MED 9 Italian Destroyers
Fulmine 0115: Sunk by 6in gunfire of RN cruisers in 37-00N 18-10E
Libeccio 1048: Returned to pick up survivors, torpedoed by RN submarine *Upholder* and stern blown off; taken in tow but capsized and sank at 1119 (36-50N 18-10E)

The 17-month career of the mainstay of Force 'H', the carrier *Ark Royal*, was ended on the afternoon of 13 November 1941, as she was returning to Gibraltar from one of her numerous aircraft ferry missions to Malta. Good damage control practices could have saved her but were not available within the ship.

The loss of the *Ark Royal* marked the beginning of a period of almost unrelieved disaster for the Royal (and US) Navies.

13 RN Aircraft-Carrier
Ark Royal 1540: Torpedoed (one hit) east of Gibraltar (36-06N 05-07E) by German submarine *U.81*; taken in tow but foundered at 0600 on the 14th – one man lost

NW EUROPE 13 Russian Destroyer
Surovy Mined off Hangö

14 Russian Destroyer
Gordy Mined off Naisaari, Gulf of Finland

Russian Minesweeper
Verp Mined off Hangö

Uncertainty surrounds the fate of a number of vessels lost between 1939 and 1945 but few have provoked such interest as the loss of the Australian Navy cruiser *Sydney*. That she was sunk by the armed raider *Kormoran* is beyond question; how she came to expose herself to surprise attack at short range must remain a mystery, in the absence of any survivors.

INDIAN O. 19 RAN Cruiser
Sydney 1700: Sunk off Western Australia (in about 26S 111E) by torpedo and gunfire of German raider *Kormoran*

German Raider
Kormoran Damaged by 6in gunfire of HMAS *Sydney*; fires spread out of control and resulted in her loss – 315 men survived

HMS *Devonshire* made no mistakes in sinking the raider *Atlantis*, long before details of the *Sydney*'s loss became available. The Royal Navy cruiser exploited the longer range of her 8in guns and pounded the raider from a distance of 17,000 yards (15,700 metres).

ATLANTIC 22 German Raider
Atlantis 1118: Sunk 300 miles (560 km) north-west of Ascension Is (04-02S 18-29W) by gunfire of RN cruiser *Devonshire*; survivors rescued by U-boats which the raider was replenishing

24 RN Cruiser
Dunedin 1226: Sunk 900 miles west of Freetown (in about 03N 26W) by German submarine *U.124*; 72 men rescued on the 27th by US merchant ship – over 300 lost

MED 25 RN Battleship
Barham 1630: Torpedoed off Libyan coast (32-34N 26-24E) by German submarine *U.331*; capsized and blew up in less than 5 minutes; 862 men lost, 450 rescued

Italian Minesweeper (ex-Yugoslav)
Zirona Damaged at Benghazi by air raid and beached
(ex-*Jastreb*)

27   RAN Sloop   MED
     Parramatta   0100: Torpedoed off Bardia (32-20N 24-35E) by German submarine
                       U.559 – 20 men survived

DECEMBER 1941

1   Italian Destroyer
    Alvise da   0940: Sunk 75 miles (140 km) north-east of Tripoli (33-53N 12-28E)
     Mosto   by 6in gunfire of RN Force 'K' (see 9 November 1941)

2   Russian Escort Vessel (ex-Latvian Minesweeper)   NW EUROPE
    Virsaitis   Mined off Hangö

7   RCN Corvette   ATLANTIC
    Windflower   1250: Lost by collision in fog with merchant ship SS **Zypenberg** in
                   mid-Atlantic (46-19N 49-30W)

*Japanese carrier aircraft attacked the US Navy Fleet base at Pearl Harbor, Oahu, Hawaian Is, between 0800 and 1000 (1800–2000, 7 December in Europe). The damage to US warships was inflicted almost entirely by the aircraft of Carrier Divisions 1 (**Akagi, Kaga**) and 2 (**Hiryu, Soryu**), while those of Carrier Division 5 (**Shokaku, Zuikaku**) attacked airfields and shore installations. Despite the destruction of the US Pacific battlefleet, the absence of the US aircraft-carriers and many of the modern cruisers from Pearl Harbor at the time of the attack deprived the Japanese Navy of the absolute victory which it required in a war with a more powerful nation.*

7   *US Battleships*   PACIFIC
    Arizona   *Hit in forward magazine by bomb and blew up with very heavy loss of life*
    Oklahoma   *Hit by 5 torpedoes and sank in shallow water – not repaired*
    West Virginia *Hit by 6 or 7 torpedoes and 2 bombs: sank in shallow water in 5 minutes – raised and repaired*
    California   *Hit by 2 torpedoes and 1 bomb – sank slowly in shallow water – raised and repaired*
    Nevada   *Hit by 1 torpedo and 6 bombs (at least) and beached in harbour entrance to prevent sinking – repaired*

    US Destroyers
    Cassin   *Sunk by fire and flooding in dry dock – both salvaged and repaired*
    Downes   *Bombed in floating dock (2 hits), bow broke off when forward*
    Shaw   *magazine exploded; stern section salvaged and repaired with new bow section*

8   *US Minesweeper*
    Penguin   *Sunk at Guam by land-based Japanese Naval Air Force (JNAF) air attack*

    RN River Gunboat
    Peterel   *(disarmed at Shanghai); 0745: sunk at Shanghai by gunfire of Japanese cruiser* **Izumo**

The Japanese Naval Air Force's long-range land-based anti-shipping units proved themselves to be the equal in efficiency of their carrier counterparts on 10 December 1941, when at a distance of 600 miles (1,100 km) they sank one of the most modern battleships in existence, as well as an older battlecruiser.

10 *RN Battleship*
    Prince of   *1144–1320; Sunk east of Malaya (03-34N 104-26E) by JNAF*
     Wales   *torpedo aircraft*

    RN Battlecruiser
    Repulse   *1223–1233: Sunk with HMS* **Prince of Wales** *(03-37N 104-21E)*

PACIFIC — *US Minesweeper*
Bittern — *Damaged at Cavite Navy Yard, Luzon, by JNAF air attack; scuttled later in the same month*

Japanese Minesweepers
W.10 — *Sunk off west coast of Luzon (17-32N 120-22E) by US Army Air Force (USAAF) air attack*

W.19 — *Damaged by USAAF air attack and beached on west coast of Luzon (18-22N 121-38E)*

MED — 11 — Italian Torpedo-Boat
Alcione — Torpedoed north of Crete by RN submarine **Truant**; stern blown off, ship towed to coast of Crete and beached in 35-29N 24-11E

The defence of the mid-Pacific Wake Island (18-47N 164-42E) provided the US Marine Corps with its first WWII epic, a handful of fighter-bombers and a small coast defence battery inflicting the Japanese Navy's first appreciable losses.

11 — *Japanese Destroyer*
Hayate — *0610: Damaged off Wake Is by 5in gunfire of US Marine Corps (USMC) shore battery and beached (total loss)*

Kisaragi — *0740: Sunk off Wake Is (19-16N 166-37E) by USMC air attack*

Up-to-date intelligence enabled the Royal Navy to set up an ambush off Tunisia on the night of 12/13 December 1941. The four destroyers, operating inshore of the two Italian cruisers, which were laden with aviation spirit bound for Tripoli, obtained complete surprise

PACIFIC — 12 — *RN River Gunboat*
Moth — *Scuttles as blockship in Hong Kong Dockyard; raised and repaired by Japanese; recommissioned as **Suma** (see 19 March 1945)*

MED — 13 — Italian Cruisers
Alberico da Barbiano
Alberto di Giussano — 0230: Intercepted 2 miles (3,700 metres) east of Cape Bon by RN destroyers **Sikh, Maori, Legion** and Dutch **Isaac Sweers**; **da Barbiano** hit by torpedoes from all 3 RN ships and **di Giussano** by one torpedo from **Legion** and 4.7in gunfire. Italian torpedo-boat **Cigno** undamaged and recovered 500 of the 650 survivors; 900 men lost

14 — RN Cruiser
Galatea — 2359: Torpedoed 30 miles west of Alexandria (31-12N 29-15E) by German submarine **U.557**; sank almost immediately – 144 survivors rescued by RN destroyers

PACIFIC — 16 — *RN Destroyer*
Thracian — *Damaged by Japanese Army Air Force (JAAF) air attack off Hong Kong; beached in Repulse Bay and sabotaged but later salvaged and repaired by Japanese as Patrol Vessel **P.101***

18 — *Japanese Destroyer*
Shinonome — *Mined in Dutch field off Miri, Borneo (04-24N 114-00E)*

Force 'K's' anti-shipping campaign in the Central Mediterranean came to an abrupt close in the early hours of 19 December 1941, in an Italian minefield laid on the 100-fathom (180-metre) line off Tripoli. Four of the five RN ships struck mines and although only one cruiser and one destroyer were lost, the damage caused to the survivors resulted in the disbanding of the Force.

MED — 19 — RN Cruiser
Neptune — 0030–0400: Struck 4 mines 20 miles (37 km) north of Tripoli (33-15N 13-30E), capsized and sank – 763 men lost, 1 survivor taken prisoner. Cruisers **Aurora** and **Penelope** both mined and damaged but reached Malta under their own steam

RN Destroyer   MED
Kandahar   0115: Mined attempting to go alongside HMS **Neptune**; 174 men
                 rescued under difficult conditions by HMS **Jaguar**, which scuttled
                 Kandahar by torpedo at 0430

19 RN Escort Destroyer   ATLANTIC
    Stanley   0345: Torpedoed west of Portugal (38-12N 17-23W) while
                    escorting convoy HG 76 by German U-boat **U.574**; blew up with
                    violent explosion – only 25 survivors

The Italian Fleet had been unable to make an effective challenge to the supremacy of
the British Mediterranean Fleet since the early days of the war in the Mediterranean,
but on the night of 18/19 December 1941 a handful of 'frogmen' succeeded in putting
both the remaining battleships at Alexandria out of action. Good security prevented the
extent of the damage from becoming known to the Axis, who remained unaware of the
weakness of the Fleet.

19 RN Battleship   MED
    Queen   0610: mined in Alexandria harbour by explosive charges laid by
    Elizabeth   Italian Navy swimmers; four boiler-rooms and a magazine flooded
                     and the ship settled on the bottom of the harbour. Subsequently
                     refloated, repaired and returned to service. (HMS **Valiant** was less
                     seriously damaged in the same attack)

21 *RN River Gunboat*   PACIFIC
    Cicala   *Dive-bombed off Hong Kong by Japanese Army aircraft*

21 RN Escort Carrier   ATLANTIC
    Audacity   2035: Sunk 500 miles west of Cape Finisterre (44N 20W) while
                     escorting convoy HG 76 by German submarine **U.741**

22 *Japanese Patrol Boats (ex-Destroyers)*   PACIFIC
    No. 32
    No. 33   *Damaged off Wake Island by 5in gunfire of USMC shore batteries;
                     beached on reef but subsequently slid off and sank (Wake Island
                     was overrun and captured on the following day)*

23 German Minesweeper   NW EUROPE
    M.557   Foundered north-east of Rügen Is, Baltic, in a blizzard

24 *Japanese Destroyer*   PACIFIC
    Sagiri   *Sunk off Kuching, Sarawak, by Dutch submarine* **K.16** *(02-34N
                     110-21E)*

24 RN Corvette   MED
    Salvia   0135: Sunk 100 miles west of Alexandria (31-46N 28-00E) by
                     German submarine **U.568**; had embarked many survivors of a
                     torpedoed prisoner-of-war transport – only wreckage found

24 *Japanese Minesweeper*   PACIFIC
    W.6   *Sunk off Kuching, Sarawak (01E 110E) by Dutch Army Air Force air
                     attack*

JANUARY 1942

7 Russian Minesweeper   NW EUROPE
   Vzryvatyel   Damaged by German artillery fire off Eupatoria, Black Sea, and
                     beached

9 RN Escort Destroyer
   Vimiera   1415: Mined in Thames Estuary, off East Spile Buoy (51-28N 00-
                     55E)

PACIFIC   **11**   *Dutch Minelayer*

Prins van   *Sunk south of Boengoe Island, Tarakan, by 5in gunfire of Japanese*
Oranje   *destroyer* **Yamakaze** *and 4.7in gunfire of* **Patrol Boat No. 38**

The sinking, on 12 January 1942, of two Japanese minesweepers supporting the invasion of Tarakan action had a most unpleasant consequence: the Dutch garrison commander had surrendered but the news had not reached the Karoengan Battery as the telephone lines had been cut by gunfire. The incensed Japanese invaders executed all 84 artillerymen of the battery.

   12   *Japanese Minesweepers*
W.13
W.14   *Sunk by gunfire of Dutch Army coastal battery off Tarakan, Borneo*

MED   **17**   *RN Destroyer*
Gurkha*(ii)*   0735: Torpedoed north of Bardia (31-50N 26-14E) by German submarine *U.133*; sank at 0913 with few casualties

NW EUROPE   **17**   *RN Destroyer*
Matabele   2327: Torpedoed in Barents Sea (69-21N 35-34E) by German submarine *U.454* – heavy loss of life

PACIFIC   **24**   *Japanese Escort Destroyer*
Patrol Boat   *Sunk in shallow water of Balikpapan, E. Borneo (01-24S 117-12E)*
No 37   *by gunfire and torpedoes of US destroyers* **Pope** *and* **Parrot***; raised*
*(ex-***Hishi***)*   *and broken up*

So successful was the Royal Navy's mining of the inshore channels off the Belgian coast by Motor Launches that the German Navy was obliged to use the outer channels. This re-routing was promptly countered by the laying of three fields in the Outer Ruytingen Channel by the minelayer HMS *Plover.*

NW EUROPE   **25**   *German Destroyer*
Bruno   2113: Mined west of Ostend (51-16N 02-15E) in field laid by HMS
Heinemann ***Plover***; struck second mine at 2125, abandoned at 2200 – 94 men lost

To supply their advancing Army, the Japanese occupied the port of Endau, on the east coast of Malaya on 26 January, the landings being supported by an aircraft-carrier, a heavy cruiser, five light cruisers and five destroyers. Costly daylight air attacks by the RAF failed to inflict more than insignificant damage and on the night of 26/27 January the Royal Navy could muster only two aged destroyers to attack the harbour. One was sunk within 20 minutes, the other, HMAS **Vampire***, escaped undamaged behind her own smokescreen.*

PACIFIC   **27**   *RN Destroyer*
Thanet   *pre-dawn: Sunk off Endau, Malaya (02-40N 103-42E), by gunfire of Japanese destroyers* **Amagiri, Hatsuyuki** *and* **Shirayuki** *– 57 survivors*

ATLANTIC   **31**   *RN Escort Destroyer*
Belmont   2210: Torpedoed off Halifax, Nova Scotia, (42-02N 57-18W) by German submarine *U.82*

     RN Cutter (ex-US Coast Guard Cutter)
Culver   2230: Torpedoed south-west of Ireland (48-43N 20-14W) by German submarine *U.105*

FEBRUARY 1942

PACIFIC   **2**   *Japanese Minesweeper*
W.9   *Mined in Dutch minefield off Ambon (03-42S 128-10E)*

5	RN Corvette		ATLANTIC
	Arbutus	2135: Torpedoed south of Iceland (55-05N 19-43W) by German submarine **U.136**	

8   *Japanese Destroyer*   PACIFIC
    Natsushio   *Torpedoed 22 miles (40 km) south of Macassar, Celebes (05-10S 119-16E) by US submarine **S.37***

8   Free French Corvette   ATLANTIC
    Alysse   2330: Torpedoed in N. Atlantic (45-50N 44-48W) by German submarine **U.654**; taken in tow, foundered on the 10th

9   *RN Survey Ship (ex-Sloop)*   PACIFIC
    Herald   *Damaged by air raid and scuttled at Singapore; salvaged by Japanese and commissioned as escort/survey ship **Heiyo**; see 14 November 1944*

11 RCN Corvette   ATLANTIC
    Spikenard   0035: Torpedoed south of Iceland (56-10N 21-07W) by German submarine **U.136**

12 *RN Destroyer*   MED
    Maori   Sunk by German air raid at Malta: caught fire and blew up, damaging HMS **Decoy**

13 *RN River Gunboat*   PACIFIC
    Scorpion   *Sunk in Banka Strait, off Sumatra, by gunfire of Japanese destroyers; approximately 20 survivors taken prisoner*

14 *RN River Gunboat*
    Dragonfly   *Severely damaged off Rusuk Buaja Is., east of Sumatra, by Japanese air attack; abandoned at anchor and later sank*

14 *RN River Gunboat*
    Grasshopper   *Sunk off Rusuk Is., Sumatra, by Japanese air attack; capsized in less than ten minutes, leaving very few survivors*

15 *Dutch Destroyer*
    Van Ghent   *Stranded on Banka Island, Java, and abandoned*

17 *Dutch Destroyer*
    Van Nes   *Sunk by Japanese air attack, Banka*

18 US Destroyer   ATLANTIC
    Truxtun   0410: Ran aground in entrance to Placentia Bay, Newfoundland, in a blizzard – very few survivors. USN Transport **Pollux** also wrecked. Destroyer **Wilkes** ran aground but got off with slight damage

19 *Dutch Destroyer*   PACIFIC
    Piet Hein   *Sunk in Badoeng Strait, off Bali, by 5in gunfire of Japanese destroyers **Asashio, Oshio** and **Michishio***

After the fall of Singapore and southern Sumatra on 15 February 1942, the Japanese Navy sought to isolate Java. On 19 February the Japanese carrier fleet struck at Darwin, N. Australia, the nearest Allied 'safe' base area to the Netherlands East Indies. The harbour installations were severely damaged and ten merchant ships and auxiliaries were sunk, but few warships were present and only one was sunk.

19 US Destroyer
    Peary   *Sunk by Japanese carrier aircraft at Darwin*

In an action to the north of Java on 27 February 1942, the Allied Fleet in the Netherlands East Indies was practically destroyed as a fighting force by Japanese cruiser gunfire and destroyer torpedoes. Most of the individual units which survived the Battle of the Java Sea were sunk during the following days, in harbour or attempting to escape.

PACIFIC 27 Dutch Destroyer
Kortenaer *1735: Torpedoed 43 miles (80 km) south of Bawean Island by Japanese cruiser* **Haguro** *and sank immediately – 113 survivors rescued*

RN Destroyer
Electra *1846: Sunk south-west of Bawean Is. (06-45S 112-06E) by 5in gunfire of Japanese destroyer* **Asagumo**. *The Japanese destroyer had been stopped by* **Electra**'s *4.7in shells but almost immediately scored lethal hits on the latter, which caught fire and sank rapidly – 54 survivors rescued by US submarine* **S.38**

RN Destroyer
Jupiter *2125: Mined in Dutch minefield off Soerabaja; sank 4 hours later in 06-45S 112-06E*

Dutch Cruisers
Java *2335: Torpedoed 40 miles (74 km) west-south-west of Bawean Island by Japanese cruiser* **Nachi**
De Ruyter *2335: Torpedoed by Japanese cruiser* **Haguro** *and sank very quickly*

NW EUROPE 27 German Battlecruiser
Gneisenau Severely damaged by fire and explosion in RAF air raid on Kiel; in dry dock following mine damage off Terschelling on 12 February: not repaired

ATLANTIC 28 US Destroyer
Jacob Jones 0600: Torpedoed off New Jersey coast (38-37N 74-32W) by German submarine ***U.578***; sank an hour later – 11 survivors

MARCH 1942

After a day's respite, on 28 February, most of the surviving ships of the American-British-Dutch-Australian Fleet were destroyed in Javanese waters on 1 March 1942 by an enemy who was superior in every department except courage.

PACIFIC 1 US Cruiser
Houston *0035: Sunk in Sunda Strait (06S 106E) by gunfire and torpedoes of Japanese cruisers* **Mogami** *and* **Mikuma** *and destroyers – over 300 survivors*

RAN Cruiser
Perth *0108: Sunk with USS* **Houston** *(05-45S 106-13S) – 307 survivors*

Dutch Destroyer
Evertsen *pre-dawn: Damaged off north coast of Java by 5in gunfire of Japanese destroyers* **Shirakumo** *and* **Murakomo** *and beached on Sebuku Besar Island, Sunda Strait*

Japanese Minesweeper
W.2 *Mined in Dutch minefield in Bantam Bay, Java*

RN Cruiser
Exeter *1020–1100: Damaged off Bawean Is, Java Sea (05-00S 111-00E), by 8in gunfire of Japanese cruisers* **Nachi** *and* **Haguro** *and torpedo from destroyer* **Ikazuchi**; *scuttled – 300 men rescued by Japanese*

RN Destroyer
Encounter *1135: Sunk with* **Exeter**, *by gunfire of Japanese cruisers* **Myoko** *and* **Ashigara**

US Destroyer
Pope *1230: Damaged off Bawean Island by 8in gunfire of cruisers* **Myoko** *and* **Ashigara**; *scuttled*

	US Destroyers		PACIFIC
	Edsall	*Sunk south of Java by 14in gunfire of Japanese battleships **Hiei** and **Kirishima** – it is possible that some of her crew were rescued by the Japanese, but none survived the war*	
	Pillsbury	*Sunk south of Java by 8in gunfire of Japanese cruiser **Ashigara** – no survivors*	
2	*Dutch Destroyers*		
	Banckert	*(Previously damaged by air raid). Scuttled in dry dock at Soerabaja*	
	Witte de With	*(Unable to proceed to sea due to mechanical defects). Scuttled at Soerabaja*	
2	*US Destroyer*		
	Stewart	*(Previously damaged by gunfire). Scuttled in dry dock at Soerabaja; salvaged and repaired by Japanese – commissioned as Patrol Boat **P.102***	
3	*US Escort (Patrol Gunboat)*		
	Asheville	*Sunk south of Java (12-33S 111-35E) by surface action – no survivors*	
4	*RN Destroyer*		
	Stronghold	*2315: Sunk 220 miles (405 km) south of Sunda Strait (11-30S 109-03E) by gunfire of Japanese cruisers and destroyers*	
	RAN Sloop		
	Yarra	*Sunk south of Java with HMS **Stronghold**, together with a motor minesweeper (**MMS 51**) and two naval auxiliaries*	
6	*Dutch Minesweepers*		
	Jan van Amstel	*Sunk in Madura Strait by surface action*	
	Pieter de Bitter	*Scuttled at Soerabaja*	
	Eland Dubois	*Scuttled in Gili Genteng Roads, Java*	
6	Russian Destroyer		BLACK SEA
	Smyshleny	Mined in Kerch Straits, Black Sea	
10	*Japanese Armed Merchant Cruiser*		PACIFIC
	Kongo Maru	*Sunk at Salamaua, New Guinea (06-49S 147-02E), by aircraft from US carriers **Lexington** and **Yorktown***	
11	RN Anti-Aircraft Cruiser		MED
	Naiad	2000: Torpedoed north of Mersa Matruh (32-00N 26-19E) by German submarine *U.565*	
15	RN Escort Destroyer		NW EUROPE
	Vortigern	0100: Torpedoed off Cromer, N. Sea (53-06N 01-22E) while escorting convoy FS.749 by German E-Boat *S.104*	
20	RN Escort Destroyer		MED
	Heythrop	1100: Torpedoed 40 miles (74 km) north-east of Bardia (32-33N 25-33E) by German submarine *U.652*; sank 5 hours later, in tow of HMS *Eridge*	
23	Italian Destroyers		
	Scirocco	0545: Foundered in storm in Ionian Sea (35-50N 17-35E). Destroyer *Geniere*, in company, sustained weather damage and lost several members of her crew	
	Lanciere	1007: Foundered, separately, in storm in Ionian Sea (35-35N 17-15E)	
24	RN Escort Destroyer		
	Southwold	1117: Mined off Zonkor Point, Malta (35-53N 14-35E); sank at 1800	

MED 26 RN Destroyer
Jaguar 0445: Torpedoed off Sidi Barrani (31-53N 26-18E) by German submarine **U.652** – 53 survivors rescued

RN Destroyer
Legion (Damaged by air attack on 23 March). Sunk in air raid on Grand Harbour, Malta

NW EUROPE 28 RN Escort Destroyer
Campbeltown Expended as blockship in raid on St. Nazaire; rammed lock gates and subsequently blown up

29 German Destroyer
Z.26 0920: Sunk in Barents Sea (72-07N 32-15E) by 6in gunfire of RN cruiser **Trinidad** and 4.7in gunfire of destroyers **Fury** and **Eclipse**, escorting convoy PQ 13 (HMS **Trinidad** suffered torpedo damage, from one of her own torpedoes which circled after firing, in the action but reached Murmansk)

APRIL 1942

MED 1 Italian Cruiser
Giovanni delle 0900: Torpedoed 11 miles (20 km) south-east of Stromboli Island,
Bande Nere Tyrrhenian Sea, by RN submarine **Urge**; hit by 2 torpedoes, broke in half and sank almost immediately

BLACK SEA 2 Russian Cruiser
Chervonaya (Beached in shallow water at Sevastopol, following previous
Ukraina bomb damage). Destroyed by German air attack

nk Russian Destroyer
Shaumyan Ran aground at Gelendzhik, Black Sea

In early April the hitherto triumphant Japanese carrier fleet delivered two strikes on British naval bases in Ceylon, attacking Colombo on the 5th and Trincomalee on the 9th. Despite the wealth of targets at the former, only two warships were sunk, another damaged and just one merchant ship damaged, out of 34 ships present. The chance sighting of two RN heavy cruisers gave the Japanese dive-bombers the opportunity to make up for what was otherwise a rather ineffective performance.

PACIFIC 5 *RN Armed Merchant Cruiser*
Hector *0800: Sunk in shallow water in Colombo Harbour by aircraft from carriers* **Akagi, Soryu** *and* **Hiryu***; raised and scrapped*

RN Destroyer
Tenedos *Sunk in Colombo Harbour by carrier aircraft – 33 men lost*

RN Cruisers
Cornwall *1340–1355: Sunk south of Ceylon (01-54N 77-45E) by dive-*
Dorsetshire *bombers from carriers* **Akagi, Soryu** *and* **Hiryu***; 190 men lost from* **Cornwall***, 234 from* **Dorsetshire** *– 1,122 survivors rescued 30 hours after sinkings*

Although the Japanese carrier fleet could mount only 'hit and run' strikes against its distant targets, the Axis air forces were able to sustain a prolonged bombing campaign against the British naval and air bases on Malta, barely 100 miles (180 km) to the south of Sicily. Few ships which had been damaged elsewhere and had entered Malta Dockyard for repairs survived.

MED 5 RN Destroyer
Lance (In dry dock, damaged) Damaged beyond repair in German air raid on Malta Dockyard (a further raid on the 9th added to the damage)

RN Minesweeper
Abingdon (Damaged on the 4th) Sunk in German air raid on Malta Dockyard

| 6 | RIN Sloop | | PACIFIC |
| | **Indus** | *Sunk off Fakir Point, Akyab (20-07N 92-54E) by JAAF air attack* | |

| 6 | RN Destroyer | | MED |
| | **Havoc** | 0415: Ran aground on sand-bank off Kelibia, Tunisia (36-48N 11-08E), at 30 knots; one man lost, crew and 100 passengers bound for Gibraltar interned by Vichy French | |

The Japanese carrier force returned to the attack of Ceylon on 9 April, after refuelling, undertaking a strike on Trincomalee. Most of the shipping had been dispersed in anticipation of the raid and only one merchant ship and a floating dock were sunk. As on the 5th, the greatest success of the day was scored by the dive-bombers against targets discovered by chance, some 65 miles (120 km) to the south of the main target.

9	RN Carrier		PACIFIC
	Hermes	*1100—20: Sunk off Batticaloa, Ceylon, (07-50N 81-49E) by aircraft from carriers* **Akagi, Hiryu, Shokaku** *and* **Zuikaku,** *which scored over 40 hits with 500lb (227kg) bombs; 307 men lost*	
	RAN Destroyer		
	Vampire	*1130: Sunk with HMS* **Hermes** *by dive-bombers – 8 men lost. The nearby hospital ship* **Vita** *was respected by the Japanese and rescued over 600 survivors from these ships*	
	RN Corvette		
	Hollyhock	*1200: Sunk 30 miles (55 km) south-south-east of Batticaloa (07-30N 81-57E) by aircraft from carrier* **Soryu** *– 53 men lost*	

| 11 | RN Destroyer | | MED |
| | **Kingston** | (Damaged on 22 March by Italian gunfire and by bombs on 5 and 7 April) Sunk in dry dock at Malta by German air raid | |

| 26 | US Destroyer | | ATLANTIC |
| | **Sturtevant** | 1515: Mined in USN minefield off Marquesas Key, Key West, Florida – 15 men lost; three merchant ships were subsequently lost in this 'friendly' field | |

| 27 | RN Minesweeper | | NW EUROPE |
| | **Fitzroy** | 1210: Mined 40 miles (75 km) east-north-east of Great Yarmouth (52-39N 02-46E), possibly on British mine; sank in 9 minutes with few casualties | |

MAY 1942

| 1 | RN Destroyer | | ATLANTIC |
| | **Punjabi** | 1345: Sunk in fog east of Iceland (66-00N 08-00W) in collision with RN battleship **King George V** – 205 men rescued; **KGV** damaged by explosion of the destroyer's depth-charges | |

| 2 | Japanese Seaplane-Carrier | | PACIFIC |
| | **Mizuho** | *Torpedoed off Cape Omaisaki, Honshu (34-26N 138-14E), by US submarine* **Drum** | |

2	RN Cruiser		NW EUROPE
	Edinburgh	(Damaged by torpedo 30 April – **U.456**) 0457: Torpedoed in Barents Sea (72-05N 35-02E) by German destroyer **Z.24**; abandoned at 0550 and scuttled by HMS **Foresight** – 58 men lost	
	German Destroyer		
	Hermann Schoemann	Severely damaged in Barents Sea by 4.7in gunfire of RN destroyers **Foresight** and **Forester**; scuttled by **Z.24** (72-20N 35-15E)	

The US Army held out on the Bataan Peninsula until 9 April and then retreated to the fortified island of Corregidor, in the entrance to Manila Bay. On 4 May, after three days' preparatory air and artillery bombardment, the Japanese landed on the fortress; the defenders fought stubbornly but there could be no relief and the last organized resistance to the Japanese in the Philippines ended on 6 May.

PACIFIC | 4 | USN Minesweeper
Tanager   Sunk in Manila Bay by Japanese artillery fire

4 | Japanese Destroyer
Kikuzuki   *0815: Badly damaged at Tulagi, Solomon Is, (09-07S 160-12E) by aircraft from US carrier* **Yorktown**; *beached and abandoned*

5 | USN Minesweeper
Pigeon   Sunk in Manila Bay (14-23N 120-36E) by JAAF air attack (this ship was in service as a submarine rescue vessel)

US Navy River Gunboat
Mindanao   Sunk at Corregidor by Japanese Army air attack

British Commonwealth forces invaded northern Madagascar on 5 May 1942 to secure the Vichy French harbour of Diego Suarez (or, rather, to prevent its use by the Axis navies). In the course of the 48-hour operation, all the French naval forces were destroyed or taken, RN carrier aircraft being responsible for most of the losses, which included two submarines and an armed trawler. One RN minesweeping corvette was sunk.

INDIAN O. | 5 | French Armed Merchant Cruiser
Bougainville   Torpedoed and sunk at Diego Suarez by RN aircraft (HMS ***Illustrious***)

RN Corvette
Auricula   am: Mined in Courrier Bay, north-west coast of Madagascar (12-12S 49-19E); remained afloat, with back broken, until the 6th – no casualties

PACIFIC | 6 | US Minesweepers
Finch   *Sunk at Corregidor by Japanese artillery fire; salvaged by Japanese Navy April 1943 and commissioned as Patrol Boat* **P.103** *– sunk 12 January 1945*

Quail   *Scuttled at Corregidor to avoid capture*

6 | US Navy River Gunboat
Luzon   *Scuttled at Corregidor; raised and repaired by Japanese as* **Karatsu** *and sunk at Manila on 3 February 1945*

6 | US Navy River Gunboat
Oahu   *Scuttled at Corregidor*

INDIAN O. | 6 | French Aviso
D'Entre-   Sunk in shallow water, Diego Suarez Bay, by RN aircraft (HMS
casteaux   ***Indomitable***) and 4.7in gunfire of destroyer ***Laforey***

In early May a US carrier force arrived in the Coral Sea to counter a Japanese attempt to land on the south coast of New Guinea. Although US unit losses were heavier, they were compensated by the thwarting of the Japanese strategic intention.

PACIFIC | 7 | Japanese Light Carrier
Shoho   *1110: Sunk off Woodlark Is, Coral Sea (10-29S 152-55E) by USN aircraft from carrier* **Yorktown**; *hit by a dozen bombs and up to 7 torpedoes – sank in less than 10 minutes*

US Destroyer
Sims   *1130: Sunk in Coral Sea by Japanese aircraft from carriers* **Shokaku** *and* **Zuikaku** *– 14 survivors.*

*(The oiler **Neosho**, identified as a carrier, was also sunk by this strike, the first in which Carrier Division 5 achieved sinkings without the assistance of the more experienced CarDivs 1 and 2, albeit needing 60 sorties to sink the two ships)*

8   US Carrier
     Lexington   *1120: Damaged and set on fire in Coral Sea by Japanese torpedo-bombers from carriers **Shokaku** and **Zuikaku**; fires could not be controlled and ship was abandoned at 1700 following major explosions. Scuttled at 2000 by US destroyer **Phelps***

9   German Minesweeper
     M.533   Sunk north-west of Boulogne in collision with motor minesweeper **R.45**

11   Japanese Minelaying Cruiser
     Okinoshima   *Sunk in St George's Channel, New Britain, (05-06S 153-48E) by US submarine **S-42***

An attempt on 11 May 1942 by four Royal Navy destroyers from Alexandria to intercept an Axis convoy bound for Benghazi ended in disaster, the ships being subjected to repeated dive-bombing attacks. Land-based RAF fighters were unable to provide adequate defence and only one ship survived.

11   RN Destroyers
     Lively   1645: Sunk 100 miles (185 km) north-east of Tobruk (33-24N 25-38E) by German air attack; sank immediately – 76 men lost
     Jackal   2007: Damaged 60 miles (110 km) north of Mersa Matruh (32-38N 26-20E) by German air attack; taken in tow, still on fire, by HMS **Jervis**, which had to scuttle her at 0455 on the 12th
     Kipling   2007: Sunk in company with **Jackal** by air attack – went down quickly. HMS **Jervis** rescued 650 men from the three ships and brought them safely to Alexandria

A German convoy coast-crawling from the Hook of Holland to Le Havre was intercepted by RN coastal forces between Dover and Boulogne in the early hours of 13 May. Screening E-boats failed to prevent the MTBs from breaking through and two valuable torpedo-boats were lost. RAF fighter-bombers sank two M-class minesweepers of the escort, continuing to Cherbourg, on the following day.

13   German Torpedo-Boats
     Iltis   0404: Torpedoed north of Boulogne (50-46N 01-34E) by RN **MTB 221** – 34 men lost
     Seeadler   0409: Torpedoed with **Iltis** (50-48N 01-32E) by **MTB 219** – 84 men lost

14   Russian Destroyer
     Dzerzhinski   Mined off Sevastopol

     RN Cruiser
     Trinidad   (Damaged by her own torpedo on 29 March) am: Severely damaged in Barents Sea, 100 miles (185 km) north of Murmansk (73-37N 23-27E), by air attack and scuttled by HMS **Matchless** – 81 men lost

     German Minesweepers
     M.26   Sunk off Cap de la Hague, Normandy, by RAF air attack
     M.256   Badly damaged by air attack off Cap de la Hague, towed to Cherbourg Harbour, where she later sank. (Subsequently refloated, repaired and restored to service)

MED 29 Italian Destroyer
Emanuele 0330: Torpedoed 78 miles (145 km) north-north-west of Benghazi
Pessagno by RN submarine **Turbulent**; hit in bow and amidships, she sank
in less than one minute

JUNE 1942

Although the Battle of the Coral Sea in early May had imposed a check on Japanese expansion and provided the Allies with a welcome, if pyrrhic, victory, Japanese naval strength was little diminished. At the beginning of June the Japanese Navy was able to send to sea four large carriers and four smaller carriers (with 350 aircraft), 8 battleships, 19 cruisers and 74 destroyers: the purposes of this deployment were the near-simultaneous occupation of the Aleutian Islands and, more important, Midway Island, 1,360 miles (2,500 km) north-west of Hawaii. Against one wing of this divided armada, the US Navy was able to concentrate just three carriers (with 230 aircraft), 8 cruisers and 14 destroyers: the great equalizer was the unsuspected American ability to read the Japanese naval cypher. The battle of Midway was a very close-run thing but it produced the first Allied strategic victory in the Pacific.

PACIFIC 4 *Japanese* *Attacked about 200 miles (370 km) north-east of Midway Island*
Carriers
Akagi *1026: Hit by two bombs (aircraft from USS* **Enterprise***); fires could not be controlled and ship was scuttled just before dawn on the 5th (30-30N 178-40E) – 263 men lost*
Kaga *1028: Hit by four bombs (aircraft from USS* **Enterprise***); abandoned soon after the attack and sank at 1926 (30-20N 179-17E) – about 800 men lost*
Soryu *1029: Hit by three bombs (aircraft from USS* **Yorktown***); abandoned from 1050 and sank at 1910 (30-42N 178-38E) – 718 men lost*
Hiryu *1705: Hit 200 miles (370 km) north-east of Midway by four bombs (aircraft from USS* **Enterprise***); abandoned early on the 5th, torpedoed by destroyers at dawn and sank at 0900 (31-27N 179-23E) – 416 men lost*

6 *Japanese Cruiser*
Mikuma *(Damaged early on 5 June in collision with cruiser* **Mogami** *and by USMC aircraft during that day)*
0900–1500: Hit by up to eight bombs, abandoned and sank after nightfall (29-20N 173-30E). Sister-ship **Mogami** *survived the collision and six 1,000lb (455kg) bombs, repaired and returned to service 1943*

US Carrier
Yorktown *(Damaged at 1200 and 1445 on 4 June by torpedoes and bombs, abandoned and taken in tow on the 5th)*
1335, 6 June: Torpedoed 200 miles (370 km) east-north-east of Midway by Japanese submarine **I-168** *and sank by slow flooding at 0500 on the 7th*

US Destroyer
Hammann *1335: Torpedoed while alongside* **Yorktown** *by* **I-168***; sank in less than 4 minutes*

MED 8 Italian Destroyer
Antoniotto 2125: Torpedoed north of Cape Bon (38-09N 11-00E) by mistake by
Usodimare Italian submarine **Alagi**; broke in half and sank rapidly

9	Free French Corvette		ATLANTIC
	Mimosa	0215: Torpedoed in N. Atlantic (52-15N 32-37W) by German submarine *U.124*	

10 Russian Destroyer   BLACK SEA
   Svobodny   Sunk by air attack in Korabelnya Bight, Sevastopol

12 RN Escort Destroyer   MED
   Grove   0540: Torpedoed in Gulf of Sollum (32-05N 25-30E) by German submarine *U.77*

13 Russian Minesweeper   BLACK SEA
   T.413   Sunk by air attack off Cape Feolenta, Black Sea

In mid-June 1942 convoys left Gibraltar and Alexandria simultaneously to relieve Malta. Both came under heavy sustained air attack: the eastbound ('Harpoon') convoy was protected by two carriers until dusk on the 14th, but the westbound ('Vigorous') convoy had no continuous fighter protection. The Italian Fleet sortied on the 15th and the 'Vigorous' convoy, threatened by the stronger enemy force, was recalled.

15 RN Destroyer   MED
   Bedouin   0700: Damaged south-west of Pantelleria by 6in gunfire of Italian cruisers *Montecuccoli* and *di Savoia*, while escorting 'Harpoon'. 1200: torpedoed by Italian torpedo aircraft and sank quickly (36-17N 11-41E)

   Italian Cruiser
   Trento   (Badly damaged east of Malta at 0616 by RAF Beaufort torpedo-bomber (No 217 Squadron) attack and taken in tow) 1010: torpedoed by RN submarine *Umbra*, forward magazine blew up and ship sank in less than 5 minutes (35-10N 18-40E)

   RN Destroyer
   Hasty   0525: Damaged south-east of Crete (34-05N 22-00E) while escorting 'Vigorous', by E-boat (*S.55*) and scuttled

   RN Escort Destroyer
   Airedale   1525: Damaged south of Crete (33-50N 23-50E) while escorting 'Vigorous', by German air attack; latter scuttled by HMS *Aldenham* (torpedo) and *Hurworth* (gunfire)

   RAN Destroyer
   Nestor   1806: Damaged south of Crete (33-36N 24-27E) while escorting 'Vigorous', by German air attack; later scuttled by RN forces

16 RN Anti-Aircraft Cruiser
   Hermione   0127: Torpedoed south of Crete (33-30N 26-10E) while escorting 'Vigorous', by German submarine *U.205*

   Polish Escort Destroyer
   Kujawiak   0100: Mined east of Grand Harbour, Malta (35-53N 14-35E), while escorting 'Harpoon'; sank in less than 3 minutes

17 RN Escort Destroyer   ATLANTIC
   Wild Swan   2005: Damaged by German air attack 100 miles (185 km) south of Bantry Bay, Ireland (49-52N 10-44W). 2305: sank after collision with Spanish fishing vessel

21 Italian Destroyer   MED
   Strale   0100: Ran aground near Cape Bon, Tunisia, during RN air attack (830 Squadron, shore-based on Malta); salvage impractical and hulk destroyed by RN submarine *Turbulent* on 8 August 1942

24 RN Minesweeper   NW EUROPE
   Gossamer   am: Sunk in Kola Inlet by air attack (68-59N 33-03E); sank in 8 minutes – 23 men lost

PACIFIC 25 *Japanese Destroyer*
Yamakaze *Torpedoed 60 miles (110 km) south-east of Yokosuka (34-34N 140-26E) by US submarine* **Nautilus**

BLACK SEA 26 Russian Destroyer
Bezuprechny Sunk off Yalta by German air attack

MED 29 Italian Aviso
Diana 1120: Torpedoed 100 miles (185 km) north-west of Tobruk (33-30N 23-39E) by RN submarine ***Thrasher***; sank in less than 15 minutes

JULY 1942

BLACK SEA 2 Russian Flotilla leader
Tashkent (Damaged by air attack off the Crimea on 28 June 1942); foundered at Novorossisk owing to flooding caused by further air attack , damage

2 Russian Destroyer
Bditelny Sunk at Novorossisk by German air attack

PACIFIC 4 *Japanese Destroyer*
Nenohi *Torpedoed off Agattu, Aleutian Is (52-15N 173-51E) by US submarine* **Triton**

5 *Japanese Destroyer*
Arare *Torpedoed in Kiska Bay, Aleutian Is (52-00N 177-40E) by US submarine* **Growler**; *the destroyers* **Katumi** *and* **Shiranui** *were severely damaged in the same attack on this anchorage*

ATLANTIC 5 RN Minesweeper
Niger 2105: Mined in RN minefield off Iceland (66-35N 23-14W). (Four Allied merchant vessels were also lost in this incident)

BLACK SEA 16 Russian Cruiser
Komintern (Badly damaged on 2 July by air attack at Novorossisk) Damaged beyond repair by German air attack at Poti: subsequently sunk as breakwater

July had been deceptively peaceful, if judged by the number of warships lost. Early in the month, however, the RN had sustained a major defeat in the Arctic, where convoy PQ.17 had been dispersed in the face of a threat from the German battleship ***Tirpitz*** and the greater part of the merchant ships had been sunk by air attack and U-boats. On the other flank of the Russian front, the German Army finally subdued and captured the important naval base of Sevastopol, despite the considerable sacrifices made by the Soviet Navy in attempting to reinforce the besieged port by sea. August was to see the Royal Navy return in force to the Mediterranean to relieve Malta, while the US Navy went over to the offensive in the South-West Pacific.

AUGUST 1942

PACIFIC 4 *US Destroyer*
Tucker *Mined in US minefield at the entrance to Espiritu Santo harbour, New Hebrides*

US Marines, supported by the greater part of the US Pacific Fleet and units of the RAN, landed on Guadalcanal Island on 7 August 1942, the main objective being to capture a half-finished airfield.

No one could have envisaged that this operation would have led to the succession of naval battles which followed and cost both sides such a large proportion of their operational fleets. Months were to elapse before the Allies were able to find an effective counter to the Japanese Navy night-fighting tactics, which had first been encountered off Java. The first heavy defeat came off Savo Island, less than 48 hours after the initial landings on Guadalcanal. The sole consolation was the sinking of one of the retiring Japanese cruisers by a US submarine.

9 *RAN Cruiser*   PACIFIC
   Canberra   *0143: Badly damaged south of Savo Is (09-15S 159-40E) by 8in gunfire of Japanese cruisers (***Chokai, Aoba, Kako, Kinugasa** and **Furutaka***) and torpedoes; scuttled at 0800 by US destroyer ***Ellet** – 84 men lost*
                     *US cruiser **Chicago** damaged by torpedo*

   US Cruisers
   Quincy   *0155–0220: Hit by Japanese gunfire and torpedoes east of Savo Is;*
   Vincennes   ***Quincy** sank at 0235, **Vincennes** at 0250 and **Astoria**, under tow*
   Astoria   *but still on fire, at 1215. 1,203 men lost from the three ships*

   US Destroyer
   Jarvis   *(Damaged by JNAF torpedo attack off Guadalcanal on the 8th and by 4.7in gunfire of destroyer **Yunagi** as she passed near the Savo Is action early on the 9th)*
                     1300: Torpedoed by JNAF aircraft south of Guadalcanal (09-42S 158-59E) – 247 men lost, no survivors

10 *Japanese Cruiser*
   Kako   *0908: Torpedoed off New Ireland (02-15S 152-15E) by US submarine **S-44***

The RN despatched a convoy to Malta for Gibraltar as the echoes of the first battle for Guadalcanal died. Three carriers, two battleships, seven cruisers and 26 destroyers formed a close escort which broke up most of the air attacks until the carriers turned back at dusk on 12 August, to the north of Tunisia. Thereafter, the remaining cruisers and destroyers had to face submarine, air and surface attacks. Five of the fourteen merchant ships reached Malta.

11 RN Carrier   MED
   Eagle   1115: Torpedoed 65 miles (120 km) south of Majorca (38-05N 03-02E) by German submarine *U.73*; sank in 8 minutes, survivors rescued by HMS *Laforey, Lookout* and tug *Jaunty*

12 RN Destroyer
   Foresight   1850: Torpedoed north of Bizerta (37-40N 10-00E) by Italian aircraft; taken in tow by HMS *Tartar* but scuttled on following day, 13 miles (24 km) south-west of Galita Is

   RN Anti-Aircraft Cruiser
   Cairo   1955: Torpedoed north-east of Bizerta (37-40N 10-06E) by Italian submarine *Axum*; stern blown off and had to be scuttled on following day (cruiser HMS *Nigeria* was damaged by the same salvo)

13 RN Cruiser
   Manchester   0105: Torpedoed 4 miles (7,400 metres) off Kelibia, Tunisia (36-50N 11-10E), by Italian motor-torpedo boats *Ms16* and *Ms22*; scuttled at 0400 – most survivors rescued by HMS *Somali* and *Pathfinder*

The amphibious raid on Dieppe on 19 August 1942 proved to be an expensive means of gaining experience, but although the troops (particularly the Canadian units) suffered heavily, the Royal Navy lost only one major unit to air attack.

| NW EUROPE | 19 | RN Escort Destroyer | |
| | | **Berkeley** | 1318: Severely damaged 4 miles north-west of Dieppe (49-57N 01-04E) by air attack; back broken by near-miss bombs – scuttled by HMS **Albrighton** |

PACIFIC 22 US Destroyer
Blue *0400: Torpedoed off Savo Island by Japanese destroyer* **Kawakaze**; *towed to Tulagi but scuttled (in 09-17S 160-02E) after dark on the 23rd on approach of Japanese surface force*

MED 22 Italian Torpedo-Boat
Generale Antonio Cantore 1005: Mined 10 miles (18 km) north-east of Bomba, Libya, in field laid by RN submarine **Porpoise** on 5 August

ATLANTIC 22 US Destroyer
Ingraham 2225: Sunk off Nova Scotia (42-34N 60-05W) in collision in fog with oiler **Chemung**; heavy loss of life due to explosion of depth-charges – only 11 survivors. Destroyer **Buck** had been damaged only seconds before in a collison with a troopship of the same convoy

Not until mid-August was the Japanese Navy able to assemble a carrier fleet to contest the US foothold on Guadalcanal. It arrived in the area on the 24th and immediately sought action. The Battle of the Eastern Solomons was not to provide a dramatic result, for although one of the two US carriers was damaged and had to withdraw for repairs and a Japanese seaplane-carrier was very seriously damaged, there was only one ship lost outright.

PACIFIC 24 Japanese Carrier
Ryujo *1620: Damaged north of Santa Isabel Is, Solomons (06-20S 160-50E) by four bombs and one torpedo (aircraft from USS **Saratoga**); abandoned after attack and sank 6 hours later*

NW EUROPE 24 Russian Torpedo-Boat
Burya Mined off Suursaari Island, Gulf of Finland

Russian Minesweeper
Fugas Mined in Gulf of Finland

PACIFIC 25 Japanese Destroyer
Mutsuki *Sunk 40 miles (75 km) north of Santa Isabel Is (07-47S 160-13E) by USAAF B-17 aircraft (the first success by this type of aircraft against a Japanese warship in the Solomons campaign)*

NW EUROPE 25 German Minelayer
Ulm 2234: Sunk 100 miles (185 km) east of Bear Is by 4.7in gunfire of RN destroyers **Marne, Martin** and **Onslaught**; 60 men rescued

PACIFIC 28 Japanese Destroyer
Asagiri *1800: Sunk 60 miles (110 km) north-north-east of Savo Is (08-00S 160-10E) by USN aircraft (ex-**Enterprise** shore-based on Guadalcanal). Destroyer **Shirakumo** severely damaged and towed back to base*

MED 29 RN Escort Destroyer
Eridge 0500: Damaged off Daba, Eastern Mediterranean (31-07N 28-26E) by E-boat torpedo; towed to Alexandria by HMS **Aldenham** – not repaired

PACIFIC 30 US Fast Transport
Colhoun *1515: Sunk off Guadalcanal (09-24S 160-01E) by JNAF aircraft – 51 men lost*

SEPTEMBER 1942

1   Russian Torpedo-Boat   NW EUROPE
Purga   Sunk in shallow water off Marja, Lake Ladoga, by air attack; machinery salvaged and installed in *Vikhr* (see 21 September 1941)

4   Italian Torpedo-Boat   MED
Polluce   0505: Damaged 50 miles (90 km) north of Tobruk (32-38N 23-38E) by air attack: one bomb detonated ready-use ammunition on quarterdeck, causing fire and flooding – sank at 0722

5   *US Fast Transports*   PACIFIC
Gregory
Little   *Sunk off Guadalcanal (09-20S 160-01E) by 5in gunfire of Japanese destroyer* **Yudachi***, which was escorting a 'Tokyo Express' transport mission; 33 men lost from the two ships*

11   *Japanese Destroyer*
Yayoi   *Sunk off Vakuta Is, Solomons (08-45S 151-25E) by RAAF and USAAF air attack*

11   RCN Corvette   ATLANTIC
Charlottetown 1100: Torpedoed in Gulf of St. Lawrence (49-12N 66-48W) by German submarine *U.517*

14   RCN Escort Destroyer
Ottawa   0005: Torpedoed in Gulf of St. Lawrence (47-55N 43-27W) by German submarine *U.91*

Between 12 and 20 September, the RN fought through a convoy to North Russia, the first since the disastrous PQ 17. The German torpedo-bomber force based in N. Norway sank eight freighters but was broken in the process – the only warships to be lost were sunk near the end of the voyage, by U-boats. As PQ 18 was fighting off the aircraft in the Arctic, an ill-planned amphibious raid on Tobruk went awry and, even further to the east and south, the US Navy lost one of its precious carriers to a Japanese submarine.

14   RN Destroyer   MED
Sikh   0510: Damaged by 88mm gunfire (Luftwaffe flak battery) off Tobruk; sank in tow of HMS *Zulu* (32-05N 24-00E). Two Motor Launches were also sunk by the flak battery

RN Anti-Aircraft Cruiser
Coventry   1120: Damaged east of Tobruk by German air attack, set on fire, abandoned and scuttled by HMS *Zulu* (32-48N 28-17E)

RN Destroyer
Zulu   1615: Damaged east of Tobruk by Italian air attack; taken in tow by HMS *Hursley* but sank at 2155 (32-00N 28-56E). Three MTBs were also sunk by aircraft

15   *US Carrier*
Wasp   *1445: Torpedoed north-west of Espiritu Santo, New Hebrides (12-25S 164-08E), by Japanese submarine* **I-19***: fires and explosions led to abandonment from 1520 and ship was scuttled at 2100 by destroyer* **Lansdowne** *– 193 men lost, 366 injured.*
The same torpedo salvo scored hits on battleship **North Carolina** *and destroyer* **O'Brien***, 10,000 yards (9,250m) beyond the* **Wasp***; although* **O'Brien** *reached Noumea, she was subsequently lost attempting the passage to Pearl Harbor (see 19 October 1942)*

NW EUROPE 20 RN Minesweeper
Leda 0520: Torpedoed west of Bear Island (Björnoya) (75-48N 06-00E) by German submarine **U.435**

RN Destroyer
Somali 1850: Torpedoed west of Bear Island (75-40N 02-00E) by German submarine **U.703**; taken in tow by HMS **Ashanti**, but after 80 hours, in which 420 miles (780 km) were covered, the **Somali** suddenly broke her back in a gale and sank at 0230 on the 24th (69-11N 15-32W)

PACIFIC 25 *RAN Destroyer*
Voyager *Ran aground on Timor Is (09-11S 125-43E): could not be towed off before she was damaged by JAAF air attack; demolished by her crew*

ATLANTIC 26 RN Escort Destroyer
Veteran 0735: Torpedoed south of Iceland (54-51N 23-04W) by German submarine **U.404**; lost with all hands, plus up to 80 merchant survivors

27 German Merchant Raider
Stier Sunk north-west of Tristan da Cunha (28-08S 20-01W) by 4in gunfire of US merchant ship **Stephen Hopkins**, which scored 35 hits on the raider before she had to be abandoned; German survivors rescued by German oiler **Tannenfels**, US seamen reached S. America a month later

OCTOBER 1942

2 RN Anti-Aircraft Cruiser
Curacoa 1312: Sunk off north-west Ireland (55-50N 08-38W) by collision with RMS **Queen Mary**

Late on 11 October 1942 US cruisers and destroyers intercepted a Japanese force which was covering a Guadalcanal reinforcement operation. The Japanese never gained the initiative in the Battle of Cape Esperance, off the northern point of Guadalcanal, and suffered their first real defeat in a night surface encounter. Two out of three destroyers sent to look for survivors were found and sunk by USN and USMC aircraft on the following day.

PACIFIC 11 *Japanese Destroyer*
Fubuki *2355: Sunk west of Savo Is (09-06S 159-38E) by 8in and 6in gunfire of US cruisers* **San Francisco, Salt Lake City, Helena** *and* **Boise**

Japanese Cruiser
Furutaka *2355: Torpedoed by US destroyer* **Duncan**, *following 6in and 8in gunfire damage; 0040: capsized and sank (09-02S 159-34E)*

US Destroyer
Duncan *2355: Damaged off Savo Is by 8in gunfire of Japanese cruiser* **Furutaka**, *5in gunfire of destroyer* **Hatsuyuki** *and, probably, gunfire of US ships; abandoned at 0200 and sank about 10 hours later – survivors rescued by USS* **McCalla**, *48 men lost*

12 *Japanese Destroyers*
Murakumo *0800: Torpedoed 90 miles (165 km) west-north-west of Savo Is (08-40S 159-20E) by USN aircraft (ex-***Saratoga** *shore-based on Guadalcanal); abandoned and scuttled*

Natsugumo	*1645: Sunk 8 miles (15 km) west-south-west of Savo Is (09-10S 159-40E) by USMC aircraft*	PACIFIC

14 German Merchant Raider | NW EUROPE
Komet 0115: Sunk 5 miles (9 km) north of Cap de la Hague by RN **MTB.236**

15 *US Destroyer* | PACIFIC
Meredith *1215: Sunk off San Cristobal Is, Solomons, by aircraft from carrier* **Zuikaku** *– 73 survivors rescued by destroyers* **Grayson** *and* **Gwin**, *185 men lost*

16 *Japanese Destroyer*
Oboro *Sunk 30 miles (55 km) north-east of Kiska, Aleutians (52-17N 178-08E), by USAAF air attack*

19 *US Destroyer*
O'Brien *0740: Foundered off Samoa (13-30S 171-18E) following major structural failure (see 15 September 1942)*

19 Italian Destroyer | MED
Giovanni da 1300: Torpedoed south of Pantelleria (35-52N 12-02E) by RN
Verazzano submarine **Unbending**; stern blown off and ship sank at 1450

In late October came the critical point of the US campaign to hold the Guadalcanal beach-head. The Japanese mounted a major operation in which their carrier fleet would co-ordinate its activities with those of the land-based JNAF units and support the Army, whose main task was to capture the vital airfield. The US troops held the airfield and the depleted carrier force, although it lost another ship, forced the Japanese carriers to withdraw, having lost most of their aircraft and with two ships damaged.

25 *Japanese Cruiser* | PACIFIC
Yura *1300–1700: Damaged off Savo Is by USN, USMC and USAAF aircraft; scuttled by destroyers* **Harusame** *and* **Yudachi** *30 miles (55 km) north-north-east of Savo Is (08-40S 160-00E)*

26 *US Carrier*
Hornet *0910: Damaged north of Santa Cruz Is by torpedo aircraft from* **Shokaku** *and dive-bombers from* **Zuikaku**; *abandoned and taken in tow but attacked and damaged again (by aircraft from* **Junyo***) at 1515, 1555 and 1705. US destroyers were unable to scuttle her before the Japanese Fleet arrived at 2100. Finally sunk by torpedoes of destroyers* **Akigumo** *and* **Makigumo**

US Destroyer
Porter *1005: Torpedoed north of Santa Cruz by Japanese submarine* **I-21***; 1100: abandoned and scuttled by destroyer* **Shaw** *– 15 men lost*

NOVEMBER 1942

4 Italian Torpedo-Boat | MED
Centauro noon: Sunk alongside mole at Benghazi by air raid

6 Italian Minesweeper (ex-Yugoslav)
Selve 1500: Damaged at Benghazi by RAF air raid and burned out
(ex-**Galeb**)

The Royal Navy returned to Algeria on 8 November 1942, to land Anglo-US troops. The French Navy, nursing its memories of July 1940, fought fiercely in the opening stages of the invasion and both sides sustained losses.

MED 8 RN Cutters
Walney 0300: Damaged by Vichy French gunfire from shore batteries and destroyers, abandoned in Oran Harbour. 0945: blew up and sank

Hartland 0315: Damaged in Oran Harbour by gunfire of French destroyer **Typhon**, abandoned and sank at 1025

French Flotilla Leader
Épervier 0545: Damaged off Oran by 6in gunfire of RN cruiser **Aurora** and beached

French Destroyers
Tramontane 0540: Sunk off Oran by 6in gunfire of HMS **Aurora**
Tornade 0540: Damaged by 6in gunfire of HMS **Aurora**; sank at 0727
Typhon Scuttled in Oran Harbour, following cruiser gunfire damage

French Aviso
La Surprise Sunk off Oran (35-55N 01-05W) by 4.7in gunfire of RN destroyer **Brilliant**

RN Destroyer
Broke 0830: Damaged off Algiers Harbour (36-50N 03-00E) by Vichy French shore batteries; abandoned and scuttled at 1900 (36-50N 00-40E)

The US Navy was entirely responsible for the invasion of Morocco. The Vichy French Navy defended the naval base of Casablanca resolutely but again suffered heavy losses at the hands of the more powerful attacker

ATLANTIC 8 French Flotilla Leader
Milan 0930: Damaged off Casablanca by 5in gunfire of US destroyer **Wilkes** and beached

French Destroyers
Fougueux 1000: Sunk off Casablanca by 16in gunfire of US battleship **Massachusetts** and 8in gunfire of cruiser **Tuscaloosa**
Boulonnais 1012: Sunk off Casablanca by gunfire of USS **Massachusetts**

French Cruiser
Primauget 1100–1120: Damaged off Casablanca by 8in gunfire of US cruiser **Augusta** and 6in gunfire of cruiser **Brooklyn**; returned to Casablanca Harbour and beached

French Flotilla Leader
Albatros 1100: Damaged off Casablanca by gunfire of USS **Augusta** and **Brooklyn** and beached

French Destroyers
Brestois
Frondeur 1100–1120: Badly damaged by US ships' gunfire, sank in Casablanca Harbour. (French battleship **Jean Bart** was severely damaged in harbour by US 16in gunfire)

MED 9 RN Corvette
Gardenia Sunk off Oran (35-49N 01-05W) in collision with RN trawler **Fluellen**

RN Minesweeper
Cromer 1715: Mined off Mersah Matruh (31-26N 27-16E) – blew up

The Axis response to the Allied invasion of North Africa was swift, submarines and aircraft concentrating on the warships and transports, and from 10 November the casualties mounted steadily until the appropriate defensive organizations could be established.

10	RN Destroyer	MED

Martin 0354: Torpedoed 85 miles (155 km) north-east of Algiers (37-53N 03-57E) by German submarine **U.431**; possibly hit by three torpedoes – 63 survivors

RN Sloop
Ibis 1000: Torpedoed by Italian aircraft 10 miles (18 km) north of Algiers (36-55N 03-05E); capsized almost immediately – 102 survivors

11	*Japanese Armed Merchant Cruiser*	INDIAN O.

Hokoku Maru *0600: Sunk 550 miles (1,000 km) south-south-west of the Cocos Is, Indian Ocean (20-00S 93-00E) by 3in gunfire of RIN minesweeper* **Bengal** *and 4in gunfire of Dutch tanker* **Ondina**

12	RN Anti-Aircraft Ship	MED

Tynwald (Previously damaged by air attack) 0600: Torpedoed off Bougie (36-42N 05-10E) by Italian submarine **Argo**

US Escort   ATLANTIC
Erie 0200: Torpedoed off Curacao (12-04N 68-57W) by German submarine **U.163**; ship beached – later refloated but capsized on 5 December while under tow

Between 12 and 15 November 1942 the Japanese made their last major effort to eject US forces from Guadalcanal, sending battleships as well as the usual cruisers and destroyers to shell the USMC airfield and sweep aside US Navy units in preparation for the arrival of a large reinforcement convoy. The two major battles which resulted cost the US Navy dearly (two cruisers and seven destroyers), but the Japanese lost both of their battleships and failed to neutralize the airfield. USMC aircraft from the island and USN aircraft from USS **Enterprise** *made their greatest contribution by destroying the troop convoy – only 2,000 Japanese soldiers, out of 11,000 despatched, reached Guadalcanal.*

The first night action, on 12/13 November, degenerated into a hideous melée, with the USN's lack of sound night-fighting doctrine once again exposed: out of thirteen US ships engaged, only three escaped undamaged. Two nights later, two US battleships were sent in to meet the 'Tokyo Express' and although one was put out of action early in the engagement and three out of four destroyers were sunk, the Japanese lost their second battleship. The decision as to the outcome of the Guadalcanal campaign was thus reached in a few minutes in the early hours of 15 November. The US Navy had established dominance, despite much heavier losses than its opponent, by making it plain that it would accept attrition in order to attain its aim: the Japanese Navy, lacking the seemingly endless resources of the USN, had to acknowledge strategic defeat.

13	*US Anti-Aircraft Cruiser*	PACIFIC

Atlanta *0150: Severely damaged south of Savo Is by 14in gunfire of Japanese battleship* **Hiei** *and torpedo from destroyer* **Akatsuki**; *reduced to a wreck and scuttled 3 miles (5½ km) off Guadalcanal 12 hours later*

US Destroyers
Barton *0152: Torpedoed by Japanese destroyer – sank almost immediately, with very heavy loss of life*
Cushing *0155: Damaged by Japanese gunfire, abandoned at 0315 and remained afloat, on fire until she blew up at 1700 – 69 men lost*
Laffey *0155: Torpedoed by Japanese destroyer and hit by 14in gunfire from battleship* **Hiei**; *sank almost immediately, with very heavy loss of life*

PACIFIC | **Monssen** | *0200: Damaged by Japanese gunfire, abandoned at 0220 and remained afloat, on fire, until she blew up at noon – 130 men lost*

Japanese Destroyers
Akatsuki | *0150: Sunk by 5in gunfire of US cruiser **Atlanta** and 5in gunfire of destroyer **O'Bannon** (09-17S 158-56E)*
Yudachi | *0155–0236: Sunk by 5in gunfire of US destroyers and 8in gunfire of cruiser **Portland** (09-14S 159-52E)*

US Anti-Aircraft Cruiser
Juneau | *(Damaged by gunfire in night action) 1100: Torpedoed north of Guadalcanal by Japanese submarine **I-26**: blew up and sank immediately – 10 survivors, 700 men lost*

Japanese Battleship
Hiei | *(Damaged by 85 shell hits in night action and unable to withdraw) 0615–1430: Hit by at least 4 bombs and 4 torpedoes from USMC and USN aircraft based on Guadalcanal, sank at 1900 (09-00S 159-00E) – 450 men lost*

MED | 13 | Dutch Destroyer
Isaac Sweers | 0615: Torpedoed 60 miles (110 km) north-west of Algiers (37-23N 02-12E) by German submarine ***U.431***

PACIFIC | 14 | *Japanese Cruiser*
Kinugasa | *0800: Torpedoed 15 miles (28 km) west of Rendova Is, Solomons, by USN aircraft (from **Enterprise**, shore-based on Guadalcanal); later hit by bombs (aircraft from **Enterprise**) and sank at 1020 (08-45S 157-00E). **Enterprise** dive-bombers also badly damaged cruisers **Chokai, Maya** and **Isuzu** but all reached base and were repaired*

US Destroyers
Preston | *2330: Hit south of Savo Is by 5.5in gunfire of Japanese cruiser **Nagara**; sank in 15 minutes – 131 survivors rescued, 116 men lost*
Walke | *2332: Torpedoed by Japanese destroyers, sank at 2345 – 75 men lost*
Benham | *2338: Torpedoed by Japanese destroyers; bow blown off and she made for Espiritu Santo under her own steam.*
*1500/15th: ship began to break up, abandoned and scuttled by USS **Gwin**, which was the only US destroyer to survive the battle. (US battleship **South Dakota** was badly damaged by 42 14in and 8in shell hits)*

Japanese Destroyer
Ayanami | *2332: Hit south of Savo Is (09-10S 159-52E) by 16in gunfire of US battleship **Washington** and 5in gunfire of destroyers; sank at 2340*

| 15 | *Japanese Battleship*
Kirishima | *0001: Damaged west of Savo Is by 16in gunfire of USS **Washington** – 9 hits (and up to 40 5in hits); 0320 scuttled (09-05S 159-42E) – 250 men lost*

MED | 15 | RN Minesweeper
Algerine | 0350: Torpedoed off Bougie, Algeria (36-15N 05-08E) by Italian submarine ***Ascianghi***

ATLANTIC | | RN Escort Carrier
Avenger | 0415: Torpedoed west of Gibraltar (36-15N 07-45W) by German submarine ***U.155***; hit in bomb-room and blew up – only 12 survivors

RCN Escort Destroyer
Saguenay   Damaged beyond repair in collision east of Newfoundland with SS **Azara**; explosion of depth-charges destroyed ship's stern – towed to St Johns, Newfoundland, and then to Halifax, to be used as training hulk. (The **Azara** sank, crew rescued by the **Saguenay**)

18   Norwegian Corvette
Montbretia   0800: Torpedoed south-west of Iceland (53-37N 38-15W) by German submarine **U.262**

Russian Gunboat
Kraznoye   Torpedoed off Lavansaari Island, Gulf of Finland, by Finnish MTB;
Znamya   salved and recommissioned post-war

22   Russian Destroyer
Sokrushitelny   Foundered in storm in the Barents Sea

24   *Japanese Destroyer*
Hayashio   *Sunk in Huon Gulf, New Guinea (07-00S 147-30E), by USAAF air attack*

25   German Minesweeper
M.101   1805: In collision with SS **Levante** west of Namsos (64-09N 10-07E), capsized at 1813 and sank at 1845

27   French Aviso
Granit   Scuttled at Toulon; raised, repaired and commissioned into German Navy as **SG.21**

27   Italian Torpedo-Boat
Circe   0130: Sunk in Gulf of Castellammare Siculo (38-14N 12-57E) by collision with Italian SS **Citta di Tunisi**; two convoys met head-on and **Circe** was rammed and cut in two by a ship of the other group; 66 men lost, 99 rescued by destroyer **Folgore**

Early on 27 November the French Fleet at Toulon was scuttled to prevent the ships from falling into German hands. The operation was a national gesture and not a pro-Allied contribution, but it undoubtedly denied the Axis navies some very useful warships, particularly destroyers and minesweeping avisos. It is highly questionable whether either the German or Italian navies would have been able to find the crews or oil fuel for the capital ships, cruisers and flotilla leaders – the last were also very mechanically demanding and would have placed a considerable burden on base engineering staffs, to judge by Allied experience of supporting the type. The real tragedy lay in the decision to scuttle, rather than attempt a break-out by serviceable surface units, if not to rally to the French faction in North Africa, then to seek internment in Spain or the Balearic Islands, to await Allied victory – a now reasonable expectation.

French ships Scuttled and not Salvaged:

Battleships	Flotilla Leaders	Destroyers
Provence	**Aigle**	**Casque**
Dunkerque	**Cassard**	**Mameluck**
Strasbourg	**Gerfaut**	**Le Bordelais**
	Guépard	**Le Mars**
Seaplane-Carrier	**Kersaint**	**La Palme**
Commandant Teste	**Lynx**	
	Mogador	Torpedo-Boat
Cruisers	**Tartu**	**La Poursuivante**
Algérie	**Vauban**	
Colbert	**Vauquelin**	Avisos
Dupleix	**Vautour**	**D'Iberville**
Foch	**Verdun**	**Les Eparges**
Marseillaise	**Volta**	**Yser**

MED   French ships Refloated but not returned to active service:

Cruisers

Jean de Vienne   Allocated to Italian Navy as **FR.11**; refloated but still at Toulon on 9 September 1943 and abandoned to Germany

La Galisson-nière   To Italian Navy as **FR.12**, fate as **FR.11**

Flotilla Leader

Panthère   To Italian Navy as **FR.22**; towed to La Spezia, scuttled on 9 September 1943

Valmy   To Italian Navy as **FR.24**; captured by Germans at Savona on 9 September 1943, while under tow from Toulon to Genoa

Destroyers

Siroco   To Italian Navy as **FR.32**; captured by Germans at Genoa on 9 September 1943, while under repair

L'Adroit   To Italian Navy as **FR.33**; captured at Toulon by Germans on 9 September 1943

Cyclone   To Italian Navy as **FR.34**; captured by Germans at Imperia on 9 September 1943, while under tow to Genoa: became German **TA.34**

Bison   To Italian Navy as **FR.35**; as **FR.33**

Foudroyant   To Italian Navy as **FR.36**; as **FR.33**

Le Hardi   To Italian Navy – 'FR' number not allocated; captured at Savona with **FR.24**

Avisos

L'Impétueuse   To Italian Navy as **FR.54**; captured by Germans at Toulon on 9 September 1943

Dédaigneuse   To Italian Navy as **FR.56**; as **FR.54**

French ships commissioned for Active Service with Axis Navies:

Flotilla Leaders

Lion   (Scuttled) to Italian Navy as **FR.21** (see 9 September 1943)

Tigre   (Captured) to Italian Navy as **FR.23**; restored to French Navy 28 October 1943

L'Indompt-able   To German Navy as **SG.9**

Destroyer

Trombe   (Captured) to Italian Navy as **FR.31**; restored to French Navy 28 October 1943

Torpedo-Boats

Baliste   (Captured) to German Navy as **TA.12** (see 22 August 1943)

La Bayon-naise   (Scuttled) to German Navy as **TA.13** (see 25 August 1944)

Avisos

Chamois   (Scuttled) raised by Italian Navy as **FR.53**; abandoned to Germans at Toulon 9 September 1943 and renamed **SG.21** (see 15 August 1944)

La Curieuse   (Scuttled) raised by Italian Navy as **FR.55**; like **FR.53**, abandoned at Toulon to Germans and renamed **SG.25** (see August 1944)

28   RN Destroyer

Ithuriel   Damaged beyond repair at Bône by German air raid

30   *German Merchant Raider*
  Thor   *Burned out at Yokohama following accidental explosion and fire*
                        aboard German tanker **Uckermark** *(ex-***Altmark***)*

Although the US cruiser and destroyer force covering the Guadalcanal beach-head had
excellent intelligence to give warning of the major Japanese re-supply operation on the
night of 29/30 November 1942, was in an ideal position for the actual interception and
even made the initial radar detection in ample time, the Japanese destroyers,
encumbered with drums of fuel, fought back so effectively that four out of the five US
cruisers were severely damaged. US Navy tactics and leadership were no better than
they had been in August but damage control had improved and only one of the ships
torpedoed was lost.

30   *Japanese Destroyer*
  Takanami   *2330: Damaged 10 miles (18 km) south-south-west of Savo Is (09-*
                        10S 159-45E) by 8in and 6in gunfire of US cruisers; sank 0140 on 1
                        December, survivors rescued by **Oyashio** *and* **Kuroshio**

  US Cruiser
  Northampton   *2348: Damaged south of Savo Is by two 24in torpedoes fired by*
                        destroyer **Oyashio***; abandoned at 0240 and sank at 0305/1*
                        December (09-12S 159-50E) – 773 men rescued, 58 lost
                        (US cruisers **Minneapolis, Pensacola** *and* **New Orleans** *were also*
                        damaged by torpedoes)

DECEMBER 1942

1   *RAN Minesweeper*
  Armidale   *1530: Sunk off Timor (10-00S 128-00E) by JNAF bombers and*
                        torpedo aircraft; approximately 30 survivors rescued by HMAS
                        Kalgourlie *and RAAF flying-boat*

The Allied invasion of Algeria had opened a Second Front in North Africa. The German
Army occupied Tunis and its port of Bizerta, which had the advantage as a supply base
of being close to the Italian ports, as well as to the front-line. It was also close to
advanced British naval bases, in Malta and Algeria.
  In the first of a series of surface ship attacks on the Axis traffic, an Italian convoy
consisting of four transports bound from Palermo to Bizerta, escorted by three
destroyers and two torpedo-boats, was intercepted off Tunisia early on 2 December
1942 by three cruisers and two destroyers from Bône. All four transports and one
destroyer were sunk and another destroyer and a torpedo-boat were damaged. While
retiring, the RN force was attacked by German aircraft and a destroyer was lost.

2   Italian Destroyer
  Folgore   0116: Sunk north of Cap Bon (37-43N 11-16E) by 6in gunfire of HMS
                        Aurora and 5.25in gunfire of RN cruisers *Argonaut* and *Sirius* –
                        126 men lost. Destroyer *da Recco* very severely damaged by
                        gunfire (118 men killed) and towed to port by *Pigafetta*; torpedo-
                        boat *Procione* also damaged by gunfire but returned to Palermo
                        under own steam

  RN Destroyer
  Quentin   0640: Sunk off Galita Is (37-40N 8-55E) by German torpedo aircraft

Italian troubles on this day were not yet over. A smaller convoy, of two merchant ships,
bound from Naples to Tripoli, escorted by two torpedo-boats, was attacked at about
1900 by RN torpedo aircraft from Malta. Both merchant ships were sunk and a destroyer
striking force, also from Malta, found one of the torpedo-boats shortly before midnight.

MED	2	Italian Torpedo-Boat

Lupo 2345: Sunk off Kerkenah Bank (N.4 Buoy) by 4.7in gunfire of RN destroyers **Jervis, Javelin, Janus** and **Kelvin**; surprised while rescuing survivors of SS **Veloce** and unable to open fire in return

NW EUROPE 3 RN Escort Destroyer

Penylan 0630: Torpedoed 5 miles (10 km) south of Start Point (50-08N 03-39W) by German E-Boat (**S.115**) while escorting a coastal convoy; 117 men rescued

MED 4 Italian Cruiser

Muzio (Badly damaged 13 August 1942 by RN submarine **Unbroken** and
Attendolo under repair)
1650: damaged at Naples by USAAF air raid; capsized at 2210 due to spread of uncontrolled flooding

The French warships based at Bizerta were not seized by the Axis until 8 December; although none was immediately fit for operational service, there was no large-scale attempt to scuttle the vessels, most of which saw some service under one or both Axis flags.

8 French Torpedo-Boats

Bombarde To Italian Navy as **FR.41**, towed to Italy; transferred to German Navy 6 April 1943 as **TA.9** (see 23 August 1944)

La Pomone To Italian Navy as **FR.42**, as **FR.41**: became **TA.10** (see 27 September 1943)

L'Iphigénie To Italian Navy as **FR.43**, as **FR.41**: became **TA.11** (see 9/10 September 1943)

French Avisos
La Batailleuse To Italian Navy as **FR.51**, towed to Naples (see 9 September 1943)
Commandant To Italian Navy as **FR.52** (see 28 May 1943)
Rivière
Elan To German Navy as **SG.19** (see 8 September 1943)

9 RN Corvette

Marigold Sunk off Algiers (36-50N 03-00E) by Italian torpedo aircraft – 40 men lost

RN Destroyer
Porcupine 2330: Torpedoed 70 miles (130 km) north-north-east of Oran (36-40N 00-04E) by German submarine **U.602**; towed to Arzeu and later to UK (bow section only) but not repaired

11 RN Escort Destroyer

Blean 1630: Sunk 60 miles (110 km) west of Oran (35-55N 01-50W) by German submarine **U.443**; 94 men rescued by HMS **Wishart**

PACIFIC 12 *Japanese Destroyer*

Teruzuki *0100: Damaged 20 miles (37 km) north-east of Kolombangara, Solomons, (07-50S 157-30E) by US MTB PT-45; stopped, set on fire and blew up at 0440*

MED 17 Italian Destroyer

Aviere 1115: Torpedoed north of Bizerta (38-00N 10-05E) by RN submarine **Splendid**; hit by two torpedoes, broke in half and sank immediately – 200 men lost, 30 survivors

ATLANTIC RN Destroyer

Firedrake 2010: Torpedoed 600 miles (1,100 km) south of Iceland (50-50N 25-15W) by German submarine **U.211**; broke in half immediately – 26 survivors rescued by HMS **Sunflower**

18   *Japanese Cruiser*   PACIFIC

     Tenryu   *Torpedoed 10 miles (18 km) east of Madang (05-11S 145-57E) by US submarine* **Albacore**

     RN Destroyer   MED

     Partridge   0817: Torpedoed 50 miles (90 km) west of Oran (35-50N 01-35W) by German submarine *U.565*; 173 survivors rescued by HMS *Penn*

19   RN Corvette

     Snapdragon   2025: Sunk off Benghazi (32-18N 19-54E) by German air attack; sank in 3 minutes – 59 survivors

29   *US Destroyer-Minesweeper*   PACIFIC

     Wasmuth   *Sunk by the accidental explosion of two of her own depth-charges in a gale off the Aleutian Is*

In a classic convoy defence action in the Barents Sea on New Year's Eve, five RN destroyers held off a much superior force of German ships, initially consisting of three destroyers and a heavy cruiser, until two RN light cruisers could come up in support. The combined defensive force then drove off the original attacking group, which had been reinforced by three more destroyers and a pocket battleship; none of the merchant ships in convoy JW 51B was lost.

31   German Destroyer   NW EUROPE

     Friedrich   1040: Sunk (in approximately 73-15N 30-20E) by 6in gunfire of RN
      Eckoldt   cruiser *Sheffield*. (German cruiser *Admiral Hipper* damaged by gunfire of HMS *Sheffield* and *Jamaica*)

     RN Minesweeper

     Bramble   1045: Sunk 15 miles (28 km) north-east of convoy (73-18N 30-06E) while detached to round up stragglers, by 11in gunfire of pocket battleship *Lützow*; no survivors

     RN Destroyer

     Achates   1116: (already damaged by gunfire) Severely damaged by gunfire of *Lützow*; abandoned at 1300 and sank at 1330 (73-18N 30-06E) – 81 survivors (RN destroyer *Onslow* severely damaged by 8in gunfire of *Hipper* but reached Kola Inlet under own steam)

JANUARY 1943

2   RN Minesweeper   MED

     Alarm   Damaged beyond repair at Bône by German air raid and beached; 4in gun removed and used by British Army to fire starshell for coast defence

3   Italian Cruiser

     Ulpio Traiano (Fitting out for service) Sunk at Palermo by explosive charges laid by RN human torpedo *Chariot No 22*

7   Italian Destroyer

     Bersagliere 1625: Sunk while moored in Palermo Harbour by air raid; capsized to starboard within 5 minutes of two bombs hitting

8   German Minesweeper   NW EUROPE

     M.489   Sunk by explosion and fire at Rotterdam (either accident or sabotage)

To tighten the blockade of Tunisia, the Royal Navy employed two of its 34-knot purpose-built minelayers and two submarines to mine the Axis shipping routes. The *Abdiel's* fields proved to be particularly effective, for between January and March 1943 they claimed seven destroyers and escorts.

MED 9 Italian Destroyer
Corsaro 2015: Mined 38 miles (70 km) north-north-east of Bizerta while escorting a convoy to Tunisia, in field laid by RN minelayer **Abdiel**; attempting to assist mined destroyer **Maestrale** when a mine blew off her rudder – a second mine broke the **Corsaro** in two and she sank rapidly.
(The **Maestrale** was towed first to Bizerta and then to Genoa, where she was still under repair on 9 September 1943)

PACIFIC 10 Japanese Destroyer
Okikaze *Torpedoed 35 miles (65 km) south-east of Yokosuka (35-02N 140-12E) by US submarine* **Trigger**

ATLANTIC 12 *US Destroyer*
Worden *0730: Stranded in Constantine Harbour, Amchitka, Aleutian Is; immediate salvage attempts were unsuccessful and she had to be abandoned in a rising sea*

MED 12 Italian Torpedo-Boat
Ardente 0400: Collided with destroyer **Grecale** 3 miles (5½ km) north of Punta Barone, Sicily; two torpedo-boats were returning to Palermo from an escort operation when they met three Italian destroyers outbound for Tunisia, in bad weather. A boiler explosion in **Ardente** was followed by a serious fire and she sank 95 minutes after the collision; **Grecale** lost her bow and was towed to Palermo

PACIFIC 13 *Japanese Patrol Boat (ex-Destroyer)*
No. 1 *(ex-* *Torpedoed 65 miles 120 km) west-south-west of Kavieng (02-51S*
Shimakaze) *149-43E) by US submarine* **Guardfish**

MED 17 Italian Destroyer
Bombardiere 1725: Torpedoed 24 miles (45 km) north-west of Marettimo Is, west of Sicily, (38-15N 11-43E) by RN submarine **United**; hit in boiler-room, broke in half and sank very quickly

PACIFIC 23 *Japanese Destroyer*
Hakaze *Torpedoed 15 miles (28 km) south-west of Kavieng, New Ireland, (02-47S 150-38E) by US submarine* **Guardfish**

MED 19 Italian Minesweeper (ex-Yugoslav)
Eso (ex-**Sokol**) 2100: Torpedoed 4 miles (7 km) east of Djerba Island by RN aircraft

PACIFIC 29 *US Cruiser*
Chicago *1940: Damaged off Rennel Is, Solomons, by JNAF torpedo aircraft (2 hits); taken in tow by USS* **Louiville**, *then tug* **Navajo**, *but torpedoed again (4 hits) at 1620 on the 30th and sank 20 minutes later. US destroyer* **LaVallette** *also damaged but towed to Espiritu Santo*

MED 29 RN Auxiliary AA Ship
Pozarica 1950: Damaged 30 miles (55 km) north-west of Bougie by torpedo aircraft; towed to Bougie by HMS **Cadmus**. Capsized 13 February during salvage operations

30 RN Corvette
Samphire 0020: Torpedoed 30 miles (55 km) north-east of Bougie (37-07N 05-32E) by German submarine **U.596**; 4 survivors rescued by HMS **Zetland**

30   Italian Minesweeper (ex-Yugoslav)   MED
      Unie (ex-   1405: Destroyed at Bizerta by explosion following USAAF air raid
      Kobac)

31   Italian Corvette
      Procellaria   1120: Mined in the Sicilian Channel (37-20N 10-37E) in field laid by
                          RN minelayer **Welshman**; slowly flooded and sank at 1430.
                          Procellaria was escorting a Sicily-bound group which included the
                          damaged destroyer **Maestrale** (see 9 January), in tow of the
                          Animoso

      Italian Torpedo-Boat
      Generale   1730: Mined 18 miles (33 km) south-east of Cani Island while
      Marcello   proceeding from Bizerta to the aid of the **Procellaria**, in same
      Prestinari   minefield; sank at 1825

FEBRUARY 1943

1   *US Destroyer*   PACIFIC
      DeHaven   *1500: Sunk 2 miles (4 km) south-east of Savo Is by JNAF dive-*
                          bombers – 167 men lost

The evacuation of Japanese troops from Guadalcanal began on the night of 1/2
February. One of the 20 destroyers employed was badly damaged by USN air attack and
another was mined, but the remaining eighteen carried out the operation successfully.

      Japanese Destroyer
      Makigumo   *Mined 3 miles (5½ km) south-south-west of Savo Is (09-15S 159-*
                          47E) while evading US PT-boats' attack

1   RN Minelayer   MED
      Welshman   1840: Torpedoed 45 miles (83 km) east of Tobruk (32-12N 24-52E)
                          by German submarine **U.617**; mine deck flooded and ship capsized
                          suddenly at 2035 and sank within 3 minutes – 152 men lost

3   Italian Torpedo-Boat
      Uragano   0938: Mined 27 miles (50 km) north-east of Cani Rocks (37-35N 10-
                          37E) in field laid by RN minelayer **Abdiel**; steering gear wrecked
                          and ship sank at 1335

      Italian Destroyer
      Saetta   0950: Mined while attempting to assist the **Uragano** – broke into
                          three sections and sank in less than one minute. Three surviving
                          torpedo-boats, escorting a tanker, did not make a second attempt
                          to assist the **Uragano**

6   RCN Corvette
      Louisburg   1925: Torpedoed 60 miles (110 km) north-east of Oran (36-15N 00-
                          15E) by German aircraft – 50 men rescued. First RCN warship to be
                          sunk by aircraft and in the Mediterranean

9   RN Corvette
      Erica   Mined between Benghazi and Derna (32-48N 21-10E) on British
                          mine, laid in July 1941 by submarine **Rorqual** – all 71 members of
                          ship's company rescued

20   *Japanese Destroyer*   PACIFIC
      Oshio   *Sunk 70 miles (130 km) north-west of Manus Island, Admiralty Is*
                          (00-50S 146-06E) by US submarine **Albacore**

ATLANTIC   22   RCN Corvette

             Weyburn   1056: Mined 4 miles (7 km) west of Cape Spartel (35-46N 06-02W); explosion of her depth-charges damaged HMS **Wivern**

BLACK SEA   28   Russian Minesweeper

             Gruz   Torpedoed off Cape Myshako, Black Sea, by German E-boats (1st S-boote Flotille)

MARCH 1943

The Axis forces on the Tunisian run were being whittled away in ones and twos as they attempted small convoys at frequent intervals, while accurate USAAF air raids were beginning to inflict noticeable losses in harbour, where the Italian Navy had enjoyed relative immunity since the end of 1940.

MED   1   Italian Destroyer

             Geniere   1330: Sunk in dry dock at Palermo; USAAF air raid destroyed the dock gates and the destroyer and several minor craft were inundated. Salvaged 1943/44 and towed to Taranto

             Italian Torpedo-Boat

             Monsone   1800: Sunk at Naples by USAAF air raid

The Japanese situation in New Guinea was scarcely less desperate. As the Allied troops advanced overland and in a series of amphibious 'hooks', one major operation was undertaken to restore the situation. In early March a Japanese Army division was despatched in eight transports from Rabaul, with a strong destroyer and air escort. USAAF and Royal Australian Air Force aircraft attacked the convoy repeatedly from 2 to 4 March, sinking all eight transports and four destroyers. Of the 7,000 Japanese troops, fewer than 1,000 reached New Guinea.

PACIFIC   3   *Japanese Destroyers*

             Shirayuki

             Tokitsukaze   *Sunk 55 miles (100 km) south-east of Finschhafen (07-15S 148-30E) by USAAF and Royal Australian Air Force air attack*

          4   *Japanese Destroyers*

             Arashio   *(Damaged on 3rd) Sunk 55 miles south-east of Finschhafen by USAAF B-17 aircraft*

             Asashio   *Sunk 45 miles (83 km) south-east of Finschhafen (07-15S 148-15E) by USAAF B-25 aircraft*

          6   *Japanese Destroyers*

             Minegumo   *0100-0115: Sunk off Vila, Kula Gulf, (08-01S 157-14E) by 6in gunfire of US cruisers* **Monpelier** *and* **Cleveland**

             Murasame   *0100-0110: Sunk with* **Minegumo***, by 6in gunfire of US cruisers* **Cleveland** *and* **Denver** *and torpedo fired by US destroyer* **Waller***. Only 49 men survived from the two Japanese destroyers*

             Japanese Patrol Boat (ex-Destroyer)

             No. 34 *(ex-*   *Badly damaged south of Kavieng in collision with target ship*

                Susuki)   **Yakaze***; sunk at Truk on 3 July 1944 by USN air attack, while awaiting repairs*

MED   7   Italian Torpedo-Boat

             Ciclone   1310: Mined 70 miles (130 km) north-east of Bizerta while rescuing survivors from a merchant ship mined in the same field, laid by RN minelayer **Abdiel**; abandoned at 1405 – 15 men lost; taken in tow by **Groppo** but sank at 1325 on the 8th in heavy seas

11	RN Escort Destroyer	ATLANTIC
	Harvester (Immobilized early on the 11th by explosion in **U.444**, which she had rammed) 1200: Sunk in N. Atlantic (51-23N 28-40W) by German submarine **U.432**	

12 RN Destroyer   MED
    Lightning   2220: Torpedoed off Bizerta (37-53N 09-50E) by German E-boat (7th Flotilla) –170 men rescued by HMS **Legion**

19 RN Escort Destroyer
    Derwent   Dusk: Torpedoed in Tripoli Harbour by air-dropped circling torpedo and beached with machinery flooded. Salvaged and towed to Plymouth but repairs never completed

20 *Japanese Armed Merchant Cruiser*   PACIFIC
    Bangkok Maru *1500: Torpedoed east of Jaluit Atoll, Marshall Is (05-47N 169-42E) by US submarine* **Pollack**

24 Italian Destroyers   MED
    Lanzerotto   0730: Mined 28 miles (52 km) north of Cap Bon, in field laid by RN
      Malocello minelayer **Abdiel**; broke in two and sank at 0845
    Ascari   0800 & 1300: Mined while assisting **Malocello**; struck three mines which blew off her bows and stern – sank at 1320, 53 survivors. 100 German troops were also rescued, but 550 others were lost, together with 397 men of the destroyers' crews

27 RN Escort Carrier   NW EUROPE
    Dasher   1645: Lost off Little Cumbraes Is, Clyde (55-40N 04-57W), by accidental petrol explosion and fire; sank in 3 minutes – 149 survivors rescued

APRIL 1943

1 Italian Destroyer (ex-Yugoslav)   MED
    Lubliana (ex- 0400: Stranded in bad weather 1 mile (1,850 m) east of Ras el
      Ljubljana)   Ahmar, while entering the Gulf of Tunis; badly damaged by heavy seas and abandoned

The Japanese Navy reinforced its 11th Air Fleet in the Rabaul area with its rebuilt carrier air groups in order to support Army operations in Papua New Guinea. The first strike was delivered on 7 April 1943 and was intended to neutralize the Guadalcanal base. No fewer than 67 dive-bombers, escorted by 110 fighters, attacked shipping in the roads, but the JNAF aircrew were no longer the power they had been and they sank only one destroyer, a Royal New Zealand Navy minesweeping trawler and a USN oiler.

7 *US Destroyer*   PACIFIC
    Aaron Ward *1515: Badly damaged off Guadalcanal by JNAF dive-bombers,*
      (ii)   *towed towards Tulagi but sank at 2135 due to progressive flooding – 27 men lost*

9 *Japanese Destroyer*
    Isonami   *Torpedoed 35 miles (65 km) south-east of Wangiwangi, Celebes (05-26S 123-04E) by US submarine* **Tautog**

10 Italian Cruiser   MED
    Trieste   1435: Damaged at La Maddalena, Sardinia, by USAAF air raid; bridge wrecked, hull holed underwater – attempts at salvage failed and ship rolled to starboard and sank at 1613

ATLANTIC 11 RN Escort Destroyer
Beverley (Damaged on the 9th in collision with merchant ship)
0400: Torpedoed south-west of Iceland (52-28N 40-32W) while escorting convoy ON.176 by German submarine **U.188** – heavy loss of life

NW EUROPE 14 Norwegian Escort Destroyer
Eskdale 0300: Torpedoed 12 miles (22 km) east-north-east of the Lizard, English Channel (50-03N 04-56W) while escorting convoy PW.323, by German E-Boats **S.65, S.90** and **S.112**

A brisk action, in which the honours were even, was fought off the west coast of Sicily during the early hours of 16 April 1943, when two RN destroyers encountered two Italian torpedo-boats covering a convoy bound for Tunisia.

MED 16 Italian Torpedo-Boat
Cigno 0300: Stopped by 4in gunfire and sunk 15 miles (28 km) south of Marettimo Is (37-45N 12-13E) by a torpedo fired by RN destroyer **Pakenham**; 103 men rescued (out of 105)
Torpedo-boat **Cassiopea** was badly damaged and fires were not brought under control until 0500; towed to Trapani by **Climene**

RN Destroyer
Pakenham 0300: Damaged by 3.9in gunfire (4 hits) of Italian **Cigno**; taken in tow by HMS **Paladin** after the latter had damaged and driven off the Italian **Cassiopea**.
Scuttled by **Paladin** (torpedo) at about 0800, 12 miles (22 km) off Cape Granitola, Sicily (37-26N 12-30E) due to threat of German air attack

16 Italian Torpedo-Boat
Giacomo 1330: Sunk at Catania by USAAF air raid
Medici

19 Italian Destroyer
Alpino 0100: Sunk at commercial harbour of La Spezia by RAF air raid; set on fire by incendiary bombs and hit by one high-explosive bomb which caused flooding – sank at 0235

PACIFIC 23 Japanese Patrol Boat (ex-Destroyer)
No. 39 Torpedoed 150 miles (280 km) north-east of Formosa (23-45N
(ex-**Tade**) 122-45E) by US submarine **Seawolf**

28 Japanese Auxiliary Seaplane-Carrier
Kamikawa 0100: Torpedoed north of New Ireland (01-40S 150-24E) by US
Maru submarine **Scamp**

MED 28 Italian Torpedo-Boat
Climene 0935: Torpedoed 35 miles (65 km) west-north-west of Marettimo Is (37-45N 11-53E) by RN submarine **Unshaken**; ship broke in half and sank in 3 minutes – 53 men lost

The desperate straits of the Axis armies in Tunisia obliged their navies to risk daylight resupply by destroyers. Two separate operations were attempted on 30 April 1943, 600 German troops being ferried from Pozzuoli, near Naples, aboard two destroyers, while a third ship left Trapani with 50 tons of ammunition. Fighter cover was provided but this was brushed aside by the US Tactical Air Force, whose fighter-bombers scored a victory smaller in scale but no less important than that obtained early in March in the Bismarck Sea by the Far East air forces.

30 Italian Destroyer
Leone 1230: Sunk 2 miles (3,700 metres) north-north-east of Cap Bon by
Pancaldo USAAF air attack; 124 men lost, 156 rescued, as well as most of the German troops (Second sinking – see 10 July 1940)

German Destroyer (ex-Greek)   MED
Hermes (ZG.3) 1230: Damaged 2 miles off Cap Bon by USAAF air attack; reached
(ex-**Vasilevs** Korbus under own steam and anchored but damage to machinery
Georgios I) was not repairable locally and the ship was scuttled on 7 May

Italian Destroyer
Lampo (Second sinking – see 16 April 1941)
1700: Damaged 6 miles (11 km) east of Ras Mustafa, Tunisia, by
USAAF air attacks; cargo of ammunition on quarterdeck set on fire
and ship abandoned at 1735 – sank at 1912, with loss of 60 men

MAY 1943

4   Italian Torpedo-Boat
Perseo 0100: Sunk 7 miles (13 km) east of Kelibia by 4.7in gunfire of RN
destroyers **Nubian, Petard** and **Paladin** while escorting a freighter
to Tunisia – 133 men lost. The freighter, carrying ammunition,
blew up

6   Italian Escort Destroyer
Tifone 1830: Severely damaged off La Goulette, Gulf of Tunis, by USAAF
air attack; towed to Korbus with wrecked stern and steering gear.
Crew unable to repair her to enable escape to Sicily under own
steam; no tug available, so she was scuttled at 2200 on 7 May, as
Allied troops entered Tunis

*In the early hours of 7 May three US destroyer-minelayers laid a field in the Blackett
Strait, off Rendova Is, a passage frequently used by Japanese destroyers sortie-ing
down 'The Slot' to resupply Army Solomons Is garrisons or harass American activities.
The minefield almost immediately paid for itself.*

8   *Japanese Destroyers*   PACIFIC
Kuroshio *(dawn) Struck 3 mines off Rendova and sank almost immediately
(08-05S 156-55E)*

Kagero *Damaged by mines off Rendova (08-06S 156-55E) and sunk later in
the day by shore-based USN and USMC dive-bombers*

Oyashio *Sunk by US dive-bombers while assisting the* **Kuroshio** *and*
Kagero. *A fourth destroyer, the* **Michishio**, *attempting to assist
the damaged destroyers, was damaged by air attack but managed
to return to base*

14   German Minesweeper   NW EUROPE
M.8 0340: Torpedoed off the Hook of Holland (52-04N 03-55E) by RN
MTB 232

Early in 1943 the Royal Air Force's Coastal Command formed a dedicated shipping
strike 'Wing' armed with Bristol Beaufighter aircraft. Individual squadrons within the
Wing, which was based at North Coates, in East Anglia, specialized in torpedo, bomb
and rocket attack, and all three forms of attack, supported by cannon-firing aircraft to
suppress the strong flak defences of German convoys, were used in strikes. The first
successful strike occurred on the afternoon of 17 May 1943; by coincidence, it was
followed by the first night sinking by a lone roving patrol.

17   German Minesweeper
M.414 1630: Torpedoed off Texel (53-09N 04-38E) by RAF Coastal
Command air attack (North Coates Wing)

NW EUROPE   18   German Minesweeper

M.345   0100: Sunk off Gravelines (51-03N 02-02E) by RAF Coastal Command air attack (No 415 Squadron – Hampden)

MED   20   RN Minesweeper

Fantôme   Damaged by mine off Cape Bon – stern blown off; towed to Bizerta, where she was written off as a constructive total loss

25   Italian Escort Destroyer

Groppo   1130: Damaged in Messina Harbour by USAAF air raid; flooded and capsized at 1430

27   French Destroyer

Léopard   Ran aground north-north-east of Benghazi (32-27N 20-27E) while escorting Malta-Alexandria convoy; badly damaged and could not be refloated

28   Italian Corvette (ex-French Aviso)

FR.52 (ex-   1230: Sunk at Livorno (Leghorn) by USAAF air raid (Refloated by
Command-   Germans and renamed *SG.22* but not recommissioned and
ant Rivière)   scuttled in May 1945)

Italian Torpedo-Boats

Angelo   1300: Sunk at Livorno by USAAF air raid
Bassini

Antares   1300: Damaged at Livorno by USAAF air raid; towed away from mole to prevent the latter from being obstructed and sank some hours later in shallow water, with superstructure above water

JUNE 1943

2   Italian Torpedo-Boat

Castore   0145: Damaged one mile (1,800 metres) off Cape Spartivento, Italy, by 4.7in gunfire of RN destroyer *Jervis* and Greek destroyer *Vasilissa Olga*; T/B set on fire and steering gear destroyed – sank at 0315.

Castore was escorting a convoy of two ships from Taranto to Messina – both merchant ships were sunk by the Allied destroyers

PACIFIC   *8*   *Japanese Battleship*

Mutsu   *Sank in Hiroshima Bay due to magazine explosion probably caused by unstable 16in ammunition*

11   *Australian Minesweeper*

Wallaroo   *Sunk in collision off Fremantle with SS* **Gilbert Costin**

ATLANTIC   13   US Coast Guard Cutter

Escabana   Lost off Ivigtut, Greenland (60-50N 52-00W) by accidental explosion

NW EUROPE   15   German Minesweeper

M.483   Sunk 16 miles (30 km) south of Alderney, Channel Is (49-27N 02-15W) by RAF Fighter Command air attack (No 263 Squadron – Whirlwinds)

15 Russian Minesweeper   BLACK SEA
    Zashchitnik   Sunk off Tuapse, Black Sea, by German submarine **U.24**

28 Italian Cruiser   MED
    Bari   Sunk in shallow water in Livorno Harbour by USAAF air raid;
                      broken up by Germans after September 1943

JULY 1943

5   US Destroyer   PACIFIC
    Strong   *0040: Torpedoed off Bairoko, Kula Gulf, Central Solomons (08-05S
                      157-15E), by Japanese destroyer; sank at 0122 – 46 men lost, about
                      240 rescued by USS* **Chevalier**

*A Japanese reinforcement operation on the night of 5/6 July was intercepted by the US
Navy in Kula Gulf, between Kolombangara and New Georgia. Three light cruisers and
four destroyers surprised ten Japanese destroyers, seven of which were being used as
transports. Although the leading Japanese destroyer was smothered by 6in gunfire in
the opening minutes and the other two ships of the covering group were damaged, their
torpedoes hit and sank one of the US cruisers. One other Japanese destroyer, slightly
damaged, ran aground off Vila, Kolombangara, and was destroyed during the day by air
attack.*

6   Japanese Destroyer
    Niizuki   *0157: Sunk 5 miles (9 km) north-east of Kolombangara Is (07-57S
                      157-12E) by 6in gunfire of US cruisers* **Honolulu, Helena** *and* **St
                      Louis;** *300 men lost*

    US Cruiser
    Helena   *0204: Torpedoed 10 miles (19 km) north-north-east of
                      Kolombangara (07-46S 157-11E) by Japanese destroyers* **Suzukaze**
                      and **Tanikaze** *(3 hits); broke in half and sank at 0340 – 745 men
                      rescued by USS* **Nicholas** *and* **Radford,** *88 more on the 7th by USS*
                      Gwin *and* **Woodworth** *and 165 on the 15th by USS* **Taylor, Dent**
                      and **Waters**

    Japanese Destroyer
    Nagatsuki   *Stranded near Bambari Harbour, 5 miles (9 km) north of Vila,
                      Kolombangara (08-02S 157-12E); sunk during afternoon of same
                      day by USMC aircraft*

10 German Minesweeper   NW EUROPE
    M.153   0250: Sunk 45 miles (83 km) north-east of Ushant (48-50N 04-05W)
                      by 4in gunfire of RN escort destroyers **Melbreak, Wensleydale** and
                      Glaisdale

The first Allied invasion of Axis home territory began early on 10 July, with landings in
Sicily. One US Navy destroyer was sunk shortly before dawn but, such was the Allied air
supremacy, she was the only such casualty of the first day and only one more warship
was to be sunk during the assault phase, although several were severely damaged.

10 US Minesweeper   MED
    Sentinel   0430: Damaged off Licata, Sicily (37-06N 13-55E) by German dive-
                      bombers and sank at 1050 after further damage from near-miss
                      bombs

    US Destroyer
    Maddox   0458: Sunk off Gela, Sicily (36-52N 13-56E), by German air attack;
                      hit aft by two heavy bombs, she sank in less than 2 minutes, with
                      the loss of 210 men – 74 rescued

MED   Italian Minesweeper (ex-Yugoslav)

Oriole (ex-   2015: scuttled at Augusta following damage sustained in air
    Labud)   attack south of Messina

In the early hours of 13 July 1943 yet another 'Tokyo Express' run was intercepted by the US Navy to the north-east of Kolombangara and again, but for the last time, the Japanese destroyers scored an impressive tactical victory thanks to their long-range torpedoes. Strategically, however, it was a narrow Allied victory, for the four transport destroyers failed to get through to Vila.

PACIFIC   13 Japanese Cruiser

Jintsu   *0145: Sunk 14 miles (26 km) north of Kolombangara (07-41S 157-15E) by 6in and 5in gunfire and torpedoes of Allied task group – 483 men lost*

US Destroyer

Gwin   *0214: Torpedoed north of Kolombangara by Japanese destroyers; scuttled at 0900 by USS* **Ralph Talbot** *(07-41S 157-27E) – 61 men lost. Cruisers USS* **Honolulu, St Louis** *and HMNZS* **Leander** *were all damaged by torpedoes between 0122 and 0211; two destroyers also sustained minor damage in a collision*

   17 Japanese Destroyer
Hatsuyuki   *Sunk off Kahili, Bougainville, (06-50S 155-47E) by US air attack*

NW EUROPE 17 German Minesweeper
M.346   *Torpedoed off Gamvik, Tanafjord, N. Norway (71-07N 28-19E) by Russian submarine* **S.51** *– 32 men lost*

The Allied losses in the Battle of Kolombangara (13 July) gave the Japanese a temporary local naval superiority which could not be challenged effectively by the US Navy destroyers. Land-based aircraft became the most effective method of interdicting the 'Tokyo Express' resupply runs.

PACIFIC   20 Japanese Destroyers
Kiyonami   *Sunk 42 miles (78 km) north-north-west of Kolombangara (07-13S 156-45E) by USMC air attack*
Yugure   *Sunk 55 miles (102 km) north of Kolombangara (07-25S 156-45E) by USMC air attack*

   22 Japanese Seaplane-Carrier
Nisshin   *Sunk 17 miles (32 km) west of Cape Alexander, Bougainville Is (06-35S 156-10E) by US air attack*

MED   22 Italian Minelayer
Durazzo   *0910: Torpedoed off Pinarello, east coast of Corsica, by RN submarine* **Safari***; hit again at 1000, broke in half and sank*

NW EUROPE 23 German Minesweeper
M.152   1513: Mined off the Gironde

MED   24 Italian Corvette
Cicogna   *1345: Severely damaged at Messina by USAAF air raid; beached with much of hull flooded and extensive fire damage – hulk abandoned*

PACIFIC   27 Japanese Minelayer
Hirashima   *Torpedoed off Osezaki, Fukueshima (32-32N 127-41E) by US submarine* **Sawfish**

Japanese Destroyers
Ariake   *Stranded on reef off Cape Gloucester, New Britain (05-27S 148-*
Mikazuki   *25E); destroyed 28th by USAAF air attack*

AUGUST 1943

4	Italian Torpedo-Boat	MED

Lince — Stranded on spit opposite Punta Alice lighthouse, Gulf of Taranto; salvage had not commenced before the ship was torpedoed on 28 August by RN submarine **Urge**

Italian Torpedo-Boat

Pallade — Damaged at Naples by USAAF air raid; salvage attempts could not cope with flooding and the ship capsized at 0920 on the 5th

4   RN Escort Destroyer

Arrow — 1540: damaged beyond repair in Algiers Roads by the explosion of the SS **Fort la Montee** which she had been assisting – 34 men killed and 80 wounded; the destroyer was beached and subsequently scrapped at Taranto

5   Italian Corvette

Gazzella — 0508: Mined off Asinara, Sardinia (40-54N 08-38E) in a recently laid field; sank in less than one minute

Fresh destroyers reinforced the Allied naval forces in the Solomons in early August and on the night of the 6th/7th, six of them intercepted four Japanese destroyers attempting to resupply the Kolombangara garrison. Using the enemy's own preferred weapon, the torpedo, the US ships surprised the Japanese and scored a significant victory without incurring any damage.

6   Japanese Destroyers   PACIFIC

Hagikaze *2345: Torpedoed close inshore off east coast of Vella Lavella (07-*
Arashi *50S 156-55E) by US destroyers* **Dunlap**, **Craven** *and* **Maury**.
Kawakaze **Kawakaze** *was again torpedoed at 0005 on the 7th by USS* **Stack** *and sank immediately.* **Hagikaze** *and* **Arashi** *blew up and sank at about 0010 – no survivors from crew or embarked soldiers. Destroyer* **Shigure** *was damaged by 5in gunfire but escaped and returned to base*

8   Italian Destroyer   MED

Freccia — 0125: Sunk at Genoa by RAF air raid; hit by 2 bombs and sank in 20 minutes

9   Italian Destroyer

Vincenzo — 1835: Torpedoed 5 miles (9 km) south-west of Punta Mesco, La
Gioberti — Spezia, by RN submarine **Simoom**; torpedoes were fired at the cruiser **Giuseppe Garibaldi**, which took avoiding action – the destroyer had no time to manoeuvre and sank quickly. **Gioberti** was the 44th and last Italian destroyer to be lost during hostilities before the Armistice

22   German Torpedo-Boat (ex-French)

TA.12 — Sunk off Rhodes (35-08N 27-53E) by air attack
(ex-**Baliste**)

27   RN Sloop   ATLANTIC

Egret — 1300: Sunk 30 miles (56 km) west of Vigo (42-10N 09-22W) by German air attack – 35 survivors. **Egret** was the first ship to be sunk by the Henschel Hs 293A glider-bomb; in the same attack, HMCS **Athabaskan** was damaged by an Hs 293A but rescued the sloop's survivors and returned to base under her own steam

28   Italian Torpedo-Boat   MED

Lince — 0815: Torpedoed while aground in the Gulf of Taranto (see 4 August) by RN submarine **Urge**

On 28 August 1943 the Danish Government refused German demands for the imposition of martial law and capital punishment for acts of sabotage. The German Army took over the administration of the country, against opposition in certain areas:

ships of the Royal Danish Navy at sea sought asylum in Swedish ports, while most of those in Danish bases were scuttled. The loss of the minesweeping force was a serious matter for the German Navy, which now had to stretch its limited resources in the western Baltic to fill the gap left.

NW EUROPE   28   Danish Sloop
               Ingolf   Scuttled in the Great Belt; raised and towed to Kiel, where she was destroyed by air raid in 1944

       29   Danish Ships scuttled at Copenhagen:

             Coast Defence Ships
             Niels Iuel   Salvaged by Germans and refitted as training ship **Nordland**; sunk 3 May 1945
             Peder Skram   Salvaged, became German **Adler**; bombed April 1945

             Sloops (all salvaged)
             Hejmdal
             Freja
             Lindormen

             Minelayer
             Lossen   Salvaged and put into service as a merchant vessel

SEPTEMBER 1943

PACIFIC   2   *Japanese Escort Vessel*
            Mutsure   *Torpedoed 85 miles (160 km) north-north-west of Truk, Caroline Is (08-40N 151-31E) by US submarine* **Snapper**

             Japanese Patrol Boat (ex-Destroyer)
            No. 35   *Sunk in Lae Harbour, New Guinea, by USAAF air attack*
            *(ex-***Tsuta***)*

ATLANTIC   6   RN Escort Destroyer
            Puckeridge   1915: Torpedoed 40 miles (75 km) east of Gibraltar (36-06N 04-44W) by German submarine **U.617**; sank in 6 minutes – 129 survivors rescued by Spanish merchant vessel

A substantial proportion of the Italian 'establishment' and people had been less than happy from the outset with their country's involvement in what they saw as a 'German war' and it was clear by mid-1943 that Italy's considerable sacrifices had been to no material avail – the Axis was unquestionably losing. Mussolini was deposed on 15 July and the Provisional Government, after taking careful stock of the overall situation, began to seek an armistice. This was signed on 3 September (the day that the first landings were made in mainland Italy) and came into force at 1730 on the 8th.

One condition of the Armistice was that the Italian Fleet and merchant navy should be transferred to the Allies, to be at their disposal for the prosecution of the war against Germany. This was faithfully observed by the Italian Navy and every seaworthy warship which could get away from La Spezia, Genoa and Taranto sailed on the evening of 8 September for Malta. A few very determined ships' companies even managed to escape from the Adriatic, despite the German domination of the shores of this narrow land-locked sea. Most of the ships which could not get away were scuttled or sabotaged, but a number were unavoidably seized by the Germans. The latter were not prepared to let the Fleet which had got away fall into the Allies' hands without loss and inflicted serious casualties on the main fleet and the detached units. Italian losses might have been greater had German forces not been distracted by the simultaneous Allied invasion at Salerno.

The precise sequence of scuttlings, captures and sinkings by the erstwhile allies is somewhat confusing and not until 16 September did a clear picture of losses emerge: for that reason, although the losses under way are listed in chronological sequence the ships scuttled and captured are listed separately, at the end of the month.

| 8 | German Escort (ex-French Aviso) | | MED |

SG.19
(ex-**Elan**) — Interned in Turkey to avoid capture in Aegean following Italian acceptance of Allied Armistice terms

9 Italian Corvette

Berenice — 0900: Sunk in Trieste Harbour by German artillery while attempting to leave the port to escape to Malta. The **Berenice** had only just completed fitting-out but had a full crew

Italian Minelayer

Pelagosa — Sunk 7 miles (12.7 km) off Genoa by German artillery while attempting to escape to an Allied port

Italian Minelayers

Buccari — Scuttled at La Spezia

Crotone — Captured at La Spezia; found scuttled there

Italian Minesweeper   PACIFIC

Lepanto — *Scuttled at Shanghai. Raised 1944 and commissioned as Japanese gunboat **Okitsu**; surrendered August 1945 and handed to China*

The main body of the Italian Fleet from La Spezia (three battleships, six cruisers and thirteen destroyers) was located off the west coast of Corsica during the forenoon of 9 September and attacked during the afternoon by a specialist Luftwaffe anti-shipping unit (KG 100) based at Toulouse, which introduced a new weapon – a guided armour-piercing bomb – which scored an immediate success.

9 Italian Battleship   MED

Roma — 1510: Sunk in Gulf of Asinara, Sardinia (41-10N 08-40E) by German air attack; hit by two FX.1200 guided bombs which caused a severe fire in the after magazine as well as flooding – ship went down in 50 minutes. One cruiser and six escorts remained to rescue survivors (see 11 September)

Two destroyers were ordered to proceed direct to the Straits of Bonifacio, between Sardinia and Corsica, to interdict German shipping. At 1600 on the 9th they engaged artillery ferries and motor launches but were taken under fire by German-manned coastal batteries which scored hits on both destroyers.

9 Italian Destroyers

Antonio da Noli — 1715: (slightly damaged by gunfire) Mined 5 miles (9 km) off Pertusato lighthouse, Bonifacio Straits; broke in half and sank rapidly

Ugolino Vivaldi — 1700: Damaged off Maddalena by gunfire of coastal batteries and brought to a standstill 30 minutes later, still within range of the batteries, on fire and with damage to boilers. Got under way at 1900 at 10 knots but damaged by German air attack which brought her to a stop again; abandoned during the forenoon of the 10th and sank at 1130 – crew rescued by RN submarine **Sportsman**

RN Minelayer

Abdiel — 2300: Mined in Taranto harbour while landing Army occupation forces – very heavy casualties

10 German Torpedo-Boat (ex-French)

TA.11 (ex-**Iphigénie**) — Damaged by Italian artillery on the 9th. Sunk off Piombino, Elba, by Italian MAS while escorting a northbound convoy

MED   Italian Minelayer
Fasana   Captured at Trieste; commissioned by German Navy as **Kiebitz** – found scuttled at Tagliamento in May 1945

11 US Destroyer
Rowan   0001: Torpedoed off Salerno by German E-boats; sank in less than one minute with loss of over 200 men

Italian Minelayer
Viesti   Captured at Naples; scuttled by German Navy before the liberation of the port

PACIFIC   *11* *Japanese Minesweeper*
W.16   *Mined 60 miles (110 km) south of Makassar, Celebes (06-08S 119-20E)*

The Italian squadron which had been left to rescue the survivors of the **Roma** arrived off the Balearics at noon on 10 September to land the wounded. The Spanish authorities refused permission to enter the harbours of Pollensa and Port Mahon to refuel as well as land the wounded: the light cruiser **Attilio Regolo** had sufficient fuel to continue to Gibraltar, but on the 11th three destroyers proceeded into Port Mahon and internment, while two torpedo-boats and an escort destroyer went to Pollensa where one was interned and the other two scuttled themselves rather than go into internment.

MED   11 Destroyers
Mitragliere
Fuciliere
Carabiniere Interned at Port Mahon, Minorca; restored to Italy, January 1945

Torpedo-Boats
Orsa   Interned at Pollensa, Majorca
Pegaso   0720: Scuttled in Pollensa Bay after landing wounded and non-essential members of her own crew

Escort Destroyer
Impetuoso 0730: scuttled in Pollensa Bay with **Pegaso**

Italian Torpedo-Boats (ex-Yugoslav, ex-Austro-Hungarian)
T-8   pm: Sunk off Punta Olipa, 20 miles (37 km) north-west of Dubrovnik, by German air attack
T-6   1800: Scuttled 16 miles (30 km) north of Rimini as insufficient fuel remained to reach an Allied port

Italian Destroyer
Quintino Sella 1745: Torpedoed 30 miles (55 km) south of Venice by German E-boat (**S.54** or **S.61**) which approached under cover of a merchant ship and hit with 2 torpedoes; the **Sella** sank almost immediately

13 Italian Corvette
Lucciola Sabotaged at Castellamare do Stabilia, Adriatic; not repaired by Germans and scuttled by them in May 1945

14 Italian Torpedo-Boat
Giuseppe
  Sirtori 0910: Badly damaged off Corfu by German air attack and beached off Potamos Point; burned-out hulk destroyed on 25 September to prevent it falling into German hands

The German U-Boat Command, beaten in the spring 1943 North Atlantic campaign, committed its submarines to a fresh offensive in September. All the boats were armed with a new acoustic homing torpedo, intended specifically for use against the convoy escorts, and they scored an immediate success against the escort of convoy ON.202. Only six merchant ships were sunk, however, against three U-boats lost and the RN rapidly introduced an effective decoy and countermeasures tactics.

20   RN Frigate   ATLANTIC
Lagan   0305: Damaged south-west of Iceland (57-09N 27-28W) by German submarine *U.270* (homing torpedo); towed to UK, arrived 24th – not repaired

RCN Destroyer
St. Croix   1756: Damaged by German submarine *U.305* (homing torpedo) and brought to a standstill; sunk at 1855 by the same submarine (in 57-30N 31-10W) – survivors rescued by HMS *Itchen*

RN Corvette
Polyanthus   2236: Torpedoed south-west of Iceland (57-00N 31-10W) by German submarine *U.952* (homing torpedo) – sank almost immediately

22   RN Frigate
Itchen   2355: Torpedoed south of Greenland (53-25N 39-42W) by German submarine *U.666* (homing torpedo); forward magazine blew up and only 3 men survived from crews of *Itchen* and *St. Croix*

23   German Torpedo-Boat (ex-French)   MED
TA.10 (ex-   0110: Damaged 10 miles (18 km) south of Rhodes (36-25N 28-17E)
    La Pomone)   by 4.7in gunfire of RN destroyer *Eclipse*; anchored in Prassos Bay with machinery burned out – scuttled on the 26th (*Eclipse* reported that she had engaged a merchant ship)

German Escort (ex-French Seaplane-Tender)   NW EUROPE
SG.2   Sunk at Nantes by USAAF air raid (one of four 'Sans Souci'-class
   (*Saturnus*)   ships taken over in a St. Nazaire shipyard in 1940 and completed as escorts)

24   Italian Torpedo-Boat   MED
Francesco   pm: Damaged off Corfu by German air attack; brought to a
   Stocco   standstill and sank at 1920 8 miles (15 km) off Corfu due to gradual flooding

25   US Minesweeper
Skill   Torpedoed off Salerno (40-20N 14-35E) by German submarine *U.593*

26   *Japanese Torpedo-Boat*   PACIFIC
Kasasagi   *2300: Torpedoed 25 miles (46 km) south of Flores Sea (05-50S 121-57E) by US submarine* **Bluefin**

26   Italian Torpedo-Boat (under German control)   MED
Rosolino Pilo   Defected to the Allies while escorting a German convoy in the Adriatic

The Allied occupation of the Dodecanese islands of Kos and Leros gave the German Air Force its last opportunity to demonstrate the lethality of air attack by well-trained units on warships without air cover.

26   Greek Destroyer
Vasilissa Olga 0915: Sunk in Leros Harbour by German air attack – 70 men lost
RN Destroyer
Intrepid   (Damaged at 0915 but repairs effected)
                 1700: Damaged at Leros by German air attack and abandoned – 15 men lost; capsized at 0200 on the 27th

27   German Escort (ex-Minesweeper)   NW EUROPE
Jungingen   (See 9 May 1940) Pre-dawn: Sunk 3 miles (5,500m) west of Berck-
   (ex-*M.534*,   sur-Mer (50-28N 01-27E) by RN *MTB*s *202, 204* and *231*
   ex-*M.134*)

MED   27   Italian Torpedo-Boat
           Enrico Cosenz (Damaged on the 25th in collision with merchant ship) Damaged in Lastovo Harbour, Adriatic, (42-40N 16-54E) by German air attack; local repairs not possible and ship scuttled at 2045

PACIFIC   *28*   *Japanese Minelayer*
           Hoko   Sunk 20 miles (37 km) east of Buka Island, Solomons (04-35S 152-11E) by USAAF air attack

ITALIAN UNITS SCUTTLED OR CAPTURED, 9–16 SEPTEMBER 1943

—————————————————— 9 September ——————————————————

MED   Captured by German Forces

Cruisers
Bolzano   At La Spezia (under repair – badly damaged); not taken into German service – scuttled April 1945

Gorizia   As **Bolzano** – sunk 26 June 1944 by explosive charges placed by Anglo-Italian 'frogmen'

Destroyers
Turbine   At Piraeus; renamed **TA.14** (see 15 September 1944)
Francesco Crispi   At Piraeus (sabotaged); renamed **TA.15** (see 8 March 1944)
Dardo   At Genoa (damaged – see 23 September 1941); renamed **TA.31**, not repaired and scuttled April 1945
Premuda   At Genoa (under repair); renamed **TA.32**, not repaired and scuttled April 1945
Sebenico   At Venice (under repair); renamed **TA.43**, not repaired and scuttled at Trieste May 1945
FR.32 (ex-**Siroco**)   At Genoa (under repair); not renamed or repaired, scuttled April 1945

Torpedo-Boats
Castelfidardo   At Suda, Crete; renamed **TA.16** (see 2 June 1944)
Solferino   At Suda; renamed **TA.18** (see 19 October 1944)
San Martino   At Piraeus; renamed **TA.17** (see 12 October 1944)
Calatafimi   At Piraeus (sabotaged); renamed **TA.19** (see 9 August 1944)
Generale Achille Papa   At Genoa (under repair and sabotaged); renamed **SG.20**, not repaired and scuttled, April 1945
T.3   At Fiume; renamed **TA.48** (see 20 February 1945)
T.7   At Gravosa; handed over to 'puppet' Croatian Navy (see 24 June 1944)

Corvettes (all at Livorno under repair)
Camoscio   Renamed **Uj.6081** (see 17 August 1944)
Antilope   Renamed **Uj.6082** (see 16 August 1944)
Artemide   Renamed **Uj.2226**, not repaired and scuttled, April 1945

Minesweeper
Crotone   At La Spezia (damaged); beached at La Spezia after air raid May 1944, not repaired

Scuttled

Cruiser
Taranto   At La Spezia; immediately refloated for use as a blockship but sunk by Allied air raid on 23 October 1943 and again on 23 September 1944 after being refloated for the second time

Destroyers

Nicolo Zeno   At La Spezia (unserviceable); not raised

Corazziere   At Genoa (under repair); raised in January 1944, sunk again by Allied air raid, 4 September 1944

Maestrale   At Genoa (under repair – see 9 January 1943); raised by Germans but scuttled in April 1945

FR.21   At La Spezia (under repair); not raised
(ex-**Lion**)

FR.22 (ex-   As **FR.21**
Panthère)

Escort Destroyer

Ghibli   At Genoa (unserviceable); raised by Germans but not put into service – scuttled at Genoa, April 1945

Torpedo-Boats

Generale   At La Spezia (unserviceable); apparently not raised
Antonio
Cascino

Generale   At La Spezia (unserviceable); raised by Germans but not repaired
Carlo   – sunk again at La Spezia on 4 October 1944 (Allied air raid?)
Montanari

Lira   At La Spezia (unserviceable); raised by Germans but not put into service – sunk again at La Spezia by Allied air attack on 4 November 1944

Procione   At La Spezia (unserviceable); not raised before the end of the war

Corvettes

Persefone   At La Spezia (under repair); raised and commissioned by German Navy as **Uj.2227** – scuttled at Genoa, April 1945

Euterpe   As **Persefone**, commissioned as German **Uj.2228** – scuttled at Genoa, April 1945

FR.51 (ex-   At La Spezia; raised, renamed **SG.23** and transferred to Genoa –
Aviso **La**   scuttled April 1945
Batailleuse)

──────────────── 10 September ────────────────

Captured

Destroyer

Antonio   At Fiume (under repair); sabotaged but repaired by Germans and
Pigafetta   put into service as **TA.44** (see 17 February 1945)

Torpedo-Boats

Insidioso   At Pola (out of fuel); sabotaged but repaired by Germans, renamed **TA.21** and put into service on 8 November 1943 (see 5 November 1944)

Giuseppe   At Durazzo, Albania, after engagement with German artillery and
Missori   armour; renamed **TA.22** but initially continued to serve under the Italian flag, with an Italian crew supervised by a German detachment. Sabotaged at Trieste by Italian crew; after repair, manned by German Navy from January 1944 until scuttled at Trieste, May 1945

———————————————————————— 11 September ————————————————————

Captured

  Old Cruiser
  Cattaro   At Pola, renamed **Niobe** (see 22 December 1944)

  Torpedo-Boats
  Giuseppe la   At Naples (under repair)
  Masa
  Partenope   At Naples (under repair, in drydock). Neither of these two ships
                     could be repaired before the Allies captured Naples

  Corvette
  Vespa   At Pozzuoli (sabotaged); renamed **Uj.2221** and repaired by
                     Germans at Genoa, where scuttled in April 1945

——————————————————————————— 12 September ———————————————————————————

Captured

  Torpedo-Boat
  Audace   At Venice (unserviceable); renamed **TA.20** and repaired (see 1
                     November 1944)

——————————————————————————— 16 September ———————————————————————————

Captured

  Escort Destroyers
  Impavido   At Portoferraio, Corsica (unserviceable); repaired by Germans and
                     renamed **TA.23** (see 25 April 1944)
  Ardito   At Portoferraio, (unserviceable); repaired by Germans and
                     renamed **TA.25** (see 15 June 1944)

  Torpedo-Boat
  Giuseppe   At Fiume (under repair – sabotaged); repaired by Germans and
  Dezza   renamed **TA.35** (see 17 August 1944)

German forces also captured an appreciable number of torpedo-boats and corvettes,
and one escort destroyer, in various stages of construction. Those that were later
completed and saw service under the German ensign are listed below, by type, in 'TA'
numerical order (note that the 'TA' numbers given to the ex-**Ardito** and ex-**Intrepido**
have been inadvertently reversed in previous published lists).

  Escort Destroyer
  (at Genoa, 9 September)
  Intrepido   Renamed **TA.26** – see 15 June 1944

  Torpedo-Boats
  (at Genoa, 9 September)
  Arturo   Renamed **TA.24** – see 18 March 1945
  Auriga   Renamed **TA.27** – see 15 May 1944
  Rigel   Renamed **TA.28** – see 4 September 1944
  Eridana   Renamed **TA.29** – see 18 March 1945
  Dragone   Renamed **TA.30** – see 15 June 1944

  (at Fiume, 10 September)
  Stella Polare Renamed **TA.36** – see 15 March 1944
  Gladio   Renamed **TA.37** – see 7 October 1944
  Spada   Renamed **TA.38** – see 13 October 1944
  Pugnale   Renamed **TA.40** – see 20 February 1945
  Daga   Renamed **TA.39** – see 16 October 1944
  Spica   Renamed **TA.45** – see 13 April 1945

Corvettes   MED
(at Genoa, 9 September)
Tuffetto   Renamed **Uj.2222** – see 23 April 1945
Marangone   Renamed **Uj.2223** – see 16 August 1944

(at Monfalcone, 10 September)
Egeria   Renamed **Uj.201** – see 29 February 1944
Melpomene   Renamed **Uj.202** – see 1 November 1944
Spingarda   Renamed **Uj.208** – see 1 November 1944

OCTOBER 1943

1   Italian Destroyer
     Euro   1115: Sunk at Partheni Bay, Leros, by German air attack; hull holed
                        by fragments from near-miss bombs, ship settled in shallow water
3   US Destroyer   PACIFIC
     Henley   *1815: Torpedoed off Cape Cretin, Finschhafen, New Guinea (07-
                        40S 148-06E), by Japanese submarine* **RO-103**; *back broken, sank
                        in 15 minutes – 15 men lost*

3   RN Escort Destroyer
     Sherwood   Beached as a stripped hulk inside Spurn Head, Humber Estuary
                        (58-37N 00-05W) for use as a Coastal Command air-sea rocket target

5   Italian Minelayer   MED
     Legnano   0830: Sunk at Port Laki, Leros, by German air raid; caught fire and
                        magazine exploded
In late September/early October 1943, the German Army was forced to evacuate the
Kuban Peninsula, to the east of the Crimea. Despite continuous air attacks, over 280,000
personnel, 115,000 tons of material, 49,000 vehicles, 1,800 guns and 80,000 animals
were ferried across the Kerch Straits, for the loss of just *two* of the 240 craft involved.
Two attempts were made by Russian destroyers to intercept the traffic around the
south of the Crimea: neither found any convoys at sea, but on the second occasion the
three ships closed the coast to bombard German-held ports. German E-boats attempted
to attack two of the ships and although these were beaten off, the Russians' departure
from the area was delayed and the group was still close inshore at dawn, when a
German dive-bomber *Gruppe* began a series of 'shuttle' attacks.

6   Russian Flotilla Leader   BLACK SEA
     Kharkhov   0700: Damaged south of Feodosiya, Crimea, by German air attack;
                        taken in tow by **Sposobny** but damaged again at 0930 – sank after
                        3rd attack, at about noon

     Russian Destroyers
     Bezposh-   0930: Damaged south of Feodosiya by German air attack; taken in
     chadny   tow by **Sposobny** but sank after 4th attack, in the afternoon
     Sposobny   noon: Damaged by 3rd German air attack, brought to a stop – sunk
                        by 4th attack

     US Destroyer   MED
     Buck   0036: Torpedoed 40 miles (75 km) south of Sorrento (39-57N 14-
                        28E) by German submarine **U.616**; hit by two torpedoes and sank
                        in 4 minutes – 57 men rescued, over 150 lost

11   RN Minesweeper
     Hythe   0200: Torpedoed off Bougie (37-04N 05-00E) by German
                        submarine **U.371**

12   US Destroyer
     Bristol   0423: Torpedoed 40 miles (75 km) north-east of Bougie (37-19N 06-
                        19E) by German submarine **U.371** – 241 men rescued, 52 lost

PACIFIC 17 German Merchant Raider
Michel   *0200: Torpedoed off Chichi Jima, Bonin Is (33-42N 140-08E), by US submarine* **Tarpon**
The **Michel** *was the last active German disguised merchant raider*

MED 17 German Escort Vessel (ex-RN Minesweeper)
Uj.2109   2330; Sunk in Kalymnos harbour by 4.7in gunfire of RN destroyers
(ex-**Widnes**) **Jervis** and **Penn**

ATLANTIC 21 RCN Minesweeper
Chedabucto   Damaged in St. Lawrence (48-14N 69-16W) in collision with SS **Lord Kelvin**; beached but declared a total loss

MED 22 RN Escort Destroyer
Hurworth   2200: Mined east of Kalymnos (36-59N 27-06E) in new German field; 80 survivors landed in Turkey

Greek Escort Destroyer
Adrias   2200: Damaged by mine, in company with the **Hurworth**; bows blown off and beached at Gumushuk, Turkey – 20 men lost. Refloated and left 1 December under own steam for Alexandria – not repaired

The last action against the 'Tokyo Express' was fought late on 6 October 1943. On this occasion six Japanese destroyers were covering a transport group evacuating Vella Lavella, in the Central Solomons. The US Navy received intelligence of the operation too late to provide timely reinforcements for the three destroyers already on patrol. The latter attacked the Japanese support group with torpedoes and succeeded in sinking one destroyer; the other Japanese ships disengaged, although they had an unrepeatable opportunity to annihilate the entire US destroyer division, all three ships of which were damaged. The Japanese evacuation group carried out its task undisturbed.

PACIFIC 6 Japanese Destroyer
Yugumo   2300: Sunk 15 miles (28 km) north-west of Vella Lavella (07-33S 156-14E) by torpedoes and 5in gunfire of US destroyers

US Destroyer
Chevalier   2301: Damaged 18 miles (33 km) north-west of Vella Lavella (07-30S 156-14E) by torpedo fired by **Yugumo** and ramming by USS **O'Bannon**; bow blown off by torpedo and machinery spaces flooded by collision – scuttled by USS **LaVallette** at about 0200, 54 men lost. USS **Selfridge**, continuing alone after the **Chevalier** and **O'Bannon** had collided, had her bow blown off at about 2310 by a torpedo fired by the **Shigure** or **Samidare**, but returned to Guadalcanal under her own steam

ATLANTIC 8 Polish Destroyer
Orkan   0605: Torpedoed south-west of Iceland (56-30N 26-25W) by German submarine **U.378** (homing torpedo); sank in 5 minutes – 44 survivors

MED 9 RN Anti-Aircraft Cruiser
Carlisle   1205: Severely damaged south of Scarpanto Strait (35-48N 27-36E) by German air attack – 20 men lost; towed to Alexandria by HMS **Rockwood** - not repaired

RN Destroyer
Panther   'Sunk by German air attack in company with the **Carlisle**'

RN 'Hunt'-class Escort Destroyers operating in the English Channel were reinforced by Fleet destroyers from the Home Fleet to deal with the faster, more powerful German torpedo-boats and destroyers based at Brest and Cherbourg. The latter were competently handled and in the first encounter they damaged two of the RN destroyers. A small cruiser was sent to strengthen the squadron in the Channel, but she was lost on her first operation, an attempt to intercept a convoy off the north coast of Brittany.

23	RN Anti-Aircraft Cruiser		NW EUROPE
	Charybdis	0145: Torpedoed 18 miles (33 km) north-east of Roscoff, Brittany (48-59N 03-39W), by German torpedo-boats *T.23* and *T.27*; two torpedoes hit and she capsized quickly, sinking at 0230 with the loss of 464 men – 107 survivors	

RN Escort Destroyer

Limbourne   0152: Torpedoed one mile north-east of *Charybdis* by German torpedo-boat *T.22*; bows blown off and scuttled at 0640 by torpedo from HMS *Talybont* and 4.7in gunfire of HMS *Rocket* after unsuccessful attempts to take her in tow; 42 men lost, 100 survivors

23	RN Minesweeper		MED
	Cromarty	1124: mined in western approaches to Bonifacio Straits, N. Sardinia; 62 survivors rescued	
24	*Japanese Destroyer*		PACIFIC
	Mochizuki	*Sunk 90 miles (170 km) south-south-west of Rabaul (05-42S 151-40E) by USMC air attack*	
24	RN Destroyer		MED
	Eclipse	0050: Mined east of Kalymnos (37-01N 27-11E) – see 22 October; transporting 200 troops to Leros, of whom 140 were lost	
31	German (ex-Danish) Sloop		NW EUROPE
	Heimdal	Sabotaged at Copenhagen	

NOVEMBER 1943

1	US Destroyer		ATLANTIC
	Borie	Damaged by ramming German submarine *U.405* (sunk in 49-00N 31-14W); forward engine-room flooded and ingress of water forward could not be checked. Abandoned in a gale in the evening of the 2nd – crew rescued by USS *Goff* and *Barry* but 27 men lost during transfer	

The US Marines invaded Bougainville on 1 November and that night a Japanese striking force (two heavy cruisers, two light cruisers and six destroyers) approached to bombard the beach-head. Thanks to good intelligence, the US Navy was able to intercept with four large light cruisers and eight destroyers and enjoyed surprise when they opened fire, but the torpedo attacks were unsuccessful and gunfire accounted for the two Japanese ships sunk. The melée yet again degenerated into chaos, with three separate collisions between consorts and exchanges of gunfire between 'friends', but the US Navy force scored an undeniable victory at the cost of just one destroyer damaged by torpedo.

2	*Japanese Light Cruiser*		PACIFIC
	Sendai	*0252: Damaged off Empress Augusta Bay (06-10S 154-19E) by 6in gunfire of US cruisers and stopped, on fire; sunk at 0350 by 5in gunfire of US destroyer **Ausburne***	

Japanese Destroyer

Hatsukaze   *0307: Damaged by collision with cruiser **Myoko** and bow broken off.*
*0430–0540: sunk off Empress Augusta Bay (06-01E 153-58E) by 5in gunfire of US destroyer **Spence** and others*

(Japanese damage)   *Japanese cruiser **Haguro** damaged at 0130 by USN air attack; **Myoko** damaged by collision with **Hatsukaze**; destroyers **Samidare** and **Shiratsuyu** badly damaged by collision*

PACIFIC   *(USN damage)* US destroyer **Foote** *hit by Japanese torpedo at 0308 and stern blown off – towed to base; destroyer* **Spence** *hit by 5in shell, speed reduced;* **Spence** *and* **Thatcher** *collided at high speed, but neither sustained serious damage*

2   Japanese Minesweeper
     W.26   *Severely damaged at Rabaul by USAAF air attack; not repaired – sunk at Rabaul by air attack on 17 February 1944*

Rabaul was attacked by aircraft from the USS **Saratoga** *and* **Princeton** *from 0900 on 5 November. No Japanese warships were sunk, but the 22 dive-bombers and 23 torpedo-bombers nevertheless scored a high percentage of hits, putting six cruisers out of action:*

Maya	*Bombed*	**Atago**	*Near-miss bombs*
Takao	*Bombed*	**Agano**	*Bombed*
Mogami	*Bombed*	**Noshiro**	*Torpedoed*

MED   6   US Destroyer
     Beatty   1805: Torpedoed 40 miles (75 km) west-north-west of Philippeville, Algeria (37-12N 06-16E) by German aircraft; broke in two at 2305 and sank – 12 men lost

US carriers returned to Rabaul on 11 November, unaware of the extent of the damage inflicted on the 5th. Five carriers were involved, with correspondingly larger striking forces, but although one destroyer was sunk, the overall result was disappointing.

PACIFIC   11   Japanese Destroyer
     Suzunami   *0830: Sunk at Rabaul by dive-bombing (USS* **Essex***). Cruiser* **Agano** *and destroyer* **Naganami** *damaged by torpedoes*

MED   11   RN Escort Destroyer
     Rockwood   0030: Damaged 15 miles (25 km) south of Kos (36-25N 26-52E) by Hs 293A glider-bomb which failed to explode; towed out of area by HMS ***Petard***, effected local repairs in Turkish waters and was then towed to Alexandria by HMS ***Blencathra*** – not repaired

13   RN Escort Destroyer
     Dulverton   0130: Damaged 5 miles (9 km) east of Kos (36-50N 27-30E) by glider-bomb – 109 survivors rescued by HMS ***Echo*** and ***Belvoir***; scuttled at 0415

15   RN Destroyer
     Quail   am: Mined in entrance to Bari Harbour and beached; salvaged but capsized in Gulf of Taranto (40-05N 17-52E) while in tow to Taranto on 18 June 1944

PACIFIC   16   Japanese Minelayer
     Ukishima   *Lost by unknown cause, 10 miles (19 km) south-east of Hatsushima (34-55N 139-22E), possibly in minefield laid in December 1942 by US submarine* **Sunfish**

17   US Fast Transport (APD)
     McKean   *0340: Torpedoed off Empress Augusta Bay (06-31S 154-52E) by JNAF aircraft; sank, on fire, 2 hours later – survivors rescued by USS* **Sigourney** *and* **Talbot**

18   Japanese Escort Destroyer
     Sanae   *Torpedoed 90 miles (165 km) south of Basilan Island, Philippines (04-52N 122-07E) by US submarine* **Bluefish**

18   RN Sloop
     Chanticleer   1530: Torpedoed 250 miles (460 km) east-north-east of San Miguel Is, Azores (39-47N 20-12W) by German submarine ***U.515*** (homing

torpedo); towed to Azores with stern blown off – 28 men lost. Ship was not repaired but was laid up at Horta as a base ship and renamed **Lusitania**

22   RN Minesweeper
Hebe   Mined off Bari (41-08N 16-52E) – 38 men lost (36 of 72 survivors injured)

23   *Japanese Escort*
Wakamiya   *Torpedoed 70 miles (130 km) south of Shushan Island, China (28-49N 122-11E), by US submarine* **Gudgeon**

The US Fifth Fleet began the main offensive drive in the Pacific on 20 November 1943 with the invasion of the Gilbert Islands. The landing on Tarawa became synonymous with heavy casualties, with the US Marines losing 1,056 men in 76 hours; the US Navy lost only one ship, with very heavy loss of life.

24   *US Escort Carrier*
Liscombe Bay *0513: Torpedoed off Butariti Atoll, Gilbert Islands (02-58N 172-26E), by Japanese submarine* **I-175***; bomb room exploded and ship sank in 23 minutes – 644 men lost*

24   German Torpedo-Boat (ex-French)
TA.12   Under repair, destroyed at Toulon by USAAF air raid
(ex-**Baliste**)

The Japanese attempted to evacuate personnel from Buka, the northernmost island in the Solomons chain, on the night of 24/25 November. The US Navy again had good intelligence of the operation and five destroyers intercepted the five Japanese ships – three destroyers carrying personnel and two in support – to the south-east of Cape St. George, New Ireland, and sank both the escorts and, an hour later, one of the transports.

25   *Japanese Destroyers*
Onami   *0200: Torpedoed 55 miles (100 km) east-south-east of Cape St. George by US destroyers* **Ausburne**, **Claxton** *and* **Dyson** *– blew up and sank immediately*
Makinami   *0200: Torpedoed with* **Onami***; sunk at 0255 by US destroyers* **Converse** *and* **Spence**
Yugiri   *0300-0328: Sunk 50 miles (93 km) east of Cape St. George by 5in gunfire of USS* **Ausburne**, **Claxton** *and* **Dyson**

29   *US Destroyer*
Perkins   *0150: Sunk off Cape Vogel, New Guinea (09-39S 150-04E) in collision with Australian transport* **Duntroon***; 9 men lost, 229 rescued by the transport*

DECEMBER 1943

4   *Japanese Escort Carrier*
Chuyo   *Torpedoed 260 miles (480 km) south-east of Yokosuka (32-37N 143-39E) by US submarine* **Sailfish**

11   RN Frigate
Cuckmere   1313: Torpedoed off Algiers (36-55N 03-01E), while escorting convoy KMS.34, by German submarine **U.223**; towed to Algiers, not repaired

12   RN Escort Destroyers
Tynedale   0710: Torpedoed off Bougie (37-10N 06-05E) while escorting KMS.34, by German submarine **U.593** (homing torpedo) – sunk

MED		***Holcombe***	1455: Torpedoed off Bougie (37-20N 05-50E) by German submarine ***U.593*** (homing torpedo) – sunk

MED   ***Holcombe***   1455: Torpedoed off Bougie (37-20N 05-50E) by German submarine ***U.593*** (homing torpedo) – sunk

NW EUROPE   13   German Torpedo-Boat
     T.15   Sunk at Kiel by USAAF air raid

MED   18   RN Minesweeper
     Felixstowe   Mined 3 miles (5,500m) east of Cape Ferro, Sardinia (41-10N 09-40E) – no casualties

PACIFIC   *19*   *Japanese Destroyer*
     Numakaze   *Torpedoed 50 miles (90 km) east-north-east of Okinawa (26-29N 128-26E) by US submarine* **Grayback**

     20   *Japanese Destroyer*
     Fuyo   *Torpedoed 60 miles (110 km) west of Manila (14-44N 119-55E) by US submarine* **Puffer**

MED   22   German Escort (ex-Yugoslav old cruiser)
     Niobe ex-   (Aground near Silba Island, Adriatic) Torpedoed by RN ***MTB 226***
     Cattaro*, ex-**   and ***MTB 228. (The German Navy still had a ***Niobe*** in service, the
     Dalmacija)   old ex-Dutch cruiser ***Gelderland***, operating as an AA ship in the Baltic – see 16 July 1944)

     German Minelayer (ex-Yugoslav Seaplane-Tender)
     Drache (ex-   Sunk off Samos, Aegean, by RAF air attack
     Zmaj)

NW EUROPE   23   RN Destroyer
     Worcester   2230. Mined off Smith's Knoll, North Sea, towed to Yarmouth with extreme stern blown off – damaged beyond economical repair

PACIFIC   *Japanese Gunboat (ex-RN Minesweeper)*
     Nanyo *(ex-*   *Sunk by USAAF air attack 35 miles (63 km) south of Formosa*
     Lyemun)   *(25-30N 119-30E)*

ATLANTIC   24   US Destroyer
     Leary   0010: Torpedoed 420 miles (780 km) north-north-east of the Azores (45-00N 22-00W) by German submarine ***U.275*** (homing torpedo); abandoned at 0225, torpedoed again by German submarine ***U.382*** and sank immediately – 97 men lost

     RN Escort Destroyer
     Hurricane   2000: Torpedoed in N. Atlantic (45-10N 22-05W) by German submarine ***U.415*** (homing torpedo); in no danger of sinking but immobilized – HMS ***Watchman*** scuttled her at 1300/25th, on orders of CinC Western Approaches

PACIFIC   *26*   *US Destroyer*
     Brownson   *1420: Sunk 8 miles (15 km) north of Cape Gloucester, New Ireland (05-20S 148-25E), by JNAF air attack; went down in 40 minutes – 108 men lost*

The German battlecruiser ***Scharnhorst*** attempted to intercept convoy JW 55B off northern Norway on 26 December 1943. Her first two approaches to the convoy were driven off by the cruisers of the close cover, which then shadowed the German ship until the distant cover (a battleship and a cruiser, with four destroyers) could arrive and come into action. The Battle of the North Cape was the last open-sea capital ship action.

NW EUROPE   26   German Battlecruiser
     Scharnhorst   1650-1928: Severely damaged by 14in gunfire of RN battleship ***Duke of York*** and 6in gunfire of cruiser ***Jamaica***; sunk (in 72-16N 28-41E) by cruiser and destroyer torpedoes at 1945 – 1,803 men lost, 36 rescued by RN ships

On the day after the loss of the **Scharnhorst**, a powerful force of German destroyers and torpedo-boats sortied into the Bay of Biscay to shepherd into port an inbound blockade runner from the Far East. The latter had been sunk by RAF air attacks late on the 27th, but the German destroyer force was not aware of this when it was intercepted on the 28th by two RN cruisers. Although numerous and supported by aircraft which released glider-bombs at the RN cruisers, the German ships were not handled resolutely and after an hour under fire withdrew, in two groups. The cruisers pursued one group of four ships, sinking three, and broke off only when ammunition ran low.

28	German Destroyer		NW EUROPE
	Z.27	1400-1500	
	German Torpedo-Boats		
	T.25	1355-1540: 85 men lost	
	T.26	1355-1540: 3 men lost	
		Sunk south-west of Ushant by 6in gunfire of RN cruisers **Glasgow** and **Enterprise**; 168 survivors from the three ships were rescued	
31	RN Minesweeper		MED
	Clacton	0832: mined off the east coast of Corsica (42-39N 09-39E) and sank immediately; 43 survivors rescued by RN minesweeper **Polruan**	

JANUARY 1944

3	US Destroyer		ATLANTIC
	Turner	0616: Lost at anchor off the Ambrose Light Vessel, New York, by magazine fire and explosion (at 0742) – approximately 120 men lost	
7	RN Frigate		
	Tweed	1613: Torpedoed 600 miles (1,100 km) west of Cape Ortegal (44-18N 21-19W) by German submarine **U.305** (homing torpedo); sank in 2 minutes, 52 men rescued by HMS **Nene**	
11	*Japanese Cruiser*		PACIFIC
	Kuma	*0913: Torpedoed off Penang (05-28N 99-55E) by RN submarine* **Tally Ho!** *– 2 hits*	
14	*Japanese Destroyer*		
	Sazanami	*Torpedoed 300 miles (550 km) south-east of Yap, Caroline Is (05-15N 141-15E) by US submarine* **Albacore**	
22	US Minesweeper		MED
	Portent	Mined off Anzio (41-24N 12-44E)	
23	RN Destroyer		
	Janus	1815: Torpedoed off Anzio (41-26N 12-38E) by German aircraft; magazine blew up and ship sank with heavy loss of life. (HMS **Jervis** was severely damaged by a glider-bomb in the same raid, but reached Naples under her own steam)	
26	*Japanese Destroyer*		PACIFIC
	Suzukaze	*Torpedoed 140 miles (260 km) north-north-west of Ponape, Caroline Is (08-51N 157-10E) by US submarine* **Skipjack**	
29	RN Anti-Aircraft Cruiser		MED
	Spartan	1820: Sunk in Anzio Bay (41-26N 12-41E) by Hs 293A glider bomb; fires could not be brought under control and the ship sank in about an hour – 523 men rescued	
30	*Japanese Minelayer*		PACIFIC
	Nasami	*Torpedoed west of Truk (09-50N 147-06E) by US submarine* **Trigger**	

NW EUROPE 30 RN Destroyer
Hardy 0405: Torpedoed 60 miles (110 km) south of Bear Island (73-37N 18-06E) by German submarine **U.278** (homing torpedo); magazine blew up after 3 minutes but ship had to be scuttled – 40 men lost

31 German Minesweeper
M.451 Ran aground near Porkkala, Finland, in a storm – total loss

FEBRUARY 1944

PACIFIC 1 *Japanese Destroyer*
Umikaze *Torpedoed south of Truk (07-10N 151-43E) by US submarine* **Guardfish**

NW EUROPE 6 German Minesweeper
M.156 1045: Sunk at Abervrach, Brittany, by RAF air attack (No 266 Squadron – Typhoons)

PACIFIC 10 *Japanese Destroyer*
Minekaze *Torpedoed 85 miles (160 km) north-north-east of Formosa (23-12N 121-30E) by US submarine* **Pogy**

16 *Japanese Cruiser*
Agano *1350: Torpedoed 160 miles (300 km) north of Truk (10-11N 151-42E) by US submarine* **Skate**

On 17 and 18 February 1944 the nine carriers of Task Force 58 attacked the Japanese Navy's advanced anchorage at Truk, in the Caroline Islands. The heavy units of the Combined Fleet had recently removed to Singapore; although the US Navy was disappointed by the small number of warships sunk, the aircraft sank numerous auxiliaries in the lagoon, which never again regained its importance as a base.

17 *Japanese Training Cruiser*
Katori *(Damaged by air attack off Truk while attempting to escape): (pm) Sunk 40 miles (74 km) north-west of Truk (07-45N 151-20E) by 8in gunfire of US cruisers* **Minneapolis** *and* **New Orleans** *and torpedoes of destroyers* **Radford** *and* **Burns**

Japanese Destroyer
Maikaze *Sunk in company with* **Katori** *(07-45N 151-20E)*

Japanese Armed Merchant Cruiser
Akagi Maru *Sunk north-west of Truk (07-54N 151-25E) by USN aircraft*

Japanese Cruiser
Naka *Sunk 35 miles (65 km) west of Truk (07-15N 151-15E) by aircraft from USS* **Bunker Hill** *and* **Cowpens**

Japanese Destroyers
Fumizuki *Sunk by aircraft from USS* **Enterprise** *south-west of Truk (07-24N 151-44E)*
Oite *Sunk by aircraft west of Truk (07-40N 151-45E)*
Tachikaze *Sunk by aircraft at Truk (07-04N 151-55E)*

Japanese Minesweeper
W.26 *(Already severely damaged – see 2 November 1943). Sunk at Rabaul by aircraft*

MED 18 RN Cruiser
Penelope 0730: Torpedoed 35 miles (65 km) west of Naples (40-55N 13-25E) by German submarine **U.410**; sank 10 minutes later after major explosion (probably after magazine) – 250 men rescued

20	RN Sloop		ATLANTIC
	Woodpecker	0001: Torpedoed south-west of Ireland (48-49N 22-11W) by German submarine **U.764** (homing torpedo); stern blown off and taken in tow but sank at 0910 on 27 February off Scilly Isles (49-51N 06-46W) in a gale	

RN Escort Destroyer
Warwick   1145: Torpedoed 20 miles (37 km) south-west of Trevose Head, Cornwall (50-29N 05-25W), by German submarine **U.413**; sank very quickly after heavy explosion – 93 men rescued

22	*Japanese Minelayer*		PACIFIC
	Natsushima	*Sunk off Kavieng, New Ireland (02-40S 149-40E) by 5in gunfire of US destroyers* **Ausburne, Dyson** *and* **Stanley**	

25	RN Destroyer		MED
	Inglefield	(dusk) Sunk off Anzio (41-26N 12-38E) by Hs 293A glider bomb – 157 men rescued	
	RN Destroyer		NW EUROPE
	Mahratta	2210: Torpedoed 280 miles (520 km) west of the North Cape (71-17N 13-30E) by German submarine **U.956** (homing torpedo) – 16 survivors	

29	German Corvette (ex-Italian)		MED
	Uj.201 (ex-**Egeria**)	Damaged at Monfalcone by air raid; not repaired before the end of the war	

MARCH 1944

1	RN Frigate		ATLANTIC
	Gould	1920: Torpedoed 480 miles (890 km) north-north-east of the Azores (45-46N 23-10W) by German submarine **U.358** (homing torpedo); the sinking came near the end of a 14-hour hunt – **U.358** surfaced to sink the **Gould** and was in turn sunk by HMS **Affleck**	

3	*Japanese Minelayer*		PACIFIC
	Shirakami	*Sunk south of Urup Island, Kuriles (43-30N 150-00E) by collision in a gale with Army transport* **Nichiran Maru**	

8	German Torpedo-Boat (ex-Italian Destroyer)		MED
	TA.15 (ex-**Francesco Crispi**)	1900: Sunk off Heraklion, Crete (35-20N 25-10E) by RAF air attack (rocket projectiles); raised and repaired (see 12 October 1944)	

9	RN Corvette		ATLANTIC
	Asphodel	0130: Torpedoed 390 miles (725 km) west-north-west of Cape Finisterre (45-24N 18-09W) by German submarine **U.575** (homing torpedo) – 5 survivors rescued by HMS **Clover**	

US Destroyer Escort
Leopold   2100: Torpedoed 360 miles (670 km) south-south-west of Iceland (58-36N 25-57W) by German submarine **U.255** (homing torpedo); remained afloat with back broken until 0145, when the stern broke off and sank – bow section not scuttled until 0845/10th, but only 28 survivors rescued by USS **Joyce**

13	*Japanese Cruiser*		PACIFIC
	Tatsuta	*Torpedoed 145 miles (270 km) south-south-west of Yokosuka (32-58N 138-52E) by US submarine* **Sandlance**	

NW EUROPE	14	German Minesweeper	
		M.10	2145: Sunk 3 miles (5,500m) off Dunkirk by RN **MTB 353** in an attack on a convoy

PACIFIC	*16*	*Japanese Destroyer*	
		Shirakumo	*Torpedoed 170 miles (315 km) east of Muroran, Hokkaido (42-25N 144-55E) by US submarine* **Tautog**

MED	18	German Torpedo-Boat (ex-Italian)	
		TA.36 (ex- **Stella Polare**)	2025: Mined 15 miles (28 km) south-south-west of Fiume (45-07N 14-21E)

	27	German Corvette (ex-Italian)	
		Uj.205 (ex- **Colubrina**)	Sunk at Venice by USAAF air raid

	30	RN Destroyer	
		Laforey	0110: Torpedoed 60 miles (110 km) north-east of Palermo (38-54N 14-18E) by German submarine *U.223* (homing torpedo) at the end of a 5½-hour hunt, the U-boat being sunk by HMS **Tumult, Blencathra** and **Hambledon**; only 69 survivors were picked up from the *Laforey*, which was the last RN vessel to be sunk in the Mediterranean by submarine

The US fast carriers attacked Japanese air and naval bases in the Western Caroline Islands at the end of March 1944. The harbour in the Palau Islands was the most important left to the Japanese in the South-West Pacific, but, as at Truk in February, there were no major warships present. The results were thus less than had been hoped for, but the bombs and air-laid mines (used by US carrier aircraft for the first time) cost the Japanese three valuable Fleet oilers and a unique fast repair ship, as well as a number of smaller craft.

PACIFIC	*30*	*Japanese Patrol Boat (ex-Destroyer)*	
		No. 31 *(ex-* **Kiku***)*	*Sunk off Palau (07-30N 134-30E) by USN carrier aircraft*
		Japanese Destroyer	
		Wakatake	*Sunk 60 miles (110 km) north of Palau (07-50N 134-20E) by USN carrier aircraft*

APRIL 1944

NW EUROPE	10	German Minesweeper	
		M.459	Sunk off Narva, Gulf of Finland, by Russian air attacks. *M.413* was badly damaged but reached harbour

PACIFIC	*11*	*Japanese Destroyer*	
		Akigumo	*Torpedoed 30 miles (56 km) south-east of Zamboanga, Philippines (06-43N 122-23E) by US submarine* **Redfin**

MED	11	US Destroyer Escort	
		Holder	2340: Torpedoed 40 miles (75 km) east-north-east of Algiers (37-01N 03-50E) by German aircraft – 16 men lost; towed to Algiers and then to New York but not repaired

PACIFIC	*14*	*Japanese Destroyer*	
		Ikazuchi	*Torpedoed 200 miles (370 km) south-south-east of Guam (10-13N 143-51E) by US submarine* **Harder**

15 Japanese Minesweeper   PACIFIC
    W.7   *Torpedoed south-east of Port Blair, Andaman Is (11-34N 93-08E)*
                    by RN submarine **Storm**

20 US Destroyer   MED
    Lansdale   2105: Torpedoed 40 miles (75 km) east of Algiers (37-02N 03-51E)
                    by German aircraft; abandoned at 2125 and sank soon afterwards
                    – 49 men lost, 233 survivors rescued by USS ***Newell*** and ***Menges***

21 German Minesweeper (ex-Dutch)   NW EUROPE
    M.553 (ex- Mined in the Baltic
    **Willem van
    Ewijck (ii)**)

23 Japanese Destroyer   PACIFIC
    Amagiri   *Mined 55 miles (100 km) south of Balikpapan, Borneo (02-10S 116-45E)*
                    in minefield laid by US submarine **Tautog** *on 7 March 1943*

25 German Torpedo-Boat   MED
    TA.23 (ex- 0145: Mined west of Capraia (43-02N 09-45E) in field laid by Italian
    Impavido) torpedo-boat ***Sirio*** operating under Allied control; 0645: scuttled
                    by ***TA.29***

26 German Torpedo-Boat   NW EUROPE
    T.29   0420: Sunk north of the Ile de Batz, Brittany (48-53N 03-33W) by 4.7in
                    gunfire of RCN destroyer ***Haida*** – 135 men lost

27 Japanese Cruiser   PACIFIC
    Yubari   *Torpedoed off Palau (05-20N 132-16E) by US submarine* **Bluegill**

    Japanese Minelayer
    Kamome   *Torpedoed west of Tokunoshima, Nansei Shoto (27-37N 128-11E)*
                    by US submarine **Halibut**

29 French Aviso
    Tahure   *Torpedoed off Indo-China (13-02N 109-28E) by US submarine*
                    Flasher

Three days after sinking the ***T.29***, HMCS ***Haida*** was again off the Ile de Batz, covering a
minelaying operation. The ***T.24*** and ***T.27***, both of which had been damaged during the
previous encounter, were intercepted en route from St Malo to Brest and the ***Haida*** repeated
her success, although not until her sister-ship had been torpedoed, with heavy loss of life.

28 RCN Destroyer   NW EUROPE
    Athabaskan 0415: Torpedoed about 12 miles (22 km) north of the Ile Vierge, Brittany
                    (48-43N 04-31W), by German torpedo-boat ***T.24***; hit again at 0417 and
                    blew up – 85 men rescued

    German Torpedo-Boat
    T.27   0435: Damaged by 4.7in gunfire of RCN destroyer ***Haida*** and
                    driven ashore off Pontusval, Brittany (48-40N 04-23W). Damaged
                    again by RAF air attack on 3 May and destroyed by RN ***MTB.673***'s
                    torpedo on 7 May

MAY 1944

2   US Destroyer   ATLANTIC
    Parrott   1636: Collided in fog off Norfolk Naval Base, Virginia (36-51N 76-
                    18W) with merchant ship SS ***John Morton***; beached, then towed to
                    Portsmouth Navy Yard, Va. – not repaired

ATLANTIC	3	US Destroyer Escort	
		Donnell	1200: Torpedoed 280 miles (890 km) south-west of Cape Clear (47-48N 19-55W) by German submarine *U.765* (homing torpedo); both propellers blown off, towed to the Clyde but not repaired – 27 men lost
NW EUROPE	4	RN Minesweeper	
		Elgin	pm: Mined 9 miles (17 km) east of Portland (50-28N 02-11W), acoustic mine exploded 50 yards from stern – no casualties; ship towed to Portsmouth but not repaired
MED	5	US Destroyer Escort	
		Fechteler	0446: Torpedoed off Alboran Island (36-07N 02-40W) by German submarine *U.967* (homing torpedo); abandoned at 0515, sank at 0600 – 186 men rescued
ATLANTIC	7	RCN Frigate	
		Valleyfield	0435: Torpedoed 40 miles (75 km) south-east of Cape Race (46-03N 52-24W) by German submarine *U.548* (homing torpedo) – 121 men lost, 38 men rescued by HMCS *Giffard*
PACIFIC	10	*Japanese Destroyer*	
		Karukaya	*Torpedoed 35 miles (65 km) west-north-west of Iba, Luzon (15-38N 119-25E) by US submarine* **Cod**
NW EUROPE	12	German Minesweeper	
		M.372	Sunk off Swinemünde (54-41N 12-31E) by Russian air attack
PACIFIC	14	*Japanese Destroyer*	
		Inazuma	*Torpedoed off Tawi-Tawi, Borneo (05-08N 119-38E) by US submarine* **Bonefish**
NW EUROPE	14	German Minesweeper	
		M.435	Sunk north of Ameland (53-35N 05-43E) by RAF Coastal Command (Langham Wing) air attack
PACIFIC	17	*Japanese Patrol Boat (ex-Destroyer)*	
		No. 36 *(ex-Fuji)*	*Damaged at Soerabaja by RN and USN aircraft (HMS* **Illustrious** *and USS* **Saratoga***); not repaired*
	22	*Japanese Destroyer*	
		Asanagi	*Torpedoed 200 miles (370 km) west-north-west of Chichi Jima, Bonin Is (28-20N 138-57E) by US submarine* **Pollack**
NW EUROPE	22	German Minesweeper	
		M.515	Mined west of Fehmarn, W. Baltic (54-34N 10-45E) by RAF-laid ground mine
PACIFIC	22	*Japanese Gunboat*	
		Hashidate	*Torpedoed off Pratas Reef, South China Sea (21-08N 117-20E) by US submarine* **Picuda**
	24	*Japanese Escort*	
		Iki	*Torpedoed in South China Sea, 240 miles (445 km) east of Singapore (01-17N 107-53E) by US submarine* **Raton**
NW EUROPE	24	German Torpedo-Boat	
		Greif	0030: Damaged north-west of Ouistreham (49-21N 00-19W) by RAF air attack (415 Squadron) and abandoned and scuttled following collision with torpedo-boat *Falke*
		German Minesweeper	
		M.39	0240: Torpedoed by RN *MTBs* *354* and *361* off Dunkirk

29	US Escort Carrier		ATLANTIC

Block Island   2013: Torpedoed 420 miles (780 km) south of the Azores (31-13N 23-03W) by German submarine **U.549** (3 'straight-running' torpedo hits); carrier sank at 2045 – 6 men lost, 951 rescued by DEs **Ahrens** and **Robert I. Paine**.

DE **Barr** was torpedoed by **U.549** during the subsequent hunt (at 2033) but was towed to Casablanca and repaired

31	*Japanese Escort*		PACIFIC

Ishigaki   *Torpedoed 70 miles (130 km) west of Matsuwa, Kuriles (48-30N 151-30E) by US submarine* **Herring**

31	German Minesweeper		NW EUROPE

M.13   Mined in the Gironde estuary

JUNE 1944

2	*Japanese Escort*		PACIFIC

Awaji   *Torpedoed off Yasho Island, Formosa (22-34N 121-51E) by US submarine* **Guitarro**

2	German Torpedo-Boat (ex-Italian)		MED

TA.16 (ex-   (Severely damaged by RAF air attack 10 miles (18 km) north of
Castel-   Heraklion at 1830/1st). 1800: Sunk at Heraklion by explosion of
fidardo   ammunition ship SS **Gerhard** during RAF air raid

4	German Minesweeper		NW EUROPE

M.37   0010: Torpedoed off Narva, Gulf of Finland, by Russian MTBs

5	USN Minesweeper		

Osprey   Mined 30 miles (55 km) north-west of Cap d'Antifer (50-13N 01-26W), Normandy

The main Japanese fleet, now known as the 'Mobile Fleet', concentrated at Tawi Tawi, in the Sulu Sea, in mid-May 1944. The location was chosen for its central position, from which the Fleet could sortie to drive off a US thrust towards the Marianas Islands or western New Guinea, the most obvious objectives in the drive towards Japan itself, and also for its proximity to the oil fuel supplies from Tarakan. The Tawi Tawi anchorage and its surrounding sea areas were, however, ill-placed for anti-submarine operations and the US Pacific Fleet submarines were ordered to watch the Mobile Fleet and inflict attrition.

6	*Japanese Destroyer*		PACIFIC

Minazuki   *Torpedoed 150 miles (280 km) east-north-east of Tarakan, Celebes (04-05N 119-30E) by US submarine* **Harder** – *sank in 4 minutes*

Japanese Escort

No. 15   *Torpedoed south-east of Cape St. Jacques, Indo-China (08-58N 109-30E) by US submarine* **Raton**

While the Japanese Fleet awaited the US Pacific Fleet's next major move, the Allies in Europe were mounting the largest amphibious invasion of all, on five separate beaches in Normandy. Eight hundred and eighty-two major and minor warships supported over 4,000 landing ships and craft and 1,250 transports of all sizes. The German Navy reacted swiftly and vigorously, but although the three torpedo-boats of the 5. *Torpedo-Flotille* found the plum naval target – the old battleships of the RN bombardment group – their torpedoes hit only one of the screening destroyers. Allied warship losses to enemy action in the early stages of Operation 'Neptune' were few, belying the difficulty and danger of the work.

NW EUROPE	6	Norwegian Destroyer
		Svenner 0440: Torpedoed 35 miles (65 km) west-north-west of Le Havre (49-27N 00-15W) by German torpedo-boats **Möwe**, **Jaguar** and **T.28**
		RN Escort Destroyer
		Wrestler 0645: Mined 20 miles (37 km) west-north-west of Le Havre (49-36N 00-28W); damaged beyond repair but towed to Portsmouth
		US Destroyer
		Corry 0633: Mined off 'Utah' Beach, Normandy (49-31N 01-12W); sank at 0640 – 22 men lost, 260 rescued by USS **Fitch** and **Hobson**, under fire from German artillery
PACIFIC	7	*Japanese Destroyer*
		Hayanami *noon: Torpedoed 35 miles (65 km) east of Tawi-Tawi, Borneo (04-43N 120-03E) by US submarine* **Harder** *– sank in less than one minute*
NW EUROPE	7	USN Minesweeper
		Tide am: Mined off 'Utah' Beach, Normandy (49-37N 01-05W)
PACIFIC	8	*Japanese Destroyer*
		Harusame *Sunk off Dampier Strait, West New Guinea (00-05S 132-45E) by USAAF air attack*
		Japanese Destroyer
		Kazegumo *Torpedoed off Davao Gulf, Mindanao (06-03N 125-57E) by US submarine* **Hake**
NW EUROPE	8	US Destroyer
		Meredith (ii) 0152: Mined off 'Utah' Beach, Normandy – 35 men lost; towed to anchorage area and salvage begun – damaged early on the 9th by near-miss bomb and sank at 1010 (49-33N 01-06N)
		RN Frigate (Assault HQ Ship)
		Lawford 0445: Sunk off 'Juno' Beach, Courseulles, Normandy (49-26N 00-24W) by German air attack
		US Destroyer
		Glennon 0803: Mined off Quineville, Normandy – 25 men lost; ship settled by the stern, which grounded, preventing a tow, and abandoned at anchor. Sunk by German artillery on the 9th (49-33N 01-06W)
		US Destroyer Escort
		Rich 0920: Mined attempting to assist **Glennon**; detonated two mines and broke in half, both portions sinking near Iles Marcouf (50-32N 01-12W) – 89 men lost, 126 rescued
PACIFIC	9	*Japanese Destroyer*
		Matsukaze *Torpedoed 70 miles (130 km) south-east of Chichi Jima, Bonin Islands (26-59N 143-13E) by US submarine* **Swordfish**
		Japanese Destroyer
		Tanikaze *2130: Torpedoed in Sibutu Passage, 90 miles (165 km) south-west of Basilan Island (05-42N 120-41E) by US submarine* **Harder**
NW EUROPE	9	RN Auxiliary AA Ship
		Alynbank Expended as blockship
	9	German Destroyers
		ZH.1 (ex-Dutch 0210: Damaged and brought to a stop west of the Ile de Batz (48-
		Gerard Cal- 47N 04-07W) by 4.7in gunfire; torpedoed by RN destroyer
		lenburgh) **Ashanti**. 140 survivors rescued by RN ships, 29 reached the Ile de Batz
		Z.32 0420: Damaged by 4.7in gunfire of RCN destroyers **Haida** and **Huron** and driven ashore on the Ile de Batz, after all ammunition

and torpedoes expended – approximately 30 men lost. Sub- NW EUROPE
sequently destroyed by RAF air attack (Coastal Command
Beaufighters of 144 and 404 Squadrons – rocket projectiles). *Z.24*
and *T.24* were both damaged but escaped to Brest

As the first stage of the laying of the artificial harbours off the Normandy invasion
beaches, 53 old merchant ships and warships were scuttled stem to stern about 1,500
yards offshore, giving a total of 4 miles (7 km) of limited shelter; of this, 2,000 feet (600m)
was formed by the four Allied warships scuttled off the Anglo-Canadian sector.

RN Battleship – Target Ship	Netherlands Cruiser
Centurion	**Sumatra**
RN Cruiser	French Battleship
Durban	**Courbet**

9   German Torpedo-Boat (ex-Italian)   MED
    TA.27 (ex-   1200: Damaged at Portoferrario, Elba (42-49N 10-20E) by USAAF
    Auriga)   air attack; capsized during the night of 9th/10th

9   RN Minesweeper
    Kellett   0130: damaged beyond economical repair by grounding on Peveril
    Ledge, Swanage Bay, while returning from Seine Bay assault area

11 RN Frigate   NW EUROPE
    Halsted   0315: Torpedoed off Normandy by German E-Boats of *9.
    Schnellboot Flotille*; bows blown off and returned to Portsmouth
    astern under her own power – not repaired

12 *Japanese Torpedo-Boat*   PACIFIC
    Otori   *Sunk 180 miles (335 km) north-west of Saipan (17-32N 144-00E) by
    USN carrier aircraft*

13 RN Escort Destroyer   NW EUROPE
    Boadicea   0445: Torpedoed 12 miles (22 km) south-west of Portland Bill (50-26N
    02-46W) by German aircraft; hit by two torpedoes and blew up – only
    12 survivors

14 *Japanese Destroyer*   PACIFIC
    Shiratsuyu   *Sunk 90 miles (165 km) south-east of Surigao Strait (09-09N 126-
    51E) by collision with oiler* **Seiyo Maru**

14 German Minesweepers   NW EUROPE
    M.83   0140: Sunk off Cap de la Hague by 4.7in gunfire of RN destroyer
    Ashanti and Polish **Piorun** – 24 men rescued
    M.343   0230: Sunk south of Jersey by the same destroyers. **M.412** was
    badly damaged in this running battle

14/15
    German Torpedo-Boats (ex-Italian)   MED
    TA.26 (ex-**Intrepido**)
    TA.30 (ex-   Torpedoed 17 miles (31 km) west of La Spezia (44-04N 09-32E) by
    Dragone)   three USN MTBs of 29th PT Squadron (probably **PT**s **552**, **558**, **559**)
    – 167 survivors from the two torpedo-boats

The German light forces based on the Channel ports constituted a threat to the Anglo-
US amphibious build-up in the Bay of the Seine and had already inflicted losses by
minelaying and direct attack. The RAF's considerable might was called upon to deliver
concentrated attacks on the two major bases on successive nights. Striking at such
short ranges, the heavy bombers were able to achieve a high degree of accuracy; they
were, however, much assisted by the local flak commander, who forbade the AA
defences to open fire on the first wave as Luftwaffe minelaying aircraft were also in the
area. The German Navy's losses were crippling.

NW EUROPE 15 German Torpedo-Boats
Falke
Jaguar
Möwe   0045; Sunk at Le Havre by RAF air raid (325 Lancasters); **Möwe** flooded and capsized at 0500 – 12 dead. The other two ships were hit by 4-5 bombs each and sank immediately – combined total of 42 men lost. This raid also sank eleven E-boats, 20 miscellaneous patrol craft and 19 tugs. The torpedo-boat **Kondor**, damaged by mine on 24 May, was further damaged and had to be scuttled on 28 June; torpedo-boat **T.28** was slightly damaged but managed to escape in late July – the only significant survivor of the German flotillas based in France

German Minesweeper
M.103   0557: Sunk off the Ems estuary (53-35N 06-16E) by RAF air attack (Coastal Command Beaufighters of North Coates and Langham Wings). E-boat depot ship **Nachtigall** and brand-new MV also sunk

RN Frigate
Mourne   1145: Torpedoed 40 miles south-south-west of the Lizard (49-25N 05-30W) by German submarine **U.767** (homing torpedo); bows blown off and sank in one minute

RN Frigate
Blackwood   1910: Torpedoed 23 miles (43 km) south-south-east of Portland Bill (50-04N 02-15W) by German submarine **U.764** (homing torpedo); bows blown off and taken in tow but sank at 0410 on the 16th, 23 miles (42 km) south-east of Portland Harbour

German Minesweepers
M.402
M.507
M.550   2300: Sunk at Boulogne by RAF air raid (274 Lancasters and Halifaxes). Seven R-boats and 17 miscellaneous auxiliaries and small craft also sunk

17 German Minesweeper
M.546   Sunk north-west of Boulogne by air attack (possibly No 415 Squadron RCAF).

18 German Minesweeper
M.133   0200: Torpedoed south-west of Jersey by RN **MTB**s **727** and **748**; towed to St. Malo – not repaired and scuttled on 6 August

The Japanese carriers sortied from Tawi Tawi for what was to be their last battle on 11 June 1944. The US landings on Saipan began on the 14th and five days later the first, defensive phase of the Battle of the Philippine Sea was fought by the US fast carriers. No ships were sunk by aircraft on that day, the kills going to the US submarines which had up to the opening of the battle performed their scouting duties to perfection.

PACIFIC 19 *Japanese Carriers*
Taiho   *0900: Torpedoed 180 miles (333 km) north-north-west of Yap (12-22N 137-04E) by US submarine **Albacore**; only one hit and ship continued in formation, but aviation fuel tanks were ruptured and inept damage control permitted inflammable vapour to spread. **Taiho** blew up at 1532 and sank at 1706 (12-05N 138-12E) – 1,650 men lost*

Shokaku   *1220: Torpedoed 140 miles (260 km) north of Yap, Caroline Is (11-50N 137-57E) by US submarine **Cavalla**; 3 hits started extensive fires and ship disintegrated at 1510 when the bomb-room exploded (11-40N 137-40E)*

The German Navy supported the seaward flank of the Finnish defences, bombarding Russian positions ashore and patrolling to prevent landings on the offshore islands. On the night of 18/19 June, the patrols were strengthened by the presence of a torpedo-boat which fought one successful action at the head of the Gulf of Finland but was less fortunate in a second clash. The loss of *T.31* obliged the Germans to rely thereafter upon smaller craft to support their ally.

19	German Torpedo-Boat		NW EUROPE
	T.31	0230: Torpedoed off Biorko Island, Gulf of Finland (60-26N 28-17E) by Russian MTBs – 105 men lost	

The US carriers went over to the offensive on 20 June but delays in locating the Japanese fleet resulted in only one major strike being launched. Attacking at dusk, the results disappointed the US Navy, who were as yet unable to realize that the slaughter of the Japanese air groups on the previous day had reduced the enemy carrier force to a state of impotence from which it could not recover.

20	Japanese Carrier		PACIFIC
	Hiyo	*1845: Torpedoed 450 miles (835 km) north-west of Yap (15-30N 133-50E) by USN aircraft (USS* **Belleau Wood***); set on fire and sank at 2030.*	
		Carriers **Zuikaku** *and* **Chiyoda** *were also hit and set on fire by US carrier bomber aircraft, but both eventually brought the fires under control and were repaired at Kure. The battleship* **Haruna** *and heavy cruiser* **Maya** *were also damaged and two Fleet oilers had to be scuttled*	

21	Torpedo-Boat (ex-Italian Escort Destroyer)		MED
	TA.25 (ex-*Ardito*)	0230: Torpedoed in an almost unrecorded surface action 8 miles (15 km) west of Viareggio (43-49N 10-12E) by US Navy PT-boats; 107 men rescued	

Although the surface patrols and RAF bomber raids on the French ports had reduced the German capability for direct attack on the amphibious reinforcement shipping, air and sea-laid mines (particularly the new and virtually unsweepable pressure-actuated 'Oyster' mines) inflicted serious casualties in late June. Besides the warships sunk or damaged beyond repair, the Allies lost the services of the Norwegian-manned escort destroyer *Glaisdale*, the French frigate *La Surprise* and two minesweepers. Three merchant vessels were also sunk.

21	RN Destroyer		NW EUROPE
	Fury	1045: Mined off 'Sword' Beach, Normandy; taken in tow but broke away in a gale and went ashore at 2300 – total loss	
	German Minesweeper		
	M.538	Severely damaged off Viborg by Russian air attack and towed to Königsberg – laid up, unrepaired, and scuttled in April 1945	

22	Italian Cruiser		MED
	Bolzano	(Damaged and not in commission – intended by Germans for use as a blockship) pre-dawn: Sunk at La Spezia by explosive charge placed by RN human torpedo ('Chariot')	

23	RN Anti-Aircraft Cruiser		NW EUROPE
	Scylla	2300: Mined off 'Sword' Beach (49-25N 00-24W); extensive shock damage throughout midships section and loss of all power, towed to Portsmouth – constructive total loss	

24	RN Destroyer		
	Swift	0735: Mined off 'Sword' Beach, 5½ miles (10 km) north of Ouistreham (49-22N 00-17W), 17 men lost; later broke in half and sank.	

NW EUROPE		The minesweeping trawler **Lord Austin** and Motor Minesweeper (MMS) **No. 8** and two large freighters were also sunk on this day

MED   Croat Torpedo-Boat (ex-Yugoslav)

T.7   2200: Severely damaged by gunfire of RN **MGB**s **662** and **659** and **MTB 670**; beached on Murter Island, N. Adriatic, and abandoned

25   German Torpedo-Boat (ex-Italian)

TA.22 (ex-   am: Severely damaged off Trieste by USAAF air attack while
Giuseppe   running trials after extensive repairs; paid off, unrepaired, and
Missori)   scuttled May 1945

French Destroyer (under German control)

Bison   (Hulk used as smoke-screen platform). Rammed at Toulon by German submarine and sank in harbour

NW EUROPE   RN Frigate

Goodson   1415: Torpedoed 40 miles (75 km) south-east of Start Point by German submarine **U.984** (homing torpedo); stern blown off, towed to Portland by HMS **Bligh** – not repaired

MED   26   Italian Cruiser

Gorizia   (Damaged and not in commission – intended by Germans for use as a blockship). Sunk at La Spezia by explosive charges placed by Anglo-Italian 'frogmen'

NW EUROPE   27   RN Corvette

Pink   1515: Torpedoed 20 miles (37 km) east-north-east of Barfleur (29-48N 00-49W) by German submarine **U.988** (homing torpedo); propeller and shaft blown off, towed to Portsmouth – not repaired

NW EUROPE   28   German Torpedo-Boat

Kondor   (Damaged by mine on 24 May and by bomb on 15 June). Scuttled at Le Havre

PACIFIC   28   *Japanese Escort*

No. 24   *Torpedoed 30 miles (56 km) west of Iwo Jima, Bonin Islands (24-44N 140-20E) by US submarine* **Archerfish**

29   *Japanese Minelayer*

Tsugaru   *Torpedoed west of Morotai (02-19N 127-57E) by US submarine* **Darter**

JULY 1944

4   *Japanese Minelayer*

Sarushima   *Sunk off Anijima, Bonins (27-10N 142-10E) by US carrier aircraft (Task Group 58.1)*

Japanese Minesweeper

W.25   *Sunk off Bonins (28-35N 141-04E) by US carrier aircraft*

NW EUROPE   German Minesweeper

M.469   am: Torpedoed north-west of Vlieland (53-21N 04-57E) by RN **MTB 458**; blew up when hit by two torpedoes

PACIFIC   6   *Japanese Destroyer*

Hokaze   *Torpedoed 105 miles (195 km) north-north-east of Menado, Celebes (03-24N 125-28E) by US submarine* **Paddle**

RN Frigate
Trollope   0123: Torpedoed 10 miles (18 km) west of Cap d'Antifer by German E-boat; towed to Arromanches Harbour and beached, then towed to Portsmouth – not repaired

On the night of 5/6 July the German Navy introduced a new weapon to harass the Normandy anchorages – the 'human torpedo'. These craft, which had a maximum endurance of about 10 hours at 3 knots, were launched from German-occupied beaches on the north shore of the Seine Bay. Although they could not submerge, they were difficult to spot in the darkness and inflicted several losses, although at a high cost to themselves.

6   RN Minesweepers
    Magic   0353: 7 miles north of Ouistreham (49-25N 00-15W)
    Cato   0511: 5 miles north of Hermanville (49-25N 00-17W)
    Torpedoed off 'Sword' Beach, Normandy, by German midget submarines ('*Neger*' type)

8   *Japanese Destroyer*
    Tamanami   *Torpedoed 150 miles (280 km) west-south-west of Manila (13-55N 118-30E) by US submarine* **Mingo**

    Japanese Destroyer
    Usugumo   *Torpedoed 330 miles (610 km) west-south-west of Paramushiro, Kurile Islands (47-43N 147-55E) by US submarine* **Skate**

8   Polish Cruiser
    Dragon   0428: Torpedoed off 'Sword' Beach by German midget submarine; beached off Arromanches Mulberry Harbour and declared a total loss on 11 July

    RN Minesweeper
    Pylades   0500: Torpedoed at anchor 8 miles north of Ouistreham, 'Sword' Beach (49-26N 00-15W) by German midget submarine – 11 men lost

9   US Minesweeper
    Swerve   Mined off Anzio (41-31N 12-28E) while clearing swept channel in low visibility

16   Russian Minesweeper
    T.218   Torpedoed by German E-boats off Narva, Gulf of Finland

    German Anti-Aircraft Ship (ex-Dutch cruiser)
    Niobe (ex-   1620: Sunk north of Kotka, Gulf of Finland, by Russian air attack –
    Gelderland)   60 men lost; the German Navy estimated that 102 attack aircraft and 30 fighters took part in the strike, which began at 1545

18   German Minesweeper
    M.264   Sunk off the estuary of the Weser, N. Germany, by RAF Coastal Command air attack (North Coates Wing). Three merchant vessels and a patrol launch were also sunk by this strike

19   *Japanese Cruiser*
    Oi   *1110: Torpedoed 570 miles (1,000 km) south of Hong Kong (12-45N 114-20E) by US submarine* **Flasher**; *sank 4 hours later*

20   RN Destroyer
    Isis   1800+: Probably mined while at anchor 6 miles north of Arromanches (49-27N 00-41W); loss not known until 0209 on 21st, when HMS **Hound** recovered 20 survivors. (There is a possibility that a German midget submarine was responsible)

NW EUROPE   German Minesweeper
M.20   Sunk in Narva Bay, Gulf of Finland, by Russian air attack

21   RN Minesweeper
Chamois   am: Mined in the Seine Bay; towed to Portsmouth – not repaired

German Minesweeper
M.307   2100: Sunk north of Spiekeroog (53-53N 07-55E) by RAF air attack (first successful dusk strike by Coastal Command Beaufighter Wing). The German convoy consisted of 9 merchant vessels escorted by 21 minor warships – one merchant vessel was sunk

German Minesweeper
M.413   Sunk off Narva by Russian air attack

24   RN Escort Destroyer (serving as HQ Ship)
Goathland   pre-dawn: Mined in the Seine Bay, 17 miles (31 km) north-north-east of Courseulles – towed to Portsmouth but not repaired

PACIFIC   25   *Japanese Minelayer*
Sokuten   *Sunk at Malakal, Palau Islands (07-20N 134-27E) by US carrier aircraft*

Japanese Destroyer
Samidare   *Ran aground in Palau Is (08-10N 134-38E) avoiding carrier air attack – torpedoed 25 August, before she could be salvaged, by US submarine* **Batfish**

27   *Japanese Fast Transport*
T.1   *Sunk off the Palau Islands (07-30N 134-30E) by US carrier aircraft*

NW EUROPE   29   German Torpedo-Boats
T.2
T.7   Sunk at Bremen by USAAF air raid. *T.2* was raised on 27 September 1944 but repairs were not completed before the end of the war. *T.7* was raised on 25 October 1944 but was hulked and not repaired

AUGUST 1944

ATLANTIC   2   US Destroyer Escort
Fiske   1535: Torpedoed 470 miles (870 km) north-north-west of the Azores (47-10N 32-40W) by German submarine *U.804* (homing torpedo); broke in half at 1640, bow section sinking immediately, while stern had to be sunk by gunfire – 33 men lost, 183 rescued by USS *Farquhar*

On the night of 2/3 August the German Navy's 'Small Battle Units' made their biggest effort. Fifty-eight *'Neger'* human torpedoes and 32 *'Linsen'* explosive motor boats set out to attack the anchorage as the tide turned. One 'Hunt'-class escort destroyer and a minesweeping trawler (HMS *Gairsay*) were sunk by the torpedoes and one Landing Craft (Gun) by the motor-boats: these small returns cost 41 *'Neger'* and 22 *'Linsen'*.

NW EUROPE   3   RN Escort Destroyer
Quorn   0251: Sunk in the Seine Bay by German human torpedo ('*Neger*')

4   *Japanese Destroyer*
Matsu   *Sunk 50 miles (93 km) north-west of Chichi Jima, Bonin Islands (27-40N 141-48E) by 5in gunfire of US destroyers* **Ingersoll**, **Knapp** *and* **Cogswell**

	Japanese Fast Transport	PACIFIC
	T.4	*Sunk off Chichi Jima (27-07N 142-12E) by USN aircraft (TG 58.1)*

4   German Minesweepers   NW EUROPE

M.271

M.325   Sunk at Pauillac, Gironde, by RAF air raid

M.422   1945: Capsized at Pauillac following air raid

5   *Japanese Fast Transport*   PACIFIC

T.2   *Sunk off Chichi Jima (27-05N 142-09E) by USN aircraft (TGs 58.1 and .3)*

6   German Minesweepers   NW EUROPE

M.263

M.486   0040: Sunk 32 miles (60 km) south-south-west of St. Nazaire by 5.25in gunfire of RN cruiser **Bellona** and 4.7in gunfire of RN destroyers **Ashanti** and **Tartar** and RCN destroyers **Haida** and **Iroquois**. Four small ships in German convoy also sunk

German Escort (ex-French Seaplane-Tender)

SG.3 (Jupiter)   Severely damaged by gunfire in the above action and, during
(ex-**Sans**   daylight on the 6th, at Les Sables d'Olonne, Brittany, by RAF air
Pareil)   attack (Coastal Command Beaufighters of 236 Squadron) – burned out

German Minesweeper

M.133   (Damaged by MTB – see 17/18 June) Scuttled at St. Malo

7   *Japanese Cruiser*   PACIFIC

Nagara   *Torpedoed 35 miles (65 km) south of Nagasaki (32-09N 129-53E) by US submarine* **Croaker**

Japanese Escort

Kusagaki   *Torpedoed 60 miles (111 km) west of Manila (14-51N 119-59E) by US submarine* **Guitarro**

8   German Minesweepers   NW EUROPE

M.366

M.367

M.428

M.438   pm: Sunk off Noirmoutiers, south of St. Nazaire, by RAF air attack (Coastal Command Beaufighters of Nos 236 and 404 Squadrons)

RCN Corvette

Regina   2225: Torpedoed off Trevose Head, Cornwall (50-42N 05-03W) by German submarine **U.667** (homing torpedo), while escorting a coastal convoy; ship rolled over and sank almost immediately

9   German Torpedo-Boat (ex-Italian)   MED

TA.19 (ex-   1800: Torpedoed off Port Vathi, Samos (37-45N 26-59E) by Greek
Calatafimi)   submarine **Pipinos** – 5 men lost

German Torpedo-Boat (ex-Italian)

TA.21 (ex-   Severely damaged off Cape Salvore, Istria, by aircraft gunfire; laid
Insidioso)   up, unrepaired (see 5 November)

11   German Minesweeper   NW EUROPE

M.27   1955: Mined off Pauillac, Gironde (45-15N 01-15W) – 41 men lost

German Minesweepers

M.84   (Damaged and in dock) Scuttled at Le Havre

M.384   (Damaged) Scuttled at Nantes as no tug available to evacuate her

MED   12   German Minesweeper
M.468   0400: Mined off Namsos (64-29N 10-31E) – probably on drifting mine

NW EUROPE   German Minesweeper
M.370   Sunk off Royan by RAF air attack (Coastal Command Mosquitoes of 235 and 248 Squadrons – bombs)

Russian Minesweepers (ex-USN)
T.118   1905: Torpedoed in the Kara Sea (72-30N 66-00E) by German submarine *U.365* (homing torpedo)
T.114   2345: Torpedoed close to *T.118* by German submarine *U.365* (conventional torpedo). A Soviet freighter was also sunk

   13   German Minesweeper
M.383   0620: Sunk off Langeroog (53-50N 07-45E) by RAF air attack (Coastal Command Beaufighters of the Langham Wing and 254 Squadron)

   14   German Minesweeper
M.444   Sunk in Brest Roads – possibly mined during RAF Bomber Command air raid

German Minesweeper
M.206   (Damaged by air attack on 4 August) Scuttled at St. Malo

   15   German Minesweeper
M.385   0300: Damaged off Sables d'Olonne, north-west of La Pallice, Brittany, by 6in gunfire of RN cruiser *Mauritius* and 4.7in gunfire of RN destroyer *Ursa* and RCN destroyer *Iroquois*; beached as a total loss.
A Sperrbrecher (*No. 157*) and a small coaster were also sunk; *M.275* badly damaged by gunfire but reached La Pallice

Allied landings in the South of France, to the east of Marseilles, began early on 15 August. Heavy air raids on Toulon had virtually eliminated the U-boats as a threat and the light forces in the area could not offer serious opposition to the huge Anglo-American invasion force, which also enjoyed overwhelming air superiority. Nevertheless, the German Navy did make two attempts to harass detached units operating close inshore.

MED   15   German Corvette (ex-Italian)
Uj.6081 (ex-   0440: sunk south of Port Cros, off Toulon, by 5in gunfire of US
Camoscio)   destroyer *Somers*. US boarding party removed charts and orders before the corvette sank – 99 men rescued. A second *U-jäger* (the ex-French *Escahoet*) was sunk in this action

German Escorts (ex-French Avisos)
SG.21 (ex-
Chamois)
SG.25 (ex-*La*
Curieuse)   Sunk at Toulon by USAAF air raid

   17   German Torpedo-Boat (ex-Italian)
TA.35 (ex-   0500: Mined west of Pola, Istria (44-53N 13-47E): broke in half and
Giuseppe   sank – 71 men lost
Dezza)

German Corvette (ex-Italian)
Uj.6082 (ex-   0500: Sunk in the Bay of Ciotat, 15 miles (28 km) east of Marseilles,
Antilope)   by 6in gunfire of RN gunboats *Aphis* and *Scarab* and 5in gunfire of US destroyer *Endicott*.

A second U-jäger (ex-Turkish yacht **Kemid Allah**) was sunk by the **Endicott**; 211 men were rescued   MED

German Corvette (ex-Italian)

Uj.2223 (ex-   Sunk at Genoa by USAAF air raid
Marangone)

18   Japanese Escort Carrier   PACIFIC

Taiyo   *Torpedoed 22 miles (41 km) south-west of Cape Bojeador, Luzon (18-16N 120-20E) by US submarine* **Rasher**

Japanese Cruiser

Natori   *Torpedoed 250 miles (460 km) north-east of Surigao, Philippines (12-29N 128-49E) by US submarine* **Hardhead**

The German Navy, which had suffered the loss of nearly every one of its principal units based west of the Straits of Dover (only the **T.28** escaped from Le Havre to return to Germany), experienced a major disaster on the Eastern Front, in the Baltic, when three torpedo-boats supporting the Army in the Gulf of Narva ran into a German-laid minefield and were lost, with heavy casualties.

18   German Torpedo-Boats   NW EUROPE
    T.22   Mined (59-42N 27-44E) – 143 men lost
    T.30   Mined (59-43N 27-44E) – 114 men lost
    T.32   Mined (59-42N 27-43E) – 137 men lost

21   RN Sloop

Kite   0650: Torpedoed 220 miles (410 km) south-west of Bear Island, Norwegian Sea (73-01N 03-57E) by German submarine **U.344** (homing torpedo); sank almost immediately – 9 men rescued

RN Corvette

Orchis   0830: Mined off Courseulles, Normandy; bows blown off back to the 4in gun – beached as a total loss

RCN Corvette

Alberni   1141: Torpedoed 25 miles (46 km) south-east of St. Catherine's Point, Isle of Wight (50-18N 00-51W) by German submarine **U.480** (homing torpedo); hit amidships and sank in less than 30 seconds

German Destroyer

Z.23   (Decommissioned 0930, unseaworthy) pm: Sunk at La Pallice (46-10N 01-12W) by RAF Coastal Command air attack

German Minesweeper

M.292   Sunk off Le Verdon, at the entrance to the Gironde, by RAF air attack (Coastal Command Mosquitoes of 235 and 248 Squadrons)

German Escort (ex-French Aviso)   MED

SG.16 (ex-   (Not in commision) Scuttled at Marseilles
**Amiral
Sénès**)

22   Japanese Escorts   PACIFIC

Sado   *Torpedoed 35 miles (65 km) west of Manila (14-15N 120-25E) by US submarine* **Haddo**

Hiburi   *Torpedoed in company with* **Sado** *by US submarine* **Harder**

Matsuwa   *Torpedoed 55 miles (102 km) west-south-west of Manila (14-15N 120-05E) by US submarine* **Harder**

22   RCN Escort Carrier   NW EUROPE

Nabob   0020: Torpedoed 120 miles (220 km) west-north-west of the North Cape, Norway (71-42N 19-11E) by German submarine **U.354**

NW EUROPE   (homing torpedo); returned 1,000 miles (1,850 km) to UK under own steam but not repaired

RN Frigate
Bickerton   0022: Torpedoed with **Nabob**; stern wrecked but ship salvageable – scuttled for tactical reasons (Force commander did not wish to be hampered by two crippled ships) 3 hours after the attack

RN Minesweeper
Loyalty   1606: Torpedoed 27 miles (50 km) south of the Nab Tower, Spithead (50-09N 00-41W – within about 10 miles of the position of the sinking of HMCS **Alberni**, see 21 August) – by German submarine **U.480** (homing torpedo); capsized in less than 7 minutes

PACIFIC   23   *Japanese Destroyer*
Asakaze   *Torpedoed 20 miles (37 km) south-west of Cape Bolinao, Luzon (16-06N 19-44E) by US submarine* **Haddo**

NW EUROPE   23   German Torpedo Boat (ex-French)
TA.9 (ex-   Sunk at Toulon by USAAF air raid
Bombarde)

MED   24   German Escort (ex-French Aviso)
SG.14 (ex-   1645: Sunk off Capraia (40-35N 14-12E) by air attack
**Matelot
Leblanc**)

NW EUROPE   German Destroyer
Z.24   pm: Severely damaged off Le Verdon (45-31 01-06W) by RAF air attack (Coastal Command Beaufighters of 236 and 404 Squadrons); capsized and sank at 0100 on the 25th

German Torpedo-Boat
T.24   Sunk off Le Verdon (45-31N 01-05W) with **Z.24**

PACIFIC   25   *Japanese Destroyer*
Yunagi   *Torpedoed 20 miles (37 km) north-north-east of Cape Bojeador, Luzon (18-46N 120-46E) by US submarine* **Picuda**

NW EUROPE   25   German Torpedo-Boat (ex-French)
TA.13 (ex-**La**   Scuttled at Toulon
Bayonnaise)

German Minesweeper
M.347   2100: Torpedoed off Schiermonnikoog (53-34N 06-01E) by RAF aircraft (Coastal Command Beaufighters of the Langham and North Coates Wings)

25   German Destroyer
Z.37   (Damaged and out of commission) Scuttled in drydock at Bordeaux

German Minesweepers scuttled at Bordeaux
M.262
M.304   (Mined 18 August in Gironde)
M.344
M.363   (Mined 0020/17 August in Gironde)

25   German Minesweeper
M.463   Scuttled at Bordeaux with **M.262,** etc.

These scuttlings marked the end of the German Navy's surface forces on the English Channel and French Atlantic coasts. Of the 38 ubiquitous 'M'-class minesweepers based in French waters on 6 June 1944, only one (**M.155**) escaped to return to Germany. Twenty-one were either sunk by Allied action or scuttled. The remainder were paid off and their crews and removable weapons used for local defence; after the war, these sixteen ships were repaired and entered service with Allied navies.

26 German Minesweeper
    M.266   Sunk at Kiel by RAF air raid; salvaged and returned to service (see 11 March 1945)

A breakdown in communications and poor staff work were responsible for one of the most serious British 'Own Goals'. Royal Air Force reconnaissance reported that the ships 'appeared to be friendly' but the naval staff responsible for the security of the assault area were unaware of the change in the minesweeping programme which had taken the 1st Minesweeping Flotilla into an area in which there were not known to be any Allied ships – the Royal Navy therefore ordered the attack on its own ships!

27 RN Minesweepers
    Britomart
    Hussar   1345: Sunk 12 miles (22 km) west of Cap d'Antifer (49-41N 00-05E) by RAF air attack (Tactical Air Force Typhoons)
    Salamander   Damaged beyond repair – stern blown off by Typhoon's rocket projectiles. HMS *Jason* and trawler *Colsay* were slightly damaged

29 *Japanese Minesweeper*
    W.28   *Torpedoed 70 miles (130 km) north-west of Menado, Celebes (02-15N 123-29E) by US submarine* **Jack**

31 *Japanese Escort (ex-Minelayer)*
    Shirataka   *Torpedoed west of Itbayat, Luzon Strait (20-55N 121-07E) by US submarine* **Sealion**

SEPTEMBER 1944

1 RN Corvette
    Hurst Castle   0825: Torpedoed 11 miles (20 km) north of Tory Island, Donegal (55-27N 08-12W) by German submarine *U.482* (homing torpedo); stern wrecked and sank in 6 minutes – 105 survivors rescued by HMS *Ambuscade*

2 Russian Minesweeper
    Vzryv (T.410)   0552: Torpedoed off Constanta, Rumania, by German submarine *U.19*

4 German Torpedo-Boat (ex-Italian)
    TA.28 (ex-   (In dock) Sunk at Genoa by USAAF air raid; salvaged but not
    Rigel)   returned to service and scuttled in May 1945

German Corvette (ex-Italian)
    Uj.6085 (ex- Sunk at Genoa by USAAF air raid. The destroyer *TA.33* (ex-
    Renna)   *Corsaro II*), approaching completion, was damaged beyond repair in the same raid

5 German Minesweepers
    M.274
    M.276   Scuttled at the mouth of the Schelde

12 *US Fast Transport*
    Noa   *Sunk by collision with US destroyer* **Fullam** *off the Palau Islands (07-01N 134-30E)*

Japanese Destroyer
    Shikinami   *Torpedoed 240 miles (445 km) south-east of Hong Kong (18-16N 114-49E) by US submarine* **Growler**

PACIFIC		*Japanese Escort* **Hirado** *Torpedoed 250 miles (460 km) south-east of Hong Kong (17-54N 114-49E) by US submarine* **Growler**

PACIFIC — *Japanese Escort*
Hirado — *Torpedoed 250 miles (460 km) south-east of Hong Kong (17-54N 114-49E) by US submarine* **Growler**

NW EUROPE — 12 — German Minesweepers
M.426
M.462 — Sunk off Lister, S. Norway, by RAF Coastal Command air attack (Banff Wing). One of the ships was torpedoed and the other sunk by rockets; two more M-class were claimed as seriously damaged

PACIFIC — 13 — *US Destroyer Minesweeper*
Perry — *Mined off Peleliu, Palau Is (06-53N 134-00E)*

ATLANTIC — 13 — US Destroyer
Warrington — Foundered in a hurricane off the Bahamas (26-00N 74-00W); she lost all power at about 0430 when the machinery spaces flooded and sank 10 hours later – 251 men lost, 68 rescued two days later

PACIFIC — 14 — *Japanese Fast Transports*
T.3 — *Stranded on reef south of Mindanao (05-34N 125-23E)*
T.5 — *Sunk in Davao Gulf, Mindanao (06-10N 126-00E) by USN carrier aircraft*

15 — *Japanese Escort Carrier*
Unyo — *2300: Torpedoed 220 miles (760 km) south-east of Hong Kong (19-18N 116-26E) by US submarine* **Barb** *(which sank an 11,000 dwt tanker with the same salvo)*

MED — 15 — German Torpedo-Boat (ex-Italian Destroyer)
TA.14 (ex-**Turbine**) — Sunk at Salamis (37-57N 23-32E) by USAAF air raid

NW EUROPE — 17 — German Torpedo-Boat
T.18 — 0710: Sunk north-west of Paldiski (Baltic Port) – (59-22N 24-03E) by Russian air attack (R/Ps) – 30 men lost

PACIFIC — 18 — *Japanese Armed Merchant Cruiser*
Saigon Maru — *Torpedoed off Manila Bay (14-20N 120-05E) by US submarine* **Flasher**

MED — 18 — German Torpedo-Boat (ex-Italian)
TA.17 (ex-**San Martino**) — Damaged beyond repair at Piraeus by RAF air attack (sunk 12 October by further air attack)

PACIFIC — 19 — *Japanese Cruiser (ex-Chinese)*
Ioshima *(ex-Ning Hai)* — *0800: Torpedoed south of Honshu (33-40N 138-18E) by US submarine* **Shad**

NW EUROPE — 20 — German Minesweeper
M.132 — 2235: Torpedoed off Egeroy, Norway (58-27N 05-51E) by RN submarine **Sceptre**

PACIFIC — 21 — *Japanese Destroyer*
Satsuki — *Sunk in Manila Bay (14-35N 120-55E) by US carrier aircraft*

Japanese Escort
No.5 — *Sunk off Masinloc, Luzon (150-25N 119-50E) by US carrier aircraft*

NW EUROPE — 23 — Russian Escort (ex NKVD Patrol Vessel)
Brilliant (**SKR.29**, ex-**PS.3**) — 0015: Torpedoed off Kravkova Island, Kara Sea (77-30N 87-30E) by German submarine **U.957**

24   *Japanese Escort (ex-Minelayer)*   PACIFIC
     Yaeyama   *Sunk south of Mindoro, Philippines (12-15N 121-00E) by US carrier aircraft*

    Japanese Torpedo-Boat
    Hayabusa   *Sunk 110 miles (205 km) south-south-east of Manila (13-00N 122-00E) by US carrier aircraft*

    Japanese Seaplane-Tender
    Akitsushima   *0730: Sunk in Coron Bay, Calamian Island, Philippines (11-59N 120-02E) by US carrier aircraft*

1   *Japanese Minelayer*
    Ajiro   *Torpedoed WNW of Osagawara Gunto, Bonin Is. (28-20N 139-25E) by US submarine* **Snapper**

24   Russian Minesweeper (ex-USN)   NW EUROPE
    T.120   0900: Torpedoed off the Yenisei Gulf, Kara Sea (76-30N 84-50E) by German submarine ***U.739*** (homing torpedo)

25   German Minesweeper
    M.471   Sunk in the Marsdiep, Den Helder, by RAF Coastal Command air attack (North Coates and Langham Wings – rockets)

26   *Japanese Escort (ex-Minelayer)*   PACIFIC
    Aotaka   *Torpedoed 120 miles (220 km) north-north-east of Labuan (07-00N 116-00E) by US submarine* **Pargo**

27   *Japanese Escort*
    No.10   *Torpedoed 100 miles (185 km) north-north-west of Amami-o-Shima (29-26N 128-50E) by US submarine* **Plaice**

27   RN Escort Destroyer (Aircraft Target Ship)   NW EUROPE
    Rockingham 0446: Mined 30 miles (55 km) south-east of Aberdeen (56-47N 01-30W); taken in tow but abandoned at 2026 and sank in 56-29N 00-57W

OCTOBER 1944

3   *US Destroyer Escort*   PACIFIC
    Shelton   *0810: Torpedoed off Morotai (02-33N 129-18E) by Japanese submarine* **RO.41**; *capsized under tow at 2145 – 13 men lost (US submarine* **Seawolf** *was sunk by USS* **Rowell** *during the subsequent hunt)*

4   RCN Frigate   ATLANTIC
    Chebogue   2204: Torpedoed 550 miles (1,020 km) west-south-west of Cape Clear, S. Ireland (49-20N 24-20W) by German submarine ***U.1227*** (homing torpedo); stern blown off – 7 men lost. The damaged ship was towed 890 miles (1,650 km) to Port Talbot, S. Wales, where she was laid up, unrepaired

6   *Japanese Escort*   PACIFIC
    No. 21   *Torpedoed 140 miles (260 km) north-west of Cape Bojeador, Luzon (19-45N 118-22E) by US submarine* **Seahorse**

6/7 German Torpedo-Boat (ex-Italian)   MED
    TA.37 (ex- Sunk 35 miles (65 km) north of Skiathos, Gulf of Salonika (40-36N
      Gladio)   22-46E) while escorting a small convoy, by 4.7in gunfire of RN destroyers ***Termagant*** and ***Tuscan***

7   *Japanese Minelayer*   PACIFIC
    Ikitsushima *Torpedoed south-east of Bawean Island, Java Sea (05-26S 113-48E) by Dutch submarine* **Zwaardvisch**

	8	RN Minesweeper	
		Mulgrave	Mined off Normandy and beached; later salvaged and towed to English port, not repaired
MED	9	German Torpedo-Boat (ex-Italian)	
		TA.38 (ex-*Spada*)	Damaged in the Peliti Channel, near Volos, by RN aircraft (809 Squadron, HMS *Stalker*) and possibly by mine; scuttled at Volos (39-21N 22-56E) on 13 October
NW EUROPE		German Escort (ex-Dutch Gunboat)	
		K.2	0715: Torpedoed west of Egersund (58-17N 05-45E) by RAF aircraft (Coastal Command Beaufighters of the Banff Wing); stern destroyed and towed to port. At Delfzijl, out of commission, in May 1945
PACIFIC	10	*Japanese Escort (ex-Minelayer)*	
		Takashima	*Sunk off Okinawa (26-39N 127-52E) by US carrier aircraft*
		Japanese Escort (ex-Destroyer)	
		Kali *(ex-Kashi)*	*Sunk off Okinawa by USN aircraft*
NW EUROPE	11	German Minesweeper	
		M.303	Sunk off Kiberg, N. Norway, by Russian MTBs
MED	12	RN Destroyer	
		Loyal	Severely damaged by acoustic mine in the Tyrrhenian Sea – all machinery and armament suffered shock damage – constructive total loss
	12	German Torpedo-Boats (ex-Italian)	
		TA.17 (ex-*San Martino*)	Scuttled at Piraeus, following further bombing damage (see 16 September)
		TA.15 (ex-*Francesco Crispi*)	(Salvaged after sinking off Crete – see 8 March 1944) Sunk at Piraeus by air raid
ATLANTIC	14	RCN Frigate	
		Magog	1325: Torpedoed in the mouth of the St. Lawrence River (49-12N 67-19W) by German submarine *U.1223* (homing torpedo); stern blown off – 2 men lost, towed to port, not repaired
NW EUROPE	15	German Cruiser	
		Leipzig	Damaged in collision off Gdynia with cruiser *Prinz Eugen*; not repaired
PACIFIC	16	*Japanese Torpedo-Boat*	
		Hato	*Sunk 130 miles (240 km) east-south-east of Hong Kong (21-54N 116-30E) by US carrier aircraft*
MED	16	German Torpedo-Boat (ex-Italian)	
		TA.39 (ex-*Daga*)	0142: Mined 45 miles (83 km) south of Salonika
PACIFIC	17	US Destroyer-Minesweeper	
		Montgomery	*Mined east of the Palaus (10-56N 125-12E)*
	18	*Japanese Escort (ex-Minelayer)*	
		Maeshima	*Damaged off Salomague, Luzon (17-46N 120-25E) by US carrier aircraft and beached*
		RAN Minesweeper	
		Geelong	*Sunk in collision off New Guinea (06-04S 147-50E) with SS **York***

The force of ex-Italian torpedo-boats which the German Navy had been operating in the Aegean since September 1943 had steadily been whittled away during the autumn of 1944 and the last unit was destroyed late on 19 October 1944.

| 19 | German Torpedo-Boat (ex-Italian) | | MED |

TA.18 (ex-**Solferino**)   2250: Damaged off Skiathos by 4.7in gunfire of RN destroyers **Termagant** and **Tuscan**, driven ashore (in 37-45N 26-59E) and destroyed by gunfire at 2340

| 21 | German Minesweeper | | NW EUROPE |

M.31   Sunk off Honningsvaag, N. Norway, by Russian MTBs

23   *Japanese Seaplane-Carrier*   PACIFIC

Kimikawa Maru   Torpedoed west of Luzon (18-58N 118-46E) by US submarine **Sawfish**

The US Army landing on Leyte Island, Philippines, began on 20 October 1944, after five days of 'precursor' operations. The Japanese Navy had devised a complex plan to counter the invasion, employing two powerful surface striking forces to destroy the supporting warships, while the once-powerful carrier fleet would be used as a decoy to draw off the US Fast Carrier Task Force, present in its usual striking and covering role. The Japanese carriers had few aircraft embarked and the surface attack squadrons would rely primarily on shore-based air support, which included a major (and successful) tactical surprise element. The efficient US submarines struck first.

23   *Japanese Cruiser*

Aoba   *0330: Torpedoed 12 miles (22 km) south of Cape Calavite, W. Luzon, by US submarine* **Bream***; severely damaged and repairs not complete before she was again damaged at Kure by air attack in March 1945 and then sunk in July 1945*

Japanese Cruisers

Atago   *0533: Torpedoed in the Palawan Passage, W. Philippines (09-28N 117-17E) by US submarine* **Darter***; 5 hits*

Takao   *0534: Torpedoed with* **Atago** *by* **Darter***; 4 hits claimed, ship reached Singapore via Brunei but was not repaired (see also 31 July 1945)*

(The **Darter** *ran aground on Bombay Shoal while pursuing the damaged* **Takao** *and had to be abandoned – subsequently destroyed by 6in gunfire of US submarine* **Nautilus***)*

Maya   *0556: Torpedoed near* **Atago** *(09-22N 117-07E) by US submarine* **Dace***; blew up and sank very quickly*

24   *US Light Carrier*

Princeton   *0938: Damaged east of Polillo Islands, Philippines (15-12N 123-36E) by land-based JNAF dive-bomber; abandoned by all but firefighters at 1020, torpedo-room blew up at 1523, inflicting 600 casualties and extensive damage on cruiser* **Birmingham***, alongside. Scuttled at 1700 by cruiser* **Reno** *– 108 men lost*

The US Fast Carrier Task Force, alerted by the submarines' reports, delivered five strikes on the largest Japanese force – the 'Centre Force' – on 24 October. Japanese losses were less than might have been expected from the weight of attack, but the force was delayed by 7 hours, which could not be made up, and the rather delicate timetable for the operation was irretrievably upset.

Japanese Battleship

Musashi   *1026-1550: Attacked in Sibuyan Sea, Philippines, by US carrier aircraft – numerous torpedo and bomb hits stopped her at about 1450. Sank at 1935 (in 12-50N 122-35E)*

Japanese Destroyer
Wakaba   *Sunk off west coast of Panay Island, Philippines (11-50N 121-25E) by US carrier aircraft (USS* **Franklin***)*

The first Japanese attack force (the 'Southern Force'), spearheaded by two old battleships, approached Leyte Gulf through the Surigao Strait. The Allied ships of the US 7th Fleet were aware of the threat and were lying in wait.

25   *Japanese Battleship*
Fuso   *0300: Sunk in Surigao Strait (10-25N 125-23E) by US destroyer torpedoes – blew up at 0420*

Japanese Destroyer
Michisio   *0301: Torpedoed in Surigao Strait by US destroyer;*
0355: sunk by US destroyer **Hutchings** *(10-25N 125-23E)*

Japanese Battleship
Yamashiro   *0315-0410: Damaged by US destroyer torpedoes in Surigao Strait.*
0353-0408: Hit by 16in and 14in gunfire of US battleships **West Virginia, Tennessee, Maryland** *and* **California***, as well as 8in and 6in gunfire of seven US and one RAN cruisers. Sank at 0419 (10-22N 125-21E)*

Japanese Destroyers
Yamagumo   *0330: Torpedoed in Surigao Strait (10-16N 125-23E) by US destroyer* **McDermut** *– sank 10 minutes later*
Asagumo   *0407: Torpedoed in Surigao Strait by US destroyers*
0721: sunk by 6in gunfire of US cruiser **Denver** *(10-04N 125-21E)*

Japanese Cruiser
Mogami   *0418: Damaged by 6in gunfire of US cruisers and 5in gunfire of destroyers;*
0525: Damaged by collision with cruiser **Nachi***, which was also seriously damaged;*
0910: Damaged by US carrier aircraft – stopped and scuttled at 1230 (09-40N 124-50E)

The delayed Japanese 'Centre Force' which passed through the San Bernardino Strait unopposed was too late to affect the battle fought in the Surigao Strait but it surprised one of the 7th Fleet's escort carrier task units off the island of Samar. Only the devotion of the carriers' screen and the aircrew, whose doggedness forced the Japanese commander into an unexpected retreat, saved Task Unit 77.4.3 from total destruction.

US Destroyers
Johnston   *0720+: Damaged by gunfire of Japanese 'Centre Force', abandoned at 0945 and sank at 1010 (11-40N 126-20E) – 185 men lost. One of her torpedoes blew the bows off the cruiser* **Kumano** *(see also 26 October and 25 November)*
Hoel   *0725+: Damaged by gunfire of Japanese 'Centre Force' – at least 40 hits; sank at 0855 – 268 men lost (11-46N 126-33E)*

Japanese Cruiser
Suzuya   *0730: Torpedoed by US carrier aircraft (TU.77.4.2) while standing by the damaged cruiser* **Kumano***; scuttled by destroyer* **Okinami** *(11-50N 126-25E)*

25   *US Escort Carrier*
Gambier Bay   *0810-0825: Damaged by 8in gunfire of Japanese cruisers; set on fire, machinery spaces flooded and she capsized and sank at 0907 – 100 men lost (11-31N 125-12E)*

US Destroyer Escort

Samuel B.   *0851+: Damaged by major calibre shells (at least 20 hits);*
   Roberts   *abandoned at 0935 and sank at 1005 – 94 men lost (11-40N 126-20E)*

Japanese Cruisers

Chikuma   *0853: Torpedoed by US carrier aircraft (TU.77.4.2); sank at about 0905 (11-22N 126-16E)*

Chokai   *0905: Torpedoed by US carrier aircraft (USS* **Kitkun Bay***); scuttled by destroyer* **Fujinami** *(11-26N 126-15E)*

The Japanese began to retreat at about 0920, leaving the five surviving USN escort carriers, two of them seriously and two others slightly damaged, to lick their wounds undisturbed. The reprieve was, however, brief, for 90 minutes after the last shells were fired, the next Japanese surprise was sprung upon the same group of ships.

The failure of conventional air attack during the Battle of the Philippine Sea in June 1944 had led the JNAF to the desperate step of training suicide attack units for the next battle. The first two missions attacked Task Unit 77.4.3 at 1050 and 1110 on 25 October and besides sinking the only carrier to have come undamaged through the gun battle, severely damaged two others.

25   US Escort Carrier

St. Lo   *1050: Hit by Kamikaze east of Samar (11-10N 126-05E); uncontrollable fires and explosions resulted in her loss at 1125*

The shambles off Samar had been made possible by the success of the Japanese diversionary force in drawing off the US Fast Carrier Task Force. Admiral Halsey, obsessed with his ambition to score a major victory over the Japanese carriers, had failed to take the most elementary precautions against the appearance of the 'Centre Force' in his, and the 7th Fleet's, rear. While Task Unit 77.4.3 was undergoing its ordeal, his aircraft were sinking the aircraft-less Japanese carriers, who carried out their sacrificial role to its logical conclusion. This one-sided action was known as the 'Battle of Cape Engano'.

25   Japanese Light Carrier

Chitose   *0800: Damaged by US carrier aircraft (USS* **Essex** *and* **Lexington***); set on fire and sank 235 miles (435 km) east of Cape Engano at 0937 (19-20N 126-20E)*

Japanese Carrier

Zuikaku   *0815: Torpedoed by US carrier aircraft (USS* **Intrepid** *or* **San Jacinto***); 1310: again torpedoed by USN aircraft (USS* **Lexington** *and* **Cowpens***); sank 220 miles (407 km) east-north-east of Cape Engano (19-20N 125-51E) at 1414*

Japanese Light Carriers

Chiyoda   *0945: Damaged by US carrier aircraft (USS* **Lexington** *and* **Franklin***); brought to a standstill, on fire, at 1018;*
   1700: Sunk 260 miles (480 km) south-east of Cape Engano (18-37N 126-45E) by 6in and 8in gunfire of cruisers **Santa Fe**, **Wichita**, **New Orleans** *and* **Mobile**

Zuiho   *1310-1330: Sunk 215 miles (400 km) east-north-east of Cape Engano (near* **Zuikaku***) by US carrier aircraft (USS* **Essex**, **Langley***, etc)*

Japanese Destroyer

Hatsutsuki   *Damaged by US carrier aircraft; 2046: sunk east-north-east of Cape Engano (20-24N 126-20E) by gunfire of US cruiser group (see* **Chiyoda***)*

Even when the aircraft attacks ceased, due in part to the exhaustion of the aircrew, several of whom flew three sorties during the day, the surviving ships were harried by the pursuing cruiser and destroyer group and then ran over a submarine patrol line.

PACIFIC   25   Japanese Destroyer

Akizuki   Dusk: Torpedoed north-east of Cape Engano (20-29N 126-36E) by US submarine **Halibut**

Japanese Cruiser

Tama   (Damaged by carrier aircraft) 2315: Torpedoed 320 miles (590 km) north-east of Cape Engano (21-32N 127-19E) by US submarine **Jallao**

26   Japanese Destroyer

Nowaki   0030: Damaged by 6in gunfire of US cruisers and sunk 65 miles (120 km) south-south-east of Legaspi, Luzon (13-00N 124-54E) by destroyer **Owen**'s torpedoes at 0135

ATLANTIC   25   Canadian Escort Destroyer

Skeena   0200: Stranded on Videy Island, Reykjavik, after dragging her anchors in a gale – several men lost. Salvage could not be attempted in the prevailing bad weather and she was declared a total loss in December

MED   German Torpedo-Boat (ex-Italian Destroyer)

TA.31 (ex-   Damaged beyond repair at Genoa by USAAF air raid; scuttled
Dardo)   April 1945

The pursuit of the remnants of the beaten Japanese fleet was taken up from dawn on 26 October by the escort carriers of Task Group 77.4 and the fast carriers of Task Force 38. Five ships were sunk by dive-bombers and the cruiser **Kumano**, *her bows previously blown off by the destroyer's* **Johnston**'s *torpedo, was left with only one boiler after a bomb hit but managed to reach Manila.*

PACIFIC   26   Japanese Light Cruisers

Noshiro   0910: Sunk off Batban Island (11-35N 121-45E) by US carrier aircraft (USS **Wasp** and **Hornet** – TF 38)

Kinu   Sunk 44 miles (80 km) south-west of Masbate (11-46N 123-11E) by US carrier aircraft (TG 77.4)

Abukuma   (Damaged off Panaon Island, Surigao Strait, by US MTB **PT-137** at 0315 on 25 October) Sunk 10 miles (18 km) south-east of Los Negros Island (09-20N 122-30E) by US carrier aircraft (TG 77.4)

Japanese Destroyers

Uranami   Sunk 70 miles (130 km) north-east of Iloilo (11-50N 123-00E) by US carrier aircraft (TG 77.4)

Hayashimo   Stranded 40 miles (75 km) south-east of Mindoro (12-05N 121-50E) and destroyed by US carrier aircraft (TF 38)

ATLANTIC   26   Norwegian Corvette

Rose   (pre-dawn) Sunk by collision with RN frigate ***Manners*** 540 miles (1,000 km) east of Cape Race (45-50N 40-15W)

PACIFIC   27   Japanese Destroyers

Fujinami
Shiranuhi   Sunk 80 miles (150 km) north of Iloilo (12-00N 122-30E) by US carrier aircraft (USS **Essex** – TF 38)

NW EUROPE   27   German Minesweeper

M.433   Sunk off Vegafjord (65-30N 12-00E) by RN carrier aircraft (HMS ***Implacable***)

28   US Destroyer Escort
      Eversole   *0230: Torpedoed off Leyte (10-18N 127-37E) by Japanese*
                        submarine **I-45***; sank in 15 minutes with heavy loss of life – 139*
                        men rescued by USS **Richard S. Bush** *while DE* **Whitehurst** *hunted*
                        and sank **I-45**

NOVEMBER 1944

1   US Destroyer
      Abner Read   *1342: Sunk in Leyte Gulf (10-47N 125-22E) by JNAF suicide aircraft*
                        ('kamikaze'); sank in 36 minutes – 22 men lost, 56 injured

      RN Frigate
      Whittaker   0220: Torpedoed off Lough Swilly (55-30N 07-39E) by German
                        submarine *U.483* (homing torpedo); magazine explosion blew off bow
                        and wrecked the structure forward of the bridge – 92 men lost,
                        including all officers. Towed to N. Ireland and laid up at Belfast

Although eliminated from the Aegean, the German Navy still possessed a number of ex-
Italian torpedo-boats and corvettes in the northern Adriatic, to protect and support the
garrisons along the Yugoslav coast. The Royal Navy's 'Hunt'-class escort destroyers
also operated off the Dalmatian coast, patrolling in support of the MTBs and MGBs
which were hunting the enemy's light craft and transports. On the night of 1/2
November 1944 a German force ran into an ambush.

      German Torpedo-Boat (ex-Italian)
      TA.20 (ex-
        Audace)

      German Corvettes (ex-Italian)
      Uj.202 (ex-
        Melpomene)
      Uj.208 (ex-   2230: Sunk west of Pag Island, Adriatic (44-34N 14-44E) by 4in
        Spingarda)   gunfire of RN escort destroyers *Avon Vale* and *Wheatland*; 71
                         men rescued by the RN from the three ships

3   Japanese Destroyer
      Akikaze   *Torpedoed 160 miles (300 km) west of Cape Bolinao, Luzon (16-*
                         48N 117-17E) by US submarine **Pintado**

4   Japanese Minesweeper
      W.5   *Torpedoed in Malacca Straits, 90 miles (166 km) south of Penang*
                         (03-44N 99-50E) by RN submarine **Terrapin**

4   German Torpedo-Boat (ex-Italian)
      TA.47 (ex-   (Under repair, not in commission) Sunk at Genoa by USAAF air raid
        Lira)

5   Japanese Cruiser
      Nachi   *(Damaged 26 October in collision with* **Mogami***)* Sunk in Manila
                         Bay, 5 miles (9 km) west of Corregidor Island (14-23N 120-25E) by
                         US carrier aircraft (USS **Lexington***)*

6   German Torpedo-Boat (ex-Italian)
      TA.21 (ex-   (Laid up at Fiume – see 9 August) Sunk by USAAF air raid
        Insidioso)

8   Japanese Torpedo-Boat
      Sagi   *Torpedoed 60 miles (110 km) west-south-west of Cape Bolinao,*
                         Luzon (16-09N 118-56E) by US submarine **Gunnel**

PACIFIC 10 Japanese Escort
No. 11   Sunk off Ormoc, Leyte (10-51N 124-32E) by USAAF aircraft

Japanese Patrol Boat (ex-Destroyer)
No. 46 (ex-   Torpedoed 75 miles (140 km) south-west of Yokosuka (34-30N
Yugao)   138-34E) by US submarine **Greenling**

US Ammunition Ship
Mount Hood   Blew up at Manus, Admiralty Islands

NW EUROPE 10 RN Minesweeper
Hydra   Mined off Ostend; abandoned as she seemed likely to founder but
later towed to Sheerness – not repaired

Seeking to check the US Army invasion of Leyte, the Japanese despatched reinforcement convoys from Manila to Ormoc, a small port on the west coast of Leyte Island. USAAF aircraft were unable to halt the traffic and when a larger movement, by half-a-dozen transports escorted by seven destroyers and a minesweeper, was detected the fast carriers were recalled from their replenishment area, 700 miles to the east, to strike at this convoy on 11 November 1944. The first wave, of nearly 350 aircraft, sank all the transports and the second sank four of the destroyers and the minesweeper; more than 10,000 Japanese soldiers were lost. The three destroyers which escaped were dealt with two days later, after the carriers had completed their postponed refuelling.

PACIFIC 11 Japanese Destroyers
Hamanami
Naganami
Shimakaze
Wakatsuki   noon: Sunk in Ormoc Bay, west of Leyte Island (10-50N 124-35E)
by US carrier aircraft (TF 38)

Japanese Minesweepers
W.30   Sunk in Ormoc Bay (10-50N 124-31E) by US carrier aircraft
W.22   Mined, position uncertain

The last major German warship outside the Baltic was destroyed on 12 November 1944. The battleship **Tirpitz** had spent her entire operational career in Norwegian waters, making just three sorties of any significance in nearly three years but exerting an influence which could not be measured against miles steamed. First seriously damaged (by midget submarine attack) in September 1943, she was thereafter repeatedly damaged by air attack. On 15 September 1944 an RAF raid scored a hit which wrecked her bow; unfit for operations, the **Tirpitz** was towed to Tromsö, where she was moored as a floating fortress.

NW EUROPE 12 German Battleship
Tirpitz   0941-0943: Sunk off Haakoy Island, Tromsö, by RAF air attack
(Bomber Command Lancasters of 9 and 617 Squadrons); hit by
three 12,000lb (5.4-tonne) bombs, capsized at 0952 – over 1,000
men lost

At the other end of Norway a Home Fleet cruiser force, assisted by good intelligence, intercepted a German convoy in waters which had been for so long dominated by the German Air Force.

12 German Minesweepers
M.416
M.427   2359: Sunk off Listerfjord, south-east of Egersund (58-14N 06-12E)
by gunfire of RN cruiser **Kent** (8in), cruiser **Bellona** (5.25in) and
destroyers **Verulam** and **Algonquin** (4.7in) and **Myngs** and
Zambesi (4.5in). Two transports and two armed trawlers were
also sunk by the striking force

After the disaster off Ormoc on 11 November, the Japanese Navy assembled a fresh convoy in Manila Bay. Before this could sail, the US fast carrier aircraft returned: seven transports were sunk, harbour installations were wrecked and the escort forces suffered further heavy losses.

13   Japanese Cruiser   PACIFIC

       Kiso   Sunk in Manila Bay (14-35N 120-50E) by US carrier aircraft

       Japanese Destroyers

       Akebono

       Akishimo

       Okinami

       Hatsuharu   Sunk with **Kiso**, 8 miles (15 km) west of Manila, by carrier aircraft

Although the Japanese losses to the carrier strikes were heavy, the latter could not be sustained and for most of the rest of November 1944 the US submarines applied the pressure.

14   Japanese Escort

       No.7   Torpedoed 165 miles (305 km) north-west of Cape Bolinao, Luzon (17-46N 117-57E) by US submarine **Ray**

14   Japanese Escort (ex-RN Survey Ship)

       Heiyo   Mined in Java Sea

       (ex-RN **Herald**)

17   Japanese Torpedo-Boat

       Hiyodori   Torpedoed 140 miles (260 km) east-north-east of Cape Tourane, Indo-China (16-56N 110-30E) by US submarine **Gunnel**

       Japanese Escort Carrier

       Shinyo   2305: Torpedoed 140 miles (260 km) north-east of Shanghai (33-02N 123-33E) by US submarine **Spadefish**

20   Japanese Minesweeper

       W.38   Torpedoed 75 miles (140 km) south-west of Taiwan (21-21N 119-45E) by US submarine **Atule**

20   German Torpedo-Boat   NW EUROPE

       T.34   Mined off Cap Arkona, Hamburg (54-40N 13-29E) on RAF-laid mine – 62 men lost

21   Japanese Battleship   PACIFIC

       Kongo   0300: Torpedoed 65 miles (120 km) north-west of Kiirun, Formosa (26-09N 121-23E) by US submarine **Sealion II** – blew up and sank at about 0515

       Japanese Destroyer

       Urakaze   Torpedoed with **Kongo** by USS **Sealion II**; hit by stern salvo fired immediately after bow salvo had been fired at the battleship

21   Russian Minesweeper   NW EUROPE

       Shpil   Sunk off Sorve Peninsula, Oesel Island, Gulf of Riga, by 105mm gunfire of German minesweeper *M.328* and gunfire of patrol craft

24   RCN Corvette

       Shawinigan 0115: Torpedoed in the Cabot Strait, off Cape Breton (47-34N 59-11W) by German submarine *U.1228* (homing torpedo) – lost with all hands

25   Japanese Destroyer   PACIFIC

       Shimotsuki 0220: Torpedoed 220 miles (410 km) east-north-east of Singapore (02-21N 107-20E) by US submarine **Cavalla**

       Japanese Escort

       No. 38   Torpedoed 60 miles (110 km) west of Manila (14-22N 119-57E) by US submarine **Hardhead**

PACIFIC

Japanese Patrol Boat (ex-Destroyer)

No. 38 (ex-   Torpedoed 100 miles (185 km) north of Cape Engano (20-12N 121-
Yomogi)   51E) by US submarine **Atule**

The fast carriers of Task Force 58 returned to the Luzon area on 25 November 1944 for their final round of strikes in the month. Although they mopped up a few ships, it was at a cost of two carriers seriously damaged (**Intrepid** and **Cabot**) and two others superficially damaged (**Essex** and **Hancock**) by Kamikazes. The JNAF suicide aircraft had scored hits on seven fast carriers and four escort carriers since the campaign had begun exactly a month earlier and, although only one escort carrier had been sunk, eight ships had been forced to withdraw for repairs.

25   Japanese Coast Defence Ship (ex-Chinese Cruiser)
Yasoshima   Sunk in Santa Cruz Bay, Luzon (15-40N 119-45E) by US carrier
(ex-**Ping**   aircraft (TG 38.3)
Hai)

Japanese Cruiser
Kumano   (Severely damaged 25 and 26 October) Sunk in Dasol Bay, Luzon
(15-45N 119-48E) by US carrier aircraft (USS **Ticonderoga**)

Japanese Fast Transports
T.6
T.10   Sunk in Balanacan Harbour, Mindoro (13-32N 121-52E) by US
carrier aircraft (TF 38)

Japanese Minesweeper
W.18   Sunk off Hainan Island (16-52N 108-30E) by USAAF air attack (XIV
Air Force based in China)

Although German submarines operated in the Baltic throughout the war against the Soviet Union, few opportunities for attacks were offered by the Russian Navy and the 440-ton minesweeper **T.217** was their only known success against a warship.

NW EUROPE   27   Russian Minesweeper
T.217   Sunk off Paldiski, Estonia (59-26N 24-00E) by German submarine
U.679

PACIFIC   29   Japanese Carrier
Shinano   0318: Torpedoed by US submarine **Archerfish** – 6 hits; her damage
control arrangements were elaborate, but were as yet incomplete
and all power was lost due to flooding at about 0600 and the
Shinano, the largest warship to be sunk by submarine torpedo,
capsized at 1100, 160 miles (295 km) south-east of Cape Muroto,
Shikoku (32-00N 137-00E)

NW EUROPE

German Minesweeper
M.584   Mined in the Kattegat (56-53N 10-48E) on RAF-laid mine

30   RN Frigate
Duff   Mined north-west of Ostend – 3 men lost; returned to Harwich
under own power but laid up, unrepaired

DECEMBER 1944

After two convoys intended for Ormoc had been destroyed by air attack, the Japanese Navy attempted to use destroyers to reinforce and supply their troops on Leyte, as they had done with some success in the Solomon Islands. These runs were intercepted by US destroyers but although US Navy tactics were much improved, the Japanese Navy could still inflict casualties in night battles and the Kamikazes were always ready to take advantage of any gaps in the protective air cover.

3   Japanese Escort Destroyer
    Kuwa   *0020: Sunk in Ormoc Bay (10-50N 124-35E) by 5in gunfire of US
                    destroyers* **Cooper, Allen M. Sumner** *and* **Moale**

    US Destroyer
    Cooper   *0030: Torpedoed in Ormoc Bay (10-54N 124-36E) by Japanese
                    destroyer (possibly* **Kuwa***); broke in half and sank almost
                    immediately – 191 men lost. Destroyer* **Moale** *was damaged by
                    gunfire in this action*

    Japanese Escort
    No. 64   *Torpedoed south-east of Hainan (18-36N 111-54E) by US
                    submarine* **Pipefish**

4   Japanese Destroyer
    Kishinami   *Torpedoed 270 miles (500 km) west-south-west of Luzon Straits
                    (13-12N 116-37E) by US submarine* **Flasher**

6   RN Frigate
    Bullen   0950: Torpedoed 7 miles (13 km) north-east of Cape Wrath, NW.
                    Scotland (58-42N 04-12W) by German submarine ***U.775*** (homing
                    torpedo); hit amidships and broke in half, the stern portion sinking
                    2 hours later – 97 men rescued by HMS ***Hesperus***

7   US Destroyer
    Mahan   *0950: Hit in Ormoc Bay (10-50N 124-30E) by three suicide aircraft
                    and set on fire; abandoned by 1025 and scuttled at 1150 by USS*
                    Walke *– 6 men lost*

    US Fast Transport
    Ward   *1000: Hit in Ormoc Bay (10-51N 124-33E) by suicide aircraft and
                    set on fire; abandoned and scuttled by USS* **O'Brien** *(whose
                    captain had previously commanded the* **Ward***)*

    Japanese Fast Transport
    T.11   *Sunk 5 miles (9 km) north of Leyte (11-23N 124-18E) by USAAF
                    aircraft*

11 US Destroyer
    Reid   *1700: Hit in the western Surigao Strait (09-50N 124-55E) by two
                    Kamikazes; after magazine blew up and the ship sank in 2 minutes
                    – 152 men rescued*

12 Japanese Destroyers
    Uzuki   *Torpedoed 50 miles (93 km) north-east of Cebu Island (11-03N 124-
                    23E) by US MTBs* **PT-490** *and* **PT-492**
    Yuzuki   *Sunk 65 miles (120 km) north-north-west of Cebu (11-20N 124-10E)
                    by USMC aircraft*

The German *6. Zerstörer-Flotille* was ordered to thicken up the existing minefields off
Reval (Tallinn) on the night of 11/12 December 1944, to close the channels used by
Russian ships leaving and entering Reval. In rough weather two of the ships ran into
one of these minefields and were lost – the weather and the danger from the mines
prevented rescue by the one remaining destroyer (***Z.43***) and two torpedo-boats and
there were no survivors.

12 German Destroyers
    Z.36   0151: Mined 12 miles (22 km) north-east of Reval (59-37N 24-51E);
                    sank on fire at 0215
    Z.35   0155: Mined in same field as ***Z.36*** (59-34N 24-49E), struck 2 mines
                    and blew up

NW EUROPE		Norwegian Corvette	
		Tunsberg Castle	1005: Mined 110 miles (205 km) north-west of the Kola Inlet (70-45N 30-09E); stern blown off and the ship sank at 1145

PACIFIC 13 *Japanese Fast Transport*
T.12 *Torpedoed 200 miles (370 km) south-east of Takao, Formosa (20-34N 118-45E) by US submarine* **Pintado**

14 *Japanese Escort*
No. 28 *Torpedoed 3 miles (5½ km) west of Hermana Island, Luzon (15-46N 119-45E) by US submarine* **Blenny**

MED 14 RN Escort Destroyer
Aldenham 1530: Mined 45 miles (83 km) south-east of Pola, Adriatic (44-30N 14-50E); 63 men rescued by HMS *Atherstone*

The next stepping-stone in the Philippines after Leyte was the island of Mindoro, needed to provide airfields to support the main Luzon landings. The assault force was attacked by suicide aircraft from 13 December (D-Day was the 15th) but although several major warships were damaged, no ship larger than an LST was sunk during the first fortnight of the campaign. Task Force 38's fast carriers supported the Mindoro invasion principally by attacking the Kamikazes' home bases and found only one Japanese warship before, on 17 December, a typhoon was encountered, with tragic results.

PACIFIC 15 *Japanese Escort*
No. 54 *Sunk in Luzon Straits (19-25N 121-25E) by US carrier aircraft*

Japanese Escort Destroyer
Momo *Torpedoed 140 miles (260 km) west-south-west of Cape Bolinao, Luzon (16-00N 117-39E) by US submarine* **Hawkbill**

18 *US Destroyers*
Spence *c1100: Capsized east of Luzon (in about 15-00N 128-00E) after her rudder jammed hard-a-starboard in typhoon; a modern ship, she was caught with only 15% of her fuel remaining and little water ballast to compensate – 23 men survived*
Hull *c1200: Broached and capsized east of Luzon – 62 men survived (* **Hull** *had 70% of her fuel remaining)*
Monaghan *(time unknown): Capsized east of Luzon – 6 men survived.*
Fifty-five men were rescued during the typhoon by the destroyer escort **Tabberer,** *which lost her foremast in the 115-knot (210-km) wind and heavy seas. Other ships damaged included four light carriers, four escort carriers, a light cruiser, seven destroyers and two more destroyer escorts, while 146 aircraft were wrecked or jettisoned by the carriers*

NW EUROPE 18 German Torpedo-Boat
T.10 (In floating dock at Gdynia, following bomb damage at Libau on 28 November)
2200: Severely damaged when dock sunk by RAF air raid; ship flooded and sank at 0320 on the 19th – salvage impractical

PACIFIC 19 *Japanese Carrier*
Unryu *1650: Torpedoed 200 miles (370 km) south-east of Shanghai (28-59N 124-03E) by US submarine* **Redfish***; hit abreast forward magazine and disintegrated in a massive explosion*

22 *Japanese Torpedo-Boat*
Chidori *Torpedoed 90 miles (167 km) west-south-west of Yokosuka (34-33N 138-02E) by US submarine* **Tilefish**

23	German Minesweeper		NW EUROPE
	M.489	Torpedoed off Mosterhavn, Bommelnfjord, Norway by Norwegian MTBs	

24	*Japanese Fast Transport*		PACIFIC
	T.8	*Sunk off Chichi Jima, Bonin Islands (25-10N 141-00E) by 5in gunfire of US destroyer* **Case**	

24	RCN Minesweeper		ATLANTIC
	Clayoquot	1337: Torpedoed off Halifax, Nova Scotia (44-30N 63-20W) by German submarine *U.806* (homing torpedo) – 64 men rescued	

25	RN Frigate		NW EUROPE
	Dakins	2110: Mined 14 miles (26 km) north-west of Ostend (51-25N 02-44E); flooded forward and returned to base under own power but not repaired	

The Japanese Navy gathered together the most effective available striking force to raid the Mindoro beach-head in late December. Just six destroyers could be made serviceable to screen one heavy cruiser and one light cruiser – a far cry from the still-powerful squadrons which could be assembled as recently as two months previously. The 'Penetration Force' reached Mindoro on 26 December, carried out an ineffectual bombardment of the airfields and retired after losing a single destroyer but with all the other ships damaged to varying extents.

26	*Japanese Destroyer*		PACIFIC
	Kiyoshimo	*Sunk 145 miles (260 km) south of Manila (12-20N 121-00E) by USAAF aircraft and torpedo fired by US MTBs*	

26	RN Frigates		NW EUROPE
	Capel	1237: Torpedoed off Cap de la Hague, Normandy (49-50N 01-41W) by German submarine *U.486* (homing torpedo); hit forward – magazine blew up, forcing bridge structure on to funnel; ship sank slowly, capsizing at 1602	
	Affleck	1252: Torpedoed (in 49-48N 01-43W) while hunting *U.486*; homing torpedo wrecked 60ft (18m) of the frigate's stern – reached Cherbourg under own power but later towed to Portsmouth and laid up, unrepaired	

22	*Japanese Fast Transport*		PACIFIC
	T.7	*Sunk off the Bonin Islands (24-47N 141-20E) by 5in gunfire of US destroyers*	

30	*Japanese Escort*		
	No. 20	*Sunk north-west of San Fernando, Luzon (16-43N 120-18E) by USAAF air attack*	
	Japanese Destroyer		
	Kuretake	*Torpedoed 65 miles (120 km) south-east of Formosa (21-00N 121-24E) by US submarine* **Razorback**	

31	German Minesweeper		NW EUROPE
	M.445	Sunk at Hamburg by RAF air raid	

?	Russian Escort		
	Korall	Believed to have been lost in 1944; exact date and cause unknown	

JANUARY 1945

The next amphibious 'jump' in the Pacific was to Lingayen Gulf, on the west coast of Luzon. The assault force left Leyte on 2 January 1945 and on the next day the fast carriers began supporting operations, attacking airfields on Formosa and the Philippines to reduce the threat posed by the Kamikazes. The weather favoured the

Japanese, who were able to mount strong attacks against the invasion shipping, while it was en route, during pre-assault minesweeping in Lingayen Gulf (on 6 and 7 January) and during the landing phase (from the 9th)

PACIFIC 2 Japanese Escort
No. 138 *Sunk off San Fernando, Luzon (16-37N 120-19E) by USAAF air attack*

4 Japanese Minesweeper
W.41 *Damaged in Formosa Strait by US carrier aircraft of TF 38 and beached near Takao*

US Escort Carrier
Ommaney Bay *1712: Hit off Mindoro by JNAF suicide aircraft; abandoned from 1750 as fires could not be controlled and scuttled at about 1830 (in 11-25N 121-19E) by destroyer **Burns***

5 Japanese Escort Destroyer
Momi *1745: Torpedoed 28 miles (52 km) west-south-west of Manila (14-00N 120-20E) by US carrier aircraft of TG 77.4 (escort carriers) (JNAF and JAAF suicide aircraft damaged two escort carriers, two heavy cruisers, two destroyers and a destroyer escort on this day)*

6 US Destroyer-Minesweeper
Long *1215: Hit in Lingayen Gulf (16-12N 120-11E) by JNAF suicide aircraft and abandoned; taken in tow but hit again at 1730 and sank slowly – one man lost*

US Fast Transport
Brooks *1252: Hit in Lingayen Gulf (16-20N 120-10E) by JNAF suicide aircraft; fires extinguished in 30 minutes and towed out of Gulf by HMAS **Warramunga** – 3 men lost. The ship was not repaired (On this day suicide aircraft also damaged two battleships, three heavy cruisers, a light cruiser, five destroyers and another destroyer-minesweeper)*

NW EUROPE 6 RN Escort Destroyer
Walpole 0730: Mined off Flushing (52-33N 03-06E)– 2 men lost; boiler room flooded and ship towed to Sheerness – damaged beyond economical repair

PACIFIC 7 US Destroyer-Minesweeper
Hovey *0430: Torpedoed in Lingayen Gulf (16-20N 120-10E) by JNAF aircraft and sank in 3 minutes – 46 men lost (including 24 **Brooks** and **Long** survivors)*

US Destroyer-Minesweeper
Palmer *1835: Sunk in Lingayen Gulf (16-20N 120-10E) by JAAF air attack; sank in less than 6 minutes – 28 men lost*

Japanese Escort Destroyer
Hinoki *2245: Sunk off Manila Bay (14-30N 119-30E) by 5in gunfire of US destroyers **Charles Ausburne**, **Shaw**, **Braine** and **Russell**. (This was the last surface engagement between US and Japanese warships)*

9 Japanese Escort
No. 3 *Sunk off Kiirun, Formosa (25-10N 121-45E) by US carrier aircraft of TF 38*

10 Japanese Escort
No. 42 *Torpedoed 100 miles (185 km) west of Okinawa (27-01N 126-34E) by US submarine **Puffer***

11 *US Fast Transport*
    Belknap   *0753: Hit in Lingayen Gulf (16-20N 120-10E) by suicide aircraft – 48 men lost; towed to Leyte but not repaired*

Task Force 38 had passed into the South China Sea on the night of 9/10 January and, undetected, reached a position from which to launch attacks on shipping off Indo-China. Targets were plentiful and the US carrier pilots enjoyed one of the best days of their war, with a score exceeded only during the February 1944 Truk strike.

12 *French Cruiser*
    Lamotte-   *Sunk in Cam Ranh Bay, Indo-China by carrier aircraft of TG 38.2*
    Picquet

    Japanese Training Cruiser
    Kashii   *Sunk 55 miles (102 km) north of Cape Varella (13-50N 109-20E) by US carrier aircraft of TG 38.3. (Nine laden tankers were also sunk by this strike)*

    Japanese Escorts
    No. 23   *Sunk off Quinhon Bay, 80 miles (150 km) north of Cape Varella (14-15N 109-19E) by US carrier aircraft of TG 38.3*
    No. 51   *Damaged with **No. 23** and sunk by the explosion of her own depth-charges*

    Japanese Escort (ex-US Minesweeper)
    Patrol Boat *Sunk 7 miles (13 km) south-west of Cape Padaran (11-10N*
    No. 103 *(ex-* *108-55E) by US carrier aircraft of TG 38.3*
    Finch*)*

    Japanese Escorts
    No. 35
    No. 43   *Sunk with **Patrol Boat No. 103***

    Japanese Minesweeper (ex-RN)
    W.101 *(ex-* *Sunk with **Patrol Boat No. 103** (One laden tanker and a submarine-*
    Taitam*)*   *chaser were also sunk by this strike)*

    Japanese Escorts
    Chiburi   *Sunk 45 miles (83 km) east of Cape St. Jacques (10-20N 107-50E) by*
    No. 17   *US carrier aircraft from USS **Ticonderoga**. (Three tankers, two*
    No. 19   *freighters and one landing ship were also sunk by this strike)*

12 RN Minesweeper
    Regulus   1350: Mined off Sista Is, southern Corfu channel (39-24N 20-10E); propellers apparently blown off and taken in tow but sank 46 minutes after explosion

    German Minesweeper
    M.273   c0100: Sunk off Nordbyfjord, Bergen, by gunfire of RN cruisers **Norfolk** and **Bellona** and destroyers **Onslow**, **Orwell** and **Onslaught**

    German Minesweeper
    M.1   Sunk off Nordbyfjord, Bergen by RAF air attack (Coastal Command Beaufighters of the Dallachy Wing)

14 *Japanese Minelayer*
    Yurijima   *Torpedoed 70 miles (130 km) south-east of Khota Baru, Malaya (05-51N 103-16E) by US submarine* **Cobia**

15 *Japanese Destroyer*
    Hatakaze   *Sunk in Takao Harbour, Formosa, by US carrier aircraft of TF 38*

PACIFIC

Japanese Fast Transport
T.14   *Sunk with* **Hatakaze**

Japanese Destroyer
Tsuga   *Sunk at Makung, Pescadores Islands (23-33N 119-33E) by US carrier aircraft of TF 38*

NW EUROPE 15 RN Escort Carrier
Thane   1330: Torpedoed in the Firth of Clyde (55-10N 05-30W) by German submarine **U.482** (homing torpedo) – 10 men lost; towed to Greenock and laid up, unrepaired

16 Russian Destroyer (ex-RN, ex-US)
Dyeyatelny   2030: Torpedoed 60 miles (110 km) east of the Kola Inlet, N. Russia,
(ex-   (68-56N 36-31E) by German submarine **U.997** (homing torpedo)
Churchill, ex-
Herndon)

PACIFIC 17 *Japanese Fast Transport*
T.15   *Torpedoed off Kagoshima, Kyushu (31-06N 130-34E) by US submarine* **Tautog**

NW EUROPE 21 German Minesweeper
M.305   Capsized in the Baltic in a storm

PACIFIC 24 *Japanese Destroyer*
Shigure   *Torpedoed 160 miles (300 km) east of Khota Bharu, Malaya (06-00N 103-48E) by US submarine* **Blackfin**

NW EUROPE 26 RN Frigate
Manners   0945: Torpedoed in the Irish Sea, 21 miles (39 km) west of Anglesey, by German submarine **U.1051** (homing torpedo) – 36 men lost; stern blown off, towed to Barrow-in-Furness and laid up, unrepaired. (**U.1051** was hunted down and sunk 5 hours later)

PACIFIC 28 *Japanese Escort*
Kume   *Torpedoed SE of Tsingtau, E China Sea (33-54N 122-55E) by US submarine* **Spadefish**

NW EUROPE 29 German Escort
F.5   Mined 16 miles (30 km) south-east of Sassnitz (54-20N 13-55E) on RAF-laid magnetic mine

PACIFIC 31 *Japanese Escort Destroyer*
Ume   *Sunk 20 miles (37 km) south of Formosa (22-30N 120-00E) by USAAF air attack (XIV Air Force, based in China)*

The Fairmile 'D'-class motor-torpedo-boats manned by the Royal Norwegian Navy undertook extended patrols in the Leads to the north of Bergen from the late autumn of 1944. Lying up under camouflage during the day, they emerged under cover of darkness to ambush German convoys. One such attack, on the night of 30/31 January 1945, was not detected before or after the torpedoes were fired and the German Navy ascribed the loss of yet another 'M'-class ship to a mine.

NW EUROPE 31 German Minesweeper
M.382   pre-dawn: Sunk in Ravnefjord, north of Molde, Norway (63-06N 07-32E) by Norwegian **MTB 715**

FEBRUARY 1945

PACIFIC 2 *Japanese Escort*
No. 144   *Torpedoed east of Kuantan, Malaya (04-11N 104-35E) by US submarine* **Besugo**

7	*Japanese Escort* **No. 53**	Torpedoed off Camranh Bay, Indo-China (11-55N 109-20E) by US submarine **Besugo**	PACIFIC

9   *Japanese escort*
No. 61   *Damaged beyond repair by mine 10nm (18km) off Cap St Jacques, Indo-China (10-10N 106-55E); towed to Saigon and laid up*

11   *RN Destroyer*
Pathfinder   *Damaged in Pakseik Taungmaw river mouth south of Akyab, Burma, by JAAF air attack; near-miss bombs in shallow water caused severe mining-type damage and the ship was immobilized and towed to Chittagong – not repaired*

12   RN Anti-Aircraft Cruiser
Delhi   0540: Damaged in Split harbour, Yugoslavia, by explosive motor-boat; the rudder and rudder head were cracked and substantial underwater damage was inflicted – not repaired

German Minesweeper
M.381   Torpedoed off Kristiansand North, Norway (63-07N 07-32E) by RN submarine ***Venturer***

13   RN Corvette
Denbigh Castle   am: Torpedoed in entrance to Kola Inlet (69-20N 33-33E) by German submarine ***U.992*** (conventional torpedo); hit right forward and bow submerged during tow. Beached 7 hours after hit but soon afterwards slid off into deeper water and sank

German Minesweeper
M.421   Mined in German defensive field at the entrance to Kolberg harbour, Baltic

14   *Japanese Escort*
No. 9   *Torpedoed south-west of Chezhu do (Quelpart Island), (32-43N 125-37E) by US submarine* **Gato**

15   Italian Battleship
Conte di Cavour   (Laid up for use as a blockship) Sunk at Trieste by USAAF air raid

16   *Japanese Minelayer*
Naryu   *Torpedoed south of Honshu (32-10N 135-54E) by US submarine* **Sennet**

17   *Japanese Escort*
No. 56   *Torpedoed 5 miles (9 km) east of Miyakejima, N. Bonins (33-54N 139-43E) by US submarine* **Bowfin**

17   German Torpedo-Boat (ex-Italian Destroyer)
TA.44 (ex-***Antonio Pigafetta***)   Sunk at Trieste by RAF air attack

German Torpedo-Boat (ex-Italian)
TA.41 (ex-***Lancia***)   Damaged beyond repair at San Rocco, Trieste, by RAF air attack. Scuttled 1 May 1945

RN Sloop
Lark   1034: Torpedoed off the Kola Inlet (69-30N 34-33E) by German submarine ***U.968*** (homing torpedo); stern blown off and towed to Rosta, where she was partially dismantled and then handed over to the Soviet Navy on 13 June 1945. Regarded by the RN as damaged beyond repair, she nevertheless appears to have seen post-war service with the Russians

NW EUROPE   RN Corvette
Bluebell   1523: Torpedoed 8 miles (15 km) north-east of the Kola Inlet (69-36N 25-29E) by German submarine **U.711** (homing torpedo) and blew up immediately, probably due to the explosion of her depth-charges, and sank in less than 30 seconds – 12 men rescued

The US Marines landed on Iwo Jima, in the Bonin Islands, on 19 February. The fighting ashore was severe and the surface of the island was not cleared of the tenacious Japanese defenders until 26 March (they continued thereafter to fight on in a warren of caves and tunnels); but although the area was less than 600 miles (1,100 km) from Japan itself, the scale of Japanese conventional bombing and Kamikaze attack was less than had been experienced in the Philippines.

PACIFIC   18   *US Destroyer-Minesweeper*
Gamble   *Damaged off Iwo Jima (24-55N 141-08E) by JNAF air attack; not repaired*

      20   *Japanese Destroyer*
Nokaze   *Torpedoed off Cape Varella, Indo-China (12-48N 109-38E) by US submarine* **Pargo**

MED   20   German Torpedo-Boat (ex-Italian)
TA.40 (ex-   Damaged beyond repair at Monfalcone, Adriatic, by air attack;
Pugnale)   scuttled 4 May 1945

          German Torpedo-Boat (ex-Yugoslav, ex-Italian)
TA.48 (ex-**T.3**)   Sunk at Trieste by air raid

NW EUROPE   RN Corvette
Vervain   1155: Torpedoed 20 miles south of Waterford, Eire (51-47N 07-06W) by German submarine **U.1208** (conventional torpedo); bows blown off and ship sank 21 minutes after the hit

MED   21   *US Escort Carrier*
Bismarck Sea   *1845: Hit off Iwo Jima (24-36N 141-48E) by JNAF suicide aircraft; abandoned from 1902 due to explosions and uncontrollable fires and sank at 2200 – 218 men lost. (USS* **Saratoga** *was severely damaged by suicide aircraft (6 hits) and another escort carrier sustained minor damage from a crashing torpedo-bomber)*

NW EUROPE   22   RCN Corvette
Trentonian   1230: Torpedoed 12 miles (22 km) east of Falmouth (50-06N 04-50W) by German submarine **U.1004** (homing torpedo); damaged aft, flooded rapidly and sank 10 minutes after the hit – 6 men lost

PACIFIC   23   *Japanese Escort*
Yaku   *Torpedoed 15 miles (28 km) south of Cape Varella (12-39N 109-29E) by US submarine* **Hammerhead**

NW EUROPE   23   French Escort Destroyer
La Combat-   2345: Mined near the East Dudgeon Light Vessel, off the Wash –
tante   60 men lost

PACIFIC   25   *Japanese Escort*
Shonan   *Torpedoed south of Hainan (17-08N 110-01E) by US submarine* **Hoe**

MARCH 1945

1   *Japanese Escort (ex-Minelayer)*   PACIFIC

     Tsubame   Sunk at Ishigaki, Sakishima Gunto (24-23N 124-12E) by US carrier aircraft of TF 38

     Japanese Torpedo-Boat

     Manazuru   Sunk off Okinawa (26-17N 127-35E) by US carrier aircraft of TF 38

2   German Minesweeper   NW EUROPE

     M.575   Capsized off Oeresund, Baltic

5   *Japanese Minesweeper*   PACIFIC

     W.15   *Torpedoed off Akuseki Jima, south of Kyushu (29-30N 129-33E) by US submarine* **Tilefish**; *beached and abandoned*

6   German Destroyer   NW EUROPE

     Z.28   2300: Sunk in Sassnitz Roads (54-30N 19-40E) by RAF air raid

8   *Japanese Escort*   PACIFIC

     No. 69   *Damaged off Hainan (19-02N 110-56E) by USAAF air attack; sank in tow off Hong Kong (22-00N 113-40E) on 16 March*

On 8/9 March, four surviving serviceable 'M'-boats and nine smaller craft from the isolated Channel Islands carried out a daring but desperate raid on Granville. The US PC.564 was sunk, four small freighters were blown up in the harbour and the German raiders succeeded in bearing off their intended prize, a coastal collier, to St Helier, together with 67 'liberated' German prisoners. Their only loss was one of the 'M'-boats, which had to be blown up when she ran aground.   NW EUROPE

10 *French Avisos*   PACIFIC

     Amiral   *Scuttled at My Tho, Indo-China, to avoid capture by the Japanese*
     Charner

     Marne   *As* **Amiral Charner**, *scuttled at Can Tho*

11 German Minesweepers   NW EUROPE

     M.266   Sunk at Kiel by USAAF air raid. **M.266** had been sunk once before
     M.804   (26 August 1944) by an RAF air raid on Kiel and had only recently
     M.805   been raised and repaired

13 *Japanese Escort*   PACIFIC

     No. 66   *Sunk off Amoy, Formosa Straits (23-30N 117-10E) by USAAF air attack*

14 German Torpedo-Boats   NW EUROPE

     T.3   Mined off Hela, Gulf of Danzig (54-39N 18-47E) in field laid by
     T.5   Russian submarine **L.21**. **T.3** had been raised and restored to service after she had previously been sunk at Le Havre by RAF air raid (see 18 September 1940)

17 RCN Minesweeper   NW EUROPE

     Guysborough 1835: Torpedoed off the Bay of Biscay (46-43N 09-20W) by German submarine **U.878** (homing torpedo); sank at 2000 – 54 men lost

18 *Japanese Fast Transport*   PACIFIC

     T.18   *Missing off Mutsurejima, Kyushu, from this date; cause uncertain but probably mined*

On the night of 17/18 March the ex-Italian, ex-Yugoslav destroyer **Premuda**, in German service as **TA.32**, led two torpedo-boats to lay mines off Cape Corse, the northern extremity of Corsica. The operation was watched by coastal radar stations on the mainland of Italy and on the Cape and two RN destroyers were 'vectored' to intercept the minelayers as they returned. The resulting engagement was the last between destroyers in the European War – only the **TA.32** escaped, damaged, to return to Genoa.

MED 18 German Torpedo-Boats (ex-Italian)

TA.29 (ex-   0302: Sunk north of Corsica (43-36N 09-18E) by 4.7in gunfire of RN
Eridano)   destroyer **Lookout**

TA.24 (ex-   0352: Sunk north of Corsica (43-49N 09-24E) by 4.7in gunfire of RN
Arturo)   destroyer **Meteor**

PACIFIC 19 Japanese (ex-RN River Gunboat)

Suma   *Mined near Kiangying, Yangtse (32-00N 120-00E) by US air-laid mine*

NW EUROPE 20 RN Sloop

Lapwing   1325: Torpedoed 6 miles (11 km) off Cape Kildin, Kola Inlet (69-26N 33-44E) by German submarine **U.968** (homing torpedo); hit amidships, broke in half and sank 20 minutes later

A USAAF air raid on Kiel on 20 March 1945 further reduced the number of 'M-class minesweepers available in the Baltic, three being sunk outright and two damaged beyond repair.

20 German Minesweepers

M.15   Sunk
M.16   (Laid up, damaged – see 4 November 1943) Sunk
M.18   Damaged beyond repair
M.19   Damaged beyond repair
M.522   Sunk

21 German Torpedo-Boat (ex-Italian)

TA.42 (ex-   Sunk at Venice by USAAF air raid
Alabarda)

21 German Battleship

Schleswig-   (Aground in shallow water off Gdynia following bombing damage)
Holstein   Scuttled

PACIFIC 24 Japanese Torpedo-Boat

Tomozuru   *Sunk 130 miles (220 km) north-west of Okinawa (28-55N 124-32E) by US carrier aircraft of TG 58.1. Two freighters and two auxiliary minesweepers were also sunk by this strike*

Japanese Escort

No. 68   *1300: Sunk 150 miles (280 km) north-west of Okinawa (30-00N 126-36E) by US carrier aircraft (TG 58.1). Four freighters and an auxiliary minesweeper were also sunk by this strike*

The greatest and, as it was to prove, the last of the major Pacific amphibious campaigns began on 26 March 1945, with landings on the Kerama Retto, a group of small islands which were to provide an advanced anchorage for the invasion of nearby Okinawa, the last stepping stone before the Home Islands of Japan. Two destroyers sustained major damage from suicide aircraft attacks on the first day – a foretaste of what was to become a daily struggle.

26 US Destroyer

Halligan   *1835: Mined off Kerama Retto, Okinawa (26-10N 127-30E); sank very quickly, with the loss of about 150 men*

NW EUROPE 26 RN Coastal Escort (Corvette)

Puffin   0230: Damaged off the Schelde by ramming a midget submarine and the subsequent explosion of its warhead; laid up, not repaired

MED 27 German Corvette (ex-Italian)

Uj.205 (ex-   Sunk at Venice by USAAF air raid
Colubrina)

28   US Minesweeper   PACIFIC
     Skylark   *Mined off Kerama Retto, Okinawa (26-20N 127-41E)*

     Japanese Escort
     No. 33   *Sunk south-south-east of Miyazaki, Kyushu (31-45N 131-45E) by
                        US carrier aircraft of TF 58*

     Japanese Minesweeper
     W.11   *Sunk off Macassar, Celebes (05-06S 119-14E) by USAAF air attack*

29   *Japanese Escorts*
     No. 18   *Sunk 110 miles (205 km) north of Cape Varella, Indo-China (14-44N
                        109-16E) by USAAF air attack*

     No. 130   *Sunk 105 miles (195 km) north of Cape Varella (14-39N 109-16E) by
                        USAAF air attack*

     Japanese Escort
     No. 84   *Torpedoed 95 miles (175 km) north of Cape Varella (14-30N 109-
                        15E) by US submarine* **Hammerhead**

29   RCN Frigate   NW EUROPE
     Teme   0625: Torpedoed 6 miles (11 km) north-west of Land's End (50-07N
                        05-45W) by German submarine ***U.246*** (homing torpedo); stern
                        blown off, towed to Falmouth and laid up, not repaired – 4 men lost

USAAF B-24 bombers carried out a very damaging raid on Wilhelmshaven on 30 March
1945. Although the primary targets were the U-boat yards, surface ships in the naval
dockyard were also hit.

30   German Cruiser
     Köln
     German Escort
     F.6 (Königin Luise)
     German Minesweeper
     M.329

APRIL 1945

*The landings on Okinawa began at dawn on 1 April 1945. Suicide aircraft had severely
damaged only two major warships since the invasion of Kerama Retto, although a
number of assault transports and landing ships had been put out of action. The
Kamikazes, Army and Navy, kept up a steady pressure but did not make the expected
major effort and sank no ships on this first day. The biggest ships attacked, the US
battleship* **West Virginia** *and the RN Fleet carrier* **Indefatigable**, *shrugged the hits off
their armour and continued to operate.*

2   US Fast Transport   PACIFIC
     Dickerson   *Hit off Okinawa by JAAF suicide aircraft – 54 men lost; towed to
                        Kerama Retto, condemned as a total loss and scuttled on 4 April*

     US Destroyer
     Shaw   *Ran aground off Leyte (09-36N 123-53E); damaged beyond repair.
                        This was the second, and final, occasion of loss for the* **Shaw**,
                        *which had been one of the original Pearl Harbor casualties but had
                        seen extensive front-line service since she had been rebuilt*

     Japanese Escort
     No. 186   *Sunk off Amami-o-shima (28-07N 129-09E) by US carrier aircraft
                        (TF 58)*

     Japanese Fast Transport
     T.17   *Sunk with escort* **No. 186** *by carrier aircraft*

PACIFIC	3	*Japanese Escort*	
		Manju	*Damaged beyond repair at Hong Kong by USAAF air attack*
NW EUROPE	3	German Minesweeper	
		M.802	Sunk at Kiel by USAAF air raid
PACIFIC	4	*Japanese Escort*	
		Mokutu	*0900: Mined in the Shimonoseki Straits (33-53N 131-03E) in field laid by USAAF B-29s*
NW EUROPE	4	German Battleship	
		Schlesien	Mined off Swinemünde (RAF-laid mine) and sank in shallow water
PACIFIC	5	*Japanese Escort*	
		No.1	*Sunk 40 miles (75 km) south-east of Amoy (23-55N 117-40E) by USAAF air attack*

6 *Japanese Destroyer*
Amatsukaze *Sunk 6 miles (11 km) east of Amoy (24-30N 118-10E) by USAAF air attack*

Japanese Escort
No. 134 *Sunk 50 miles (93 km) south-south-west of Amoy (23-55N 117-40E) by USAAF air attack*

Japanese Minesweeper
W.12 *Torpedoed north of Sumbawa Island (08-13S 119-40E) by US submarine* **Besugo**

The expected mass suicide aircraft attacks ('Kikusui') on the Okinawa assault shipping and covering forces began on 6 April 1945. Just over half of the 700 aircraft launched from Japanese bases were Kamikazes and it was fortunate for the Allies that these pilots were not of the calibre of those met during the Lingayen campaign: fewer than 40 scored hits or damaging near-misses on a total of 18 ships. Two freighters and a landing ship were sunk, as were three US destroyers; three more destroyers survived but were written off. The high incidence of attack on fast well-armed targets was indicative of the indifferent tactical training of the majority of the suicide pilots, who tended to attack the first objectives sighted (the radar picket screen or inner gun and anti-submarine defence screens) instead of the transports and carriers which were essential to the success of the assault.

6 US Destroyers
Bush *1513-1745: Hit 50 miles (94 km) north of Okinawa (27-16N 127-48E) while on radar picket station (No 1) by three JNAF suicide aircraft; almost cut in half and severely on fire, she broke up and sank at about 1830 – 87 men lost*

Colhoun *1700-1800: Hit off Okinawa in company with* **Bush** *by three JNAF suicide aircraft; back broken, holed aft by a near-miss, and extensive fires – 35 men lost. Abandoned and scuttled by gunfire of USS* **Cassin Young** *at 2330*

Newcomb *1806: Hit off Okinawa (12-38N 127-28E) while screening TF 54 (gunfire support) by three suicide aircraft in quick succession; machinery spaces severely damaged, both funnels destroyed and serious fires – 40 men lost. Towed to Kerama Retto but not repaired*

Leutze *1815: Hit off Okinawa while assisting* **Newcomb** *by one suicide aircraft; exploded on quarterdeck and caused very serious flooding aft – 7 men lost. Towed to Kerama Retto settling by the stern, salvaged but not repaired*

Morris *1815: Hit south of Okinawa (25-55N 127-52E) while on anti-submarine patrol by one suicide aircraft; severely damaged and* set on fire but brought into Kerama Retto – 13 men lost. Not repaired

US Destroyer-Minesweeper

Emmons   *1603-1833: Hit off east coast of Okinawa (26-48N 128-04E) by five JNAF suicide aircraft; damaged fore and aft, bridge destroyed, severe fires – 64 men lost. Abandoned at 1930 and scuttled at 2200 by USS* **Ellyson**. **Emmons** *had been assisting DMS* **Rodman**, *hit at 1600 by two suicide aircraft; the* **Rodman** *was towed to Kerama Retto*

In addition to the **Rodman**, three destroyers and one destroyer escort were so badly damaged by Kamikazes on 6 April that they had to retire to the US for major repairs:

1612: **Witter** *(DE): S. of Okinawa – 6 men lost*
1615: **Hyman***: off E. coast – 10 men lost*
1700: **Howorth***: off E. coast*
1730: **Mullany***: off E. coast – 30 men lost; temporarily abandoned, but brought fires under control with assistance of USS* **Purdy** *and reached Kerama Retto under own steam*

In anticipation of the havoc that would be wreaked by the first mass suicide attacks, the Japanese Navy despatched the strongest force for which it could find sufficient fuel for a one-way mission – the battleship **Yamato** (still the most powerful unit afloat), a light cruiser and a screen of eight destroyers – their purpose being further to disrupt the US assault shipping. US submarines picked up the Japanese as they left the Inland Sea and as the fast carriers prepared to provide the first line of defence, six battleships of the inshore bombardment groups were deployed to intercept any ships which might break through.

   None did, the carrier strikes sinking or damaging all the Japanese ships during the early afternoon. The JNAF co-operated, attacking TF 58 in some strength at the same time that the US attacks were beginning, but succeeded in damaging only one carrier. Suicide attacks on the Okinawa area were on a much smaller scale than on the 6th but the battleship **Maryland**, a destroyer (**Bennett**) and a destroyer escort (**Wesson**) had to withdraw, seriously damaged.

7   Japanese Battleship
     Yamato   *1241-1417: Sunk 130 miles (240 km) west-south-west of Kagoshima (30-22N 128-04E) by five 1,000lb (454kg) bombs and ten torpedoes from US carrier aircraft of TF 58 – 2,497 men lost (269 rescued)*

     Japanese Cruiser
     Yahagi   *1246-1345: Sunk 30 miles north of the* **Yamato** *(30-54N 128-10E) by an estimated 12 bombs and 7 torpedoes (6 torpedo hits claimed by aircraft from USS* **Langley***); sank at 1402*

7   Japanese Light Cruiser
     Isuzu   *Torpedoed 30nm (55km) N off Soembawa Is., Java Sea, (07-38S 118-09E) by US submarines* **Charr** *and* **Gabilan**

     Japanese Destroyers
     Asashimo   *1210-1240: Sunk with* **Yahagi** *by dive-bombing*
     Hamakaze   *1248: Torpedoed with* **Yahagi** *by aircraft from USS* **San Jacinto** *and sank very quickly*
     Kasumi   *1250: Damaged with* **Yahagi** *by dive-bombing; stopped and sank at 1700*
     Isokaze   *1250: Damaged with* **Yahagi** *by bomb near-misses; stopped and scuttled at 2240*

9   Japanese Minesweeper
     W.3   *Torpedoed 65 miles (120 km) north-east of Sendai (39-07N 141-57E) by US submarine* **Parche**

By early April 1945 the German Navy had only sufficient fuel for defensive patrols, providing direct support to the Army and supplying the troops isolated in East Prussia. The forces available consisted, apart from minesweepers and minor craft, of one pocket battleship, a heavy cruiser, seven destroyers and two damaged but seaworthy torpedo-boats. A destructive Bomber Command raid on Kiel on the night of 9/10 April disposed of heavy units immobilized by lack of fuel and smaller ships under repair.

NW EUROPE 9/10 German Pocket Battleship

Admiral Scheer   Sunk at Kiel by RAF air raid; capsized in inner dockyard basin

German Torpedo-Boat

T.1   Sunk at Kiel by RAF air raid

German Cruiser

Emden   Severely damaged at Kiel by bomb near-misses and beached

German Minesweeper

M.504   Sunk at Kiel by RAF air raid; destroyed in drydock

The massive RAF Bomber Command night raids on ports supplemented the direct attacks on ships at sea by Coastal Command, whose armoury now included solitary roaming Halifax bombers, which attacked targets of opportunity in the Kattegat and western Baltic.

10   German Torpedo-Boat

T.13   pre-dawn: Sunk south-east of Laeso Is, Skagerrak, by air attack (No 58 Squadron RAF)

11   German Minesweeper

M.376   Sunk off Hela by Russian air attack

German Minesweeper

M.2   Sunk in Fedjefjord by RAF Coastal Command (Dallachy Wing) air attack

The second Japanese major suicide onslaught was launched on 12 April. The Kamikazes, Navy and Army, backed up by 'conventional' bombers, consistently penetrated the layered defences – the outer and inner fighter patrols, the radar picket ships (which attracted numerous attacks) and the inner screen of escorts – and hit 22 ships. Only one destroyer and an LCS were sunk, and of the other casualties just five had to withdraw completely from the operation, but 675 US Navy officers and men were killed or wounded.

PACIFIC 12 *US Destroyer*

Mannert L. Abele   *1445: Sunk 72 miles (133 km) north-west of Okinawa (picket stn No. 14 – 27-25N 126-59E) by JNAF suicide aircraft; hit first by a 'Zero', breaking her keel and propeller shafts, the ship was then hit less than a minute later by a 'Baka' manned rocket-bomb which caused her immediate loss – 79 men lost*

MED 13 German (ex-Italian) Torpedo-Boat

TA.45 (ex-**Spica**)   Torpedoed in the Planinski Channel, Gulf of Fiume by RN **MTB**s **670** and **697**

NW EUROPE German Torpedo-Boat

T.16   Sunk at Frederikshavn by RAF air raid

PACIFIC 14 *Japanese Escorts*

Nomi No. 31   *Torpedoed off Tsushima Island (33-25N 126-15E) by US submarine* **Tirante**. *Two ships in convoy sunk in same attack*

In the early hours of 15 April 1945 a German minesweeper collided with a U-boat off Lindesnes. The U-boat was damaged and taken in tow by the 'sweeper, which then actuated an RAF-laid mine.

15   German Minesweeper   NW EUROPE
     M.368   pre-dawn: Mined 5 miles (9 km) north-east of Lindesnes, S. Norway (58-02N 07-12E)

16   Japanese Escort   PACIFIC
     No. 73   *Torpedoed 2 miles off Todosaki, Honshu (39-36N 142-05E) by US submarine* **Sunfish**

The Japanese air forces launched their third major suicide attack on 16 April. Again the Kamikazes were attracted to the radar picket stations to the north and west of Okinawa, where they scored fifteen direct hits or damaging near-misses on eight ships. The destroyer **Laffey**, *on Station 1 with two LCS, was repeatedly attacked over a period of 80 minutes and survived seven suicide hits and four bombs. On Station 14, one destroyer was sunk and two destroyer-minesweepers were severely damaged, one of them beyond economical repair. Elsewhere, a carrier, a destroyer and a destroyer escort also sustained damage which required them to return to the USA for repairs.*

16   US Destroyer
     Pringle   *0910: Sunk by JNAF suicide aircraft 72 miles (133 km) north-west of Okinawa (picket station No 14); hit on forward torpedo-tubes, which blew up and broke ship in two – 65 men lost*

     US Destroyer-Minesweeper
     Harding   *0959: Severely damaged north-west of Okinawa (picket station No 14 – 26-42N 127-25E) by near-miss JNAF suicide aircraft – 22 men lost; not repaired*

16   RCN Minesweeper   ATLANTIC
     Esquimalt   0930: Torpedoed off Halifax, Nova Scotia (44-28N 63-10W) by German submarine **U.190** – 44 men lost

     RN Frigate   NW EUROPE
     Ekins   2125: Mined 13 miles (24 km) north-west of Ostend. Boiler-room flooded and ship immobilized; struck second mine at 2140, causing further minor flooding. Ship later got under way and returned to port under her own steam; not repaired

     German Pocket Battleship
     Lützow   Sunk in Kaiserfahrt Canal, Swinemünde, by RAF air attack; 18 Halifax aircraft, armed with 12,000lb (5,400kg) bombs, delivered a dusk strike, obtaining near-misses which caused severe flooding. The ship was refloated but was scuttled on 4 May

19   German Minesweeper
     M.403   Sunk south-east of Anholt Is, Kattegat, (56-36N 11-49E) by RAF Coastal Command (Banff Wing) air attack

22   US Minesweeper   PACIFIC
     Swallow   *1900: Sunk by JNAF suicide aircraft off Okinawa (26-10N 127-12E); capsized and sank within 7 minutes – 2 men lost*

23   US Destroyer Escort   ATLANTIC
     Frederick C.   0840: Torpedoed north-west of the Azores (43-52N 40-15W) by
       Davis   German submarine **U.546** (homing torpedo); broke in half and sank very quickly. The **Davis** was the last US warship to be lost to German submarine attack

23   German (ex-Italian) Corvette   MED
     Uj.2222 (ex-   Sunk in the Gulf of Genoa by USN motor torpedo-boats
      Tuffetto)

German resistance in northern Italy collapsed on 24 April. La Spezia was taken on that day and the German naval command in the Mediterranean ordered that the warships at Genoa and Monfalcone should be scuttled and the port facilities destroyed.

MED 24 Torpedo-Boat (ex-Italian Destroyer)
TA.31 (ex-   Scuttled at Genoa
Dardo)

Torpedo-Boat (ex-Yugoslav, ex-Italian Destroyer)
TA.32 (ex-   (See 18 March 1945) Scuttled at Genoa
Dubrovnik,
ex-**Premuda**)

Escorts (ex-French Avisos)
SG.15 (ex-   Scuttled at Genoa
**Rageot de la
Touche**)
SG.23 (ex-**La**   Scuttled at Genoa
Batailleuse)

Corvettes (ex-Italian)
Uj.2221 (ex-   Scuttled at Genoa
Vespa)
Uj.2226 (ex-   Scuttled at Monfalcone
Artemide)
Uj.2227 (ex-   Scuttled at Monfalcone
Persefone)
Uj.2228 (ex-   Scuttled at Monfalcone
Euterpe)
Uj.6083 (ex-   Scuttled at Genoa
Capriolo)
Uj.6084 (ex-   Scuttled at Genoa
Alce)

25 German Escort
SG.20   Scuttled at Oneglia
(ex-**Generale
Achille Papa**)

PACIFIC 27 *US Destroyer*
Hutchings   *pre-dawn: Severely damaged off Okinawa (26-14N 127-49E) by Japanese explosive suicide motor-boat – not repaired*

US Fast Transport
Rathburne   *2045: Severely damaged off Okinawa (26-26N 127-36E) by JNAF suicide aircraft – not repaired*

27 RN Frigate
Redmill   0925: Torpedoed 25 miles (46 km) north-west of Blacksod Bay, S. Ireland (54-23N 10-36W) by German submarine **U.1105**. The frigate's stern and propeller shafts were blown off and she was towed to Londonderry – 22 men lost; ship was not repaired

29 *US Destroyer*
Haggard   *1700: Severely damaged off Okinawa (27-01N 129-40E) by JNAF suicide aircraft – 11 men lost; towed to Kerama Retto but not repaired*

The final Royal Navy loss to U-boat attack occurred close inshore off the Russian coast, where a small wolf-pack had concentrated to intercept a convoy due to leave Murmansk. The convoy's departure was preceded by a sweep by an escort group: in less than an hour the frigates sank two U-boats but also lost one of their own number to a homing torpedo which initiated the frightful explosion that was a feature of several American-built frigate losses.

29	RN Frigate		NW EUROPE
	Goodall	2038: Torpedoed in entrance to the Kola Inlet (69-25N 33-38E) by German submarine **U.968**; magazine explosion blew forward part of ship away – abandoned and scuttled	
30	German Minesweeper		
	M.455	Sunk at Cuxhaven by RAF air raid	

MAY 1945

1	German (ex-Italian) Torpedo-Boat		MED
	TA.41 (ex-**Lancia**)	(Damaged on 17 February 1945) Scuttled at Trieste	
	German (ex-Italian, ex-Yugoslav) Torpedo-Boat		
	TA.43 (ex-**Sebenico**, ex-**Beograd**)	Scuttled at Trieste	
2	*Japanese Escort*		PACIFIC
	Mikura	*Missing in the Sea of Japan – possibly sunk by mine*	
2	German Minesweeper		NW EUROPE
	M.387	Scuttled at Lübeck	
2	German Minesweeper		
	M.293	Sunk NE of Laeso Is., Kattegat, by RAF air attack (Banff Wing Mosquitoes)	
2/3	*Japanese Escorts*		PACIFIC
	Oga		
	No. 25	*Torpedoed in the Yellow Sea, 180 miles (330 km) west-south-west of Mokpo (33-56N 122-49E) by US submarine* **Springer**	

Seventy-three miles (135 km) to the west of Okinawa, Picket Station No 10, occupied by two destroyers and two landing ships, came under attack shortly before sunset on 3 May. About 36 suicide aircraft were involved and despite the presence of fighter patrols they scored eleven hits to sink outright one of the destroyers and **LSM(R) 195**; *the other destroyer was damaged beyond repair and only* **LCS(L) 25** *escaped with minor damage; 86 men were lost and 156 were wounded.*

3	*US Destroyer-Minelayer*	
	Aaron Ward	*1822: Damaged by two suicide aircraft; 1913-1920: hit amidships by four suicide aircraft which inflicted serious superficial damage – 45 men lost; towed to Kerama Retto and then made her own way back to USA but not repaired*
	US Destroyer	
	Little	*1843: Hit amidships by four suicide aircraft and sank in 26-24N 126-15E at 1855 – 30 men lost*

3	German (ex-Italian) Torpedo-Boat		MED
	TA.22 (ex-**Giuseppe Missori**)	Scuttled off Trieste	

While the Japanese Kamikazes were exacting a small but steady toll of US Navy ships from the overwhelming might of the task forces off Okinawa, the German Navy was in its last agonies in the Baltic. The surface units still in commission had made heroic efforts to support the Army as it retreated before the Red Army, but the offensive in the west had now brought the hitherto safe waters between Kiel and the Danish islands within reach of British and US fighter-bombers; it was believed that the Germans were planning to retreat for a final desperate defence in Norway and the tactical air forces were turned loose on the concentration of surface shipping and submarines. Mines laid by RAF Bomber Command could no longer be countered by the overworked German mine-countermeasures force and these too inflicted losses, while the German Navy scuttled ships previously damaged at sea or in air raids.

NW EUROPE 3 German Destroyer
Z.43 Mined in the Geltinger Bight while under air attack and scuttled in 54-09N 09-47E

German Escort
F.3 (Hai) Sunk in Kiel Bay (54-31N 10-11E) by RAF fighter-bombers

German Minesweeper
M.14 Mined off Swinemünde on RAF-laid mine

German Cruiser
Admiral Hipper Scuttled at Kiel (previously damaged by air raid)

German Torpedo-Boats
T.8
T.9 Scuttled in Kiel Bay (54-26N 10-10E); **T.9** had been damaged by Russian forces on 10 March

German (ex-Norwegian) Minelayer
Brummer (ex-**Tryggvason**) Scuttled at Kiel

PACIFIC 4 *Japanese Minesweeper*
W.20 *Torpedoed 140 miles (260 km) south-east of Mokpo (34-16N 123-37E) by US submarine* **Trepang**

The Kamikazes inflicted considerable loss and damage on 4 May. Besides the six ships named below, they damaged a light cruiser, three destroyers and a minesweeper of the US task force and two Royal Navy armoured carriers. In total, the attacks on 4 May cost the lives of 482 Allied sailors and wounded another 618.

4 *US Destroyers*
Luce *0808: Sunk 61 miles (112 km) west-north-west of Okinawa (picket station No 12 – 26-43N 127-14E) by one direct hit and one near-miss suicide aircraft – 149 men lost.* **LSM 190** *was also sunk in this attack*

Morrison *0825: Sunk 51 miles (94 km) north of Okinawa (picket station No 1 – 27-10N 127-58E) by four suicide aircraft (two 'Zeroes' and two E7K 'Alf' floatplanes, one of which taxied up the wake before taking off and flying into an after turret) – 159 men lost.* **LSM(R) 194** *was also sunk and the destroyer* **Ingraham** *badly damaged in this attack*

US Escort Carrier
Sangamon *dusk: Damaged by suicide aircraft south-west of Kerama Retto – 46 men lost; the ship was not repaired for USN use but was converted for commercial use*

MED 4 German (ex-Italian) Torpedo-Boat
TA.40 (ex-**Pugnale**) (Damaged on 20 February) Scuttled at Monfalcone

NW EUROPE German Minesweeper
M.301 pre-dawn: Sunk in the Kattegat (57-56N 07-34E) by RAF Coastal Command air attack (No 58 Squadron)

German Torpedo-Boat
T.36 Sunk in the Gulf of Danzig (Gdansk) by Russian air attack

German Minesweeper

M.36   Sunk in the Fehmarn Belt, western Baltic, by RAF (2nd Allied Tactical Air Force) air attack

German (ex-Dutch) Escort

K.1   Sunk at Aarhus, Denmark, by RAF air attack

At 0800 on 5 May 1945 German forces in the Netherlands, north-west Germany and Denmark ceased hostilities and thereafter the only further loss in the European theatre to direct attack was a Norwegian-manned coastal minesweeper (**NYMS 382**), sunk in the Channel by a U-boat on 7 May.

7	*Japanese Minelayer*		PACIFIC

Nuwashima   *Damaged by US naval air attack off Kyushu and beached in Saeki Bay (32-56N 131-05E)*

Japanese Minesweeper

W.29   *Mined off Kinzurusaki, W. Honshu, (34-02N 130-54E)*

7   German Minesweeper   NW EUROPE

M.22   Scuttled in the Kiel Canal (54-19N 09-58E)

9   *US Destroyer Escorts*   PACIFIC

Oberrender   *1852: Severely damaged by suicide aircraft west of Okinawa (26-32N 127-20E) – 8 men lost; towed to Kerama Retto and scrapped*

England   *1853: Damaged by suicide aircraft north-west of Kerama Retto (26-18N 127-13E); towed to Kerama Retto, patched up for passage to Guam but not fully repaired thereafter*

9   RN Minesweeper   NW EUROPE

Prompt   1705: Mined 12 miles (22 km) north-west of Ostend; towed to Southend but not repaired

11   *US Destroyers*   PACIFIC

Evans   *0800: Severely damaged by four suicide aircraft 33 miles (60 km) west-north-west of Okinawa (picket station No 15 – 26-58N 127-32E) – 30 men lost; ship immobilized and towed to Kerama Retto, not repaired*

Hugh W.   *0925: Severely damaged by two suicide aircraft, a rocket bomb*
Hadley   *('Baka') and a bomb while screening the **Evans** (26-59N 127-32E) – 29 men lost; ship lost power and nearly capsized, being saved only by good damage-control – towed to Kerama Retto but subsequently scrapped*

*Shortly after the attack on Picket Station No 15, in which the two destroyers and **LCS(L) 88** were damaged, the carriers of Task Group 58.3 were attacked and two suicide aircraft hit the **Bunker Hill**. Serious fires were not brought under control for over five hours and 404 men were lost; the carrier did not return to operations before the end of the war.*

The Japanese attempted to evacuate their garrison in the Andaman Islands in mid-May but the small force was reported by a submarine. Tracked almost continuously thereafter, it was brought to bay off the Malacca Straits by the East Indies Fleet's 24th Destroyer Flotilla and despatched in a close-range gun and torpedo action.

16   *Japanese Cruiser*

Haguro   *0100: Torpedoed 45 miles (83 km) south-west of Penang (05-00N 99-35E) by RN destroyers **Saumarez**, **Venus**, **Vigilant**, **Virago** and **Verulam***

Japanese Minelayer

Hatsutaka   *Sunk off Labuan, Borneo (04-49N 103-31E) by US submarine **Hawkbill***

PACIFIC 18 *US Destroyer*
Longshaw *0719: Stranded on Ose Reef, Okinawa (26-11N 127-37E), taken under fire by Japanese shore batteries from 1100 and severely damaged – 86 men lost. Wreck subsequently sunk by US naval gunfire*

21 *Japanese Minesweeper*
W.34 *Sunk off Kepulauan, Java Sea (06-18S 116-14E), by US submarine*
Chub

The Japanese air forces launched their heaviest night offensive of the Okinawa campaign of 24/25 May, with conventional bombers concentrating on the US airfields on the island and on troop positions and, from midnight, Kamikazes attacking shipping. On this occasion, the suicide aircraft by-passed the pickets and reached the inshore groups.

25 *US Fast Transport*
Barry *0034: Severely damaged by suicide aircraft off Okinawa (26-30N 127-50E) – no fatal casualties; towed to Kerama Retto, where it was decided to anchor her offshore as a 'tethered goat' decoy for suicide aircraft (see 21 June)*

US Minesweeper
Spectacle *pre-dawn: Severely damaged by suicide aircraft off NW Okinawa (26-40N 127-52E) and abandoned on fire – 29 men lost; 0835: **LSM-135** was hit and beached on Ie Shima while carrying **Spectacle**'s survivors – 11 men lost. The minesweeper was later towed to Kerama but was not repaired*

US Destroyer-Minesweeper
Butler *Severely damaged by suicide aircraft off Okinawa (26-12N 127-50E) – no fatal casualties; ship towed to Kerama but not repaired*

US Fast Transport
Roper *Severely damaged by suicide aircraft off Okinawa (26-34N 127-36E) – no fatal casualties; ship towed to Kerama but not repaired*

US Fast Transport
Bates *1120: Severely damaged by two suicide aircraft off NW Okinawa (26-41N 127-41E) – 21 men lost; ship towed to Hagushi Wan, where she capsized and sank*
(A destroyer and a destroyer escort were also severely damaged – with the loss of 21 men – during the forenoon of 25 May but both were repaired post-war)

27 *US Destroyer-Minesweeper*
Forrest *dusk: Severely damaged by suicide aircraft off Okinawa transport anchorage (26-00N 128-00E) – 8 men lost; towed to Kerama but not repaired*

28 *US Destroyer*
Drexler *0655: Sunk by two suicide aircraft 35 miles (65 km) north-north-west of Okinawa (picket station No 15 – 27–06N 127-38E) – 158 men lost; the destroyer was hit by a twin-engined P1Y1 'Frances' bomber and the impact rolled her on her beam-ends, causing her to sink in less than 50 seconds*

29 *US Destroyer*
Shubrick *0013: Severely damaged by suicide aircraft 50 miles (92 km) west-north-west of Okinawa (picket station No 15 – 26-38N 127-05E) – 32 men lost; destroyer taken in tow in sinking condition, reached Kerama but was not repaired*

JUNE 1945

After the heavy losses of April and May, there was a distinct lull in June 1945. The Allied fast carriers in the Pacific were 'resting', in preparation for extended operations off the Japanese Home Islands; the diminished Japanese Fleet was confined to its bases by lack of fuel. In the west, off Burma and the East Indies, the Royal Navy was engaged in peripheral mopping-up operations and in containing the residue of the Japanese force based on Singapore.

The biggest single cause of US Navy casualties (though not outright loss) during the month was the weather. For the second time, Admiral Halsey led his Third Fleet (TF 38 and its logistic support units) into the eye of a typhoon and although no ships were lost on 5 June 1945, two fast carriers, two escort carriers, three cruisers, two destroyers and a destroyer escort sustained major damage, necessitating their withdrawal for repairs. Twenty-two other warships and three supply ships were damaged to a lesser extent.

6   US Destroyer-Minelayer   PACIFIC
    J. William   *1713: Severely damaged by two suicide aircraft off Nakagusuku*
      Ditter   *Wan, Okinawa (26-14N 128-01E); towed to Kerama Retto but*
                assessed as damaged beyond repair

8   Japanese Cruiser
    Ashigara   *1209: Torpedoed 14 miles (26 km) west-south-west of Muntok Is,*
                Banka Strait (01-59S 104-57E), by RN submarine **Trenchant**; *hit by*
                5 torpedoes and sank at 1239

    US Minesweeper
    Salute   *Mined off Brunei (05-08N 115-05E)*

9   Japanese Escort
    No. 41   *Torpedoed 50 miles (92 km) south-east of Mokpo, Korea (34-18N*
                127-18E) by US submarine **Sea Owl**

10 US Destroyer
    William D.   *0825: Near-missed by suicide aircraft 35 miles (65 km) north-north-*
      Porter   *west of Okinawa (picket station No 15 – 27-06N 127-38E). Mining*
                effect caused uncontainable flooding and the ship sank at 1119 –
                no fatal casualties

16 US Destroyer
    Twiggs   *2030: Torpedoed by JNAF aircraft (which then crashed on the*
                destroyer) off Okinawa (26-08N 137-35E). 2100: ship blew up and
                sank – 183 men lost

21 US Fast Transport (anchored as decoy hulk – see 25 May)
    Barry   *1845: Sunk by suicide aircraft (with* **LSM-59**) *– no fatal casualties*

26 Japanese Destroyer
    Enoki   *Mined off Fukui, Inland Sea (35-28N 135-44E)*

30 Japanese Destroyer
    Nara   *Severely damaged by mine 6 miles (11 km) west-south-west of*
                Shimonoseki (33-54N 130-49E); towed to harbour and hulked

JULY 1945

1   Japanese Escort
    No. 72   *Torpedoed off Changsan, Yellow Sea (38-08N 124-38E) by US*
                submarine **Haddo**

PACIFIC

10 Japanese Minesweeper
    W.27   Torpedoed 55 miles (100 km) south of Tadosaki (39-20N 142-07E)
                        by US submarine **Haddo**

11 Japanese Escort Destroyer
    Sakura   Mined in Osaka Harbour (34-36N 135-28E)

The US Fast Carrier Task Force (TF 38) began operations against the Japanese Home
Islands on 10 July. This offensive lasted until the end of the war, with breaks only for
replenishment in the forward area and to avoid typhoons. Supplementing the USAAF
bombing campaign, the carrier aircraft delivered a series of strikes on strategic targets.
The first of these was against the vital coal traffic between Hokkaido and Honshu – on
14 and 15 July, all twelve of the large train ferries which carried 30 per cent of the coal
were sunk or damaged and 34 other merchant vessels were hit.

14 Japanese Escort Destroyers
    Tachibana   Sunk in Hakodate Harbour, Hokkaido (41-48N 141-41E) by US
                        carrier aircraft
    Yanagi   Severely damaged off Ashizaki, Tsugaru Straits, by US carrier
                        aircraft; ran aground, salved and towed to Ominato, where she
                        was again damaged by naval air attack on 9 August

    Japanese Escorts
    No. 65
    No. 74   Sunk 15 miles (27 km) south of Muroran, Hokkaido (42-21N 140-
                        59E) by US carrier aircraft

15 Japanese Escort
    No. 219   Sunk 2 miles (3,700 m) south-west of Hakodate (41-48N 140-41E)
                        by US carrier aircraft

    Japanese Minesweeper
    W.24   Sunk near Omasaki, Hokkaido (41-38N 140-41E) by US carrier
                        aircraft

16 Japanese Torpedo-Boat
    Kari   Torpedoed 220 miles (405 km) west-south-west of Macassar (05-
                        48S 115-53E) by US submarine **Baya**

    Japanese Gunboat (ex-Dutch Minelayer)
    Nankai (ex-   Torpedoed 150 miles (275 km) west of Soerabaja by US submarine
    Regulus)

18 Japanese Escort
    No. 112   Torpedoed Aniwa Wan, Sakhalin (46-06N 142-16E) by US
                        submarine **Barb**

19 US Destroyer
    Thatcher   Severely damaged by suicide aircraft off Okinawa (26-15N 127-
                        50E); not repaired

20 Japanese Minesweeper
    W.39   Torpedoed north-west of Mokpo, Yellow Sea (35-01N 125-42E) by
                        US submarine **Threadfin**

On 24 and 28 July the US carriers struck at the surviving heavy units of the Japanese
Navy, most of which had been laid up in various inlets in the Kure area due to lack of fuel
and, in the case of the carriers, lack of trained aircrews. The Royal Navy was
deliberately excluded from what amounted to the US Navy's revenge for Pearl Harbor –
but still managed to find one attractive target in the western Inland Sea.

24 Japanese Battleship
    Hyuga   Sunk near Kure (34-12N 132-31E) by US carrier aircraft – at least 12
                        bomb hits

154

Japanese Aircraft-Carrier
Amagi   *Grounded in shallow water off Kurahashi Jima (34-11N 132-30E)
             following bomb damage – capsized on the 28th due to flooding*

Japanese Cruiser
Tone   *Sunk in shallow water near Kure (34-14N 132-27E) – hit by three
             bombs*

Japanese Escort Carrier
Kaiyo   *Severely damaged 10 miles (18 km) north-west of Oita, Beppu Wan
             (33-21N 131-32E) by RN carrier aircraft; ship was subsequently
             mined, breaking her back, but remained afloat*

US Destroyer Escort
Underhill *pm: Torpedoed 150 miles (275 km) north-east of Luzon (19-20N
             126-42E) by manned torpedo ('Kaiten') launched by Japanese
             submarine* **I-53** *– 122 men lost; scuttled by US ships' gunfire*

RN Minesweeper
Squirrel   *Mined off Phuket Island, Gulf of Thailand, and scuttled 2½ hours
             later by RN gunfire – 7 men lost*

25 *Japanese Patrol Boat (ex-Destroyer)*
No. 2   *Torpedoed 175 miles (320 km) east of Soerabaja (07-06S 115-42E)
             by RN submarine* **Stubborn**

26 *RN Minesweeper*
Vestal   *1830: Severely damaged by JAAF suicide aircraft off Phuket Island
             (07-45N 98-29E) – 20 men lost; scuttled by gunfire of RN destroyer*
             Racehorse

*The US carrier aircraft returned to strike at the Kure area on 28 July; in addition to
sinking four more immobilized heavy units, they also found and sank a destroyer, while
further to the east RN carrier aircraft attacked three escort vessels.*

28 *Japanese Battleships*
Haruna   *Sunk in shallow water 8 miles (15 km) north-west of Kure (34-15N
             132-29E) by US carrier aircraft – 12 bomb hits sustained on the 24th
             and 28th*
Ise   *Sunk 5 miles (9 km) north-west of Kure (34-12N 132-31E) – at least
             12, and possibly 20, bomb hits on the 24th and 28th*

Japanese Cruisers
Aoba   *Sunk in Kure Dockyard (repairs suspended) by US carrier aircraft;
             aground after slight damage on the 24th, four bombs demolished
             her stern and caused extensive flooding*
Oyodo   *Sunk off Edachi (34-13N 132-25E); capsized due to flooding caused
             by numerous near-miss bombs*

Japanese Escort Destroyer
Nashi   *Sunk at Mitajirizaki, Kure (34-14N 132-30E) by US carrier aircraft.
             (Raised in 1955 and commissioned 1956-1972 as Japanese
             Maritime Self-Defence Force* **Wakaba***)*

Japanese Escorts
No. 6   *Severely damaged off Toba (34-28N 136-41E) by RN carrier aircraft
             – not repaired*
No. 30   *Sunk in Yura Straits (34-20N 135-00E) by RN carrier aircraft*
No. 45   *Severely damaged off Owase (34-05N 136-15E) by RN carrier
             aircraft – not repaired*

PACIFIC 29 *US Destroyer*
Callaghan   *0041: Hit by suicide aircraft 73 miles (75 km) west of Okinawa (picket station No 9 – 25-43N 126-55E); immobilized 0045 by explosion aft and ship abandoned – 47 men lost. Ship sank at 0235*

30 *US Cruiser*
Indianapolis *Torpedoed off Tinian (12-02N 134-48E) by Japanese submarine* **I-58** *– 883 men lost*

Japanese Destroyer
Hatsushimo   *Mined in Miyatsu Wan, 12 miles (22 km) west-north-west of Maizuru (35-33N 135-12E)*

Japanese Escorts
No. 2   *Sunk in shallow water in Maizuru Harbour by RN carrier aircraft*
Okinawa   *Sunk 6 miles (11 km) north-north-west of Maizuru (35-30N 135-21E) by US carrier aircraft*

31 *Japanese Cruiser*
Takao   *Sunk in Singapore Dockyard (laid up damaged – see 23 October 1944) by charges laid by crew of RN midget submarine* **XE-3**

AUGUST 1945

Typhoon warnings and withdrawal during the period surrounding the nuclear attack on Hiroshima resulted in a suspension of attacks by the carrier task forces. These were resumed on 9 August 1945 – the day of the Nagasaki nuclear strike.

7 *Japanese Escort*
No. 39   *Sunk off Kuche Is., Korea (35-06N 129-03E) by US air attack*

9 *Japanese Escorts*
Amakusa   *Sunk in Onagawa Wan (38-26N 141-30E) by RN carrier aircraft (HMS* **Formidable***). Lieutenant RN Gray, RCNVR, was awarded a posthumous Victoria Cross in leading this attack*
Inagi   *Sunk in Hachinohe Harbour (40-32N 141-30E) by US carrier aircraft*
Ikara   *Mined in Koguchi Channel, Nanao Wan (37-05N 137-00E)*

Japanese Minesweeper
W.33   *Sunk in Onagawa Wan by RN carrier aircraft*

Japanese Fast Transport
T.21   *Severely damaged off Tsuwajima (33-59N 132-31E) by USAAF air attack – sank the following day*

10 *Japanese Escort*
Ohama   *Sunk in the Onagawa area by Allied carrier aircraft*

Japanese Minesweeper
W.1   *Sunk off Yamada, Onagawa Wan (38-26N 141-30E) by Allied carrier aircraft*

Japanese Escort
No. 63   *1830: Mined in shallow water in Nanao Wan (37-08N 136-50E)*

Japanese Escort
No. 82   *Sunk 7 miles (13 km) south-south-west of Kumsudan, NE Korea (41-21N 130-00E) by Russian air attack*

13 *Japanese Escort*
   No. 4   *Torpedoed 50 miles (92 km) off Cerion Saki, Hokkaido (42-16N 142-12E) by US submarine* **Atule**

14 *Japanese Escorts*
   No. 13
   No. 47   *Torpedoed 14nm (26km) WNW of Maizuru, Kyushu (35-41N 134-38E) by US submarine* **Torsk**

The Japanese Government accepted the Allied demand for unconditional surrender on 14 August and in the Far East a cease-fire came into effect during the forenoon of the 15th. Diehard Kamikazes made last, unsuccessful, attempts to attack the Allied carrier task force on 15 August, but the only warship losses after the official cease-fire were Japanese.

15 *Japanese Escort*
   Kanju   *Sunk off Wonsan, Korea (39-10N 127-27E) by Russian air attack*

17 *Japanese Escort*
   No. 46   *Mined off Mokpo, Yellow Sea (34-51N 126-02E)*

18 *Japanese Escort*
   No. 213   *Sunk off Pusan, S. Korea (35-10N 129-00E) by Russian air attack*

23 *Japanese Escort*
   No. 75   *Disappeared while on passage from Wakhanai to Hokkaido – possibly mined*

Part Two:

Summary of Warship Classes and Particulars

The summary of ship types and particulars is intended to give brief outline details of all the major ships and classes that suffered loss during the 1939–45 war. Full details are to be found in a number of contemporary publications, such as *Jane's Fighting Ships, Les Flottes de Combat* and subsequent books of reference. Information is provided under the class lists as follows:

Type of Vessel: Generally the intended role for which the ship was built or modified prior to the outbreak of war.

Class Name: The commonly-accepted name of the class, which is not necessarily the designation given by the parent nation.

Number Built: The number of ships in service at the beginning of hostilities or completed before the end of the war. Ships lost or disposed of prior to 1939 (or 1941 in the case of the Soviet, Japanese and US Navies) are not included.

Period: The years between the laying-down of the first ship and the entry into service of the last to be completed during the war.

Names: The names, in alphabetical order, of all ships of the class lost (by any cause), seized or scuttled to avoid capture.

Displacement	Washington Treaty 'standard displacement'.
Length	Extreme length (overall).
Beam	Maximum waterline beam.
Guns	Number of guns of each calibre (20mm and above), expressed in inches (and mm where appropriate, except when the calibre is less than 100mm/3.9in). The number of weapons is that originally fitted or intended and does not include subsequent additions or removals.

Heavy anti-aircraft guns are described in three categories:
Dual-Purpose (DP) weapons fully capable of AA and surface roles, with appropriate fire-control;
Anti-Aircraft (AA) weapons intended primarily for AA use, with or without full fire-control;
High-Angle (HA) weapons intended primarily for surface fire but in mountings permitting AA fire, with or without fire-control.

Torpedo-tubes	Number of tubes and diameter of the torpedoes; torpedo reloads are shown, with the number when less than the full initial loaded outfit.
Mines	The maximum stowage of mines (other weapons often had to be landed for reasons of deck space or topweight).
Machinery	Designed horsepower: Steam turbines – shp Steam reciprocating – ihp Diesel motors – bhp =designed maximum speed in service (usually exceeded on trials, but more representative of speed attainable in wartime conditions).
Complement	Total number of officers and men of ships' companies, but excluding admirals' staffs, etc. (usually greatly exceeded in wartime).

ARGENTINA

Buenos Aires-class destroyers (similar to
Royal Navy 'G'-class destroyers)
7 built 1936–9
Lost **Corrientes**

Displacement	1,375 tons
Length	323ft (98.5m)
Beam	32.5ft (10m)
Guns	4 × 4.7in LA
Torpedo-tubes	8 × 21in
Machinery	34,000shp = 35.5kts
Complement	162

AUSTRALIA

'County'-class heavy cruisers
2 built 1927–8
Lost **Canberra**

Displacement	9,850 tons
Length	630ft (192m)
Beam	68ft (20.9m)
Guns	8 × 8in (203mm)
	8 × 4in (102mm)
	2 × 4 2pdr AA
Torpedo-tubes	8 × 21in
Machinery	80,000shp = 31.5kts
Complement	710

Amphion-class light cruisers
3 built 1934–5
Lost **Perth, Sydney**

Displacement	6,830 tons *(Sydney)*
	6,980 tons *(Perth)*
Length	555ft (169m)
Beam	57ft (17.3m)
Guns	8 × 6in (152mm)
	8 × 4in AA
Torpedo-tubes	8 × 21in
Machinery	72,000shp = 32.5kts
Complement	550

'N'-class destroyers
4 transferred (of 8 built) in 1941
Lost **Nestor**
Particulars as Royal Navy 'J'-class

'V & W'-class destroyers
4 built 1917–18
Lost **Vampire, Voyager, Waterhen**
Particulars as Royal Navy 'V & W'-class
destroyers

Yarra-class sloops (modified RN 'Grimsby'-
class)
4 built 1935–40
Lost **Parramatta, Yarra**

Displacement	1,060 tons
Length	266ft (81.1m)
Beam	36ft (11m)
Guns	3 × 4in AA

Machinery	2,000shp = 16.5kts
Complement	100

Bathurst-class minesweeper/escorts
56 built 1940–3
Lost **Armidale, Geelong, Wallaroo**

Displacement	650 tons
Length	186ft (56.7m)
Beam	31ft (9.5m)
Guns	1 × 4in AA
	1 × 20mm AA
Machinery	2,000ihp = 16/17kts
Complement	60

CANADA

'River'-class (RN 'A'-class) destroyers
2 built 1930–1
Lost **Saguenay, Skeena**

Displacement	1,337 tons
Length	321ft (97.9m)
Beam	34ft (10.3m)
Guns	4 × 4.7in LA
	2 × 2pdr AA
Torpedo-tubes	8 × 21in
Machinery	32,000shp = 35 kts
Complement	138

'River'-class (RN 'C'-class) destroyers
Leader + 4 built 1931–2, plus 2 ex-RN 'D'-class
transferred in 1940 and 1943
Lost **Assiniboine** (Leader), **Fraser, *Margaree,
Ottawa**
Particulars as Royal Navy 'D'-class, except
Assiniboine:

Displacement	1,390 tons
Complement	175

Margaree was HMS *Diana,* transferred in 1940
to replace HMCS *Fraser*

'Tribal'-class destroyers
4 built 1941–3
Lost **Athabaskan**

Displacement	1,927 tons
Length	377ft (115m)
Beam	36.5ft (11.1m)
Guns	6 × 4.7in HA
	2 × 4in AA
	1 × 4 2pdr AA
	20mm AA
Torpedo-tubes	4 × 21in
Machinery	44,000shp = 36kts
Complement	240

Bangor-class minesweepers
60 built 1940–3
Lost **Chedabucto, Clayoquot, Esquimalt,
Guysborough, Mulgrave**

Displacement	672 tons
Length	180ft (54.8m)
Beam	28.5ft (8.7m)

Guns	1 × 4in LA
	1 × 2pdr AA
Machinery	2,400ihp = 16kts
Complement	70

'Flower'-class corvettes
116 built 1940–4
Lost *Alberni, Charlottetown, Levis,*
Louisburg, Regina, Shawinigan, Spikenard,
Weyburn, Windflower, Trentonian
Particulars as Royal Navy 'Flower'-class
corvettes except *Trentonian*:

Displacement	980 tons
Length	208ft (63.5m)
Complement	109

'River-class frigates
60 built 1942–4
Lost *Chebogue, Magog, Teme, Valleyfield*
Particulars as Royal Navy 'River'-class frigates

DENMARK

'T.1'-class torpedo-boats
6 built 1928–34
Lost *Dragen*

Displacement	290 tons
Length	200ft (61m)
Beam	20ft (6m)
Guns	2 × 75mm LA
	2 × 20mm AA
Torpedo-tubes	8 × 18in (457mm)
Mines	20
Machinery	6,000shp = 28 kts
Complement	52

Fishery Protection Sloop *Ingolf* built 1933

Displacement	1,180 tons
Length	295ft (89.8m)
Beam	35ft (10.7m)
Guns	2 × 4.7in, 2 × 57mm,
	2 × 20mm AA
Machinery	2,950ihp = 16.5kts
Complement	66

Minelayer *Lindormen* built 1938–9

Displacement	500 tons
Length	170ft (52m)
Beam	29ft (8.8m)
Guns	2 × 75mm,
	3 × 20mm Madsen AA,
	150 mines
Machinery	1,200ihp = 15kts
Complement	58

FINLAND

Vainamoinen-class coast defence ships
2 built 1929–33
Lost *Ilmarinen*

| Displacement | 3,900 tons |

Length	305ft (93m)
Beam	53.5ft (16.3m)
Guns	4 × 10in (254mm)
	8 ×4.1in (105mm) AA
	4 × 40mm AA
	4 × 20mm AA
Machinery	4,800bhp = 15kts
Complement	343

FRANCE

Courbet-class battleships
2 built 1910–13
Lost *Courbet*

Displacement	23,200 tons
Length	551ft (168m)
Beam	92ft (28.2m)
Guns	12 × 12in (305mm)
	22 × 5.4in (138mm)
	7 × 75mm (2.95in) AA
	2 × 47mm AA
Machinery	28,000shp = 16kts (by 1939)
Complement	1,069

Bretagne-class battleships
2 built 1912–15
Lost *Bretagne, Provence*

Displacement	22,200 tons
Length	545ft (166m)
Beam	89ft (27m)
Guns	10 × 13.4in (340mm)
	14 × 5.4in
	8 × 75mm AA
Machinery	43,000shp = 21kts
Complement	1,190

Dunkerque-class battleships
2 built 1932–8
Lost *Dunkerque, Strasbourg*

Displacement	26,500 tons
Length	702ft (214m)
Beam	102ft (31m)
Guns	8 × 13in (330mm)
	16 × 5.1in (130mm) DP
	8 × 37mm AA
Machinery	100,000shp = 30kts
Complement	1,431

Suffren-class heavy cruisers
4 built 1926–32
Lost *Colbert, Dupleix, Foch*

Displacement	9,938 tons
Length	638ft (194m)
Beam	64ft (19.4m)
Guns	8 × 8in (203mm)
	8 × 90mm (3.54in) AA
	8 × 37mm AA
Torpedo-tubes	6 × 21.6in (550mm)
Machinery	100,000shp = 33kts
Complement	605

Heavy cruiser *Algériè*
one unit built 1931–4

Displacement	10,000 tons
Length	609ft (186m)
Beam	65.5ft (20m)
Guns	8 × 8in
	12 × 100mm (3.9in) AA
	8 × 37mm AA
Torpedo-tubes	6 × 21.6in
Machinery	84,000shp = 31kts
Complement	729

Duguay-Trouin-class light cruisers
3 built 1922–6
Lost **Lamotte-Picquet, Primauget**

Displacement	7,250 tons
Length	595ft (181m)
Beam	57.5ft (17.5m)
Guns	8 × 6.1in (155mm)
	4 × 75mm AA
Torpedo-tubes	12 × 21.6in
Machinery	102,000shp = 33kts
Complement	578

La Galissonnière-class light cruisers
6 built 1931–7
Lost **Jean de Vienne, La Galissionnière, Marseillaise**

Displacement	7,600 tons
Length	587ft (179m)
Beam	57ft (17.5m)
Guns	9 × 6in (152mm)
	8 × 90mm AA
Torpedo-tubes	4 × 21.6in
Machinery	81,000shp = 31kts
Complement	540

Minelaying cruiser **La Tour d'Auvergne**
one unit built 1928–31

Displacement	4,775 tons
Length	500ft (152m)
Beam	51ft (15.6m)
Guns	4 × 5.4in
	4 × 75mm AA
	2 × 37mm AA
Mines	
Machinery	57,000shp = 30kts
Complement	397

Seaplane-carrier **Commandant Teste**
one unit built 1927–32

Displacement	10,000 tons
Length	548ft (167m)
Beam	88.5ft (27m)
Guns	12 × 3.9in AA
	8 × 37mm AA
Aircraft	26 (4 × catapults)
Machinery	21,000shp = 20.5kts
Complement	686

Chacal-class flotilla leaders *(contre-torpilleurs)*
6 built 1922–7

Lost **Chacal, Jaguar, Léopard, Lynx, Panthère, Tigre**

Displacement	2,126 tons
Length	416ft (127m)
Beam	37.5ft (11.4m)
Guns	4 × 5.1in LA
Torpedo-tubes	6 × 21.6in
Machinery	55,000shp = 35.5 kts
Complement	195

Guépard-class flotilla leaders
6 built 1927–31
Lost **Bison, Guépard, Lion, Valmy, Vauban, Verdun**

Displacement	2,436 tons
Length	427ft (130m)
Beam	38.5ft (11.8m)
Guns	5 × 5.4in LA
	4 × 37mm AA
Torpedo-tubes	6 × 21.6in
Machinery	64,000shp = 37kts
Complement	230

Aigle-class flotilla leaders
6 built 1928–34
Lost **Aigle, Albatros, Epervier, Gerfaut, Milan, Vautour**

Displacement	2,440 tons
Length	422ft (128.5m)
Beam	39ft (11.8m)
Guns	
& Torpedo-tubes	as 'Guépard'-class
Machinery	64,000shp = 36kts
Complement	230

Vauquelin-class flotilla leaders
6 built 1931–4
Lost **Cassard, Chevalier Paul, Kersaint, Maillé Brézé, Tartu, Vauquelin**
as *Aigle*-class, except

Length	424ft (129.3m)
Torpedo-tubes	7 × 21.6in

Le Fantasque-class flotilla leaders
6 built 1931–6
Lost **L'Audacieux, L'Indomptable, Le Malin**

Displacement	2,570 tons
Length	434ft (132m)
Beam	40.5ft (12.4m)
Guns	as 'Guépard'-class
Torpedo-tubes	9 × 21.6in
Machinery	74,000shp = 37kts
	(all exceeded
	100,000shp/43kts on
	trials)
Complement	210

Mogador-class flotilla leaders
2 built 1936–8
Lost **Mogador, Volta**

Displacement	2,884 tons
Length	451ft (137.5m)

Beam	41.5ft (12.7m)
Guns	8 × 5.4in LA
	2 × 37mm AA
Torpedo-tubes	10 × 21.6in
Machinery	92,000shp = 39kts
Complement	264

Bourrasque-class destroyers
12 built 1923–8
Lost **Bourrasque, Cyclone, Orage, Siroco, Tornade, Tramontane, Trombe, Typhon**

Displacement	1,319 tons
Length	347ft (105.8mm)
Beam	33ft (10.1m)
Guns	4 × 5.1in LA
	2 × 37mm AA
Torpedo-tubes	6 × 21.6in
Machinery	31,000shp = 33kts
Complement	138

L'Adroit-class destroyers
14 built 1925–31
Lost **L'Adroit, Bordelais, Boulonnais, Brestois, Foudroyant, Fougueux, Frondeur, Le Mars, La Palme, La Railleuse**

Displacement	1,378 tons
Length	352ft (107.2m)
Beam	33ft (10.1m)
Armament	as *Bourrasque*-class
Machinery	33,000shp = 33kts
Complement	140

Le Hardi-class destroyers
8 built 1936–40
Lost **L'Adroit**(2nd), **Bison**(2nd), **Casque, Cyclone, Foudroyant, Le Hardi, Mameluck, Siroco**

Displacement	1,772 tons
Length	384.5ft (117.2m)
Beam	33ft (10.1m)
Guns	6 × 5.1in HA
	2 ×37mm AA
Torpedo-tubes	7 × 21.6in
Machinery	58,000shp = 37kts
Complement	175

Escort destroyer **La Combattante**
built 1941–2 and transferred 1942
see Royal Navy 'Hunt'-class (Group III)

La Melpomène-class torpedo-boats
12 built 1933–8
Lost **Baliste, La Bayonnaise, Bombarde, Branlebas, L'Iphigénie, La Pomone, La Poursuivante**

Displacement	610 tons
Length	265ft (80.7m)
Beam	26ft (8m)
Guns	2 × 3.9in LA
Torpedo-tubes	2 × 21.6in
Machinery	22,000shp = 34.5kts
Complement	105

Dumont d'Urville-class colonial sloop (aviso)
8 built 1927–40
Lost **Amiral Charner, Bougainville (I), D'Entrecasteaux, D'Iberville, Rigault de Genouilly**

Displacement	1,969 tons
Length	340ft (103.7m)
Beam	42ft (12.7m)
Guns	3 × 5.4in LA
	4 × 37mm AA
Machinery	3,200bhp = 15.5kts
Complement	135

Ardent-class avisos (escorts)
2 built 1916–17 in service in 1939
Lost **Dédaigneuse, Etourdi, Tapageuse**

Displacement	266 tons
Length	197.5ft (60.2m)
Beam	24ft (7.2m)
Guns	2 × 3.9in LA
Machinery	1,500ihp = 14–16kts
Complement	60

Marne-class avisos (escorts)
4 built 1916–17 in service in 1939
Lost **Marne, Suippe, Yser**

Displacement	600 tons
Length	256ft (78m)
Beam	29ft (8.9m)
Guns	4 × 3.9in LA
	2 × 65mm (2.56in) LA
Machinery	4,000shp = 20kts
Complement	107

Arras-class avisos (escorts)
11 built 1918–20 in service in 1939
Lost **Les Eparges, Tahure, Vauquois**

Displacement	644 tons
Length	246ft (75m)
Beam	27.5ft (8.4m)
Guns	2 × 5.4in LA
	1 ×75mm AA
Machinery	5,000shp = 19kts
Complement	103

Aviso **Conquérante**
built 1917

Displacement	374 tons
Length	218ft (66.4m)
Beam	26ft (7.9m)
Guns	2 × 3.9in LA
Machinery	1,500bhp = 17kts
Complement	54

'Flower'-class corvettes
8 built 1939–41, of which 1 was from a French Navy order and the other 7 were transferred from the Royal Navy
Lost **Alysse** (ex-RN), **La Bastiaise, Mimosa** (ex-RN)
Details as RN 'Flower'-class

Granit-class avisos (minesweepers)
2 built 1918
Lost **Granit, Meulière**

Displacement	354 tons
Length	189ft (57.6m)
Beam	26ft (7.9m)
Guns	1 × 65mm LA
Machinery	550ihp = 12.5kts
Complement	63

Dubourdieu-class avisos (minesweepers)
2 built 1918
Lost **Enseigne Henri**

Displacement	433 tons
Length	197.5ft (60.2m)
Beam	27ft (8.2m)
Guns	1 × 5.4in
	1 × 3.9in LA
Machinery	2,000shp = 16.7kts
Complement	74

Elan-class avisos (minesweepers)
13 built 1936–40
Lost **La Batailleuse, Commandant Rivière, La
Curieuse, Elan, L'Impétueuse**

Displacement	630 tons
Length	256ft (78m)
Beam	28ft (8.5m)
Guns	1 or 2 3.9in AA
Machinery	4,000bhp = 20kts
Complement	90

Chamois-class avisos (minesweepers)
9 built 1936–42
Lost **Amiral Sénès, Chamois, Matelot Leblanc,
Rageot de la Touche, La Surprise**
Particulars as *Elan*-class, except:

Displacement	647 tons

Armed merchant cruisers
13 commissioned 1930–40
Lost **Bougainville (II)**

Tonnage	4,500 grt
Length	376ft (114.5m)
Beam	52ft (15.8m)
Guns	7 × 5.4in
	2 × 75mm AA
	2 × 37mm AA
Machinery	5,200bhp = 17kts

GERMANY

Schlesien-class battleships (pre-dreadnoughts)
2 built 1906–8 in service in 1939
Lost **Schlesien, Schleswig-Holstein**

Displacement	13,200 tons
Length	419ft (127.6m)
Beam	73ft (22.2m)
Guns	4 × 11in (280mm)
	6 × 4.1in (105mm) AA
	4 × 37mm AA
	4 × 20mm AA
Machinery	17,000ihp = 16kts
Complement	600

Bismarck-class battleships
2 built 1937–41
Lost **Bismarck, Tirpitz**

Displacement	41,700 tons
	42,900 tons (*Tirpitz*)
Length	822ft (250m)
Beam	118ft (36m)
Guns	8 × 15in (380mm)
	12 × 5.9in (150mm)
	16 × 4.1in AA
	16 × 37mm AA
	20mm AA
Torpedo-tubes	8 × 21in (533mm)
	(*Tirpitz*)
Machinery	163,000shp = 31kts
Complement	1,905

Scharnhorst-class battlecruisers
2 built 1936–9
Lost **Gneisenau, Scharnhorst**

Displacement	31,850 tons
Length	771ft (235m)
Beam	98ft (30m)
Guns	9 × 11in
	12 × 5.9in
	14 × 4.1in AA
	16 × 37mm AA
	20mm AA
Torpedo-tubes	6 × 21in
Machinery	160,000shp = 31kts
Complement	1,840

Deutschland-class armoured cruisers ('pocket
battleships')
3 built 1930–5
Lost **Admiral Graf Spee, Admiral Scheer,
Lützow**

Displacement	11,700 tons
	12,100 tons (*Graf Spee*)
Length	616ft (187.9m)
Beam	67.5ft (20.6m)
	70ft (21.33m) (*Graf Spee*)
Guns	6 × 11in
	8 × 5.9in
	6 × 4.1in AA
	8 × 37mm AA
	20mm AA
Torpedo-tubes	8 × 21in
Machinery	56,000bhp = 26kts
Complement	1,000

Hipper-class heavy cruisers
3 built 1937–41
Lost **Blücher, Admiral Hipper**

Displacement	14,050 tons
Length	675ft (206m)
Beam	70ft (21.33m)

Guns	8 × 8in (203mm)
	12 × 4.1in AA
	12 × 37mm AA
	20mm AA
Torpedo-tubes	12 × 21in (with reloads)
Machinery	132,000shp = 32kts
Complement	1,382

Light cruiser **Emden**
one unit built 1924–6

Displacement	5,600 tons
Length	510ft (155.5m)
Beam	47ft (14.3m)
Guns	8 × 5.9in
	3 × 88mm (3.5in) AA
	4 × 37mm AA
	20mm AA
Torpedo-tubes	4 × 21in
Mines	120
Machinery	46,000shp = 29kts
Complement	630

Königsberg-class light cruisers
3 built 1926–9
Lost **Karlsruhe, Köln, Königsberg**

Displacement	6,650 tons
Length	570ft (174m)
Beam	50ft (15.2m)
Guns	9 × 5.9in
	6 × 88mm AA
	8 × 37mm AA
	20mm AA
Torpedo-tubes	12 × 21in (with reloads)
Mines	120
Machinery	68,000shp = 32kts
Complement	610

Light cruiser **Leipzig**
one unit built 1928–30

Displacement	6,515 tons
Length	580ft (177m)
Beam	53.5ft (16.3m)
Guns	9 × 5.9in
	8 × 88mm AA
	8 × 37mm AA
Torpedo-tubes	12 × 21in (with reloads)
Machinery	66,000shp
	+ 12,400bhp = 32kts
Complement	650

'Zerstörer 1934'-class destroyers
4 built 1934–7
Lost **Z.1 Leberecht Maass, Z.2 Georg Thiele, Z.3 Max Schultz**

Displacement	2,232 tons
Length	391ft (119m)
Beam	37ft (11.3m)
Guns	5 × 5in (127mm) LA
	4 × 37mm AA
	20mm AA
Torpedo-tubes	8 × 21in (with reloads)
Mines	60

| Machinery | 63,000shp = 36kts |
| Complement | 325 |

'Zerstörer 1934A'-class destroyers
12 built 1934–8
Lost **Z.7 Hermann Schoemann, Z.8 Bruno Heinemann, Z.9 Wolfgang Zenker, Z.11 Bernd von Arnim, Z.12 Erich Giese, Z.13 Erich Koellner, Z.16 Friedrich Eckoldt**
Particulars as 'Z.34'-class, except:

Displacement	2,270 tons
Length	397ft (121m)
Beam	37ft (11.3m)

'Zerstörer 1936'-class destroyers
6 built 1936–9
Lost **Z.17 Diether von Roeder, Z.18 Hans Lüdemann, Z.19 Hermann Kunne, Z.21 Wilhelm Heidkamp, Z.22 Anton Schmitt**
Particulars as 'Z.34'-class, except:

Displacement	2,411 tons
Length	404ft (123m)
	410ft (*Z.21–Z.22*)
Beam	39ft (11.8m)

'Zerstörer 1936A'-class destroyers (also known as 'Narvik'-class)
12 built 1939–43
Lost **Z.23, Z.24, Z.26, Z.27, Z.28, Z.32**

Displacement	2,603 tons
Length	417ft (127m)
Beam	39ft (12m)
Guns	5 × 5.9in HA
	4 × 5.9in HA (*Z.26*)
	4 × 37mm AA
	20mm AA
Torpedo-tubes	8 × 21in (with reloads)
Mines	60
Machinery	70,000shp = 36kts
Complement	332

'Zerstörer 1936A (Mob.)'-class destroyers
3 built 1940–3
Lost **Z.37**
Particulars as 'Z 1936A'-class

'Zerstörer 1936B'-class destroyers
3 built 1941–4
Lost **Z.35, Z.36, Z.43**
Particulars as 'Z 1936A'-class, except:

Displacement	2,527 tons
Guns	5 × 5in
Mines	76

Callenburgh-class destroyer **ZH.1**
seized 1940 – ex-Netherlands *Gerard Callenburgh*

Displacement	1,628 tons
Length	350ft (106.7m)
Beam	35ft (10.6m)
Guns	5 × 4.7in (120mm) LA
	4 × 37mm AA

	20mm AA
Torpedo-tubes	8 × 21in
Mines	24
Machinery	45,000shp = 36kts
Complement	230

Vasilevs Georgios-class destroyer **Hermes**
seized 1941 – ex-Greek Vasilevs Georgios I
Particulars as Greek 'Vasilevs Georgios'-class,
except:

Complement	220

'Torpedoboote 1923'-class torpedo-boats (also
known as 'Möwe'-class)
6 built 1924–8
Lost **Albatros, Falke, Greif, Kondor, Möwe,
Seeadler**

Displacement	924 tons
Length	288ft (87.7m)
	285ft (87m) (*Möwe*)
Beam	27.5ft (8.4m)
Guns	3 × 4.1in LA
	4 × 37mm AA
Torpedo-tubes	6 × 21in
Mines	30
Machinery	23,000shp = 33kts
Complement	120

'Torpedoboote 1924'-class torpedo-boats (also
known as *Wolf*-class)
6 built 1926–9
Lost **Iltis, Jaguar, Leopard, Luchs, Tiger, Wolf**

Displacement	933 tons
Length	304ft (92.6m)
Beam	28ft (8.7m)
Armament	as 'T.1923'-class, except
Guns	3 × 5in LA (*Leopard, Luchs*)
Machinery	23,000shp = 34kts
Complement	129

'Torpedoboote 1935'-class
12 built 1937–40
Lost **T.1, T.2, T.3, T.5, T.6, T.7, T.8, T.9, T.10**

Displacement	844 tons
Length	286ft (87.1m)
Beam	28ft (8.6m)
Guns	1 × 4.1in AA
	5 – 8 × 20mm AA
Torpedo-tubes	6 × 21in
Mines	30
Machinery	28,000shp = 34.5kts
Complement	119

'Torpedoboote 1937'-class torpedo-boats
9 built 1938–42
Lost **T.13, T.15, T.16, T.18**
Particulars as 'T.1935'-class, except:

Displacement	853 tons
Length	289ft (88.1m)
Beam	29ft (8.9m)

'Torpedoboote 1939'-class torpedo-boats
15 built 1940–4
Lost **T.22, T.24, T.25, T.26, T.27, T.29, T.30, T.31**

Displacement	1,294 tons
Length	336ft (102.5m)
Beam	33ft (10m)
Guns	4 × 4.1in AA
	4 × 37mm AA
	9 × 20mm AA
Torpedo-tubes	6 × 21in
Mines	50
Machinery	29,000shp = 32.5kts
Complement	206

La Melpomène-class torpedo-boats (ex-French)
5 seized 1943
Lost **TA.9** (ex-*Bombarde*), **TA.10** (ex-*La
Pomone*), **TA.11** (ex-*L'Iphigénie*), **TA.12** (ex-*Baliste*), **TA.13** (ex-*La Bayonnaise*)
Particulars as French *La Melpomène*-class,
except

Guns	2 × 3.9in
	2 × 37mm AA
	4 × 20mm AA
Torpedo-tubes	(removed)
Complement	109

Torpedo-boat **TA.14** (ex-*Turbine*)
Italian destroyer seized in 1943
Particulars as Italian *Turbine*-class

Torpedo-boat **TA.15** (ex-*Francesco Crispi*)
Italian vessel seized in 1943
Particulars as Italian *Sella*-class

Curtatone-class torpedo-boats (ex-Italian)
2 seized in 1943
Lost **TA.16** (ex-*Castelfidardo*), **TA.19** (ex-*Calatafimi*)
Particulars as Italian 'Curtatone'-class, except:

Guns	2 × 4in (102mm) LA
	6 × 20mm AA
Torpedo-tubes	2 × 21in
Mines	10
Complement	130

Palestro-class torpedo-boats (ex-Italian)
2 seized in 1943
Lost **TA.17** (ex-*San Martino*), **TA.18** (ex-*Solferino*)
Particulars as Italian *Palestro*-class, except
armament alterations as *TA.16*

Torpedo-boat **TA.20** (ex-*Audace*)
Italian vessel seized in 1943
Particulars as Italian *Audace*, except:

Guns	2 × 4in LA
	8 × 20mm AA
Mines	20
Complement	138

Escort **TA.21** (ex-*Insidioso*)
Italian vessel seized in 1943
Particulars as Italian **Insidioso**

Pilo-class torpedo-boats (ex-Italian)
2 seized in 1943
Lost **T.22** (ex-*Giuseppe Missori*), **T.32, T.34,
TA.35** (ex-*Giuseppe Dezza*), **T.36**
Particulars as Italian *Pilo*-class, except

Guns	2 × 4in LA
	6 × 20mm AA
Complement	130

Animoso-class escort destroyers (ex-Italian)
3 seized in 1943
Lost **TA.23** (ex-*Impavido*), **TA.25** (ex-*Ardito*),
TA.26 (ex-*Intrepido*)
Particulars as Italian 'Animoso'-class

Ariete-class torpedo-boats (ex-Italian)
13 seized in 1943 and completed to 1944
Lost **TA.24** (ex-*Arturo*), **TA.27** (ex-*Auriga*),
TA.28 (ex-*Rigel*), **TA.29** (ex-*Eridano*), **TA.30**
(ex-*Dragone*), **TA.36** (ex-*Stella Polare*), **TA.37**
(ex-*Gladio*), **TA.38** (ex-*Spada*), **TA.39** (ex-
Daga), **TA.40** (ex-*Pugnale*), **TA.41** (ex-*Lancia*),
TA.42 (ex-*Alabarda*), **TA.45** (ex-*Spica (II)*)
Particulars as Italian *Ariete*-class

Torpedo-boat **TA.31** (ex-*Dardo*)
Italian destroyer seized in 1943
Particulars as Italian 'Dardo'-class

Torpedo-boat **TA.32** (ex-Italian *Premuda*, ex-
Yugoslav *Dubrovnik*)
former Yugoslav flotilla leader seized in 1943
Particulars as *Dubrovnik*

Torpedo-boat **TA.43** (ex-Italian *Sebenico*, ex-
Yugoslav *Beograd*)
former Yugoslav destroyer seized in 1943
Particulars as *Beograd*-class destroyers

Torpedo-boat **TA.44** (ex-*Antonio Pigafetta*)
Italian destroyer seized in 1943
Particulars as Italian *Navigatori*-class

Old torpedo-boat **TA.48** (ex-*T 7*)
ex-Italian, ex-Yugoslav vessel seized in 1943
Particulars as Yugoslav '76 T'-class

Torpedo-boat **TA.49** (ex-*Lira*)
Italian torpedo-boat seized in 1943
Particulars as Italian *Spica*-class

'F'-class escorts
10 built 1934–6
Lost **F.3** (*Hai*), **F.5**, **F.6** (*Königin Luise*), **F.9**

Displacement	768 tons
	712 tons (*F.5*)
Length	263ft (80.2m)
	249ft (76m) (*F.5*)
Beam	29ft (8.8m)
Guns	2 × 4.1in LA
	4 × 37mm AA
	4 × 20mm AA
Machinery	14,000shp = 26kts
Complement	121

Sans Souci-class fast escorts (*Schnell Geleit*)
(ex-French seaplane-tenders)
4 seized in 1940 and completed 1942–4
Lost **SG.2** (*Saturnus*), **SG.3** (*Jupiter*)

Displacement	1,372 tons
Length	312ft (95m)
Beam	40ft (12.2m)
Guns	3 × 4.1in AA
	4 × 37mm AA
	10 – 14 × 20mm AA
Machinery	3,600bhp = 16kts
Complement	178

Chamois-class fast escorts (ex-French)
2 seized in 1942
Lost **SG.14** (ex-*Matelot Leblanc*), **SG.15** (ex-
Rageot de la Touche)
Particulars as French *Chamois*-class

Elan-class fast escorts (ex-French)
2 seized in 1942
Lost **SG.19** (ex-*Elan*), **SG.23** (ex-*La Batailleuse*)
Particulars as French *Elan*-class

'Generali'-class fast escort **SG.20** (ex-*Generale
Achille Papa*)
Italian torpedo-boat seized in 1943
Particulars as Italian 'Generali'-class

Bangor-class submarine-chaser (*U-jaeger*)
Uj.2109 (ex-*Widnes*) captured 1941
Particulars as Royal Navy *Bangor*-class
minesweeper
(AA armament augmented)

Gabbiano-class submarine-chasers (ex-Italian)
seized (some incomplete) 1943
Lost **Uj.201** (ex-*Egeria*), **Uj.202** (ex-
Melpomene), **Uj.205** (ex-*Colubrina*), **Uj.208** (ex-
Spingarda), **Uj.2221** (ex-*Vespa*), **Uj.2222** (ex-
Tuffetto), **Uj.2223** (ex-*Marangone*), **Uj.2226** (ex-
Artemide), **Uj.2227** (ex-*Persefone*), **Uj.2228** (ex-
Euterpe), **Uj.6081** (ex-*Camoscio*), **Uj.6082** (ex-
Antilope), **Uj.6083** (ex-*Capriolo*), **Uj.6084** (ex-
Alce), **Uj.6085** (ex-*Renna*)

Displacement	670 tons
Length	211ft (64.4m)
Beam	28.5ft (8.7m)
Guns	1 × 3.9in (100mm) HA
	7 × 20mm AA
Machinery	3,500bhp = 17.5kts
Complement	110

'K.1'-class escort (ex-Netherlands)
3 gunboats captured (1 completed and 2

incomplete) in 1940
Lost *K.1*, *K.2*

Displacement	1,200 tons
Length	256ft (78m)
Beam	33.5ft (10.2m)
Guns	4 × 4.7in LA
	4 × 37mm AA
	12 × 20mm AA
Mines	200
Machinery	2,770bhp = 14.5kts
Complement	161

AA Ship (ex-Netherlands scout cruiser) *Niobe*
built 1896–8 as *Gelderland*

Displacement	3,500 tons
Length	311ft (94.7m)
Beam	48ft (14.7m)
Guns	4 × 2in, 4.1in HA,
	40mm Bofors,
	20mm AA
Machinery	10,000ihp = 16kts
Complement	n/k

Minelayer *Brummer (I)*
one unit built 1924–6

Displacement	2,410 tons
Length	354ft (108m)
Beam	44ft (13.4m)
Guns	4 × 4.1in AA
	2 × 88mm AA
	4 × 37mm AA
Mines	450
Machinery	8,000shp = 20kts
Complement	182

Minelayer *Bremse*
one unit built 1929–30

Displacement	1,460 tons
Length	318ft (97m)
Beam	31ft (9.5m)
Guns	4 × 5in LA
	8 × 20mm AA
Mines	350
Machinery	26,000bhp = 27kts
Complement	192

Minelayer *Brummer (II)* (ex-*Olav Tryggvason*)
Norwegian vessel seized in 1940
Particulars as Norwegian *Olav Tryggvason*,
except:

Guns	4 × 5in LA
	2 × 37mm AA
	20mm AA
Complement	168

'M-Boote Type 1915'-class minesweepers
built 1915–18
Lost *M.61*, *M.85*, *M.89*, *M.136*, *M.502*, *M.504*,
M.507, *M.511*, *M.515*, *M.522*, *M.529*, *M.533*,
M.534 (Frauenlob), *M.538*, *M.546*, *M.550*,
M.557, *M.575*, *M.584*

Displacement	590–610 tons
Length	195ft (59.3m)
Beam	24.5ft (7.4m)
Guns	1 × 4.1in LA
	2 × 20mm AA
Mines	30
Machinery	1,850ihp = 16kts
Complement	51

'M-boote Type 1935'-class
built 1936–41
Lost *M.1*, *M.2*, *M.5*, *M.6*, *M.8*, *M.10*, *M.11*,
M.13, *M.14*, *M.15*, *M.16*, *M.18*, *M.19*, *M.20*,
M.22, *M.23*, *M.37*, *M.39*

Displacement	682 tons
Length	223ft (68.1m)
Beam	28.5ft (8.7m)
Guns	2 × 4.1in LA
	2 × 37mm AA
	20mm AA
Mines	30
Machinery	3,500ihp = 18kts
Complement	104

'M-boote Type 1938'-class minesweepers
12 built 1940–1
Lost *M.25*, *M.26*, *M.27*, *M.31*, *M.36*
Particulars as 'Type 35'-class, except:

Displacement	713 tons
Length	233ft (71m)
Beam	30ft (9.2m)
Complement	97

'M-boote Type 1935/39'-class minesweepers
built 1940–2
Lost *M.83*, *M.84*, *M.101*, *M.103*, *M.132*, *M.133*,
M.152, *M.153*, *M.156*, *M.206*, *M.256*
Particulars as 'Type 35'-class, except:

Displacement	685 tons
Length	224.5ft (68.4m)

'M-boote Type 1940'-class minesweepers
131 built 1942–5
Lost *M.262*, *M.263*, *M.264*, *M.266*, *M.271*,
M.273, *M.274*, *M.276*, *M.292*, *M.293*, *M.301*,
M.303, *M.304*, *M.305*, *M.307*, *M.325*, *M.329*,
M.343, *M.344*, *M.345*, *M.346*, *M.347*, *M.363*,
M.366, *M.367*, *M.368*, *M.370*, *M.372*, *M.376*,
M.381, *M.382*, *M.383*, *M.384*, *M.385*, *M.387*,
M.402, *M.403*, *M.412*, *M.413*, *M.414*, *M.416*,
M.421, *M.422*, *M.426*, *M.427*, *M.428*, *M.433*,
M.435, *M.438*, *M.444*, *M.445*, *M.451*, *M.455*,
M.459, *M.462*, *M.463*, *M.468*, *M.469*, *M.471*,
M.483, *M.486*, *M.489*

Displacement	543 tons
Length	204ft (62.3m)
Beam	29ft (8.9m)
Guns	1 × 4.1in LA
	1 × 37mm AA
	20mm AA
Machinery	2,400ihp = 17kts
Complement	87

'M-Boote Type 1943'-class minesweeper
20 built 1944–5
Lost *M.802, M.804, M.805*
Particulars as 'Type 40'-class, except:

Displacement	582 tons
Length	222ft (67.8m)
Beam	29.5ft (9m)

'Van Amstel'-class minesweeper *M.553* (ex-*Willem van Ewijck II*)
Netherlands vessel seized incomplete in 1940
Particulars as Netherlands *van Amstel*-class

Merchant raiders
11 commissioned and operational 1939–43
Lost *Atlantis, Komet, Kormoran, Michel, Pinguin, Stier, Thor*

Tonnages	3,287grt – 8,736grt
Length & Beam	(various)
Guns	6 × 5.9in (all)
	1 × 75mm AA
	(*Atlantis, Pinguin*)
	2 – 4 × 37mm AA
	20mm AA
Torpedo-tubes	2 or 4 × 21in
Mines	60–320
Machinery	diesel engines
	= 14–17kts
Complement	345 – 420

GREAT BRITAIN

AND ALLIED NAVIES UNDER BRITISH
CONTROL

King George V-class battleships
4 built 1912–14
Lost *Centurion*

Displacement	25,000 tons
Length	596ft (181m)
Beam	89ft (27m)
Guns	Light AA only
Machinery	31,000shp = 16kts
Complement	250

Queen Elizabeth-class battleships
5 built 1913–15
Lost *Barham, Queen Elizabeth*

Displacement	30,600–32,700 tons
Length	639.75ft (195m)
Beam	104ft (31.7m)
Guns	8 × 15in (380mm)
	Barham:
	12 × 6in (152mm)
	8 × 4in (102mm) AA
	2 × 8 2pdr (40mm) AA
	Queen Elizabeth:
	20 × 4.5in (114mm) DP
	4 × 8 2pdr AA
Torpedo-tubes	2 × 21in (533mm)
	(*Barham*)
Machinery	75–80,000shp = 24kts
Complement	1,200

Royal Sovereign-class battleships
5 built 1914–16
Lost *Royal Oak*

Displacement	29,150 tons
Length	620.5ft (189m)
Beam	102.5ft (31.2m)
Guns	8 × 15in
	12 × 6in
	8 × 4in AA
	2 × 8 2pdr AA
Torpedo-tubes	4 × 21in (*Royal Oak*)
Machinery	40,000shp = 21.5kts
Complement	1,150

King George V-class battleships
5 built 1939–42
Lost *Prince of Wales*

Displacement	36,700 tons
Length	745ft (227m)
Beam	103ft (31.4m)
Guns	10 × 14in (356mm)
	16 × 5.25in (133mm) DP
	6 × 8 2pdr AA
Machinery	110,000shp = 29kts
Complement	1,560

Repulse-class battlecruisers
2 built 1914–16
Lost *Repulse*

Displacement	32,000 tons
Length	794ft (242m)
Beam	103ft (31.4m)
Guns	6 × 15in
	12 × 4in LA
	8 × 4in AA
	2 × 8 2pdr AA
Torpedo-tubes	8 × 21in
Machinery	112,000shp = 29kts
Complement	1,200

Battlecruiser *Hood*
one unit built 1918–20

Displacement	42,100 tons
Length	860.5ft (131m)
Beam	105ft (32m)
Guns	8 × 15in
	12 × 5.5in (140mm)
	8 × 4in AA
	3 × 8 2pdr AA
Torpedo-tubes	4 × 21in
Machinery	144,000shp = 31kts
Complement	1,350

Erebus-class monitors
2 built 1916–17
Lost *Terror*

Displacement	7,200 tons
Length	405ft (123.5m)
Beam	88ft (27m)
Guns	2 × 15in
	8 × 4in LA
	2 × 3in AA

Machinery	6,000shp = 12kts
Complement	315

'C' (*Caledon*)-class light cruisers
4 built 1916–17 (one sunk 1918)
Lost **Calypso**

Displacement	4,180 tons
Length	450ft (137m)
Beam	43ft (13m)
Guns	5 × 6in
	2 × 3in AA
	2 × 2pdr AA
Torpedo-tubes	8 × 21in
Machinery	40,000shp = 29kts
Complement	400

'C' (*Coventry*)-class AA cruisers
5 built 1916–18
Lost **Curlew, Coventry**

Displacement	4,200 tons
Length	451.5ft (137.6m)
Beam	43.5ft (13.3m)
Guns	10 × 4in AA
	2 × 8 2pdr AA
Machinery	40,000shp = 29kts
Complement	400

'C' (*Capetown*)-class AA cruisers
5 built 1917–22
Lost **Cairo, Calcutta, Carlisle, Curacoa**

Displacement	4,200 tons
Length	451.5ft (137.6m)
Beam	43.5ft (13.3m)
Guns	8 × 4in AA
	1 × 4 2pdr AA
Machinery	40,000shp = 29kts
Complement	400

'Improved *Birmingham*'-class heavy cruiser
5 built 1918–20 in service in 1939
Lost **Effingham**

Displacement	9,550 tons
Length	605ft (184.4m)
Beam	65ft (19.8m)
Guns	7 × 7.5in (190mm)
	4 × 4in AA
	2 × 4 2pdr
Torpedo-tubes	4 × 21in
Machinery	65,000shp = 30.5kts
Complement	720

'D'-class light cruisers
8 built 1918–22
Lost **Delhi, Dragon** (Polish), **Dunedin, Durban**

Displacement	4,850 tons
Length	472.5ft (144m)
Beam	46.5ft (14.2m)
Guns	*Delhi:*
	5 × 5in (127mm) DP
	2 × 4 2pdr AA
	others:
	6 × 6in

	3 × 4in AA
	2 × 2pdr AA
Torpedo-tubes	12 × 21in
Machinery	40,000shp = 29kts
Complement	450

'County'-class heavy cruisers
11 built 1926–9
Lost **Cornwall, Dorsetshire**

Displacement	9,750–10,000 tons
Length	630ft (192m)
Beam	66ft (20m)
Guns	8 × 8in (203mm)
	8 × 4in AA
	2 × 4 2pdr AA (*Cornwall*)
	2 × 8 2pdr (*Dorsetshire*)
	20mm AA
Torpedo-tubes	8 × 21in (*Dorsetshire* only)
Machinery	80,000shp = 32.5kts
Complement	680 (*Cornwall*)
	650 (*Dorsetshire*)

York-class heavy cruisers
2 built 1928–30
Lost **York, Exeter**

Displacement	8,300 tons
Length	575ft (175m)
Beam	58ft (17.7m)
Guns	6 × 8in
	4 × 4in AA
	2 × 4 2pdr AA (*Exeter* only)
	20mm AA
Torpedo-tubes	6 × 21in
Machinery	80,000shp = 32kts
Complement	600

Leander-class light cruisers
5 built 1931–5
Lost **Neptune**

Displacement	7,175 tons
Length	554ft (169m)
Beam	55ft (16.8m)
Guns	8 × 6in
	8 × 4in AA
	2 × 4 2pdr AA
Torpedo-tubes	8 × 21in
Machinery	72,000shp = 32.5kts
Complement	550

Arethusa-class light cruisers
4 built 1934–7
Lost **Galatea, Penelope**

Displacement	5,250 tons
Length	506ft (154m)
Beam	51ft (15.5m)
Guns	6 × 6in
	8 × 4in AA
	2 × 4 2pdr AA
Torpedo-tubes	6 × 21in

Machinery   64,000shp = 32kts
Complement   450

'Town'-class (Groups I and II) light cruisers
8 built 1935–8
Lost *Gloucester, Manchester, Southampton*
Displacement	9,100 – 9,400 tons
Length	591ft (180m)
Beam	62ft (18.9m)
Guns	12 × 6in
	8 × 4in AA
	2 × 4 2pdr AA
	20mm AA
Torpedo-tubes	6 × 21in
Machinery	75,000shp = 32kts
	(*Southampton*)
	82,500shp = 32.5kts
	(others)
Complement	700

'Town'-class (Group III) light cruisers
2 built 1937–9
Lost *Edinburgh*
Displacement	10,000 tons
Length	613ft (187m)
Beam	63ft (19.3m)
Guns	12 × 6in
	12 × 4in AA
	2 × 8 2pdr
	20mm AA
Torpedo-tubes	6 × 21in
Machinery	80,000shp = 32kts
Complement	850

'Colony'-class light cruisers
11 built 1939–42
Lost *Fiji, Trinidad*
Displacement	8,800 tons
Length	555ft (169m)
Beam	62ft (18.9m)
Guns	12 × 6in
	8 × 4in AA
	2 × 4 2pdr AA
	20mm AA
Torpedo-tubes	6 × 21in
Machinery	72,500shp = 33kts
Complement	730

'Dido'-class AA cruisers
16 built 1939–43
Lost *Bonaventure, Charybdis, Hermione, Naiad, Scylla, Spartan*
Displacement	5,450 tons
	5,770 (*Spartan*)
Length	512ft (156m)
Beam	50ft (15.4m)
Guns	10 × 5.25in DP
	8 × do. (*Bonaventure, Spartan*)
	8 × 4.5in DP
	(*Charybdis, Scylla*)
	1 × 4in AA

(*Bonaventure*)
2/3 × 4 2pdr AA
Torpedo-tubes	6 × 21in
Machinery	62,000shp = 33kts
Complement	550

Courageous-class aircraft carriers
2 built 1915–16 (as light battlecruisers)
Lost *Courageous, Glorious*
Displacement	22,500 tons
Length	786ft (240m) (hull)
Beam	90ft (27.6m)
(Flight Deck	576 × 91ft
	[161 × 27.9m])
Guns	12 × 4.7in (120mm) AA
	3 × 8 2pdr AA
Aircraft	42
Machinery	91,000shp = 29.5kts
Complement	840

Aircraft carrier ***Eagle***
one unit built 1916–23
Displacement	22,600 tons
Length	667ft (203m)
Beam	105ft (32m)
(Flight Deck	652 × 96ft
	[199 × 29.3m])
Guns	9 × 6in
	4 × 4in AA
	2 × 8 2pdr AA
Aircraft	22
Machinery	52,000shp = 24kts
Complement	950

Aircraft carrier ***Hermes***
one unit built 1918–23
Displacement	10,850 tons
Length	600ft (183m)
Beam	70ft (21.4m)
(Flight Deck	570 × 90ft
	[174 × 27.4m])
Guns	6 × 5.5in
	3 × 4in AA
	20mm AA
Aircraft	12
Machinery	43,000shp = 26kts
Complement	700

Aircraft carrier ***Ark Royal***
one unit built 1936–8
Displacement	22,000 tons
Length	800ft (244m)
Beam	95ft (28.9m)
(Flight Deck	720 × 95ft [220 × 29m])
Guns	16 × 4.5in DP
	6 × 8 2pdr AA
Aircraft	60
Machinery	103,000shp = 31.75kts
Complement	1,580

Auxiliary aircraft carrier *Audacity*
one unit converted 1941

Displacement	5,540 gross tons
Length	475ft (145m)
Beam	56ft (17m)
(Flight Deck	460 × 60ft
	[140 × 18.3m])
Guns	1 × 4in LA
	6 × 20mm AA
Aircraft	6
Machinery	4,750bhp = 15kts
Complement	180

(Simple conversion of merchant ship, without hangar: ex-German *Hanover*)

Avenger-class escort carriers
4 units converted 1941–2
Lost *Avenger, Dasher*

Displacement	11,300 tons
Length	492ft (150m)
Beam	69ft (21m)
(Flight Deck	441 × 81ft [134 × 25m])
Guns	3 × 4in AA
	20mm AA
Aircraft	16
Machinery	8,500bhp = 16.5kts
Complement	555

'Ruler'-class escort carriers
25 units built 1943–4
Lost *Nabob, Thane*

Displacement	11,450 tons
Dimensions	as 'Avenger'-class
Guns	2 × 4in AA
	8 × 2 40mm AA
	20 × 20mm AA
Aircraft	24
Machinery	9,350shp = 17 kts
Complement	555

'Admiralty' "S"-class destroyers
11 built 1918–20 in service in 1939
Lost *Stronghold, Sturdy, Tenedos, Thanet, Thracian*

Displacement	905 tons
Length	276ft (84m)
Beam	26.75ft (8.2m)
Guns	1 × 4in LA (*Tenedos* &
	1 × 3in HA *Thanet*)
	2 × 4in LA (*Stronghold*,
	1 × 2pdr AA *Sturdy* &
	Thracian)
Machinery	27,000shp = 36kts
Complement	90

'V' & 'W'-class destroyers (unmodified)
6 built 1917–20 in service in 1939
Lost *Venetia, Wakeful, Wessex, Whirlwind, Worcester, Wren*

Displacement	1,100 tons
Length	312ft (95m)
Beam	29.5ft (9m)
Guns	16 × 4in LA ('V')
	4 × 4.7in LA
	('W')
	1 × 2pdr AA
Torpedo-tubes	6 × 21in
Machinery	27,000shp = 34kts
Complement	134

'A'-class destroyers
Leader + 8 built 1929–30
Lost *Codrington* (Leader), *Acasta, Acheron, Achates, Ardent, Arrow*

(*Codrington* details in parentheses)

Displacement	1,350 tons (1,540 tons)
Length	323ft (98.5m)
	(343ft/105m)
Beam	32ft (9.8m) (34ft/10.4m)
Guns	4 × 4.7in LA (5 × 4.7in)
	2 × 2pdr AA
Torpedo-tubes	8 × 21in
Machinery	34,000shp (40,000shp)
	= 35kts
Complement	138 (185)

'B'-class destroyers
Leader + 8 built 1930–1
Lost *Keith* (Leader), *Basilisk, Blanche, Boadicea, Brazen*

(*Keith* in parentheses)

Displacement	1,360 tons (1,400 tons)
All other particulars as 'A'-class, except
Complement	140 (175)

'D'-class destroyers
Leader + 8 built 1931–3
Lost *Dainty, Daring, Defender, Delight, Diamond, Duchess,* (*Margaree* (ex-*Diana*) – RCN)

Displacement	1,375 tons
Length	329ft (100m)
Beam	33ft (10m)
Guns	4 × 4.7in LA
	2 × 2pdr AA
Torpedo-tubes	8 × 21in
Machinery	36,000shp = 35.5kts
Complement	145

'E'-class destroyers
Leader + 8 built 1933–4
Lost *Exmouth* (Leader), *Eclipse, Electra, Encounter, Escort, Esk*
Particulars as 'D'-class, except 4.7in guns were in HA mountings and except *Exmouth*:

Displacement	1,475 tons
Length	343ft (104.5m)
Beam	34ft (10.4m)
Guns	5 × 4.7in HA
Torpedo-tubes	(nil in *Esk*)
Mines	60 (*Esk*)

Machinery   38,000shp = 36kts
Complement   175

'F'-class destroyers
Leader + 8 built 1934–5
Lost **Fearless, Firedrake, Foresight, Fury**
Particulars as 'D'-class

'G'-class destroyers
Leader + 8 built 1935–6
Lost **Grenville** (Leader), **Gallant, Gipsy, Glowworm, Grafton, Grenade, Greyhound**

	(*Grenville* in parentheses)
Displacement	1,335 tons (1,485 tons)
Length	323ft (98.5m) (330ft/100.5m)
Beam	32ft (9.8m) (34.5ft/10.5m)
Guns	4 × 4.7in HA (5 × 4.7in)
Torpedo-tubes	8 × 21in 10 × 21in (*Glowworm*)
Machinery	34,000shp = 35.5kts (38,000shp = 36kts)
Complement	145 (175)

'H'-class destroyers
Leader + 8 built 1936–7
Lost **Hardy** (Leader), **Hasty, Havock, Hereward, Hostile, Hunter, Hyperion**
Particulars as 'G'-class, except *Hardy*:

Displacement	1,505 tons
Length	337ft (103m)
Beam	34ft (10.4m)

'I'-class destroyers
Leader + 8 built 1936–7; 2 requisitioned while building for Turkey 1939
Lost **Inglefield** (Leader), **Imogen, Imperial, Intrepid, Isis, Ithuriel** (ex-Turkish), **Ivanhoe**
Details as 'H'-class except:

Displacement	1,370 tons (1,530 tons *Inglefield*)
Torpedo-tubes	10 × 21in

'Tribal'-class destroyers
16 built 1936–9
Lost **Afridi, Bedouin, Cossack, Gurkha, Maori, Mashona, Matabele, Mohawk, Punjabi, Sikh, Somali, Zulu**

Displacement	1,870 tons
Length	377ft (115m)
Beam	36.5ft (11.1m)
Guns	8 × 4.7in HA 1 × 4 2pdr AA
Torpedo-tubes	4 × 21in
Machinery	44,000shp = 36kts
Complement	190–220

'J'-class destroyers
8 built 1938–9
Lost **Jackal, Jaguar, Janus, Jersey, Juno, Jupiter**

Displacement	1,690 tons
Length	356ft (108.5m)
Beam	36ft (22.9m)
Guns	6 × 4.7in HA 1 × 4 2pdr
Torpedo-tubes	10 × 21in
Machinery	40,000shp = 36kts
Complement	183

'K'-class destroyers
8 built 1938–9
Lost **Kandahar, Kashmir, Kelly, Khartoum, Kingston, Kipling**
Particulars as 'J'-class, except *Kelly*:

Displacement	1,695 tons
Complement	218

'L'-class destroyers
8 built 1940–2
Lost **Gurkha (II), Laforey, Lance, Legion, Lightning, Lively, Loyal**

Displacement	1,920 tons
Length	362ft (110.5m)
Beam	37ft (11.2m)
Guns	*Laforey, Lightning, Loyal*: 6 × 4.7in HA Others: 8 × 4in AA 1 × 4 2pdr AA (in all) 20mm AA
Torpedo-tubes	8 × 21in
Machinery	48,000shp = 36kts
Complement	221

'M'-class destroyers
8 built 1940–2
Lost **Mahratta, Martin, Orkan** (Polish)
Particulars as 'L'-class (all armed with 6 × 4.7in guns)

'P'-class destroyers
8 built 1941–2
Lost **Pakenham, Panther, Partridge, Pathfinder, Porcupine:**

Displacement	1,540 tons
Length	345ft (105m)
Beam	35ft (10.7m)
	Pathfinder, Porcupine:
Guns	4 × 4.7in HA 1 × 4 2pdr AA 20mm AA
Torpedo-tubes	8 × 21in
	Others:
Guns	5 × 4in AA 1 × 4 2pdr AA 20mm AA
Torpedo-tubes	4 × 21in
Machinery	40,000shp = 36.75kts
Complement	175 (*Pakenham* 228)

'Q'-class destroyers
8 built 1941–2 (5 to Royal Australian Navy –
none lost)
Lost **Quail, Quentin**

Displacement	1,705 tons
Length	359ft (109m)
Beam	36ft (10.9m)
Guns	4 × 4.7in HA
	1 × 4 2pdr AA
	20mm AA
Torpedo-tubes	8 × 21in
Machinery	40,000shp = 36.75kts
Complement	175

'S'-class destroyers
8 built 1942–3
Lost **Svenner** (Norwegian), **Swift**

Displacement	1,710 tons
Length	363ft (110.5m)
Beam	36ft (10.9m)
Guns	4 × 4.7in DP
	2 × 40mm AA
	20mm AA
Torpedo-tubes	8 × 21in
Machinery	40,000shp = 36.75kts
Complement	180

'V'-class destroyers
8 built 1943–4
Lost **Hardy (II)** (Leader)
Particulars as 'S'-class, except

Displacement	1,730 tons
Complement	225

'V & W'-class escort destroyers (AA
conversion)
15 converted, built 1917–18
Lost **Valentine, Vimiera, Walpole, Whitley,
Wryneck**

Displacement	1,100 tons
Length	312ft (95m)
Beam	29.5ft (9m)
Guns	4 × 4in AA
Machinery	27,000shp = 34kts
Complement	125

'V & W'-class escort destroyers (short-range
conversion)
11 converted, built 1917–18
Lost **Vortigern, Veteran, Wild Swan**

Displacement	1,150 tons
Dimensions as 'V & W'-classes	
Guns	2 or 3 × 4.7in LA
	(3 × 4in LA in
	Vortigern)
	1 × 3in AA
	2 × 2pdr AA
Torpedo-tubes	3 or 6 21in
Machinery	27,000shp = 34kts
Complement	125–135

'V & W'-class escort destroyers (long-range
conversion)
22 converted, built 1917–19
Lost **Warwick, Wrestler**

Displacement	1,120 tons
Dimensions as 'V & W'-classes	
Guns	2 × 4in LA
	1 × 3in AA
	2 × 2pdr or 20mm AA
Machinery	18,000shp = 24.5kts
Complement	130

'Shakespeare'-class escort destroyers
5 built 1917–25 (2 scrapped pre-war)
Lost **Broke**

Displacement	1,480 tons
Length	329ft (100.3m)
Beam	32ft (9.7m)
Guns	2 × 4.7in LA
	1 × 3in AA
	20mm AA
Torpedo-tubes	6 × 21in
Machinery	43,500shp = 36.5kts
Complement	165

'Town'-class escort destroyers
43 built 1917–20 transferred to RN and 7 to
Canada (*qv*) in 1940; 9 re-transferred to USSR
in 1944 (*qv*)
Lost **Bath** (Norwegian), **Belmont, Beverley,
Broadwater, Cameron, Campbeltown,
Rockingham, Sherwood, Stanley,** (**Deyatelnyi** –
USSR), (**St Croix** – RCN)
Displacement and Dimensions
Bath, Campbeltown: see US Navy *Wickes*-
class
others: see US Navy *Clemson*-class
Bath, Belmont, Broadwater, Cameron,

	Campbeltown:
Guns	3 × 4in LA
	1 × 3in AA
Torpedo-tubes	6 × 21in
Machinery	27,000shp = 35kts
Complement	146
	Others:
Guns	1 × 4in LA
	1 × 3in AA
	20mm AA
Torpedo-tubes	3 × 21in
Machinery	13,500shp = 25kts
Complement	125

'Hunt'-class (Group I) escort destroyers
20 built 1939–40
Lost **Berkeley, Exmoor, Quorn, Tynedale**

Displacement	907 tons
Length	280ft (85.3m)
Beam	29ft (8.8m)
Guns	4 × 4in AA
	1 × 4 2pdr AA
	20mm AA

Machinery	19,000shp = 26kts
Complement	146

'Hunt'-class (Group II) escort destroyers
36 built 1940–2
Lost *Dulverton, Eridge, Grove, Heythrop, Hurworth,* (*Kujawiak* Polish), *Puckeridge, Southwold*

Displacement	1,050 tons
Length	282ft (86.1m)
Beam	31.5ft (9.6m)
Guns	6 × 4in AA
	1 × 4 2pdr
	20mm AA
Machinery	19,000shp = 25kts
Complement	164

'Hunt'-class (Group III) escort destroyers
28 built 1941–3
Lost (*Adrias* – Greek), *Airedale, Aldenham, Blean, Derwent,* (*Eskdale* – Norwegian), *Goathland, Holcombe, Limbourne, Penylan, Rockwood,* (*La Combattante* – French)

Displacement	1,087 tons
Dimensions as 'Hunt' Type II	
Guns	4 × 4in AA
	1 × 4 2pdr AA
	20mm AA
Torpedo-tubes	2 × 21in
Machinery	19,000shp = 26.5kts
Complement	164

"Brazilian 'H'"-class escort destroyers
6 built 1939–40
Lost *Harvester, Havant, Hurricane*

Displacement	1,340 tons ('H'-names)
Length	323ft (98.5m)
Beam	33ft (10m)
Guns	4 × 4.7in HA
	20mm AA
Torpedo-tubes	8 × 21in
Machinery	34,000shp = 35.5kts
Complement	145
requisitioned from Brazilian order	

'Flower'-class convoy sloops
3 built 1915–16 in service in 1939
Lost *Foxglove*

Displacement	1,165 tons
Length	268ft (81.6m)
Beam	33.5ft (10.2m)
Guns	2 × 4in LA
Machinery	1,800shp = 16kts
Complement	100

'24'-class convoy sloops
2 built 1918 in service in 1939
Lost *Herald*

Displacement	1,320 tons
Length	276ft (84.3m)
Beam	35ft (10.7m)
Guns	2 × 4in LA

Machinery	2,500shp = 17kts
Complement	90

Bridgewater-class sloops
15 built 1928–33
Lost *Dundee, Penzance*

Displacement	1,050 tons
Length	262ft (80m)
Beam	34ft (10.4m)
Guns	2 × 4in AA
Machinery	2,000shp = 16kts
Complement	100

Grimsby-class sloops
9 built 1933–6
Lost *Grimsby, Indus* (RIN)

Displacement	990 tons (*Grimsby*)
	1,190 tons (*Indus*)
Length	266ft (81.1m) (*Grimsby*)
	296ft (90.4m) (*Indus*)
Beam	36ft (11m)
Guns	2 × 4.7in LA
	1 × 3in AA (not in *Indus*)
Machinery	2,000shp = 16.5kts
Complement	100

Bittern-class sloops
3 built 1934–8
Lost *Bittern*

Displacement	1,190 tons
Length	282ft (86m)
Beam	37ft (11.3m)
Guns	6 × 4in AA
Machinery	3,300shp = 18.75kts
Complement	125

Egret-class sloops
3 built 1938–9
Lost *Egret, Auckland*

Displacement	1,200 tons
Length	292ft (89.1m)
Beam	37.5ft (11.4m)
Guns	8 × 4in AA
Machinery	3,600shp = 19.25kts
Complement	188

Black Swan-class sloops
13 built 1939–43
Lost *Ibis, Woodpecker*

Displacement	1,250 tons (*Ibis*)
	1,300 tons (*Woodpecker*)
Length	300ft (91.3m)
Beam	37.5ft (11.4m)
Guns	6 × 4in AA
	1 × 4 2pdr AA (*Ibis*)
	12 × 20mm (*Woodpecker*)
Machinery	3,600shp = 19.25kts
Complement	180

'Modified *Black Swan*'-class
20 built 1943–5
Lost **Chanticleer, Kite, Lapwing, Lark**

Displacement	1,350 tons
Length	300ft (91.3m)
Beam	38.5ft (11.7m)
Guns	as *Black Swan*-class
Machinery	4,300shp = 20kts
Complement	192

Banff-class sloops (ex-US Coastguard cutters)
10 built 1927–32 transferred 1941
Lost **Culver, Hartland, Walney**

Displacement	1,546 tons
Length	256ft (78m)
Beam	42ft (12.8m)
Guns	1 × 5in LA
	2 × 3in AA (*Walney* 3)
	20mm AA
Machinery	3,200shp = 16kts
Complement	200

Abdiel-class fast minelayers
6 built 1939–43
Lost **Abdiel, Latona, Welshman**

Displacement	2,650 tons
Length	418ft (127m)
Beam	40ft (12.2m)
Guns	6 × 4in AA
	1 × 4 2pdr AA
Mines	165
Machinery	72,000shp = 34kts
Complement	245

'Hunt'-class minesweepers
26 built 1917–20 in service in 1939
Lost **Abingdon, Dundalk, Dunoon, Elgin, Fermoy, Fitzroy, Huntley, Kellett, Stoke, Widnes** (see also German *Uj.2109*)

Displacement	710 tons
Length	231ft (70.4m)
Beam	28.5ft (8.7m)
Guns	1 × 4in LA
	1 × 3in AA
Machinery	2,200shp = 16kts
Complement	73

Halcyon-class minesweepers
21 built 1933–9
Lost **Bramble, Britomart, Gossamer, Hebe, Hussar, Leda, Niger, Salamander, Skipjack, Sphinx**

Displacement	815 tons (*Hussar, Salamander, Skipjack*)
	835 tons (*Gossamer, Hebe, Leda*)
	875 tons (*Bramble, Britomart, Sphinx*)
Length	245ft (74.7m)
Beam	33.5ft (10.2m)
Guns	2 × 4in AA

Machinery	1,750shp = 17kts
Complement	80

Bangor-class minesweepers
49 built 1940–2
Lost **Clacton, Cromarty, *Cromer, *Felixstowe, Hythe, Lyemun**

Displacement	*672 tons
	656 tons (others)
Length	*180ft (54.8m)
	174ft (53m) (others)
Beam	28.5ft (8.7m)
Guns	1 × 3in AA
	1 × 2pdr AA
	*20mm AA
Machinery	2,400shp = 16kts
Complement	60

Algerine-class minesweepers
91 built 1942–5
Lost **Alarm, Algerine, Fantome, Hydra, Loyalty, Prompt, Regulus, Squirrel, Vestal**

Displacement	850 tons
Length	225ft (68.6m)
Beam	35.5ft (10.8m)
Guns	1 × 4in AA
	8 × 20mm AA
Machinery	2,000shp = 16.5kts
Complement	85

Catherine-class minsweepers
22 built in USA and transferred 1942–3
Lost **Cato, Chamois, Magic, Pylades**

Displacement	890 tons
Length	220ft (67m)
Beam	32ft (9.7m)
Guns	1 × 3in AA
	6 × 20mm AA
Machinery	3,500bhp = 18kts
Complement	80

'PC'-class coastal escorts
2 built 1918 in service in 1939
Lost **Pathan** (RIN)

Displacement	661 tons
Length	247ft (75.3m)
Beam	27ft (8.1m)
Guns	1 × 4in LA
	2 × 3in LA
Machinery	3,500shp = 20kts
Complement	66

Kingfisher-class coastal escorts (corvettes)
9 built 1935–9
Lost **Pintail, Puffin**

Displacement	580 tons
Length	243ft (74.1m)
Beam	26.5ft (8.1m)
Guns	1 × 4in LA
Machinery	3,600shp = 20kts
Complement	60

'Flower'-class corvettes
131 built 1940–2 (see also Canada)
Lost **Arbutus, Asphodel, Auricula, Bluebell, Erica, Fleur de Lys, Gardenia, Gladiolus, Godetia, Hollyhock, Marigold,** (**Montbretia** – Norwegian), **Orchis, Picotee, Pink, Polyanthus,** (**Rose** – Norwegian), **Salvia, Samphire, Snapdragon, Vervain, Zinnia,** (**Alysse** – French), (**Mimosa** – French)

Displacement	925 tons
Length	205ft (62.5m)
Beam	33ft (10m)
Guns	1 × 4in LA
	1 × 2pdr AA
Machinery	2,750ihp = 16kts
Complement	90

'Castle'-class corvettes
27 built 1943–5
Lost **Denbigh Castle, Hurst Castle,** (**Tunsberg Castle** – Norwegian)

Displacement	1,010 tons
Length	252ft (76.8m)
Beam	37ft (11.2m)
Guns	1 × 4in AA
	10 × 20mm AA
Machinery	2,880ihp = 16.5kts
Complement	120

'River'-class frigates
55 built 1942–4 (see also Canada)
Lost **Cuckmere, Itchen, Lagan, Mourne, Tweed**

Displacement	1,370 tons
Length	301ft (91.8m)
Beam	36.5ft (11.1m)
Guns	2 × 4in LA
	6 × 20mm AA
Machinery	5,500ihp = 20kts
Complement	140

'Captain'-class frigates (US **Evarts**-class destroyer escorts)
32 built and transferred 1943–4
Lost **Blackwood, Capel, Gould, Goodall, Goodson, Lawford, Manners**

Displacement	1,085 tons
Length	289ft (88m)
Beam	35ft (10.7m)
Guns	3 × 3in AA
	10 × 20mm AA
Machinery	6,000bhp = 20kts
Complement	200

'Captain'-class frigates (US **Buckley**-class destroyer escorts)
46 built and transferred 1943–4
Lost **Affleck, Bickerton, Bullen, Dakins, Duff, Ekins, Halsted, Redmill, Trollope, Whittaker**

Displacement	1,300 tons
Length	306ft (93.3m)
Beam	37ft (11.2m)
Guns	3 × 3in AA
	10 × 20mm AA
	1 × 2pdr AA (**Ekins**)

Machinery	12,000shp = 26kts
Complement	200

Armed Merchant Cruisers
56 commissioned 1939
Lost **Andania, Carinthia, Comorin, Dunvegan Castle, Forfar, Hector, Jervis Bay, *Laurentic, Patroclus, Rajputana, Rawalpindi, Salopian, Scotstoun, Transylvania, Voltaire**

Tonnage	10,500 – 20,280 grt
Guns	8 × 6in
	2 × 3in AA, except:
	*7 × 5.5in, 2 × 3in AA
	3 × 4in AA
Speed	14.5 – 17.5kts

Auxiliary AA ships
7 commissioned 1941–2
Lost **Alynbank, Foylebank, Pozarica, Springbank, Tynwald**
'Bank'-ships

Tonnage	5,150–5,580grt
Length	434ft (132m)
Beam	54–57ft (16.5–17.4m)
Guns	8 × 4in AA
	2 × 4 2pdr AA
	20mm AA
Machinery	2,500–2,900bhp = 12kts

Pozarica

Tonnage	1,895grt
Length	306ft (93.3m)
Beam	45ft (13.7m)
Guns	6 × 4in AA
	2 × 4 2pdr AA
	8 × 20mm AA
Machinery	2,640bhp = 16.25kts

Tynwald

Tonnage	2,376grt
Length	329ft (100m)
Beam	46ft (14m)
Guns	as *Pozarica*, except
	4 × 20mm AA
Machinery	8,000shp = 21kts

'Insect'-type river gunboats
10 in service 1939, built 1915–16
Lost **Cicala, Ladybird, Moth, Peterel, Cricket, Gnat**

Displacement	625 tons
Length	237ft
Beam	36ft
Guns	2 × 6in,
	1 × 3in AA
Machinery	2,000ihp = 14kts
Complement	55

Later 'Insect'-type river gunboats
4 built 1938–40
Lost: **Dragonfly, Grasshopper, Mosquito**

Displacement	585 tons
Length	197ft (60m)
Beam	33ft (10.1m)
Guns	as *Scorpion*

| Machinery | 3,800shp = 17kts |
| Complement | 74 |

River gunboat **Scorpion**

Displacement	670 tons
Length	209ft (63.6m)
Beam	34ft (10.5m)
Guns	2 × 4in LA, 1 × 3.7in howitzer, 2 × 47mm
Machinery	4,500shp = 17kts
Complement	93

GREECE

Kilkis-class battleships (pre-dreadnoughts)
2 built 1903–5
Lost **Kilkis, Lemnos**

Displacement	13,000 tons
Length	382ft (116m)
Beam	77ft (23.5m)
Guns	4 × 12in (305mm) AA
Machinery	10,000ihp = 15kts
Complement	c.600

Light cruiser **Helle**
one unit built 1910–13

Displacement	2,083 tons
Length	322ft (98.1m)
Beam	39ft (11.9m)
Guns	3 × 6in (152mm) 1 × 3in (76mm) AA
Torpedo-tubes	2 × 18in
Mines	100
Machinery	6,000shp = 21kts
Complement	230

Aetos-class destroyers
4 built 1909–12
Lost **Leon**

Displacement	1,029 tons
Length	293ft (89.3m)
Beam	27.5ft (8.4m)
Guns	4 × 4.7in (120mm) 2 × 2pdr (40mm) AA
Torpedo-tubes	6 × 21in (533mm)
Machinery	19,750shp = 28kts
Complement	102

Ydra-class destroyers
4 built 1930–2 (similar to Italian *Dardo*-class)
Lost **Psara, Ydra**

Displacement	1,329 tons
Length	315ft (96m)
Beam	32ft (9.8m)
Guns	4 × 4.7in 3 × 2pdr AA
Torpedo-tubes	6 × 21in
Mines	40
Machinery	40,000shp = 39kts
Complement	156

Vasilevs Georgios I-class destroyers
2 built 1937–9 (similar to Royal Navy 'H'-class)

Lost **Vasilevs Georgios I, Vasilissa Olga** (also known as **Queen Olga**)

Displacement	1,350 tons
Length	322ft (98m)
Beam	35ft (10.6m)
Guns	4 × 5in (127mm) 4 × 40mm AA
Torpedo-tubes	10 × 21in
Machinery	34,000shp = 36kts
Complement	136

'Hunt'-class escort destroyers
6 built 1940–2 transferred by RN in 1942
Lost **Adrias**
Particulars as Royal Navy 'Hunt'-class (Group III)

Thyella-class torpedo-boats
2 built 1905–7 in service in 1941
Lost **Thyella**

Displacement	305 tons
Length	220ft (67m)
Beam	20ft (6.3m)
Guns	2 × 88mm LA 1 × 2pdr AA
Torpedo-tubes	2 × 18in
Machinery	6,500ihp = 24kts
Complement	70

IRAN

Babr-class sloops
2 built 1935–6
Lost **Babr, Palang**

Displacement	950 tons
Length	205ft (62.5m)
Beam	26ft (8m)
Guns	2 × 4in (102mm) LA 2 × 75mm AA
Machinery	1,900bhp = 15kts
Complement	85

ITALY

Cavour-class battleships
2 built 1910–15
Lost **Conte di Cavour**

Displacement	26,140 tons
Length	612ft (186m)
Beam	92ft (28m)
Guns	10 × 12.6in (320mm) 12 × 4.7in (120mm) LA 8 × 3.9in (100mm) AA 8 × 37mm AA 20mm AA
Machinery	75,000shp = 27kts
Complement	1,236

Littorio-class battleships
3 built 1937–42
Lost **Roma**

Displacement	41,650 tons
Length	788ft (240m)
Beam	108ft (32.9m)

Guns	9 × 15in (380mm)
	12 × 6in (152mm)
	12 × 90mm (3.54in) AA
	20 × 37mm AA
	32 × 20mm AA
Machinery	130,000shp = 30kts
Complement	1,930

Coast defence ship **San Giorgio**
one unit built 1905–10 in service in 1940

Displacement	9,232 tons
Length	462ft (141m)
Beam	69ft (21m)
Guns	4 × 10in (254mm)
	8 × 7.5in (190mm)
	10 × 3.9in AA
	6 × 37mm AA
	12 × 20mm AA
Machinery	18,000ihp = 22kts

Trento-class heavy cruisers
3 built 1925–33
Lost **Bolzano, Trento, Trieste**

Displacement	10,500 tons
Length	646ft (197m)
Beam	67.5ft (20.6m)
Guns	8 × 8in (203mm) HA
	12 × 3.9in AA
	8 × 37mm AA
Torpedo-tubes	8 × 21in (533mm)
Machinery	150,000shp = 35kts
Complement	781

Zara-class heavy cruisers
4 built 1929–32
Lost **Fiume, Gorizia, Pola, Zara**

Displacement	11,500–11,900 tons
Length	600ft (183m)
Beam	67.5ft (20.6m)
Guns	8 × 8in HA
	12 × 3.9in AA
	8 × 37mm AA
Machinery	95,000shp = 32kts
Complement	830

Light cruiser **Taranto**
ex-German, built 1910–12

Displacement	3,184 tons
Length	455ft (140m)
Beam	44ft (13.5m)
Guns	7 × 5.9in (150mm)
	2 × 75mm AA
	8 × 20mm AA
Mines	120
Machinery	25,000shp = 20kts
Complement	486

'Condottieri'-class light cruisers (1st group)
4 built 1928–32
Lost **Giovanni delle Bande Nere, Alberico da Barbiano, Bartolomeo Colleoni, Alberto di Giussano**

Displacement	5,200 tons
Length	555ft (169m)
Beam	51ft (15.5m)
Guns	8 × 6in
	6 × 3.9in AA
	8 × 37mm AA
Torpedo-tubes	4 × 21in
Mines	100
Machinery	95,000shp = 30kts
	(design speed was
	37kts and 42kts was
	attained on trial, but
	these speeds could not
	be approached in
	realistic conditions)
Complement	521

'Condottieri'-class light cruisers (2nd group)
2 built 1930–3
Lost **Armando Diaz**
Particulars as 1st Group, except:

Displacement	5,400 tons
Guns	8 × 6in
	6 × 3.9in AA
	12 × 20mm AA
Complement	544

'Condottieri'-class light cruisers (3rd group)
2 built 1931–5
Lost **Muzio Attendolo**

Displacement	7,550 tons
Length	598ft (182m)
Beam	54ft (16.5m)
Guns	8 × 6in
	6 × 3.9in AA
	8 × 37mm AA
	12 × 20mm
Torpedo-tubes	4 × 21in
Mines	100
Machinery	106,000shp = 34kts
Complement	650

'Capitani Romani'-class light cruisers
3 completed 1939–43
Lost **Ulpio Traiano**

Displacement	3,747 tons
Length	466ft (142m)
Beam	47ft (14.4m)
Guns	8 × 5.3in (135mm) HA
	8 × 37mm AA
	20mm AA
Torpedo-tubes	8 × 21in
Mines	70
Machinery	110,000shp = 41kts
Complement	420

Old light cruiser **Bari** built 1913–15
(commissioned as German *Pillau*)

Displacement	3,250 tons
Length	444ft (135.3m)
Beam	45ft (13.6m)
Guns	8 × 5.9in, 3 × 3in AA,

	6 × 20mm AA,
	120 mines
Machinery	21,000shp = 24.5kts
Complement	439

Mirabello-class destroyers
2 built 1914–17 in service in 1940
Lost **Carlo Mirabello**

Displacement	1,811 tons
Length	340ft (103.7m)
Beam	32ft (9.7m)
Guns	8 × 4in (102mm) LA
	8 × 20mm AA
Torpedo-tubes	4 × 17.7in (450mm)
Mines	100
Machinery	35,000shp = 27kts
Complement	158

Leone-class destroyers
3 built 1921–4
Lost **Leone, Pantera, Tigre**

Displacement	1,742 tons
Length	372ft (113.4m)
Beam	34ft (10.4m)
Guns	8 × 4.7in LA
	2 × 2pdr (40mm) AA
	4 × 20mm AA
Torpedo-tubes	4 × 21in
Mines	60
Machinery	42,000shp = 29kts
Complement	206

Sella-class destroyers
2 built 1922–7 in service in 1940
Lost **Francesco Crispi, Quintino Sella**

Displacement	970 tons
Length	278.5ft (84.9m)
Beam	28ft (8.6m)
Guns	4 × 4.7in LA
	20mm AA
Torpedo-tubes	4 × 21in
Mines	32
Machinery	36,000shp = 32kts
Complement	152

Sauro-class destroyers
4 built 1924–7
Lost **Cesare Battisti, Daniele Manin,
Francesco Nullo, Nazario Sauro**

Displacement	1,058 tons
Length	296ft (90.2m)
Beam	30ft (9.2m)
Guns	4 × 4.7in LA
	2 × 2pdr AA
Torpedo-tubes	6 × 21in
Mines	52
Machinery	36,000shp = 31kts
Complement	156

Turbine-class destroyers
8 built 1925–8
Lost **Aquilone, Borea, Espero, Euro, Nembo,**

Ostro, Turbine, Zeffiro

Displacement	1,090 tons
Length	306ft (93.2m)
Beam	30ft (9.2m)
Armament as 'Sauro'-class	
Machinery	40,000shp = 33kts
Complement	180

'Navigatori'-class destroyers
12 built 1927–31
Lost **Lanzerotto Malocello, Alvise da Mosto,
Antonio da Noli, Leone Pancaldo, Emanuele
Pessagno, Antonio Pigafetta, Luca Tarigo,
Antoniotto Usodimare, Giovanni da
Verazzano, Ugolino Vivaldi, Nicolo Zeno**

Displacement	1,943 tons
Length	353ft (107.7m)
Beam	33.5ft (10.2m)
Guns	6 × 4.7in HA
	2 × 37mm AA
	8–10 × 20mm AA
Torpedo-tubes	4 or 6 × 21in
Mines	54
Machinery	50,000shp = 32kts
Complement	224

Dardo-class destroyers
4 built 1929–32
Lost **Dardo, Freccia, Saetta, Strale**

Displacement	1,220 tons
Length	315ft (96m)
Beam	32ft (9.8m)
Guns	4 × 4.7in HA
	8 × 20mm AA
Torpedo-tubes	6 × 21in
Mines	54
Machinery	44,000shp = 30kts
Complement	185

Folgore-class destroyers
4 built 1929–32
Lost **Baleno, Folgore, Fulmine, Lampo**
Particulars as 'Dardo'-class, except:

Displacement	1,238 tons
Mines	52

Maestrale-class destroyers
4 built 1931–4
Lost **Libeccio, Maestrale, Scirocco**

Displacement	1,640 tons
Length	350ft (106.7m)
Beam	33ft (10.1m)
Guns	4 × 4.7in HA
	6–8 × 20mm AA
Torpedo-tubes	6 × 21in
Mines	56
Machinery	44,000shp = 32kts
Complement	190

Oriani-class destroyers
4 built 1935–7
Lost **Vittorio Alfieri, Giosue Carducci,**

Vincenzo Gioberti
Displacement 1,700 tons
Dimensions as 'Maestrale'-class
Guns 4 × 4.7in HA
2 × 37mm AA
8–12 × 20mm AA
Torpedo-tubes as *Maestrale*-class
and Mines
Machinery 48,000shp = 33kts
Complement 207

'Soldati'-class destroyers (1st series)
12 built 1937–9
Lost *Alpino, Artigliere, Ascari, Aviere,*
Bersagliere, Carabiniere, Corazziere,
Fuciliere, Geniere, Lanciere
Particulars as *Maestrale*-class, except:
Displacement 1,710 tons
Mines 48
Complement 218

'Soldati'-class destroyers (2nd series)
5 completed 1940–2
Lost *Bombardiere, Corsaro, Mitragliere*
Particulars as 'Soldati'-class, Series I, except:
Displacement 1,840 tons
Guns 5 × 4.7in HA
8–10 × 20mm AA
Machinery 50,000shp = 35kts

Guépard-class destroyer *FR.21* (ex-French *Lion*)
seized 1942
Particulars as French *Guépard*-class

Flotilla leader *Premuda* (ex-Yugoslav
Dubrovnik)
seized 1941
Particulars as Yugoslav *Dubrovnik*

Beograd-class destroyers (ex-Yugoslav)
seized 1941
Lost *Lubiana* (ex-*Ljubljana*), *Sebenico* (ex-
Beograd)
Particulars as Yugoslav *Beograd*-class, except:
Guns 4 × 4.7in LA
1 × 37mm AA
4 × 20mm AA

Torpedo-boat *Audace*
built 1913–17
Displacement 829 tons
Length 287ft (87.6m)
Beam 27.5ft (8.4m)
Guns 7 × 4in LA
2 × 2pdr AA
Torpedo-tubes (removed)
Machinery 22,000shp = 27kts
Complement 127

Pilo-class torpedo-boats
7 built 1913–16 in service in 1940
Lost *Fratelli Cairoli, Giuseppe Dezza,*

Giuseppe Missori, Rosolino Pilo,
Simone Schiaffino
Displacement 616 tons
Length 240ft (73m)
Beam 24ft (7.3m)
Guns 2 × 4in LA
6 × 20mm AA
Torpedo-tubes 4 × 17.7in
Mines 10
Machinery 15,500shp = 27kts
Complement 84

Sirtori-class torpedo-boats
4 built 1916–17
Lost *Giovanni Acerbi, Vincenzo Giordano*
Orsini, Giuseppe Sirtori, Francesco Stocco
Displacement 670 tons
Length 241ft (73.5m)
Beam 24ft (7.3m)
Guns 6 × 4in LA
2 × 2pdr AA
Torpedo-tubes 4 × 17.7in
Mines 10
Machinery 15,500shp = 25kts
Complement 98

La Masa-class torpedo-boats
7 built 1916–19 in service in 1940
Lost *Angelo Bassini, Enrico Cosenz, Giuseppe*
la Farina, Giuseppe la Masa, Giacomo Medici
Particulars as 'Sirtori'-class, except:
Displacement 650 tons
Guns 2 or 3 × 4in LA
6 × 20mm AA
Torpedo-tubes 2 or 4 × 17.7in
Giuseppe La Masa:
Guns 1 × 4in
8 × 20mm AA
Torpedo-tubes 3 × 21in
2 × 17.7in

Palestro-class torpedo-boats
4 built 1917–22
Lost *Confienza, Palestro, San Martino,*
Solferino
Displacement 862 tons
Length 269ft (81.9m)
Beam 26ft (8m)
Guns 4 × 4in LA
2 × 75mm AA
20mm AA
Torpedo-tubes 4 × 17.7in
Mines 10
Machinery 22,000shp = 27kts
Complement 106

'Generali'-class torpedo-boats
6 built 1919–22
Lost *Generale Antonio Cantore, Generale*
Antonino Cascino, Generale Antonio
Chinotto, Generale Carlo Montanari,
Generale Achille Papa, Generale Marcello
Prestinari

Particulars as 'Sirtori'-class, except:

Guns	3 × 4in LA
	2 × 75mm AA
	20mm AA
Complement	106

Curtatone-class torpedo-boats
4 built 1920–4
Lost **Calatafimi, Castelfidardo, Curtatone**

Displacement	876 tons
Length	278ft (84.7m)
Beam	26ft (8m)
Guns	4 × 4in LA
	2 × 75mm AA
Torpedo-tubes	2 × 21in
Mines	16
Machinery	22,000shp = 28kts
Complement	117

Spica-class torpedo-boats
30 built 1934–8 in service in 1940
Lost *Type A* **Aldebaran, Altair, Andromeda, Antares, Perseo, Vega;** *Type B* **Castore, Centauro, Cigno, Climene;** *Type C* **Airone, Alcione, Ariel, Calipso, Canopo, Circe, Lince, Lira, Lupo, Pallade, Partenope, Pleiadi, Polluce**

Type 'A'

Displacement	642 tons
Length	269ft (82m)
Beam	27ft (8.2m)

Type 'B'

Displacement	652 tons
Length	267ft (81.4m)
Beam	27ft (8.2m)

Type 'C'

Displacement	679 tons
Length	267ft (81.4m)
Beam	26ft (7.9m)
Guns	3 × 3.9in AA
	6–10 × 20mm AA
Torpedo-tubes	4 × 17.7in
Mines	20
Machinery	19,000shp = 27–29kts
Complement	120

Ariete-class torpedo-boats
1 completed 1943, 13 seized and completed by German Navy 1942–4
(see German Navy)

'T 1/T 5'-class torpedo boats (ex-Yugoslav)
6 built 1912–15 seized in 1941
Lost **T 3, T 6, T7, T 8**
Particulars as Yugoslav '76 T'-class

Orsa-class escort destroyers
4 built 1936–8
Lost **Orsa, Pegaso, Procione**

Displacement	1,168 tons
Length	293ft (89.3m)
Beam	31ft (9.5m)
Guns	2 × 3.9in AA
	11 × 20mm AA
Mines	20
Machinery	16,000shp = 27kts
Complement	170

Animoso-class escort destroyers (Type I)
9 built 1941–3
Lost **Ardente, Ardito, Ciclone, Groppo, Tifone, Uragano**

Displacement	1,095 tons
Length	293ft (89.3m)
Beam	32ft (9.8m)
Guns	2 × 3.9in AA
	12 × 20mm AA
Torpedo-tubes	4 × 17.7in
Mines	20
Machinery	15,500shp = 25kts
Complement	180

Animoso-class escort destroyers (Type II)
6 completed 1943–3, 1 seized and completed by German Navy 1944
Lost **Ghibli, Impavido, Impetuoso, Monsone,** (**Intrepido** – see German **TA.25**)
Particulars as *Ardente*-group, except:

Displacement	1,204 tons
Guns	3 × 3.9in AA
	10 × 20mm AA

Aviso (sloop) **Diana**
one unit built 1939–40

Displacement	2,207 tons
Length	373ft (114m)
Beam	38ft (11.7m)
Guns	2 × 4in LA
	6 × 20mm AA
Machinery	30,000shp = 28kts

Escort (ex-torpedo-boat) **Insidioso**
one unit built 1912–14 in service in 1940

Displacement	550 tons
Length	240ft (73m)
Beam	24ft (7.3m)
Guns	1 × 4in LA
	4 × 20mm AA
Machinery	16,000shp = 24kts
Complement	75

Gabbiano-class corvettes
30 completed 1942–3
12 seized and completed by German Navy 1943–4 (*qv*)
Lost **Antilope, Berenice, Camoscio, Cicogna, Euterpe, Gazzella, Lucciola, Persefone, Procellaria, Vespa**

Displacement	670 tons
Length	211ft (64.4m)
Beam	28.5ft (8.7m)
Guns	1 × 3.9in AA
	7 × 20mm AA

Torpedo-tubes	2 × 17.7in (in a few early units)
Machinery	3,500bhp = 16–17.5kts
Complement	110

Elan-class escorts (ex-French)
2 seized and commissioned 1942–3
Lost **FR 51** (ex-*La Batailleuse*), **FR 52** (ex-*Commandant Rivière*)
Particulars as French *Elan*-class

Fasana-class minelayers
4 built 1924–6
Lost **Buccari, Durrazo, Fasana, Pelagosa**

Displacement	530 tons
Length	217ft (66.3m)
Beam	33ft (10m)
Guns	1 × 75mm AA
Mines	50
Machinery	700bhp = 10kts

Ostia-class minelayers
4 built 1925–7
Lost **Legnano, Lepanto, Ostia**

Displacement	615 tons
Length	204ft (62.2m)
Beam	28.5ft (8.7m)
Guns	2 × 4in LA
	1 × 75mm AA
Mines	80
Machinery	1,500ihp = 15kts

'M-boote Type 1915'-class minesweepers
2 built 1918 in service in 1940; 6 seized in 1941 from Yugoslav Navy
Lost **Crotone, Viesti, Eso** (ex-*Sokol*), **Oriole** (ex-*Labud*), **Selve** (ex-*Galeb*), **Unie** (ex-*Kobac*), **Zirona** (ex-*Jastreb*)
Particulars as German 'M Type 1915'-class minesweepers

JAPAN

Kongo-class battleships
4 built 1911–15
Lost **Haruna, Hiei, Kirishima, Kongo**

Displacement	27,613 tons
Length	704ft (231m)
Beam	92ft (28m)
Guns	8 × 14in (356mm)
	14 × 6in (152mm)
	8 × 5in (127mm) DP
	4 × 5in AA (*Hiei*)
	4 × 2pdr (40mm) AA
	25mm AA
Machinery	136,000shp = 30kts
Complement	1,437

Fuso-class battleships
2 built 1912–17
Lost **Fuso, Yamashiro**

Displacement	34,700 tons
Length	698ft (213m)
Beam	100ft (30.5m)
Guns	12 × 14in
	14 × 6in
	8 × 5in DP
	25 × 25mm AA
Machinery	75,000shp = 24.7kts
Complement	1,400

Ise-class battleships
2 built 1915–18
Lost **Hyuga, Ise**

Displacement	36,000 tons
Length	700ft (213m)
Beam	104ft (31.7m)
Guns	12 × 14in
	16 × 5.5in (140mm) LA
	8 × 5in DP
	20 × 25mm AA
Machinery	80,825shp = 25.3kts
Complement	1,376

Reconstructed 1943–4 as hybrid seaplane-carriers:

Guns	8 × 14in
	16 × 5in DP
	57 × 25mm AA
Aircraft	22

Nagato-class battleships
2 built 1917–21
Lost **Mutsu**

Displacement	38,000 tons
Length	725ft (221m)
Beam	113ft (34.4m)
Guns	8 × 16in (406mm)
	18 × 5.5in LA
	8 × 5in DP
	20 × 25mm AA
Machinery	82,300shp = 25kts
Complement	1,368

Yamato-class battleships
2 built 1937–42
Lost **Musashi, Yamato**

Displacement	64,000 tons
Length	862ft (263m)
Beam	121ft (36.9m)
Guns	9 × 18.1in (457mm)
	12 × 6.1in (155mm)
	12 × 5in DP
	24 × 25mm AA
Machinery	150,000shp = 27kts
Complement	2,800

Furutaka-class heavy cruisers
2 built 1922-6
Lost **Furutaka, Kako**

Displacement	8,700 tons
Length	607ft (185m)
Beam	52ft (15.8m)

Guns	6 × 8in (203mm)
	4 × 4.7in (120mm) AA
	8 × 25mm AA
Torpedo-tubes	8 × 24in (610mm)
Machinery	103,400shp = 33kts
Complement	650

Aoba-class heavy cruisers
2 built 1924–6
Lost **Aoba, Kinugasa**

Displacement	9,000 tons
Length	607ft (185m)
Beam	57ft (17.6m)
Armament as *Furutaka*-class
Machinery	108,500shp = 33.4kts
Complement	650

Myoko-class heavy cruisers (also known as
Nachi-class)
4 built 1924–9
Lost **Ashigara, Haguro, Nachi**

Displacement	13,000 tons
Length	668ft (204m)
Beam	68ft (20.7m)
Guns	10 × 8in
	8 × 5in DP
	8 × 25mm AA
Torpedo-tubes	8 × 24in
Machinery	130,250shp = 33.8kts
Complement	780

Takao-class heavy cruisers
4 built 1927–32
Lost **Atago, Chokai, Maya, Takao**

| Displacement | 13,400 tons |
| Dimensions and guns as *Myoko*-class |
Torpedo-tubes	16 × 24in
Machinery	133,100shp = 34.2kts
Complement	790

Mogami-class heavy cruisers
4 built 1931–7
Lost **Kumano, Mikuma, Mogami, Suzuya**

Displacement	11,200 tons
Length	656ft (200m)
Beam	66ft (20.2m)
	63ft (19.2m) (*Mikuma*)
Guns	as *Myoko*-class
Torpedo-tubes	12 × 24in
Machinery	152,000shp = 35kts
Complement	850

Tone-class heavy cruisers
2 built 1934–9
Lost **Chikuma, Tone**

Displacement	11,215 tons
Length	656ft (200m)
Beam	61ft (18.5m)
Guns	8 × 8in
	8 × 5in DP
	12 × 25mm AA
Torpedo-tubes	12 × 24in

| Machinery | 152,000shp = 35.2kts |
| Complement | 850 |

Tenryu-class light cruisers
2 built 1917–19
Lost **Tatsuta, Tenryu**

Displacement	3,230 tons
Length	468ft (143m)
Beam	40.5ft (12.3m)
Guns	5 × 5.5in LA
	1 × 3in AA
Torpedo-tubes	6 × 21in
Mines	100
Machinery	51,000shp = 33kts
Complement	332

Kuma-class light cruisers
5 built 1918–21
Lost **Kiso, Kuma, Oi, Tama**

Displacement	5,100 tons
Length	532ft (162m)
Beam	46.5ft (14.2m)
Guns	7 × 5.5in
	4 × 5.5 (*Oi*)
	2 × 3in AA
	8 × 25mm AA (*Oi*)
Torpedo-tubes	8 × 24in
	40 × 24in
	(10 × quad TT) (*Oi*)
Machinery	90,000shp = 36kts
Complement	450

Nagara-class light cruisers
6 built 1920–5
Lost **Abukuma, Isuzu, Kinu, Nagara, Natori,
Yura**
Particulars as *Kuma*-class, except:

| Displacement | 5,170 tons |
| Mines | 80 |

Sendai-class light cruisers
3 built 1922–5
Lost **Jintsu, Naka, Sendai**
Particulars as *Nagara*-class, except:

| Displacement | 5,195 tons |

Light cruiser, **Yubari**
one unit built 1922–3

Displacement	2,890 tons
Length	463ft (141m)
Beam	39.5ft (12m)
Guns	6 × 5.5in LA
	1 × 3in AA
	25mm AA
Torpedo-tubes	4 × 24in
Mines	34
Machinery	57,900shp = 35.5kts
Complement	328

Agano-class light cruisers
4 built 1940–4
Lost **Agano, Noshiro, Yahagi**

Displacement	6,652 tons
Length	571ft (174m)
Beam	50ft (15.2m)
Guns	6 × 6in
	4 × 3in AA
	32 × 25mm AA
Torpedo-tubes	8 × 24in
Machinery	100,000shp = 35kts

Light cruiser **Oyodo**
one unit completed 1941–3

Displacement	8,500 tons
Length	630ft (192m)
Beam	51ft (15.7m)
Guns	6 × 6.1in
	8 × 3.9in (100mm) AA
	12 × 25mm AA
Torpedo-tubes	(nil)
Machinery	110,000shp = 36kts

Katori-class training cruisers
3 built 1938-41
Lost **Kashii, Katori**

Displacement	5,800 tons
Length	432ft (131.7m)
Beam	52ft (16m)
Guns	4 × 5.5in
	2 × 5in DP
	4 × 25mm AA
Torpedo-tubes	4 × 21in
Machinery	8,000shp = 18kts

Ning Hai-class coast defence ships (ex-Chinese light cruisers)
2 built 1930–6, seized 1937
Lost **Ioshima** ex-**Ning Hae, Yasoshima** ex-**Ping Hai**

Displacement	2,500 tons
Length	360ft (110m)
Beam	39ft (11.9m)
Guns	6 × 5.5in
	6 × 3in AA
Torpedo-tubes	4 × 21in
Machinery	9,500shp = 22kts
Complement	340

Aircraft carrier **Kaga**
one unit built 1920–8

Displacement	38,200 tons
Length	815ft (249m)
Beam	107ft (32.5m)
Flight Deck	815 × 100ft
	(249 × 30.5m)
Guns	10 × 8in
	16 × 5in DP
	30 × 25mm AA
Aircraft	66
Machinery	127,400shp = 28.3kts
Complement	2,016

Aircraft carrier **Akagi**
one unit built 1920–7

Displacement	36,500 tons
Length	855ft (260m)
Beam	103ft (31.3m)
Flight Deck	817 × 100ft
	(249 × 30.5m)
Guns	6 × 8in
	12 × 4.7in AA
	28 × 25mm AA
Aircraft	72
Machinery	133,000shp = 31kts
Complement	2,000

Aircraft carrier **Ryujo**
one unit built 1929–33

Displacement	10,600 tons
Length	590ft (180m)
Beam	68ft (20.8m)
Flight Deck	513 × 75ft
	(156 × 23m)
Guns	8 × 5in DP
	22 × 25mm AA
Aircraft	37
Machinery	66,270shp = 29kts
Complement	924

Aircraft carrier **Soryu**
one unit built 1934–9

Displacement	15,900 tons
Length	746ft (227m)
Beam	70ft (21.3m)
Flight Deck	712 × 85ft
	(217 × 26m)
Guns	12 × 5in DP
	28 × 25mm AA
Aircraft	63
Machinery	152,000shp = 34.5kts
Complement	1,100

Aircraft carrier **Hiryu**

Displacement	17,300 tons
Length	746ft (227m)
Beam	73ft (22.3m)
Flight Deck	712 × 89ft
	(217 × 27m)
Guns	12 × 5in DP
	31 × 25mm AA
Aircraft	64
Machinery	153,000shp = 34.3kts
Complement	1,100

Zuiho-class light carriers
2 converted 1940–2
Lost **Shoho, Zuiho**

Displacement	11,260 tons
Length	672ft (205m)
Beam	60ft (18.2m)
Flight Deck	590 × 75ft
	(180 × 23m)
Guns	8 × 5in DP
	25mm AA
Aircraft	30

Machinery	52,000shp = 28kts
Complement	785

Shokaku-class aircraft carriers
2 built 1937–41
Lost **Shokaku, Zuikaku**

Displacement	25,675 tons
Length	845ft (256m)
Beam	85ft (26m)
Flight Deck	795 × 95ft
	(242 × 29m)
Guns	16 × 5in DP
	25mm AA
Aircraft	72
Machinery	160,000shp = 34.2kts
Complement	1,660

Junyo-class aircraft carriers
converted while building 1940–2
Lost **Hiyo**

Displacement	24,140 tons
Length	720ft (219m)
Beam	88ft (26.7m)
Flight Deck	690 × 89ft
	(210 × 27m)
Guns	12 × 5in DP
	25mm AA
Aircraft	53
Machinery	56,250shp = 22.5kts
Complement	1,200

Chitose-class light carriers
converted 1942–3 (from seaplane carriers built
1934–8)
Lost **Chitose, Chiyoda**

Displacement	11,900 tons
Length	631ft (193m)
Beam	68ft (20.8m)
Flight Deck	591 × 75ft
	(180 × 23m)
Guns	8 × 5in DP
	25mm AA
Aircraft	30
Machinery	44,000shp +
	12,800bhp = 29kts
Complement	800

Aircraft carrier **Taiho**
built 1941–4

Displacement	29,300 tons
Length	855ft (260m)
Beam	91ft (27.7m)
Flight Deck	845 × 98ft
	(257 × 30m)
Guns	12 × 3.9in AA
	45 × 25mm AA
Aircraft	63
Machinery	180,000shp = 33kts
Complement	1,751

Aircraft carrier **Shinano**
built 1940–4

Displacement	64,800 tons
Length	873ft (266m)
Beam	119ft (36.3m)
Flight Deck	840 × 131ft
	(256 × 40m)
Guns	16 × 5in DP
	145 × 25mm AA
Aircraft	47
Machinery	150,000shp = 27kts
Complement	2,400

Unryu-class aircraft carriers
3 completed 1942–4
Lost **Amagi, Unryu**

Displacement	17,150 tons
	17,450 tons (*Amagi*)
Length	745ft (227m)
Beam	72ft (21.9m)
Flight Deck	712 × 89ft
	(217 × 27m)
Guns	12 × 5in DP
	89 × 25mm AA
Aircraft	63
Machinery	152,000shp = 34kts

Taiyo-class escort carriers
3 converted 1940–2
Lost **Chuyo, Taiyo, Unyo**

Displacement	17,830 tons
Length	591ft (180m)
Beam	74ft (22.5m)
Flight Deck	564 × 77ft
	(172 × 23.5m)
Guns	6 × 4.7in AA (*Taiyo*)
	8 × 5in DP (others)
	8 × 25mm AA
Aircraft	27
Machinery	25,200shp = 21kts
Complement	747 (*Taiyo*)
	850 (others)

Escort carrier **Kaiyo**
converted 1942–3

Displacement	13,600 tons
Length	546ft (166m)
Beam	72ft (21.9m)
Flight Deck	525 × 78ft
	(160 × 23.9m)
Guns	8 × 5in DP
	24 × 25mm AA
Aircraft	24
Machinery	52,100shp = 23.8kts
Complement	829

Escort carrier **Shinyo**
converted 1942–3

Displacement	17,500 tons
Length	643ft (196m)
Beam	84ft (25.6m)
Flight Deck	590 × 80ft
	(180 × 24.5m)
Guns	8 × 5in DP

	30 × 25mm AA
Aircraft	33
Machinery	26,000shp = 22kts
Complement	942

Seaplane carrier *Mizuho*
Built 1937–9

Displacement	10,930 tons
Length	624ft (190m)
Beam	62ft (18.8m)
Guns	6 × 5in DP
	12 × 25mm AA
Aircraft	24
Machinery	15,200bhp = 22kts

Seaplane carrier *Nisshin*
built 1938–42

Displacement	13,500 tons
Length	634ft (193m)
Beam	65ft (19.7m)
Guns	6 × 5in DP
	18 × 25mm AA
Aircraft	25
Machinery	47,000shp = 28kts

Seaplane tender *Akitsushima*
built 1940–2

Displacement	4,630 tons
Length	386ft (117.6m)
Beam	52ft (15.8m)
Guns	4 × 5in DP
	10 × 25mm AA
Aircraft	1 flying-boat
Machinery	8,000bhp = 19kts

Auxiliary seaplane carriers
7 converted 1939–41
Lost ***Kamikawa Maru, Kimikawa Maru***

Tonnage	6,853 grt
Length	530ft (162m)
Beam	62ft (19m)
Guns	2 × 6in LA
	25mm AA
Aircraft	12
Machinery	7,600bhp = 18kts

Minekaze-class destroyers
13 built 1918–22 in service in 1941 (see also 'patrol boats')
Lost ***Akikaze, Hakaze, Hokaze, Minekaze, Nokaze, Numikaze, Okikaze, Tachikaze***

Displacement	1,215 tons
Length	336ft (102.4m)
Beam	30ft (9m)
Guns	4 × 4.7in LA
Torpedo-tubes	6 × 21in
Mines	20
Machinery	38,500shp = 36kts
Complement	148

Momi-class destroyers
3 built 1919–22 in service in 1941 (see also

'patrol boats')
Lost ***Tsuga***

Displacement	770 tons
Length	285ft (87m)
Beam	26ft (7.9m)
Guns	3 × 4.7in LA
Torpedo-tubes	4 × 21in
Machinery	21,500shp = 36kts
Complement	110

Wakatake-class destroyers
6 built 1922–4 in service in 1941 (see also 'patrol boats')
Lost ***Fuyo, Karukaya, Kuretake, Sanae, Wakatake***
Particulars as *Momi*-class, except:

Displacement	900 tons

Kamikaze-class destroyers
9 built 1921–5
Lost ***Asakaze, Asanagi, Hatakaze, Hayate, Matsukaze, Oite, Yunagi***
Particulars as *Minekaze*-class, except:

Displacement	1,270 tons
Guns	3 × 4.7in LA
	10 × 25mm AA
Torpedo-tubes	4 × 21in
Mines	16
Complement	165

Mutsuki-class destroyers
12 built 1924–7
Lost ***Fumizuki, Kikuzuki, Kisaragi, Mikazuki, Minazuki, Mochizuki, Mutsuki, Nagatsuki, Satsuki, Uzuki, Yayoi, Yuzuki***
Particulars as *Minekaze*-class, except:

Displacement	1,315 tons
Guns	2 × 4.7in HA
	10 × 25mm AA
Torpedo-tubes	6 × 24in

Fubuki-class destroyers
19 built 1926–32 in service in 1941
Lost ****Akebono, *Amagiri, *Asagiri, *Ayanami, Fubuki, Hatsuyaki, Isonami, Murakomo, *Oboro, *Sagiri, *Sazanami, * Shikinami, Shinonome, Shirakumo, Shirayuki, Uranami, Usugumo, *Yugiri***

Displacement	2,060 tons
Length	388ft (118.4m)
Beam	34ft (10.4m)
Guns	6 × 5in LA (*DP)
	25mm AA
Torpedo-tubes	9 × 24in (3 reloads)
Mines	18
Machinery	50,000shp = 34kts
Complement	197

Akatsuki-class destroyers
4 built 1931–3
Lost ***Akatsuki, Ikazuchi, Inazuma***

Displacement	1,980 tons

188

Length	371ft (113.2m)
Beam	34ft (10.4m)
Guns	4 × 5in DP
	14 × 25mm AA
Torpedo-tubes	9 × 24in (6 reloads)
Machinery	50,000shp = 34kts
Complement	200

Hatsuharu-class destroyers
6 built 1931–5
Lost *Ariake, Hatsuharu, Hatsushimo, Nenohi, Wakaba, Yugure*

Displacement	1,715 tons
Length	359ft (109.4m)
Beam	33ft (10m)
Guns	5 × 5in DP
	25mm AA
Torpedo-tubes	6 × 24in (3 reloads)
Machinery	42,000shp = 33.3kts
Complement	200

Shiratsuyu-class destroyers
10 built 1933–7
Lost *Harusame, Kawakaze, Murasame, Samidare, Shigure, Shiratsuyu, Suzukaze, Umikaze, Yamakaze, Yudachi*
Particulars as *Hatsuharu*-class, except:

Displacement	1,900 tons
Torpedo-tubes	8 × 24in (4 reloads)

Asashio-class destroyers
10 built 1935–9
Lost *Arare, Arashio, Asagumo, Asashio, Kasumi, Michishio, Minegumo, Natsugumo, Oshio, Yamagumo*
Particulars as *Fubuki*-class, except:

Displacement	2,100 tons
Torpedo-tubes	8 × 24in (6 reloads)

Kagero-class destroyers
18 built 1937–41
Lost *Amatsukaze, Arashi, Hagikaze, Hamakaze, Hatsukaze, Hayashio, Isokaze, Kagero, Kuroshio, Maikaze, Natsushio, Nowaki, Oyashio, Shiranuhi, Tanikaze, Tokitsukaze, Urakaze*
Particulars as *Asashio*-class, except:

Beam	35.5ft (10.8m)
Machinery	52,000shp = 35kts
Complement	240

Yugumo-class destroyers
20 built 1940–4
Lost *Akigumo, Akishimo, Asashimo, Fujinami, Hamanami, Hayanami, Hayashimo, Kazegumo, Kishinami, Kiyonami, Kiyoshimo, Makigumo, Makinami, Naganami, Okinami, Onami, Suzunami, Takanami, Tamanami, Yugumo*
Particulars as *Kagero*-class, except:

Torpedo-tubes	8 × 24in (8 reloads)
Complement	228

Akizuki-class destroyers
12 built 1940–5
Lost *Akizuki, Hatsutsuki, Niizuki, Shimotsuki, Teruzuki, Wakatsuki*

Displacement	2,900 tons
Length	440ft (134m)
Beam	38ft (11.6m)
Guns	8 × 3.9in DP
	4 × 25mm AA
Torpedo-tubes	4 × 24in (4 reloads)
Machinery	52,000shp = 33kts
Complement	300

Destroyer *Shimakaze*
one unit built 1941–3

Displacement	2,700 tons
Length	415ft (126.5m)
Beam	37ft (11.2m)
Guns	6 × 5in DP
	6 × 25mm AA
Torpedo-tubes	15 × 24in (no reloads)
Machinery	75,000shp = 39kts

Matsu-class escort destroyers
18 completed 1943–5
Lost *Hinoki, Kuwa, Matsu, Momi, Momo, Nara, Sakura, Ume, Yanagi*

Displacement	1,530 tons
Length	328ft (100m)
Beam	31ft (9.3m)
Guns	3 × 5in AA
	24 × 25mm AA
Torpedo-tubes	4 × 24in
Machinery	19,000shp = 27.5kts

Tachibana-class escort destroyers
14 completed 1944–5
Lost *Enoki, Nashi, Tachibana*
Particulars as *Matsu*-class

Tomozuru-class torpedo-boats
4 built 1931–4
Lost *Chidori, Manazuru, Tomozuru*

Displacement	600 tons
Length	269ft (82m)
Beam	24ft (7.4m)
Guns	3 × 4.7in LA
Torpedo-tubes	2 × 21in
Machinery	11,000shp = 30kts
Complement	113

Otori-class torpedo-boats
8 built 1934–7
Lost *Hato, Hayabusa, Hiyodori, Kari, Kasasagi, Otori, Sagi*

Displacement	910 tons
Length	290ft (88.4m)
Beam	27ft (8.2m)
Guns	3 × 4.7in HA
	1 × 2pdr (40mm) HA
Torpedo-tubes	3 × 21in

Machinery	19,000shp = 30.5kts
Complement	113

ex-*Minekaze*-class patrol boats
2 built 1919–21 (as destroyers) in service in 1941
Lost *No. 1* (ex-*Shimakaze*), *No. 2* (ex-*Nadakaze*)

Displacement	1,390 tons
Dimensions as *Minekaze*-class	
Guns	1 × 4.7in HA
	10 × 25mm AA
Machinery	19,250shp = 20kts
Complement	100 (+250 troops)

ex-*Momi*-class patrol boats
9 built 1919–22 (as destroyers) in service in 1941
Lost *No. 31* (ex-*Kiku*), *No. 32* (ex-*Aoi*), *No. 33* (ex-*Hagi*), *No. 34* (ex-*Susuki*), *No. 35* (ex-*Tsuta*), *No. 36*, *No. 37* (ex-*Hishi*), *No. 38* (ex-*Yomogi*), *No. 39* (ex-*Tade*)

Displacement	935 tons
Dimensions as *Momi*-class	
Guns	2 × 4.7in LA
	6–8 × 25mm AA
Machinery	12,000shp = 18kts
Complement	100

ex-*Wakatake*-class patrol boat *No. 46* (ex-*Yugao*)
built 1922–4 as a destroyer

Displacement	910 tons
Dimensions as *Wakatake*-class	
Guns	2 × 4.7in LA
	8 × 25mm AA
Machinery	10,000shp = 18kts
Complement	100

Patrol boat *No. 103* (ex-USS *Finch*)
US minesweeper seized in 1941
Particulars as US Navy 'Bird'-class minesweepers

Shimushu-class escort vessels
4 built 1938–41
Lost *Ishigaki*

Displacement	860 tons
Length	255ft (77.7m)
Beam	30ft (9.1m)
Guns	3 × 4.7in LA
	4 × 25mm AA
Machinery	4,200bhp = 19.7kts
Complement	150

Etorufu-class escort vessels
14 built 1942–4
Lost *Amakusa, Hirado, Iki, Kanju, Manju, Matsuwa, Mutsure, Sado, Wakamiya*
Particulars as *Shimushu*-class, except:

Displacement	870 tons
Complement	147

Mikura-class escort vessels
8 built 1943–4
Lost *Awaji, Chiburi, Kusagaki, Mikura, Nomi*

Displacement	940 tons
Length	258ft (78.6m)
Beam	29.5ft (9m)
Guns	3 × 4.7in HA
	4 × 25mm AA
Machinery	4,200bhp = 19.5kts
Complement	150

Ukuru-class escort vessels
29 completed 1944–5
Lost *Hiburi, Ikara, Inagi, Kume, Mokuto, Oga, Okinawa, Shonan, Yaku*
Particulars as *Mikura*-class, except:

Guns	3 × 4.7in HA
	6 × 25mm AA

'Type C'-class escort vessels
50 completed 1943–5
Lost *No. 1, No. 3, No. 5, No. 7, No. 9, No. 11, No. 13, No. 15, No. 17, No. 19, No. 21, No. 23, No. 25, No. 31, No. 33, No. 35, No. 39, No. 41, No. 43, No. 45, No. 47, No. 51, No. 53, No. 61, No. 63, No. 65, No. 69, No. 73, No. 75, No. 213, No. 219*

Displacement	745 tons
Length	221ft (67.4m)
Beam	27.5ft (8.4m)
Guns	2 × 4.7in HA
	4–6 × 25mm AA
Machinery	1,900bhp = 16.5kts
Complement	136

'Type D'-class escort vessels
63 completed 1943–5
Lost *No. 4, No. 6, No. 10, No. 18, No. 20, No. 24, No. 28, No. 30, No. 38, No. 42, No. 46, No. 54, No. 56, No. 64, No. 66, No. 68, No. 72, No. 74, No. 82, No. 84, No. 112, No. 130, No. 134, No. 138, No. 144, No. 186*

Displacement	740 tons
Length	228ft (69.5m)
Beam	28ft (8.6m)
Guns	as 'Type C'
Machinery	2,500bhp = 17.5kts
Complement	160

Minelayer *Shirataka*
one unit built 1927–9

Displacement	1,540 tons
Length	300ft (91.4m)
Beam	38ft (11.6m)
Guns	2 × 4.7in HA
	25mm AA
Mines	100
Machinery	2,000ihp = 16kts
Complement	175

Minelayer *Itsukushima*
one unit built 1928–9

Displacement	1,970 tons
Length	355ft (108m)
Beam	39ft (11.9m)
Guns	3 × 5.5in
	2 × 3in AA
Mines	400
Machinery	3,000bhp = 17kts
Complement	235

Kamome-class minelayers
2 built 1928–9; converted as escorts in 1943
Lost **Kamome, Tsubame**

Displacement	450 tons
Length	230ft (70m)
Beam	23.5ft (7.1m)
Guns	1 × 3in AA
Mines	120 (nil as escorts)
Machinery	2,500ihp = 19kts
Complement	56

Minelayer **Yaeyama**
one unit built 1930–2 (converted as an escort in 1943)

Displacement	1,135 tons
Length	305ft (93m)
Beam	35ft (10.7m)
Guns	2 × 4.7in AA
	25mm AA
Mines	185 (nil from 1943)
Machinery	4,800ihp = 20kts
Complement	150

Natsushima-class minelayers
2 built 1931–4
Lost **Nasami, Natsushima**

Displacement	510 tons
Length	245ft (74.6m)
Beam	24.5ft (7.5m)
Guns	2 × 3in AA
Mines	120
Machinery	2,300bhp = 19kts
Complement	80

Minelayer **Sarushima**
one unit built 1933–4; converted as escort 1943
Particulars as *Natsushima*-class, except:

Displacement	566 tons
Mines	nil as an escort
Machinery	2,100bhp = 18kts

Minelaying cruiser **Okinoshima**
one unit built 1934–6

Displacement	4,400 tons
Length	410ft (125m)
Beam	52ft (15.7m)
Guns	4 × 5.5in LA
	2 × 3in AA
Mines	500
Machinery	9,000shp = 20kts

Minelaying cruiser **Tsugaru**
one unit built 1939–41

Displacement	4,000 tons
Length	408ft (124m)
Beam	51ft (15.6m)
Guns	4 × 5in DP
	4 × 25mm AA
Mines	600
Machinery	9,000shp = 20kts

Sokuten-class minelayer/escorts
5 built 1937–40
Lost **Naryu, Shirakami, Sokuten, Ukishima**

Displacement	720 tons
Length	247ft (75.3m)
Beam	26ft (7.8m)
Guns	2 × 2pdr (40mm) AA
Mines	120
Machinery	3,600shp = 20kts
Complement	100

Hatsutaka-class minelayer/escorts
3 built 1933–41
Lost **Aotaka, Hatsutaka**

Displacement	1,608 tons
Length	298ft (90.8m)
Beam	37ft (11.3m)
Guns	4 × 2pdr AA
	4 × 25mm AA
Mines	360
Machinery	6,000shp = 20kts

Hirashima-class minelayer/escorts
9 built 1939–43
Lost **Hirashima, Hoko, Maeshima, Nuwashima, Takashima, Yurijima**
Particulars as *Sokuten*-class, except:

Guns	1 × 3in AA
	25mm AA

Minelayer/escort **Ajiro**
one unit built 1942–3
Particulars as *Hirashima*-class, except:

Machinery	3,500bhp = 20kts

W. 1-class minesweepers
4 built 1922–5
Lost **W. 1, W. 2, W. 3**

Displacement	705 tons
Length	250ft (76.2m)
Beam	26ft (8m)
Guns	2 × 4.7in LA
Machinery	4,000ihp = 20kts
Complement	91

W. 5-class minesweepers
2 built 1927–9
Lost **W. 5, W. 6**

Displacement	720 tons
Length	252ft (76.8m)
Beam	27ft (8.2m)
other particulars as *W. 1*-class	

W. 13-class minesweepers
4 built 1932–4
Lost **W. 13, W. 14, W. 15, W. 16**

Displacement	690 tons
Length	242ft (73.8m)
Beam	27ft (8.2m)
Guns	as 'W. 1'-class
Machinery	3,200ihp = 20kts

W. 17-class minesweepers
2 built 1935–6
Lost **W. 18**

Displacement	580 tons
Length	238ft (72.5m)
Beam	26ft (7.8m)
Guns	as 'W. 1'-class
Machinery	3,200shp × 19kts

W. 7-class minesweepers
6 built 1937–9
Lost **W. 7, W. 9, W. 10, W. 11, W. 12**

Displacement	630 tons
Dimensions as W. 17-class	
Guns	2 × 4.7in AA
	2 × 25mm AA
Machinery	3,850shp = 20kts
Complement	88

W. 19-class minesweepers
17 built 1940–4
Lost **W. 19, W. 20, W. 22, W. 24, W. 25, W. 26, W. 27, W. 28, W. 29, W. 30, W. 33, W. 34, W. 38, W. 39, W. 41**
Particulars as W. 7-class, except:

Displacement	650 tons
Guns	3 × 4.7in HA
	2 × 25mm AA

ex-Bangor-class minesweepers
2 seized incomplete in 1941
Lost **W. 101** (ex-Taitam)
Particulars as Royal Navy Bangor-class, except:

Guns	1 × 4.7in LA
	8 × 25mm AA

Hashidate-class gunboat
2 built 1939–41
Lost **Hashidate**

Displacement	1,204 tons
Length	257ft (78m)
Beam	32ft (9.7m)
Guns	3 × 4.7in LA,
	4 × 25mm AA
Machinery	4,600shp = 19.5kts
Complement	170

Armed merchant cruisers
13 commissioned 1941–3
Lost **Akagi Maru, Bangkok Maru, Hokoku Maru, Kongo Maru, Saigon Maru**
(Particulars are given only for one ship:

besides being typical of the type, she was the only Japanese AMC to be sunk in a surface action)
Hokoku Maru:

Tonnage	10,438
Length	520ft (158m)
Beam	66ft (20.2m)
Guns	8 × 5.5in
	25mm AA
Torpedo-tubes	4 × 21in
Machinery	13,000bhp = 21kts

T. 1 Type' fast transports
21 completed 1943–5
Lost **T. 1, T. 2, T. 3, T. 4, T. 5, T. 6, T. 7, T. 8, T. 10, T. 11, T. 12, T. 14, T. 15, T. 17, T. 18, T.21**

Displacement	1,500 tons
Length	315ft (96m)
Beam	33.5ft (10.2m)
Guns	2 × 5in DP
	15 × 25mm AA
Machinery	9,220shp = 22kts
Complement	150 + 480 troops

Ohama-class escort (ex-target ship)
2 built 1943–5
Lost **Ohama**

Displacement	3,070 tons
Length	387ft (118m)
Beam	38ft (11.6m)
Guns	2 × 4.7in HA,
	32 × 25mm AA
Machinery	52,000shp = 32.5kts
Complement	n/k

LATVIA

'M-boote Type 1915'-class minesweeper
Virsaitis
Built 1918
Particulars as German 'Type 1915'-class minesweeper, except:

Guns	2 × 88mm HA
Complement	65

LITHUANIA

'M-boote Type 1915'-class minesweeper
Prezident Smetona
Built 1918
Particulars as German 'Type 1915'-class minesweeper, except:

Guns	2 × 75mm

NETHERLANDS

Java-class light cruiser
2 built 1918–25
Lost **Java, Sumatra**

Displacement	6,670 tons
Length	510ft (155m)
Beam	52.5ft (16m)
Guns	10 × 5.9in (150mm)
	6 × 40mm AA
Mines	12
Machinery	72,000shp = 31kts
Complement	525

Light cruiser *De Ruyter*
one unit built 1933–7

Displacement	6,470 tons
Length	560ft (171m)
Beam	51ft (15.5m)
Guns	7 × 5.9in
	10 × 40mm AA
Machinery	66,000shp = 32kts
Complement	435

ex-*Evertsen*-class destroyers
8 built 1925–30
Lost *Banckert, Evertsen, Kortenaer, Piet Hein, *Van Galen, Van Ghent, *Van Nes, *Witte de With*

Displacement	1,316 tons
Length	322ft (98.1m)
Beam	31ft (9.5m)
Guns	4 × 4.7in (120mm) LA (all)
	1 × 75mm AA
	4 × 2pdr (40mm) AA
	(*2 × 3in AA
	nil 40mm)
Torpedo-tubes	6 × 21in (533mm)
Mines	(*24)
Machinery	31,000shp = 34kts
Complement	127

Callenburgh-class destroyers
3 built 1938–40
Lost *Gerard Callenburgh, *Isaac Sweers, Tjerk Hiddes*

Displacement	1,628 tons
Length	350ft (106.7m)
Beam	35ft (10.6m)
Guns	5 × 4.7in
	4 × 40mm AA
Torpedo-tubes	8 × 21in
Mines	24
Machinery	45,000shp = 36kts
Complement	157

*Completed in Britain with 6 × 4in guns

Brinio-class gunboats
3 built 1912–13
Lost *Brinio, Friso*

Displacement	540 tons
Length	172ft (52.5m)
Beam	28ft (8.5m)
Guns	4 × 4.1in (105mm) LA
Machinery	1,500bhp = 14kts
Complement	63

Flores-class gunboats
3 built 1924–7
Lost *Johan Maurits van Nassau*

Displacement	1,450 tons
Length	246ft (75m)
Beam	38ft (11.5m)
Guns	3 × 5.9in
	1 × 75mm AA
Machinery	2,000ihp = 15kts
Complement	132

Prins van Oranje-class minelayer
2 built 1930–2
Lost *Prins van Oranje*

Displacement	1,290 tons
Length	216ft (66m)
Beam	36ft (11m)
Guns	2 × 3in AA,
	2 × 40mm AA,
	150 mines
Machinery	1,750bhp = 15kts
Complement	120

Van Amstel-class minesweepers
8 built 1935–9
Lost *Jan van Amstel, Pieter de Bitter, Eland Dubois, Willem van Ewijck (I)*

Displacement	525 tons
Length	183ft (55.8m)
Beam	26ft (7.8m)
Guns	1 × 75mm AA
Mines	20
Machinery	1,600ihp = 15.5kts
Complement	46

NORWAY

Haarfagre-class coast defence ships
2 built 1896–8
Lost *Harald Haarfagre, Tordenskjold*

Displacement	3,850 tons
Length	304ft (93m)
Beam	48ft (14.7m)
Guns	2 × 8.2in (210mm)
	6 × 4.7in (1200mm)
	6 × 3in (76mm) LA
	2 × 3in AA
	2 × 37mm AA
Machinery	4,500ihp = 14kts
Complement	250

Norge-class coast defence ships
2 built 1898–1900
Lost *Eidsvold, Norge*

Displacement	4,166 tons
Length	310ft (94.6m)
Beam	50.5ft (15.4m)
Guns	2 × 8.2in (210mm)
	6 × 5.9in (150mm)
	8 × 3in (76mm) AA
	2 × 47mm

Torpedo-tubes	2 × 18in (457mm)
Machinery	4,500ihp = 16.5kts
Complement	270

Aeger-class torpedo-boats
6 built 1933–40
Lost *Aeger, Balder, Gyller, Odin, Tor*

Displacement	590 tons
	550 tons
Length	255ft (77.6m)
Beam	26ft (7.8m)
Guns	3 × 4in (102mm)
	1 × 40mm AA
Torpedo-tubes	4 × 21in (533mm)
Machinery	12,500shp = 30kts
Complement	72

Draug-class torpedo-boats
3 built 1908–11 in service in 1940
Lost *garm, Troll*

Displacement	468 tons
Length	225ft (68.6m)
Beam	24ft (7.3m)
Guns	6 × 3in
Torpedo-tubes	3 × 18in
Machinery	8,00ibhp = 27kts
Complement	76

'S'-class destroyers
2 built and transferred in 1943–4 by RN
Lost *Svenner*
Particulars as Royal Navy 's'-class destroyers

'Town'-class escort destroyers
5 manned by RNorN 1940–4
Lost *Bath*
Particulars as RN 'Town'-class (ex-US
Clemson-class) destroyers

'Hunt'-class escort destroyer *Eskdale*
manned by RNorN 1942–3
Particulars as Royal Navy 'Hunt'-class (Group
III) escort destroyers

'Flower'-class corvettes
3 transferred from RN 1941, 3 manned 1941–5
Lost *Montbretia, Rose*
Particulars as Royal Navy 'Flower'-class
corvettes

'Castle'-class corvette *Tunsberg Castle*
transferred from RN 1944
Particulars as Royal Navy 'Castle'-class
corvettes

Minelayer *Olav Tryggvason*
one unit built 1931–4

Displacement	1,596 tons
Length	319ft (97.3m)
Beam	37.5ft (11.5m)
Guns	4 × 4.7in LA
	1 × 3in AA

Torpedo-tubes	2 × 18in
Mines	280
Machinery	6,000shp = 21kts
Complement	132

Burza-class destroyers
2 built 1926–31 (similar to French *Bourrasque*-class destroyers
Lost *Wicher*

Displacement	1,515 tons
Length	348ft (106m)
Beam	33.5ft (10.2m)
Guns	4 × 5.1in (130mm) LA
	2 × 40mm AA
Torpedo-tubes	6 × 21.6in (550mm)
Mines	60
Machinery	33,000shp = 33kts
Complement	155

Blyskawica-class destroyers
2 built 1935–7
Lost *Grom*

Displacement	2,144 tons
Length	374ft (114m)
Beam	37ft (11.3m)
Guns	7 × 4.7in (120mm) HA
	4 × 40mm AA
Torpedo-tubes	6 × 21in (533mm)
Machinery	54,000shp = 37kts
Complement	190

'M'-class destroyer *Orkan*
manned by Polish Navy 1942–3
Details as RN 'M'-class destroyers

'Hunt'-class escort destroyers
3 manned 1942–5
Lost *Kujawiak*
Particulars as Royal Navy 'Hunt'-class (Group
II) escort destroyers

Minelayer *Gryf*
one unit built 1934–8

Displacement	2,227 tons
Length	399ft (103.2m)
Beam	43ft (13.1m)
Guns	6 × 4.7in HA
	4 × 40mm AA
Mines	300
Machinery	6,000bhp = 20kts
Complement	200

Klas Horn-class destroyers
(designed based on US Navy *Clemson*-class)
2 built 1927–9
Lost *Klas Horn, Klas Uggla*

Displacement	1,004 tons
Length	304ft (92.7m)
Beam	29ft (8.9m)
Guns	3 × 4.7in (120mm) LA
	4 × 25mm AA
Torpedo-tubes	6 × 21in (533mm)
Mines	20
Machinery	24,000shp = 35kts
Complement	125

Göteborg-class destroyers
6 built 1935–41
Lost **Göteborg**

Displacement	1,030 tons
Length	310ft (94.6m)
Beam	29.5ft (9m)
Guns	3 × 4.7in LA
	4 × 25mm AA
Torpedo-tubes	6 × 21in
Mines	20
Machinery	32,200shp = 39kts
Complement	130

THAILAND

Domburi-class coast defence ships
2 built 1936–8
Lost **Ahidea, Domburi**

Displacement	2,265 tons
Length	246ft (75.1m)
Beam	44ft (13.4m)
Guns	4 × 8in (203mm)
	4 × 3in (76mm) AA
	4 × 20mm AA
Machinery	5,200bhp = 15.5kts
Complement	155

Trat-class torpedo-boats
9 built 1935–8
Lost **Cholburi, Songkla, Trat**

Displacement	430 tons
Length	223ft (68m)
Beam	21ft (6.4m)
Guns	3 × 3in AA
	2 × 20mm AA
Torpedo-tubes	6 × 17.7in (450mm)
Machinery	10,000shp = 31kts
Complement	70

UNITED STATES OF AMERICA

Oklahoma-class battleships
2 built 1913–15
Lost **Nevada, Oklahoma**

Displacement	29,000 tons
Length	583ft (178m)
Beam	108ft (33m)
Guns	10 × 14in (356)
	12 × 5in (127mm) LA
	12 × 5in AA

| Machinery | 26,500sbhp = 20.5kts |
| Complement | 2,100 |

Pennsylvania-class battleships
2 built 1914–16
Lost **Arizona**

Displacement	32,600 tons
Length	612ft (187m)
Beam	106ft (32.4m)
Guns	12 × 14in
	12 × 5in LA
	12 × 5in AA
Machinery	33,375shp = 21kts
Complement	2,290

California-class battleships
2 built 1916–21
Lost **California**

Displacement	32,600 tons
Length	624ft (190m)
Beam	108ft (33m)
Guns	as *Pennsylvania*-class
Machinery	30,000shp = 21kts
Complement	2,200

Maryland-class battleships
3 built 1917–23
Lost **West Virginia**

Displacement	31,800 tons
Dimensions as *California*-class	
Guns	8 × 16in (406mm)
	10 × 5in LA
	8 × 5in AA
Machinery	31,000shp = 21kts
Complement	2,100

Northampton-class heavy cruisers
6 built 1928–31
Lost **Chicago, Houston, Northampton**

Displacement	9,050 tons
	9,300 tons (*Chicago*)
Length	600ft (183m)
Beam	66ft (20.2m)
Guns	9 × 8in (203mm)
	8 × 5in AA
	40mm & 20mm AA
Machinery	107,000shp = 32.7kts
Complement	1,100

Indianapolis-class heavy cruisers
2 built 1929–33
Lost **Indianapolis**

Displacement	9,950 tons
Length	610ft (186m)
Beam	66ft (20.2m)
other particulars as *Northampton*-class except:	
Complement	1,150

Astoria-class heavy cruisers
7 built 1931–7
Lost **Astoria, Quincy, Vincennes**

| Displacement | 9,950 tons |

9,400 tons (*Quincy, Vincennes*)

Length	588ft (179m)
Beam	62ft (18.8m)

other particulars as *Northampton*-class except:

Complement	1,050

Brooklyn-class light cruisers
9 built 1935–40
Lost **Helena**

Displacement	10,000 tons
Length	608ft (185.5m)
Beam	62ft (18.8m)
Guns	15 × 6in (152mm)
	8 × 5in AA
	40mm & 20mm AA
Machinery	100,000shp = 34kts
Complement	1,300

Juneau-class AA cruisers
8 built 1939–45
Lost **Atlanta, Juneau**

Displacement	6,000 tons
Length	541ft (165m)
Beam	53ft (16.2m)
Guns	16 × 5in DP
	10 × 40mm AA
	20mm AA
Torpedo-tubes	8 × 21in (533mm)
Machinery	75,000shp = 32kts
Complement	800

Saratoga-class aircraft carriers
2 built 1920–7
Lost **Lexington**

Displacement	36,000 tons
Length	888ft (271m)
Beam	105ft (32m)
Flight Deck	880 × 90ft
	(267 × 27.4m)
Guns	8 × 5in AA
	6 × 4 1.1in (28mm) AA
	20mm AA
Aircraft	88
Machinery	180,000shp = 34kts
Complement	3,300

Yorktown-class aircraft carriers
3 built 1934–41
Lost **Hornet, Yorktown**

Displacement	19,800 tons
Length	809ft (247m)
Beam	83ft (25.3m)
Flight Deck	781 × 80ft
	(238 × 24.4m)
Guns	8 × 5in AA
	4 × 4 1.1in AA
	20mm AA
Aircraft	79
Machinery	120,000shp = 33kts
Complement	2,200

Aircraft carrier **Wasp**
one unit built 1936–40

Displacement	14,700 tons
Length	741ft (226m)
Beam	81ft (24.6m)
Flight Deck	735 × 80ft
	(224 × 24.4m)
Guns	8 × 5in AA
	4 × 1.1in AA
	20mm AA
Aircraft	72
Machinery	75,000shp = 29.5kts
Complement	1,800

Independence-class light carriers
9 built 1941–3
Lost **Princeton**

Displacement	11,000 tons
Length	622ft (190m)
Beam	71.5ft (21.8m)
Guns	22 × 40mm AA (2 × 4,
	9 × 2)
	10 × 20mm AA
Aircraft	31–33
Machinery	100,000shp = 31.6kts
Complement	1,560

Bogue-class escort carriers
10 units built 1941–2
Lost **Block Island**

Displacement	9,800 tons
Length	496ft (151m)
Beam	70ft (21.2m)
Flight Deck	442 × 80ft
	(135m × 24.4m)
Guns	2 × 5in DP
	16 × 40mm AA
	(8 × 2)
	20 × 20mm AA
Aircraft	18–24
Machinery	8,500shp × 17–18kts
Complement	890

Casablanca-class escort carriers
50 units built 1942–4
Lost **Bismarck Sea, Gambier Bay, Liscome Bay, Ommaney Bay, St Lo**

Displacement	7,800 tons
Length	512ft (156m)
Beam	65ft (19.8m)
Flight Deck	477 × 80ft
	(145 × 24.4m)
Guns	1 × 5in DP
	16 × 40mm AA (— × 2)
	20 × 20mm AA
Aircraft	27–30
Machinery	9,000shp = 19.5kts
Complement	860

Wickes-class destroyers
21 built 1917–20 in service in 1941
Lost **Jacob Jones, Leary**

Displacement	1,090 tons
Length	314ft (96m)
Beam	32ft (9.7m)
Guns	4 × 4in (102mm)
	1 × 3in (76mm) AA
Torpedo-tubes	12/21in
Machinery	26,000shp = 35kts
Complement	153

Clemson-class destroyers
31 built 1918–22 in service in 1941
Lost **Borie, Edsall, Parrott, Peary, Pillsbury, Pope, Reuben James, Stewart, Sturtevant, Truxtun**
Particulars as *Wickes*-class, except:

Displacement	1,190 tons

Farragut-class destroyers
8 built 1933–5
Lost **Hull, Monaghan, Worden**

Displacement	1,385 tons
	1,410 tons (*Worden*)
Length	341ft (104m)
Beam	34ft (10.4m)
Guns	5 × 5inm DP
	40mm & 20mm AA added
Torpedo-tubes	8 × 21in
Machinery	42,800shp = 36.5kts
Complement	250

Porter-class destroyers
8 built 1935–7
Lost **Porter**

Displacement	1,850 tons
Length	381ft (116m)
Beam	37ft (11.3m)
Guns	8 × 5in DP
	2 × 4 1.1in AA
	(replaced by 40mm & 20mm AA)
Torpedo-tubes	8 × 21in
Machinery	50,000shp × 37kts
Complement	290

Mahan-class destroyers
18 built 1935–7
Lost **Cassin, Cushing, Downes, Mahan, Perkins, Preston, Reid, Shaw, Tucker**

Displacement	1,500 tons
	1,450 tons (*Mahan*)

other particulars as *Farragut*-class, except:

Beam	35ft (10.6m)
Torpedo-tubes	12 × 21in
Complement	172

Somers-class destroyers
5 built 1936–9
Lost **Warrington**

Displacement	1,850 tons
Length	381ft (116m)
Beam	36.5ft (11.1m)
Guns	8 × 5in DP

	2 × 4 1.1in AA
	(replaced by 40mm & 20mm AA)
Torpedo-tubes	9/21in
Machinery	52,000shp = 35kts
Complement	270

Craven-class destroyers
22 built 1936–40
Lost **Benham, Blue, Henley, Jarvis, Rowan**

Displacement	1,500 tons
Length	341ft (104m)
Beam	35.5ft (10.8m)
Guns	4 × 5in DP
	40mm & 20mm AA added
Torpedo-tubes	16 × 21in
Machinery	50,000shp = 38.5kts
Complement	255

Sims-class destroyers
12 built 1937–40
Lost **Buck, Hammann, Morris, O'Brien, Sims, Walke**

Displacement	1,620 tons
Length	348ft (106m)
Beam	36ft (11m)
Guns	5 × 5in DP
	40mm & 20mm AA added
Torpedo-tubes	8 × 21in
Machinery	50,000shp = 37kts
Complement	250

Livermore-class destroyers
16 built 1939–41
Lost **Gwin, Ingraham, Lansdale, Meredith (I), Monssen**
Particulars as *Sims*-class, except:

Torpedo-tubes	10 × 21in
Complement	276

Bristol-class destroyers
48 built 1940–3
Lost **Aaron Ward (I), Barton, Beatty, Bristol, Corry, Duncan (I), Glennon, Laffey (I), Maddox (I), Shubrick, Turner**
Displacement and dimensions as *Sims*-class

Guns	4 × 5in DP
	1 × 4 1.1in AA, or
	2 × 40mm
	5–8 × 20mm AA
Torpedo-tubes	10 × 21in
Machinery	50,000shp = 37.5kts
Complement	270

Fletcher-class destroyers
124 built 1941–5
Lost **Abner Read, Brownson, Bush, Callaghan, Chevalier, Colhoun (II), De Haven, Evans, Haggard, Halligan, Hoel, Hutchins, Johnston, Leutze, Little (II), Longshaw, Luce,**

Morrison, Newcomb, Pringle, Spence, Strong, Thatcher, Twiggs, William D. Porter

Displacement	2,050 tons
Length	376ft (114.75m)
Beam	39.5ft (12.1m)
Guns	5 × 5in DP
	2–10 × 40mm AA
	4–11 × 20mm AA
Torpedo-tubes	10/21in
Machinery	60,000shp
Complement	330

Allen M. Sumner-class destroyers
44 built 1943–5
Lost **Cooper, Drexler, Hugh W. Hadley, Mannert L. Abele, Meredith (II)**

Displacement	2,200 tons
Length	376ft (114m.6)
Beam	41ft (12.5m)
Guns	6 × 5in DP
	12 × 40mm AA
	8–11 20mm AA
Torpedo-tubes	10 × 21in
Machinery	60,000shp = 34kts
Complement	336

Wickes and *Clemson*-class destroyer-minesweepers
18 built 1918–20 and converted 1940–2
Lost **Hovey, Long, Palmer, Perry, Wasmuth**
Particulars as *Wickes* and *Clemson* classes, except:

Guns	4 × 3in AA
	20mm AA
Torpedo-tubes	(removed)
Complement	140

Bristol-class destroyer-minesweepers
24 built 1941–3
Lost **Butler, Emmons, Forrest, Harding**
Particulars as 'Bristol'-class, except:

Guns	3 × 5in DP
Torpedo-tubes	(removed)

Wickes and *Clemson*-class destroyer-minelayers
8 built 1918–20 and converted 1930–7
Lost **Gamble, Montgomery**
Particulars as *Wickes* and *Clemson* destroyer-minesweepers, except:

Mines	80
Complement	122

Sumner-class destroyer-minelayers
12 built 1943–4
Lost **Aaron Ward (II), J. William Ditter**
Particulars as *Sumner*-class destroyers, except:

Torpedo-tubes	(removed)
Mines	100
Complement	363

Buckley-class destroyer escort
68 built 1942–4
Lost **Donnell, England, Fechteler, Rich, Underhill**

Displacement	1,400 tons
Length	306ft (93.3m)
Beam	37ft (11.3m)
Guns	3 × 3in AA
	1 × 4 1.1in AA
	6–10 × 20mm AA
Torpedo-tubes	3 × 21in
Machinery	12,000shp = 23.5kts
Complement	220

Edsall-class destroyer escorts
85 built 1942–4
Lost **Fiske, Frederick C. Davis, Holder, Leopold**

Displacement	1,200 tons
Length	306ft (93,3m)
Beam	36.5ft (11.1m)
Guns	3 × 3in AA
	2 × 40mm AA
	8 × 20mm AA
Torpedo-tubes	3 × 21in
Machinery	6,000bhp = 21kts
Complement	200

John C. Butler-class destroyer escorts
83 built 1943–5
Lost **Eversole, Oberrender, Samuel B. Roberts, Shelton**

Displacement	1,350 tons
Length	306ft (93.3m)
Beam	36.75ft (11.2m)
Guns	2 × 5in DP
	4 × 40mm AA
	10 × 20mm AA
Torpedo-tubes	3 × 21in
Machinery	12,000shp = 24kts
Complement	200

'Bird'-class minesweepers
22 built 1917–19
Lost **Bittern, Finch, Penguin, Pigeon, Quail, Tanager**

Displacement	840 tons
Length	188ft (57.3m)
Beam	35.5ft (10.8m)
Guns	2 × 3in AA
Machinery	1,400ihp = 14kts
Complement	62

'Auk'-class minesweepers
73 built 1940–5
Lost **Osprey, Portent, Sentinel, Skill, Skylark, Swallow, Swerve, Tide**

Displacement	890 tons
	810 tons (*Osprey*)
Length	221ft (67.4m)
Beam	32ft (9.7m)
Guns	1 × 3in AA
	2 × 40mm AA
	2 × 20mm AA

Machinery	3,500shp = 18kts
Complement	100

Admirable-class minesweepers
112 built 1942–5
Lost **Salute, Spectacle**

Displacement	650 tons
Length	184ft (56.2m)
Beam	33ft (10m)
Guns	1 × 3in AA
	4 × 40mm AA
Machinery	1,710bhp = 15kts
Complement	100

Asheville-class patrol gunboats
2 built 1918–23
Lost **Asheville**

Displacement	1,200 tons
Length	241ft (73.5m)
Beam	41ft (12.6m)
Guns	3 × 4in LA
	4 × 3in AA
Machinery	1,200shp = 12kts
Complement	175

Erie-class patrol gunboats
2 built 1935–7
Lost **Erie**

Displacement	1,900 tons
Length	328ft (100m)
Beam	41ft (12.6m)
Guns	4 × 6in
	4 × 3in AA
	2 × 4 1.1in AA
	(replaced by 40mm &
	20mm AA)
Machinery	6,200shp = 20kts
Complement	236

US river gunboats
3 in service 1941, built 1927–8
Lost **Luzon, Mindanao, Oahu**

Displacement	560 tons (*Oahu*
	450 tons)
Length	211ft (64.2m)
	(*Oahu* 191ft (54.4m))
Beam	31ft (9.5m) (*Oahu* 28ft
	(8.6m))
Guns	2 × 3in
Machinery	3,150ihp = 16kts
	(*Oahu* 2,250ihp
	= 15kts)
Complement	70

Wickes and *Clemson*-class fast transports
(APDs)
*6 converted pre-war from destroyers built
1917–20; 26 more converted 1942–3
Lost **Barry, Belknap, Brooks, *Colhoun,
Dickerson, *Gregory, *Little, *McKean, Noa,
Rathburne, Roper, Ward**
Displacement and dimensions as *Wickes* and

Clemson destroyer:

Guns	3 × 3in AA
	2 × 40mm AA
	20mm AA
Torpedo-tubes	(removed)
Machinery	13,000shp = 25kts

Buckley-class fast transports
44 built 1942–4
Lost **Bates**
Displacement, dimensions and machinery as
Buckley-class:

Guns	1 × 5in DP
	6 × 40mm AA
	20mm AA
Complement	204

Algonquin-class cutter
6 built 1934
Lost **Escanaba**

Displacement	1,005 tons
Length	165ft
Beam	36ft
Guns	2 × 3in
	3 ×20mm
Machinery	1,500shp = 13kts
Complement	105

USSR

Gangut-class battleships
3 built 1909–15
Lost **Marat**

Displacement	25,000 tons
Length	606ft (185m)
Beam	88ft (27m)
Guns	12 × 12in (305mm)
	16 × 4.7in (120mm) LA
	6 × 3in (76mm) AA
	37mm AA
Torpedo-tubes	4 × 17.7in (450mm)
Machinery	61,000shp = 23kts
Complement	1,286

Light cruiser **Komintern**
one unit built 1901–5

Displacement	6,338 tons
Length	440ft (134m)
Beam	54.5ft (16.6m)
Guns	10 × 5.1in (130mm)
	6 × 75mm LA
	3 × 3in AA
	2 × 47mm AA
Machinery	19,500ihp = 23kts
Complement	590

Chervonaya Ukraina-class light cruisers
2 built 1913–28
Lost **Chervonaya Ukraina**

Displacement	6,934 tons
Length	520ft (158.5m)

Beam	49ft (15.3m)
Guns	15 × 5.1in
	6 × 3in AA
	3 × 47mm AA
Torpedo-tubes	12 × 21in
Mines	100
Machinery	50,000shp = 29.5kts
Complement	750

Leningrad-class flotilla leaders
6 built 1932–40
Lost *Kharkov, Minsk, Moskva*

Displacement	2,225 tons
Length	418ft (127.5m)
Beam	38.5ft (11.7m)
Guns	5 × 5.1in
	2 × 3in AA
	2 × 45mm AA
Torpedo-tubes	8 × 21in
Mines	84
Machinery	66,000shp = 36kts
Complement	250

Flotilla leader *Tashkent*
one unit built 1937–9

Displacement	2,893 tons
Length	458ft (139.8m)
Beam	45ft (13.7m)
Guns	6 × 5.1in
	6 × 45mm AA
	8 × 20mm AA
Torpedo-tubes	9 × 21in
Mines	80
Machinery	110,000shp = 42kts
	(trials)
Complement	250

Novik-class destroyer *Yakov Sverdlov*
1 built 1910–13 serving in 1941

Displacement	1,271 tons
Length	336ft (102.4m)
Beam	31ft (9.5m)
Guns	5 × 4in (102mm) LA
	1 × 75mm AA
	1 × 37mm AA
Torpedo-tubes	9 × 17.7in
Mines	60
Machinery	36,500shp = c30kts
Complement	168

'Type II'-class destroyer *Frunze*
1 built 1911–15 serving in 1941

Displacement	1,100 tons
Length	305ft (93m)
Beam	30.5ft (9.3m)
Guns	4 × 4in LA
	1 × 75mm AA
	1 × 37mm AA
Torpedo-tubes	9 × 17.7in
Mines	60
Machinery	29,800shp = 25kts
Complement	160

'Type III'-class destroyers
2 built 1913–27 serving in 1941
Lost *Kalinin, Karl Marx*

Displacement	1,354 tons
Length	351ft (107m)
Beam	31ft (9.5m)
Guns	5 × 4in LA
	1 × 75mm AA
	1 × 37mm AA
Torpedo-tubes	6 × 17.7in
Mines	80
Machinery	32,700shp = 28kts
Complement	168

'Type IV'-class destroyers
4 built 1913–28 serving in 1941
Lost *Lenin*

Displacement	1,260 tons
Length	321ft (97.8m)
Beam	31ft (9.4m)
Guns	4 × 4in LA
	1 × 75mm AA
	2 × 45mm AA
	2 × 37mm AA
Torpedo-tubes	9 × 17.7in
Mines	60
Machinery	31,500shp = 24kts
Complement	168

'Type V'-class destroyers
5 built 1914–16 serving in 1941
Lost *Artem, Engels, Volodarski*

Displacement	1,440 tons
Dimensions as 'Type IV'-class	
Guns	4 × 4in LA
	2 × 45mm AA
	2 × 37mm AA
Torpedo-tubes	6 × 17.7in
Mines	60
Machinery	32,000shp = 24kts
Complement	160

'Type VI'-class destroyers
4 built 1915–25 serving in 1941
Lost *Dzerzhinski, Shaumyan*

Displacement	1,308 tons
Length	334ft (102m)
Beam	31ft (9.5m)
Armament as 'Type V'-class	
Mines	nil
Machinery	32,500shp = 26kts
Complement	160

'Type 7', or *Gordy*-class destroyers
28 built 1934–42
Lost *Bditelny, Bezposhchadny, Bezuprechny, Bystry, Gnevny, Gordy, Smetlivy, Sokrushitelny, Steregushchy, Stremitelny*

Displacement	1,660 tons
Length	370ft (112.9m)
Beam	33.5ft (10.2m)

Guns	4 × 5.1in
	2 × 3in AA
	4 × 37mm AA
	1 × 20mm AA
Torpedo-tubes	6 × 21in (with reloads)
Mines	60
Machinery	48,000shp = 38kts
Complement	197

'Type 7U', or *Silny*-class destroyers
18 built 1936–43
Lost *Serdity, Skory, Smely, Smyshleny, Sovershenny, Sposobny, Statny, Surovy, Svobodny*

Displacement	1,686 tons
Dimensions as 'Type 7'-class	
Guns	4 × 5.1in
	3 × 3in AA
	6 × 37mm AA
Torpedo-tubes	6 × 21in (with reloads)
Mines	60
Machinery	54,000shp = 36kts
Complement	207

ex-RN 'Town'-class escort destroyers
9 transferred 1944
Lost *Dyeyatelny*
Particulars as US Navy *Wickes*-class, except:

Guns	1 × 4in LA
	1 × 3in AA
	6 × 20mm AA
Torpedo-tubes	6 × 21in
Complement	134

Uragan-class torpedo-boats
18 built 1927–36
Lost *Burya, Purga, Snieg, Tsiklon, Vikhr*

Displacement	580 tons
Length	233ft (71m)
Beam	24.5ft (7.4m)
Guns	2 × 3.9in (100mm) HA
	2 × 37mm AA
Torpedo-tubes	3 × 17.7in
Mines	24
Machinery	6,440shp = 25kts
Complement	101

Rubin-class escorts
4 built 1936 as NKVD Border Guard Patrol Vessels
Lost *Brilliant (SKR.29), Zhemchug (SKR.27)*

Displacement	550 tons
Length	203ft (62m)
Beam	23.75ft (7.2m)
Guns	1 × 4in (102mm)
	2 × 37mm AA
Machinery	2,300bhp = 17kts

'M-boote Type 1915' escorts (formerly minesweepers)
2 built 1916–17 seized in 1940
Lost *Korall* (ex-Lithuanian *Smetona*), *Virsaitis* (ex-Latvian, name unchanged)

Particulars as German 'Type 1915' minesweepers, except
Korall:

Guns	2 × 75mm LA
	2 × 45mm AA
Virsaitis:	
Guns	2 × 3.5in (88m) HA
	2 × 57mm AA

Tral-class minesweepers
41 built 1935–45
Lost *Bugel, Bui, Fugas, Gruz, Knekt, Krambol, Minrep, Patron, Shkiv, Shpil, Shtag, T.216, T.217, T.218, T.413, Verp, Vzryv, Vzryvatyel, Zaryad, Zashchitnik*

Displacement	440–475 tons
Length	203ft (62m)
Beam	24ft (7.2m)
Guns	1 × 3.9in HA
	1 × 45mm AA
Mines	31
Machinery	2,800bhp = 18kts
Complement	52

Admirable-class minesweepers
43 built and transferred by USA in 1942–3
Lost *T.114, T.118, T.120*
Particulars as US Navy *Admirable*-class minesweeper

Grozyashchy-class armoured gunboat
1 built 1895 in service in 1941
Lost *Krasnoye Znamaya*

Displacement	1,760 tons
Length	237ft (72.2m)
Beam	42ft (12.7m)
Guns	5 × 5.1in LA
	3 × 3in AA
	4 × 45mm AA
Machinery	2,000ihp = 13kts
Complement	200

YUGOSLAVIA

Old cruiser *Dalmacija*
built 1898–1900

Displacement	2,360 tons
Length	342ft (104.3m)
Beam	39ft (11.8m)
Guns	6 × 83mm (3.3in) HA
	4 × 47mm (3pdr) LA
Machinery	8,500ihp = 19kts
Complement	300

Flotilla leader *Dubrovnik*
one unit built 1930–3

Displacement	1,880 tons
Length	371ft (113.1m)
Beam	35ft (10.7m)

Guns	4 × 5.5in (140mm)
	2 × 83mm AA
	6 × 40mm AA
Torpedo-tubes	6 × 21in (533mm)
Mines	40
Machinery	42,000shp = 37kts
Complement	200

Beograd-class destroyers
3 built 1936–40
Lost **Beograd, Ljubljana, Zagreb**

Displacement	1,210 tons
Length	316ft (96.4m)
Beam	30.5ft (9.3m)
Guns	4 × 4.7in (120mm)
	4 × 40mm AA
Torpedo-tubes	6 × 21in
Mines	30
Machinery	44,000shp = 38kts
Complement	145

'76 T'-class torpedo-boats
2 built 1913–15 in service in 1941
Lost **T 1, T 3**

Displacement	250 tons
Length	187ft (57m)
Beam	19ft (5.7m)
Guns	1 × 66mm LA
	1 × 66mm HA
Torpedo-tubes	2 × 18in
Machinery	5,000shp = 28kts
Complement	52

'87 T'-class torpedo-boats
4 built 1913–15 in service in 1941
Lost **T 5, T 6, T 7, T 8**
Particulars as '76 T'-class, except:

Displacement	260 tons
Length	190ft (58m)

'M-boote Type 1915'-class minesweepers
6 built 1917–18 in service in 1941
Lost **Galeb, Jastreb, Kobac, Labud, Orao, Sokol**
Particulars as German 'Type 1915'-class
minesweeper except:

Guns	2 × 83mm AA

Seaplane Tender **Zmaj**
one unit built 1927–30

Displacement	1,870 tons
Length	246ft (75m)
Beam	42ft (12.9m)
Guns	2 × 83mm AA
	2 × 40mm AA
Aircraft	10
Machinery	3,250bhp = 15kts

Warship Armament

GUNS: CAPITAL SHIP AND HEAVY CRUISER MAIN ARMAMENT

Country	Ship	Calibre in (mm)	Projectile Weight lb (kg)	Muzzle Velocity ft/sec	Range yds (ft)	Rate of fire per min
Japan	Yamato-class	18.1 (460) 45-cal.	3,220 (1,464)	2,556	45,960	2
Japan	Nagato-class	16.1 (410) 45-cal.	2,249 (1,022)	2,560	42,000	2–3
Great Britain	Nelson-class	16 (406) 45-cal.	2,048 (931)	2,614	39,780	2
USA	North Carolina and South Dakota	16 (406) 45-cal.	2,700 (1,227)	2,300	36,900	2
USA	Iowa-class	16 (406) 50-cal.	2,700	2,500	42,345	2
Great Britain	Queen Elizabeth and Repulse classes and Hood	15 (381) 42-cal.	1,938 (880)	2,460	33,550	2
Italy	Littorio-class	15 (381) 50-cal.	1,951 (887)	2,850	46,200	1
France	Richelieu-class	14.96 (380) 45-cal.	1,950 (886)	2,720	45,600	1–2
Germany	Bismarck-class	14.96 (380) 48-cal.	1,764 (802)	2,690	38,800	2
Great Britain	King George V-class	14 (356mm) 45-cal.	1,590 (723)	2,480	38,560	2
USA	Texas, Oklahoma and Pennsylvania classes	14in (356) 45-cal.	1,500 (682)	2,600	34,300	1
Japan	Kongo, Fuso and Ise classes	14 (356) 45-cal.	1,485 (675)	2,530	38,770	2
France	Bretagne-class	13.4 (340) 46-cal.	1,268 (576)	2,560	29,100	1
France	Dunkerque-class	13 (330) 50-cal.	1,235 (561)	2,850	45,600	2–3
Italy	Cesare and Duilio-classes	12.6 (320mm) 44-cal.	1,160 (527)	2,720	31,300	2
USSR	Gangut-class	12 (305) 50-cal.	1,038 (472)	2,500	26,925	1–2
Germany	Schlesien-class	11.1 (283) 37-cal.	529 (240)	2,690	20,590	1
Germany	Deutschland-class	11.1 (283) 49-cal.	661 (300)	2,990	39,890	3
Germany	Scharnhorst-class	11.1 (283) 51-cal.	726 (330)	2,920	44,760	3–4
Finland	Vainamoinen-class	10 (254) 45-cal.	495 (225)	2,790	33,140	4
Italy	San Giorgio	10 (254) 45-cal.	500 (227)	2,850	27,300	2
Norway	Norge-class	8.2 (210) 44-cal.	313 (142)	2,300	nk	nk
Great Britain	County-class	8 (203) 50-cal.	256 (116)	2,800	30,650	5–6
USA	Northampton and Indianapolis classes, Astoria, Minneapolis and New Orleans	8 (203) 55-cal.	260 (118)	2,800	31,860	3
USA	Remaining Astoria-class, Baltimore-class, Wichita	8 (203) 55-cal.	335 (152)	2,500	30,050 (Baltimore-cl. 4)	3
France	Suffren-class	8 (203) 50-cal.	295 (134)	2,700	32,800	4
France	Algérie	8 (203) 55-cal.	295 (134)	2,750	33,000	4
Germany	Hipper-class	8 (203) 57-cal.	268 (122)	3,035	36,680	5
Italy	Trento-class	8 (203) 50-cal.	276 (125)	2,970	34,250	3–4
Italy	Zara-class	8 (203) 53-cal.	276 (125)	3,150	37,410	4
Japan	All heavy cruiser classes	8 (203) 49-cal.	277 (126)	2,750	32,150	4–5

GUNS: LIGHT CRUISER MAIN AND CAPITAL SHIP SECONDARY ARMAMENT

Country	Ship	Calibre in (mm)	Projectile Weight lb (kg)	Muzzle Velocity ft/sec	Range yds (ft)	Rate of fire per min
Great Britain	Improved *Birmingham*-class	7.5 (190) 45-cal.	200 (90.7)	2,770	21,110	nk
Italy	*San Giorgio*	7.5 (190) 45-cal.	200 (90.9)	2,835	24,000	nk
USSR	*Krasni Kavkaz, Kirov*-class	7.1 (181) 55-cal.	214 (97.5)	3,050	41,300	4–5
France	*Duguay Trouin*-class	6.1 (155) 50-cal.	124 (56.5)	2,790	28,540	4–5
Japan	*Yamato*-class, *Oyodo*	6.1 (155) 60-cal.	123 (55.9)	3,020	29,960	5
Great Britain	River gunboats, *Alcantara, Carnarvon Castle*	6 (152) 45-cal.	100 (45.5)	2,570	15,800	5
Great Britain	'C', 'D' and 'E'-class cruisers and Armed merchant cruisers	6 (152) 45-cal.	100 (45.5)	2,800	20,000	5
Great Britain	*Leander*, 'Town' and RAN *Amphion* classes	6 (152) 50-cal.	112 (50.9)	2,760	25,480	6–8
USA	*Brooklyn* and *Cleveland* classes	6 (152) 47-cal.	130 (59)	2,500	26,100	6–8
France	*Emile Bertin, La Galissonnière*-class	6 (152) 55-cal.	119 (54)	2,850	28,950	7–8
Italy	*Condottieri*-class, Groups 1–4	6 (152) 53-cal.	110 (50)	3,280	31,000	5
Italy	*Littorio*-class and *Condottieri*, Group 5	6 (152) 55-cal.	110 (50)	2,980	28,150	4–5
Japan	*Agano*-class	6 (152) 50-cal.	100 (45.4)	2,800	22,970	4–5
Germany	All light cruisers	5.9 (150) 57-cal.	100 (45.5)	3,150	28,100	6–8
Germany	Capital ships, *Deutschland*-class	5.9 (150) 52-cal.	100 (45.3)	2,870	25,150	5–8
Germany	'Z. 1936A'-class	5.9 (150) 46-cal.	88 (40)	2,870	25,700	5–8
Germany	Merchant raiders	5.9 (150) 42-cal.	100 (45.3)	2,750	21,200	nk
Netherlands	*Java, De Ruyter* and *Flores* classes	5.87 (149mm) 50-cal.	103 (46.7)	2,950	23,200	nk
Great Britain	*Hood*, AMCs	5.5 (140) 50-cal.	82 (37.2)	2,790	17,800	nk
Yugoslavia	*Dubrovnik*	5.5 (140) 56-cal.	87.5 (40)	2,890	25,600	nk
Japan	Light cruisers, Armed Merchant Cruisers	5.5 (140) 50-cal.	84 (38)	2,800	21,600	nk
France	Old avisos	5.45 (138.6) 55-cal.	87 (39.5)	2,590	17,600	5–6
France	*La Tour d'Auvergne*, flotilla leaders, *Bougainville*-class	5.45 (138.6) 40-cal.	89.5 (40.6)	2,300	18,150	5–6
	(*Vauban* and *Guépard* classes 19,900 yards)					
France	*Le Fantasque* and *Mogador* classes	5.45 (138.6) 50-cal.	89.5 (40.6)	2,625	21,870	6–7
Italy	'Capitani Romani' and *Duilio* classes	5.3 (135) 45-cal.	72 (32.7)	2,700	21,430	6–7
Great Britain	*Dido* and *King George V* classes (dual-purpose)	5.25 (133) 50-cal.	80 (36.3)	2,670	24,070 (46,500)	8–10

GUNS: DESTROYER MAIN AND GENERAL ANTI-AIRCRAFT ARMAMENT

Country	Ship	Calibre in (mm)	Projectile Weight lb (kg)	Muzzle Velocity ft/sec	Range yds (ft)	Rate of fire per min
France	Jaguar, Bourrasque, L'Adroit classes and Polish Burza-class	5.1 (130) 40-cal.	77 (35)	2,380	20,450	5–6
France	Dunkerque-class (dual-purpose) and Le Hardi-class (LA2)	5.1 (130) 45-cal.	71 (32)	2,625	22,800 (37,000 approx)	10–12
USSR	Light cruisers, Leningrad-class	5.1 (130) 55-cal.	81 (37)	2,700	21,435	8
USSR	Tashkent, 'Type 7' and 'Type 7U' classes	5.1 (130) 50-cal.	73.6 (33)	2,800	27,800	8–10
USA	Old battleships, escort carriers, Coast Guard cutters	5 (127) 51-cal.	50 (22.7)	3,150	15,850	6
USA	Old battleships, carriers and cruisers completed pre-war (AA)	5 (127) 25-cal.	54 (24.4)	2,110	14,500 (27,400)	15–20
USA	Ships of destroyer-escort size and above (dual-purpose)	5 (127) 38-cal.	55 (25)	2,600	18,200 (37,200)	15–20
Germany	'Type 1934' and 'Types 1936A & B' destroyer classes, Bremse, torpedo-boats Leopard and Luchs, Greek Vasilevs Georgios-class	5 (127) 42-cal.	62 (28)	2,720	19,030	6–8
Japan	Destroyers (high-angle)	5 (127) 50-cal.	51 (23)	3,000	20,100 (25,000 approx)	6–10
Japan	Capital ships, carriers, cruisers, escort destroyers (dual purpose)	5 (127) 40-cal.	51 (23)	2,370	16,000 (31,000)	8
Great Britain	Destroyers, sloops (low-angle or high-angle)	4.7 (120) 45-cal.	50 (22.7)	2,650	17,700 (HA 16,000 approx)	12
Great Britain	Nelson and Glorious classes (dual-purpose)	4.7 (120) 40-cal.	50 (22.7)	2,450	16,160 (32,000)	12–15
Great Britain	'L' & 'M'-class destroyers (high-angle)	4.7 (120) 50-cal.	62 (28)	2,540	21,240 (17,000 approx)	10
Netherlands	Destroyers, 'K'-class escorts –Bofors	4.7 (120) 50-cal.	53 (24)	2,950	21,300	10
Netherlands	Callenburgh-class	4.7 (120) 45-cal.	70.5 (32)	2,600	21,300	9
Italy	Leone-class	4.7 (120) 45-cal.	51 (23)	2,460	13,800	nk
Italy	Turbine, Sella and Sauro classes	4.7 (120) 45-cal.	51 (23)	2,790	16,950	8–10
Italy	Dardo, 'Navigatori', Maestrale, Oriani, 'Soldati' classes	4.7 (120) 50-cal.	52 (23.5)	3,020	21,430	6–7
Japan	Mutsuki-class and torpedo-boats	4.7 (120) 45-cal.	45 (20.5)	2,700	17,500	5

Country	Ship	Calibre in (mm)	Projectile Weight lb (kg)	Muzzle Velocity ft/sec	Range yds (ft)	Rate of fire per min
Japan	Carriers, unmodernized cruisers, escorts, minelayers and minesweepers (AA)	4.7 (120) 45-cal.	45 (20.5)	2,700	17,500 (33,000)	6
Great Britain	Battleships, carriers, *Scylla*, *Charybdis*, *Savage*, 'Z', 'Ca' and 'Battle'-class destroyers (dual-purpose)	4.5 (114) 45-cal.	55 (25)	2,450	20,700 (41,000)	12
Netherlands	*Brinio*-class	4.1 (105) 50-cal.	40 (18)	2,900	13,000	15
Germany	*Wolf*-class, *Bremse*	4.1 (105) 51-cal.	32.4 (14.7)	3,035	18,860	12
Germany	*Schlesien*-class, *Emden*, 'Type 35' & 'Type 37' torpedo-boats, minesweepers	4.1 (105) 45-cal.	33.3 (15)	2,575	16,600	12
Germany	Capital ships, heavy cruisers (AA)	4.1 (105) 60-cal.	33.3 (15)	2,950	19,360 (41,000)	15–18
Finland	*Vainamoinen*-class – Bofors (AA)	4.1 (105) 50-cal.	35.3 (16)	2,625	19,900 (39,000)	15
Great Britain	'Admiralty "S"'-class destroyers, *Halcyon*, 'Hunt', *Bangor* classes	4 (102) 40-cal. (Mk IV)	31 (14)	2,180	11,580	12
Great Britain	*Repulse, Eagle, Hermes, York, Sydney, Coventry, Curlew*, 'P' & 'O' class destroyers, *Algerine*-class minesweepers (AA)	4 (102) 45-cal. (Mk V)	31 (14)	2,390	16,400 (31,000)	15
Great Britain	'V & W'-class destroyers, *Bridgewater*, etc.-class, *Kingfisher*-class (LA)	4 (102) 45-cal. (Mk V)	31 (14)	2,640	13,800	15
Great Britain	Widespread use: capital ships, cruisers, *Abdiel*-class, 'M'-class destroyers, 'Hunt'-class escort destroyers, RAN frigates, etc. (dual-purpose and AA)	4 (102) 45-cal. (Mk XVI)	35 (15.9)	2,660	19,850 (39,000)	12
Great Britain	Corvettes, 'River'-class frigates, RAN *Bathurst*-class	4 (102) 40-cal. (Mk XIX)	35 (15.9)	1,300	9,700	12–15
USA	*Wickes* & *Clemson*-class destroyers, patrol gunboats, Greek *Aetos*-class destroyers	4 (102) 51-cal.	33 (15)	2,900	15,900	10–12
USSR	Old destroyers, some *Uragan*-class	4 (102) 60-cal.	39 (17.7)	2,700	16,400	10
Norway	Torpedo-boats – Bofors	4 (102) 50-cal.	31 (14)	2,790	20,000	15
Italy	*Mirabello*-class, torpedo-boats except *Pilo*-class	4 (102) 45-cal.	30 (13.7)	2,790	16,400	10

Country	Ship	Calibre in (mm)	Projectile Weight lb (kg)	Muzzle Velocity ft/sec	Range yds (ft)	Rate of fire per min
Italy	*Pilo*-class, *Audace, Diana*	4 (102) 35-cal.	30 (13.7)	2,460	12,800	10
France	Torpedo-boats, *Elan* and *Chamois*-classes	3.9 (100) 45-cal.	33 (15)	2,480	16,400	10
France	*Richelieu, Commandant Teste* (AA)	3.9 (100) 45-cal.	33	2,480	17,280 (32,000)	10
USSR	Some *Uragan*-class, *Tral*-class (LA); modern cruisers (AA)	3.9 (100) 53-cal.	34.4 (15.6)	2,950	24,500 (47,000)	15
Italy	*Cesare*-class, all cruisers, *San Giorgio, Spica* and *Ariete* classes, escort destroyers, corvettes (AA)	3.9 (100) 47-cal.	30.4 (13.8)	2,790	16,700 (35,000ft approx)	8–10
Japan	*Taiho, Oyodo, Akizuki*-class (dual-purpose)	3.9 (100) 65-cal.	28.7 (13)	3,310	21,300 (42,600)	15–20

Following convention, guns of calibres less than 3.9in/100mm are expressed in the form used in their country of origin

Country	Ship	Calibre in (mm)	Projectile Weight lb (kg)	Muzzle Velocity ft/sec	Range yds (ft)	Rate of fire per min
France	Cruisers (AA)	90mm (3.54in) 50-cal.	21 (9.5)	2,790	16,900 (35,000)	10
Italy	*Duilio* and *Littorio* classes (AA)	90mm (3.54in) 50-cal.	22.3 (10)	2,820	17,500 (35,400)	30
Germany	Some 'Type 40' minesweepers, Danish torpedo-boats	88mm (3.4in) 35-cal.	19.8 (9)	2,300	13,000	10–15
Germany	Light cruisers (AA)	88mm (3.4in) 72-cal.	19.8 (9)	3,110	18,800 (40,500)	10–15
Yugoslavia	*Dalmacija, Dubrovnik, Zmaj,* ex-German minesweepers – Skoda (AA)	83mm (3.26in) 55-cal.	23 (10.6)	2,625	18,000 (37,500)	15
Great Britain	'A' – 'I' class destroyers, RN and Indian *Bangor*-class (AA)	3in (76.2mm) 45-cal. (20cwt)	17.5 (8)	2,025	12,900 (25,500)	15
Great Britain	'S', 'V & W' and 'Town'-class destroyers, widespread service in minor warships (AA)	3in (76.2mm) 40-cal. (12cwt) (also known as '12pdr')	13 (5.9)	2,235	11,750 (19,000)	15
USA	Unconverted *Wickes* and *Clemson* class destroyers (HA)	3in (76.2mm) 23-cal.	13 (5.9)	1,650	10,100 (18,000)	15
USA	Converted *Wickes* and *Clemson* classes, destroyer escorts, minesweepers, widespread in minor warships (AA)	3in (76.2mm) 50-cal.	13 (5.9)	2,700	14,590 (29,900)	15–18
USSR	'Type 7' and '7U' destroyers (AA)	3in (76.2mm) 55-cal.	14.6 (6.6)	2,670	14,760 (30,000)	16–18
Norway	Coast defence ships, *Olav Tryggvason* – Bofors (AA)	76.2mm (3in) 50-cal.	12.5 (5.7)	2,890	16,500 (32,000)	20+
Italy	Minelayers	76.2mm (3in) 40-cal.	14.3 (6.5)	2,230	10,900	15

Country	Ship	Calibre in (mm)	Projectile Weight lb (kg)	Muzzle Velocity ft/sec	Range yds (ft)	Rate of fire per min
Japan	Old light cruisers, minor warships (AA)	76.2mm (3in) 40-cal.	13 (5.8)	2,235	11,800 (23,600)	13–20
Japan	*Agano*-class (AA)	76.2mm (3in) 60-cal.	13.2 (6)	2,950	14,870 (29,800)	25
France	Old battleships, *Suffren, Duquesne, Duguay Trouin*-class and many minor warships (AA)	75mm (2.95in) 50-cal.	13 (5.9)	2,790	15,420 (32,800)	10–15
Netherlands	*Evertsen, Flores* and *Van Amstel* classes (AA)	75mm (2.95in) 55-cal.	13 (5.9)	2,930	11,500 (32,000)	20+

Also intended solely for surface action were a small number of types of gun of less than 3in/75mm calibre. Although effective against small craft, they could not be regarded as 'ship-killing weapons' and are therefore omitted.

GUNS: LIGHT ANTI-AIRCRAFT ARMAMENT

Close-range anti-aircraft guns were produced in two main categories: the 37–40mm weapons which could destroy an aircraft with a single hit and the 20–25mm guns which relied upon the cumulative effect of several light shells and therefore a higher rate of fire. The maximum horizontal and vertical ranges are quoted as an indication of the power of individual weapons, but these were of significance only when the weapons were used for barrages, to provide a curtain or box of defensive fire. This form of AA defence was wasteful for weapons with high rates of fire; individual aimed fire was preferred but effective ranges were considerably less.

The maximum rate of fire, although expressed in rounds-per-minute was attainable only in relatively short bursts; although there were exceptions (such as the 40mm Bofors) few guns could sustain the maximum rate because of the need to change magazines or ammunition boxes. Short-range engagements rarely lasted more than a few seconds however, and the maximum rate is a fair yardstick of capability, if not of individual effectiveness.

Country	Ship	Calibre in (mm)	Projectile Weight lb (kg)	Muzzle Velocity ft/sec	Range yds (ft)	Rate of fire per min
USSR		45mm 46-cal.	3.1 (1.4)	2,490	10,400 (19,700)	30 single-shot
Sweden. Widely used by German and Allied navies		40mm (Bofors) 60-cal.	1.97 (0.89)	2,890	10,750 (23,500)	120 auto-matic
		(Max. Effective Range 3,500yds/3,200m)				
Great Britain. Royal Navy, RCN, RAN		40mm (Vickers) 39-cal.	1.68 (0.76)	2,400	6,800 (13,000)	115 auto-matic
		(Max. Effective Range 2,500yds/2,300m)				
Great Britain, Netherlands, Italy, Japan		40mm (Vickers) 39-cal.	2.00 (0.91)	2,040	5,000 (10,000)	90 auto-matic
France		37mm 50-cal.	1.6 (0.73)	2,790	nk (nk)	30–42 single-shot
Italy		37mm 54-cal.	1.81 (0.82)	2,625	8,530 (16,400)	120 auto-matic
		(Max. Effective Range 4,400yds/4,000m)				
USSR		37mm 67-cal.	1.61 (0.73)	2,890	8,750 (19,000)	160 auto-matic
		(Max. Effective Ceiling 4,500ft/1,400m)				

Country	Ship	Calibre in (mm)	Projectile Weight lb (kg)	Muzzle Velocity ft/sec	Range yds (ft)	Rate of fire per min
Germany. SKC/30		37mm 80-cal.	1.65 (0.75)	3,280	9,300 (22,300)	30 single-shot
Germany. Flak M42		37mm 69-cal.	1.42 (0.64)	2,770	6,600 (16,000)	160 auto-matic
		(Max. Effective Range 5,000yds/4,800m)				
Germany. Flak M43		37mm 57-cal.	1.42 (0.64)	2,690	6,500 (15,750)	240 auto-matic
USA		1.1in (28.2mm) 75-cal.	0.91 (0.42)	2,700	7,400 (19,000)	150 auto-matic
		(Max. Effective Range 3,000yds/2,700m)				
Japan		25mm 60-cal.	0.55 (0.25)	2,950	8,200 (18,000)	220 auto-matic
		(Max. Effective Range 1,650yds/1,500m)				
Switzerland. Widely used by Allies, German and Italian navies		20mm (Oerlikon) 70-cal.	0.27 (0.12)	2,750	4,800 (10,000)	465–480 auto-matic
		(Max. Effective Range 1,200yds/1,100m)				
Germany		20mm (Flak 30) 65-cal.	0.27 (0.12)	2,870	5,250 (12,000)	280–300 auto-matic
		(Max. Effective Range 1,200yds/1,100m)				
		(Later 20mm Flak 38 had higher rate of fire 450–500)				
Italy		20mm (Breda) 65-cal.	0.29 (0.13)	2,750	6,000 (9,500)	220 auto-matic
		(Max. Effective Range 2,700yds/2,500m?)				
Italy		20mm (Scotti) 77-cal.	0.28 (0.12)	2,700	5,500 (7,000)	250 auto-matic
		(Max. Effective Range 2,500yds/2,280m?)				

TORPEDOES: SURFACE- AND AIR-LAUNCHED

Country	Ship	Calibre in (mm)	Torpedo Weight lb (kg)	Warhead Weight lb (kg)	Range at yds	Speed kts
Great Britain	Nelson & Rodney	24.5 Mark I (622mm)	5,700 (2,590)	743 (338)	15,000 20,000	35 30
Japan	Old light cruisers, Mutsuki-class	24 8th Year Type (610mm)	5,207 (2,367)	759 (345)	20,000 10,000	28 38
Japan	Furutaka, Aoba and Fubuki classes	24 Type 90 (610mm)	5,730 (2,605)	825 (375)	16,400 7,500	35 46
Japan	Modern cruisers and destroyers	24 Type 93 (610mm) ('Long Lance')	5,940 (2,700)	1,080 (490)	44,000 35,000 20,000	36 40 50
USA	Aircraft, PT-boats	22.4 Mark 13 (569mm)	1,927 (876)	401 (182)	c2,000	30
USA	Aircraft, PT-boats	22.4 Mark 13–2	2,216 (1,007)	600 (273)	6,300	33.5
France	Cruisers, destroyers and torpedo-boats	21.65 Model 23D (550mm)	4,550 (2,068)	682 (310)	15,300 6,500	35 43
Great Britain	Old cruisers and destroyers, MTBs	21 Mark IV (533mm)	3,206 (1,457)	515 (234)	10,000 8,000	29 35
Great Britain	RN and RAN County-class cruisers	21 Mark VII (533mm)	4,106 (1,866)	740 (336)	16,000	33
Great Britain	Light cruisers and modern destroyers	21 Mark IX** (533mm)	2,732 (1,242)	810 (368)	15,000 11,000	35 41

Country	Ship	Calibre in (mm)	Torpedo Weight lb (kg)	Warhead Weight lb (kg)	Range at yds	Speed kts
Great Britain	Ex-Brazilian 'H', ex-Turkish 'I' classes, Polish destroyers	21 Mark X (533mm)	3,564 (1,620)	661 (300)	13,000 5,500	29 43
Great Britain	Netherlands destroyers	21in (533mm)	3,630 (1,650)	770 (350)	13,000 4,400	28 45
USA	Old destroyers, PT-boats	21 Mark 8 (533mm)	3,050 (1,386)	466 (212)	14,000	27
USA	AA cruisers, modern destroyers	21 Mark 15 (533mm)	3,840 (1,745)	825 (375)	15,000 6,000	26.5 45
USSR	Destroyers and submarines	21 Model 38 (533mm)	3,542 (1,610)	660 (300)	13,000 4,400	28.5 43.5
Germany	All surface ships and submarines	21 G7A T1 (533mm)	3,362 (1,528)	660 (300)	15,300 6,500	30 44
Germany	E-boats and submarines	21 G7A T2 (533mm) (battery-powered)	3,527 (1,603)	660 (300)	5,500	30
Italy	Cruisers and destroyers; also used by USSR	21 W or SI 270 (533mm)	3,740 (1,700)	595 (270)	13,000 4,400	30 48
Japan	Old destroyers and submarines	21 Type 89 (533mm)	3,670 (1,668)	661 (300)	11,000 6,000	35 45
Italy	Aircraft – circling torpedo; also used by Germany	19.7 (500mm)	772 (350)	264 (120)	16,400 (reducing to 4kts)	13.5
Great Britain	Aircraft, MTBs	18 Mark XII (457mm)	1,548 (704)	388 (176)	3,500 1,500	29 40
Great Britain	Aircraft, MTBs	18 Mark XV (457mm)	1,800 (819)	545 (247)	3,500 2,500	33 40
USSR	Aircraft	17.7 Model 36AN (450mm)	2,024 (920)	550 (250)	4,000	40
Germany	Aircraft	17.7 F5b (457mm)	1,786 (812)	551 (250)	2,200	40
Italy	Torpedo-boats, MAS-boats	17.7 W 200 (457mm)	2,046 (930)	440 (200)	8,800 3,300	30 44
Italy	Aircraft – also used by Germany	17.7 Type W (457mm)	1,990 (905)	441 (200)	3,300	40
Japan	Aircraft – Mitsubishi G3M 'Nell' and Nakajima B5N 'Kate'	17.7 Type 91, Mod 1 (450mm)	1,725 (784)	330 (150)	2,200	41
Japan	Aircraft – Mitsubishi G4M 'Betty'	17.7 Type 91, Mod 2 (450mm)	2,060 (935)	451 (205)	2,200	43

TORPEDOES: SUBMARINE-LAUNCHED

Country	Ship	Calibre in (mm)	Torpedo Weight lb (kg)	Warhead Weight lb (kg)	Range at yds	Speed kts
France	All submarines	21.65 Model 24 (550mm)	3,278 (1,490)	682 (310)	7,500 3,300	35 45
Great Britain	All submarines	21 Mark IV (see above)			6,000	35
Great Britain	All submarines	21 Mark VIII** (533mm)	3,450 (1,568)	805 (366)	7,000 5,000	41 45.5

Country	Ship	Calibre in (mm)	Torpedo Weight lb (kg)	Warhead Weight lb (kg)	Range at yds	Speed kts
USA	'S'-class	21 Mark 10 (533mm)	2,215 (1,007)	497 (226)	3,500	36
USA	Modern submarines	21 Mark 14 (533mm)	3,280 (1,490)	643 (292	9,000 4,500	31 46
USSR		21 Model 38, Type 3 (see above)				
Germany		21 G7a & G7e (see above)				
Germany	Submarines and E-boats	21 T.5 'Zaunkönig' (533mm)	3,290 (1,497)	660 (300)	6,200	25
Italy	All submarines	21 W 270V (533mm)	3,740 (1,700)	594 (270)	4,000 13,000	50 30
Japan		21 Type 89 (see above)				
Japan	Modern submarines	21 Type 95 (533mm)	3,663 (1,665)	890 (405)	13,000 9,000	45 51
USA	Submarines – anti-escort homing torpedo	19 Mark 27 (483mm)	720 (327)	95 (43)	5,000	12

French and Italian submarines carried 17.7in (450mm) torpedoes in addition to their larger weapons but these weapons were intended primarily for use against merchant ships and do not appear to have been employed successfully against warships.

Theatres of War

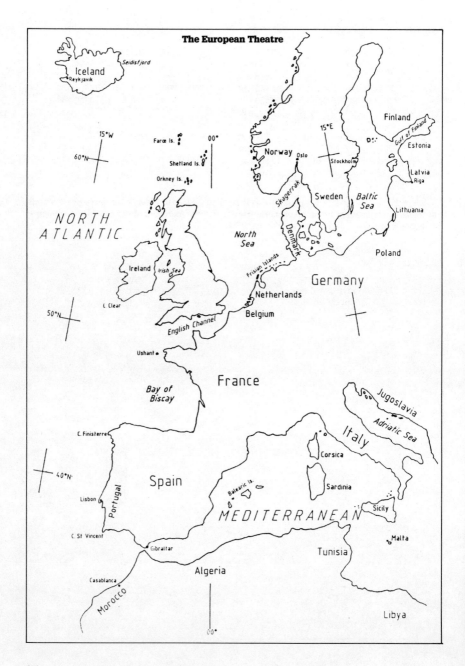

The European Theatre

The Western Baltic saw the first naval losses of the war and the last large-scale losses in the European theatre. Although Denmark (mainland and islands) acted as an effective barrier to any Anglo-French operations in support of Poland, it was no obstacle to the German Navy, which could transfer ships between the North Sea and Baltic via the *Kaiser Wilhelm Kanal*, better known elsewhere as the 'Kiel Canal'.

The North Sea was extensively mined by the German and British navies, effectively placing it out of bounds to operations by heavy surface units for the duration of the war. Although submarines scored some successes during the first year, offensive action thereafter was left mainly to the opposing air forces.

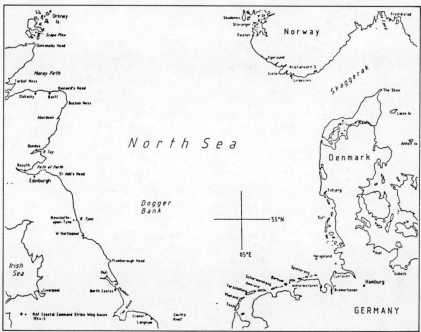

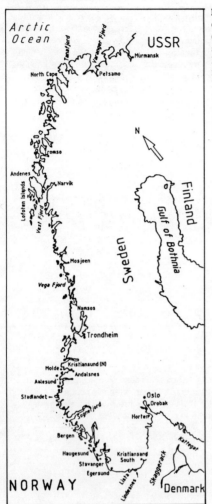

Norway lacked internal 'lines of communication' and by deciding upon the simultaneous occupation of half a dozen ports along 1,000 miles of coast the German Navy was forced to expose itself to the far greater strength of the Royal Navy's Home Fleet, which was based barely 400 miles distant.

The head of Ofot Fjord was the scene of two engagements which cost the German Navy ten of its large destroyers, unable to escape owing to lack of fuel.

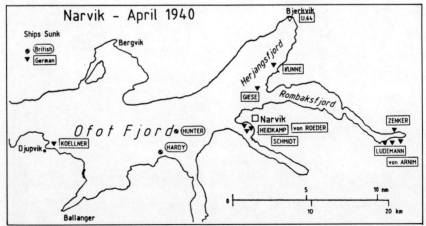

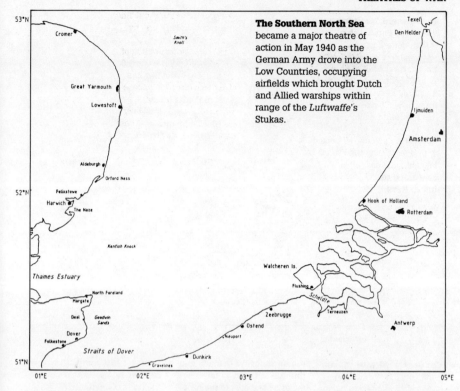

The Southern North Sea became a major theatre of action in May 1940 as the German Army drove into the Low Countries, occupying airfields which brought Dutch and Allied warships within range of the *Luftwaffe*'s Stukas.

The Route between Dunkirk and Dover was complicated by the lines of shallows off the French coast, preventing the evacuating ships from seeking sea-room to escape the dive-bombers and providing identifiable turning points at which the laden vessels could be ambushed by 'E-boats'.

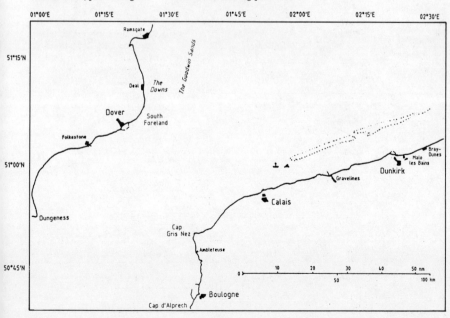

The Western Mediterranean, from Cape Bon to Gibraltar, was the operational responsibility of the French Navy until the fall of France. With the entry into the war of Italy, this area was transformed from a 'backwater' into a major maritime 'front', with the Royal Navy's Force 'H' tasked with neutralizing the French Fleet at Oran as well as containing the Italian Navy.

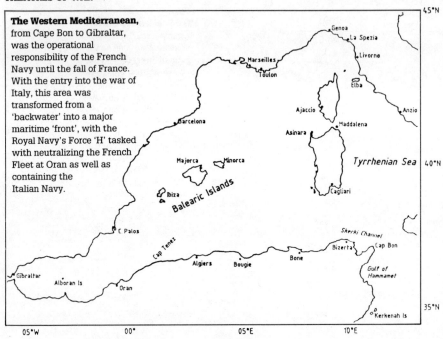

The Central Mediterranean traffic, north-south for the Italian Navy supplying its North African army, and west-east for the Royal Navy running convoys to Malta and through to Egypt, created two major crossroads, to the east and west of Malta. The majority of both sides' losses between 1940 and 1943 were suffered on the routes and in the ports of destination in the area depicted in this plan.

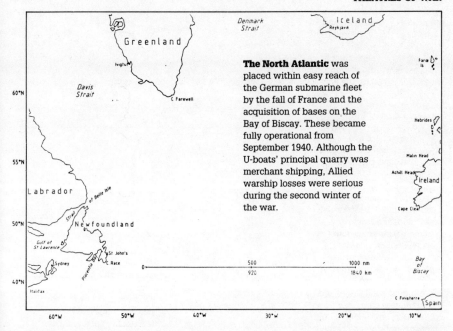

The North Atlantic was placed within easy reach of the German submarine fleet by the fall of France and the acquisition of bases on the Bay of Biscay. These became fully operational from September 1940. Although the U-boats' principal quarry was merchant shipping, Allied warship losses were serious during the second winter of the war.

The arrival of the *Luftwaffe* on Sicilian and North African airfields in early 1941 resulted in a dramatic increase in the number of Allied warships sunk or severely damaged. In the **Eastern Mediterranean**, the majority of the 57 Allied losses between June 1940 and October 1943 were due to air attack at sea. The Axis, on the other hand, lost eight ships in harbour to air attack and the 17 sunk in the open sea were mostly the victims of surface or submarine action.

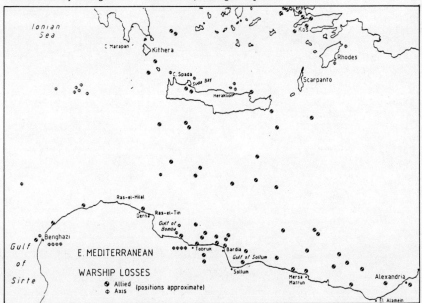

The Red Sea base at Massawa should have enabled the Italian Navy to interdict effectively the vital British supply route to the Suez Canal, upon which the Allied campaign in the Western Desert depended almost entirely. In the event, the destroyer flotilla seldom sortied and the submarines achieved very little before, in April 1941, the base was overrun by ground forces and the destroyers put to sea for a last effort, which ended in four of the six ships being scuttled off neutral Saudi Arabia.

Greece and the Aegean came within range of the *Luftwaffe* in April 1941, and by the end of May the Allies had been driven from the mainland, the minor islands and Crete with very heavy losses. When, two and a half years later, they returned to attempt to occupy the Italian-owned Dodecanese Islands, the German Air Force demonstrated off Kos, Leros and Kalymnos that it had lost little of its skill against ships without air cover.

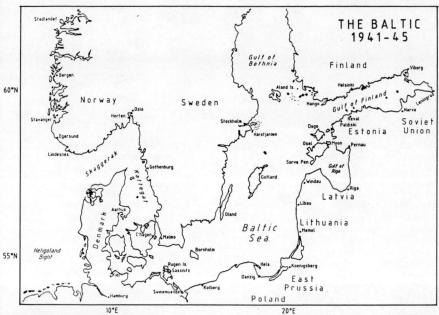

THE BALTIC
1941-45

The Baltic was a 'backwater' between October 1939 and June 1941, when Germany invaded the Soviet Union. From the outset, the opposing navies' primary role was support of the land battle, the Russians falling back as the German army swept through the Baltic States, supplied and supported by the German Navy.

The Gulf of Finland was reached in August 1941, and late in the month the Finnish Navy gave a dramatic demonstration of offensive minelaying, which cost the Soviet Navy nine ships in two days as they attempted to evacuate the encircled garrison of Reval. From beginning to end, mines were to be the most common cause of loss both to the Axis partners and to the Russians in these shallow and constricted waters.

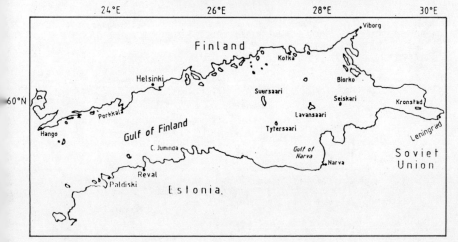

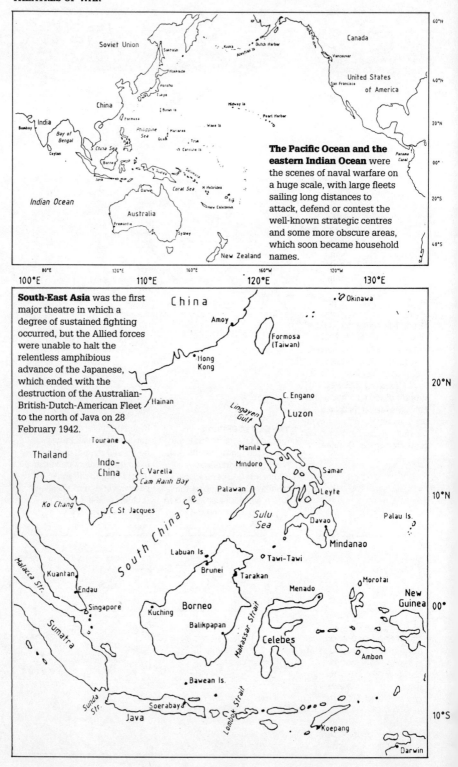

The Pacific Ocean and the eastern Indian Ocean were the scenes of naval warfare on a huge scale, with large fleets sailing long distances to attack, defend or contest the well-known strategic centres and some more obscure areas, which soon became household names.

South-East Asia was the first major theatre in which a degree of sustained fighting occurred, but the Allied forces were unable to halt the relentless amphibious advance of the Japanese, which ended with the destruction of the Australian-British-Dutch-American Fleet to the north of Java on 28 February 1942.

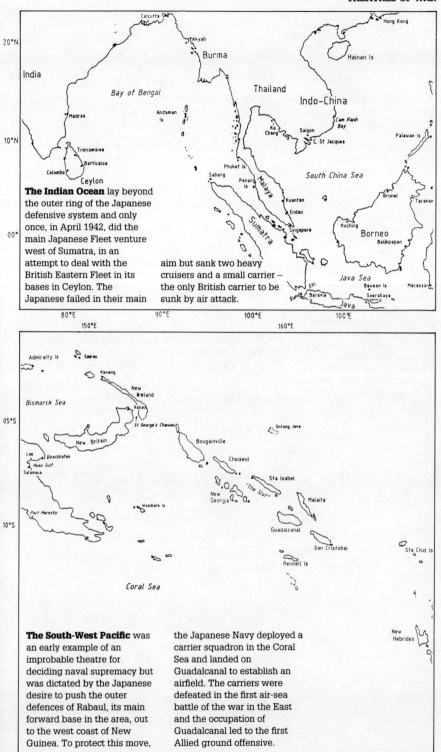

20°N

Calcutta

Hong Kong

Akyab

Burma

Hainan Is

India

Thailand

Indo-China

Bay of Bengal

Cam Ranh Bay

10°N

Madras

Andaman Is

Ko Chang

Saigon

C. St Jacques

Palawan Is

Trincomalee

Batticaloa

Colombo

Ceylon

Phuket Is

Sabang

Penang Is

Malaya

South China Sea

Brunei

Tarakan

00°

Kuantan

Kuching

Endau

Singapore

Borneo

Balikpapan

Sumatra

Java Sea

Str.

Bawean Is

Macassar

Sunda

Baravia

Soerabaya

Java

80°E   90°E   100°E   100°E

The Indian Ocean lay beyond the outer ring of the Japanese defensive system and only once, in April 1942, did the main Japanese Fleet venture west of Sumatra, in an attempt to deal with the British Eastern Fleet in its bases in Ceylon. The Japanese failed in their main aim but sank two heavy cruisers and a small carrier – the only British carrier to be sunk by air attack.

150°E   160°E

Admiralty Is   Emirau

Kavieng

New Ireland

Bismarck Sea

Rabaul

05°S

St George's Channel

Ontong Java

New Britain

Bougainville

Lae   Finschhafen

Huon Gulf

Salamaua

Choiseul

Sta Isabel

New Georgia

"The Slot"

Malaita

Port Moresby

Woodlark Is

Guadalcanal

10°S

San Cristobal

Sta Cruz Is

Rennell Is

Coral Sea

New Hebrides

The South-West Pacific was an early example of an improbable theatre for deciding naval supremacy but was dictated by the Japanese desire to push the outer defences of Rabaul, its main forward base in the area, out to the west coast of New Guinea. To protect this move, the Japanese Navy deployed a carrier squadron in the Coral Sea and landed on Guadalcanal to establish an airfield. The carriers were defeated in the first air-sea battle of the war in the East and the occupation of Guadalcanal led to the first Allied ground offensive.

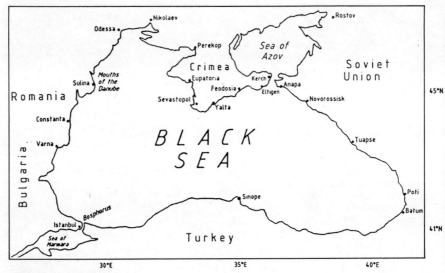

Black Sea operations were one-sided in that only the Soviet Navy sustained losses to major warships. The Axis spring 1942 offensive resulted in the German occupation of the north coast and brought the more distant Soviet naval bases within the reach of long-range bombers.

The Approaches to the Sicilian Channel saw intense activity during the Royal Navy's operations to relieve Malta. The most hard-fought convoy battles occurred in June and August 1942, with the Axis air forces and the Italian Navy forcing the heavily-escorted merchant ships to run a 300-mile gauntlet, with no assurance of safety on reaching the destination.

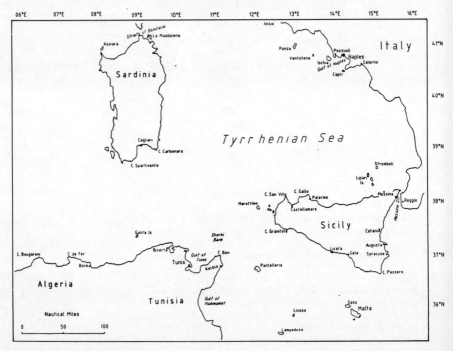

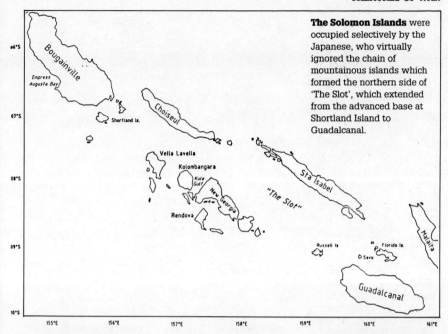

The Solomon Islands were occupied selectively by the Japanese, who virtually ignored the chain of mountainous islands which formed the northern side of 'The Slot', which extended from the advanced base at Shortland Island to Guadalcanal.

The Sicilian Channel. The French colony of Tunisia remained neutral until November 1942, when it was occupied by the Axis, but its territorial waters around the corner between Zembra Island and Kelibia were not respected by either side up to that date. Thereafter, most of the losses fell upon the Italian Navy as it attempted to run supplies to Tunis, losing ships to aircraft close inshore, to mines on the Skerki Bank and to submarines and surface ships as they skirted the Bank to avoid the minefields.

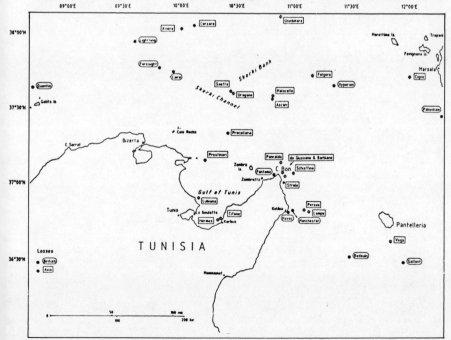

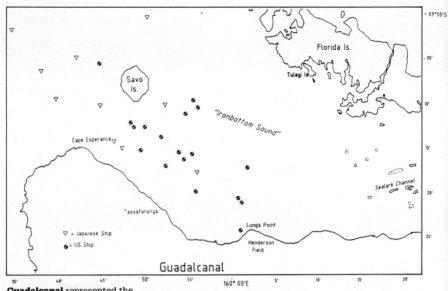

Guadalcanal

Guadalcanal represented the extreme limit of Japanese expansion in the south-west Pacific and was the scene of a four-month battle of attrition. The US Navy lost the more ships but was better able to replace matériel and personnel casualties.

The Adriatic, in which only Allied submarines had been able to operate between April 1941 and September 1943, became a theatre of general naval operations after the Italian surrender, the Allied navies supporting the armies as they advanced up the Italian peninsula and the coastal activities of the Yugoslav *Partisans*.

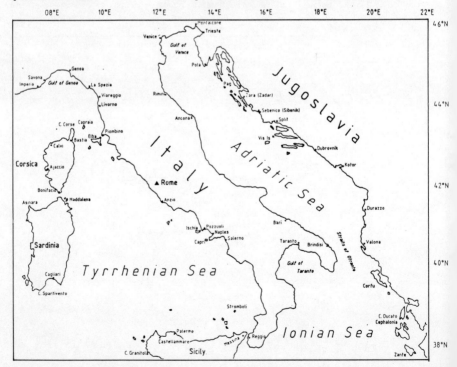

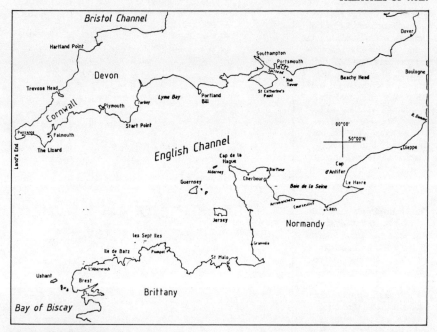

The English Channel was a major battleground from the summer of 1940, but most of the casualties were inflicted by air attack and mine. In October 1943, the Royal Navy lost a modern AA cruiser (HMS *Charybdis*) in a night surface action off the coast of Brittany and was discouraged from committing large ships to the area until the Normandy invasion.

The Normandy Landings. In view of the size and importance of the enterprise, Allied losses during the twelve weeks following the landings between Ouistreham and Quineville were not excessive. Apart from a small cluster of US Navy losses off 'Utah' Beach in the opening days, most were suffered by the Royal Navy and its Allies on or near the eastern sector, where they were exposed to a heavier scale of attack, from air-dropped mines and the German 'Small Battle Units' which were launched from Houlgate and the coast around to Le Havre.

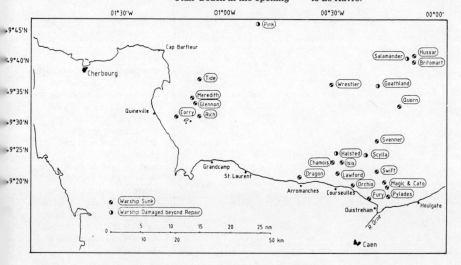

The West Coast of France was isolated from the rest of German-controlled north-west Europe by the Allied capture of Normandy. The substantial numbers of destroyers and minesweepers were hunted down relentlessly by Royal Navy and Royal Canadian Navy destroyers and MTBs and, by day, by RAF Coastal Command's Strike Wings, which could reach as far as the Gironde estuary.

The Philippine Islands had been taken by the Japanese with little opposition from the US Navy and their recapture had a symbolic significance almost as great as their strategic value. Appropriately, the first assault, on Leyte Island, initiated the war's greatest and last series of naval battles, on a 600-mile 'front' extending from the Sulu Sea to Cape Engano.

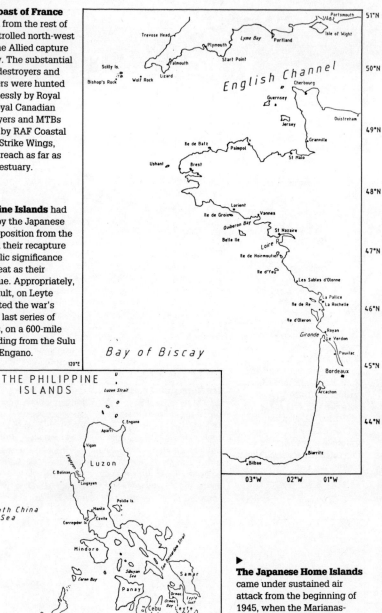

The Japanese Home Islands came under sustained air attack from the beginning of 1945, when the Marianas-based USAAF B-29s began to inflict serious industrial damage. Carrier aircraft operated occasionally, during brief but destructive strikes, up to July 1945, when they too began sustained intensive operations, in the course of which most of the surviving serviceable units of the Imperial Japanese Navy were destroyed.

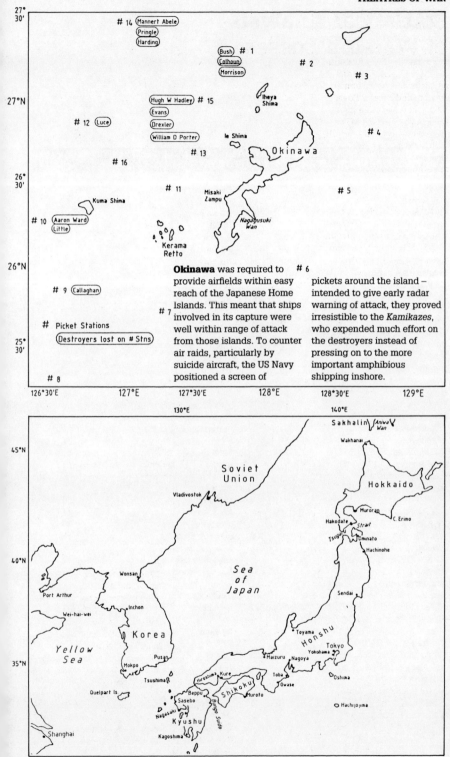

27°30'
14 (Mannert Abele)
(Pringle)
(Harding)

(Bush) # 1
(Colhoun)
(Morrison)

2

3

27°N
(Hugh W Hadley) # 15
(Evans)
(Drexler)
(William D Porter)

Iheya Shima

12 (Luce)

le Shima

4

Okinawa

13

16

26°30'
11
Misaki Zampu

5

Kuma Shima

Nagagusuki Wan

10 (Aaron Ward)
(Little)

Kerama Retto

26°N

Okinawa was required to provide airfields within easy reach of the Japanese Home Islands. This meant that ships involved in its capture were well within range of attack from those islands. To counter air raids, particularly by suicide aircraft, the US Navy positioned a screen of # 6 pickets around the island – intended to give early radar warning of attack, they proved irresistible to the *Kamikazes*, who expended much effort on the destroyers instead of pressing on to the more important amphibious shipping inshore.

7

9 (Callaghan)

Picket Stations
(Destroyers lost on # Stns)

25°30'

8

126°30'E   127°E   127°30'E   128°E   128°30'E   129°E

130°E   140°E

45°N

Sakhalin Aniva Wan

Wakhanai

Soviet Union

Hokkaido

Vladivostok

Muroran
C. Erimo

Hakodate
Strait
Tsugaru
Oomnato
Hachinohe

40°N

Sea of Japan

Wonsan

Sendai

Port Arthur

Wei-hai-wei

Inchon

Korea

Toyama

Honshu

Tokyo
Yokohama

35°N

Yellow Sea

Pusan

Maizuru
Nagoya

Mokpo

Quelpart Is.

Tsushima

Hiroshima
Kure
Toba

Shikoku

Owasi

Oshima

Beppu
Sasebo

Bungo Suido

Muroto

Nagasaki

Kyushu

Hachijojima

Shanghai

Kagoshima

Statistical Analysis of Warship Losses

WARSHIP LOSSES BY ENEMY ACTION AND NOT INCLUDING SCUTTLING, CAPTURE OR INTERNMENT 1939–1945 (TOTAL: 1,454)

By Type

Carriers		47
Cruisers		110
Other major		78
capital ships	*36*	
AMCs	*28*	
coast defence	*8*	
auxiliary AA ships	*5*	
seaplane tender	*1*	
Destroyer types		545
destroyers	*446*	
leaders	*14*	
escort destroyers	*85*	
Torpedo-boats		118
Escorts		252
frigates, etc.	*130*	
sloops	*40*	
corvettes	*54*	
gunboats	*28*	
Mine Warfare		276
minesweepers	*227*	
minelayers	*37*	
fast minecraft	*13*	
(ex-destroyers, USN)		
Fast Transports		29
(ex-destroyers, USN, IJN)		
Total		1,454

By Area

Atlantic		108
NW Europe		213
(Biscay, Channel, N Sea)		
Norway & Arctic		79
Mediterranean		332
(including Adriatic)		
SE Asia		227
(E Indies, S China Sea, Philippines)		
Indian Ocean		25
(inc. Red Sea & Gulf)		
SW Pacific		105
(Solomons & New Guinea)		
Japanese Empire		163
(Taiwan, NE China, Japan)		
Pacific Areas		78
Baltic and Black Sea		126

By Country

Royal Navies	359
US Navy	167
USSR	70
France	41
Netherlands	15
Norway	10
Poland	6
Greece	9
Germany	244
Italy	119
Japan	402
Neutrals & others	14

By Cause

Air attack		561
suicide	*45*	
air raid, inc. guided missiles	*88*	
Submarine torpedo		330
Surface action		262
gunfire & torpedo	*211*	
MTB torpedo	*41*	
ramming, artillery	*10*	
Mine		200
Accident		82
collision	*30*	
foundered	*11*	
stranded	*23*	
other: fire, etc.	*18*	
Miscellaneous		21
special forces	*8*	
human torpedo	*5*	
sabotage	*1*	
blockship	*2*	
not known	*5*	

By Year

1939	14
1940	129
1941	191
1942	259
1943	206
1944	401
1945	256
Total	1,454

MAJOR NAVIES

By Cause

	RN*	USN	Germany	Italy	Japan	USSR
Air attack	84	81	59	19	173	20
Air raid	10	–	51	21	1	–
Guided missile	5	–	–	1	–	–
Submarine torpedo	105	22	9	16	145	9
Gunfire & torpedo	29	30	50	24	39	1
MTB torpedo	11	1	19	1	3	3
Shore artillery	1	1	–	2	5	1
Mine	49	15	43	22	25	32
Special forces/human torpedo	7	1	–	3	1	–
Other or not known	1	–	2	–	3	2
Collision	6	5	5	3	2	–
Foundered	–	4	3	2	–	1
Stranded	5	4	1	4	4	1
Other accident	4	3	2	1	1	–
Total	315	167	244	119	402	70
Scuttled or captured	4	4	48	77	–	1
Total including scuttling, etc. (see page 236)	321	171	292	196	402	71

*Not including Dominion and Empire navies.

By Area

	RN*	USN	Germany	Italy	Japan	USSR
Atlantic	76	17	7	–	–	–
Arctic and Norway	27	–	36	–	–	9
NW Europe	94	6	92	–	–	–
Mediterranean	127	12	47	114	–	–
Baltic and Black Sea	–	–	58	–	–	61
Indian Ocean	12	1	2	5	1	–
SE Asia	20	30	–	–	161	–
SW Pacific	2	38	–	–	65	–
Pacific Ocean Areas	–	24	1	–	53	–
Japanese Empire	1	39	1	–	122	–
Total	356	167	244	119	402	70

*Including Dominion and Empire navies.

ATLANTIC

By Type

Carriers		4
Cruisers		2
Capital Ships		3
AMCs		16
Destroyer types		33
destroyers	*21*	
escort destroyers	*12*	
Torpedo boats		2
Escorts		42
frigates, etc.	*14*	
sloops	*10*	
corvettes	*18*	
Minesweepers		5
Auxiliary AA Ship		1
Total		108

By Country

Royal Navies		76
RCN	*16*	
US Navy		17
France		3
Norway		3
Poland		1
Germany		7
Argentina		1

By Cause

Air Attack		3
guided missile	*1*	
Submarine torpedo		73
Surface action		12
Mine		2
Accident		18
collision	*12*	
foundered	*1*	
stranded	*2*	
other: fire, etc.	*3*	

By Year

1939	3
1940	15
1941	23
1942	26
1943	17
1944	21
1945	3

Vital Statistics

7.43% of total losses

16.66% of all escort losses occurred in this theatre.

21.35% of all RN & Commonwealth losses occurred here.

22.12% of all vessels lost in this theatre were sunk by submarine.

40.00% of all losses by collision occurred here.

9.09% of all losses by marine cause (foundering, stranding).

NW EUROPE

By Type

Escort Carriers		2
Cruisers		4
Capital Ships		1
Destroyer types		68
destroyer-leaders	*3*	
destroyers	*45*	
escort destroyers	*20*	
Torpedo-boats		21
Escorts		36
frigates, etc.	*17*	
sloops	*6*	
corvettes	*9*	
gunboats	*4*	
Mine warfare		79
minesweepers	*78*	
minelayers	*1*	
Armed Merchant Cruiser		1
Auxiliary AA Ship		1
Total		212

By Country

Royal Navies	94
US Navy	6
France	13
Netherlands	5
Norway	2
Poland	1
Germany	92

By Cause

Air attack		82
direct attack	*56*	
air raid	*26*	
Submarine torpedo		21
Surface action		35
gunfire & torpedo	*18*	
MTB torpedo	*16*	
ramming	*1*	
Mine		55
Human torpedo		5

Accident		11
collision	5	
foundered	1	
stranded	2	
other: fire, etc.	3	
Expended as blockship		1
Sabotage		1

By Year

1939	6
1940	56
1941	5
1942	13
1943	15
1944	95
1945	22

Vital Statistics

14.58% of total losses.

27.50% of all mine losses occurred in this theatre.

34.07% of all minesweeper losses occurred here.

14.62% of all losses to air attack occurred here.

30.23% of all air raid losses inflicted in this theatre.

NORWAY AND ARCTIC

By Type

Carriers		2
Cruisers		7
Capital ships		2
Destroyer types		24
destroyer-leaders	1	
destroyers	22	
escort destroyers	1	
Torpedo-boats		3
Escorts		12
frigates, etc.	5	
sloops	3	
corvettes	3	
gunboats	1	
Mine warfare		27
minesweepers	25	
minelayers	2	
Coast defence ships		2
Total		79

By Country

Royal Navy	27
USSR	9
France	1
Norway	5
Poland	1
Germany	36

By Cause

Air attack		22
direct attack	21	
air raid	1	
Submarine torpedo		20
Surface action		30
gunfire & torpedo	27	
MTB torpedo	3	
Mine		4
Accident		3
collision	1	
foundered	1	
stranded	1	

By Year

1940	29
1941	4
1942	12
1943	3
1944	20
1945	11

Vital Statistics

5.43% of total losses.

11.41% of surface action losses occurred in this theatre.

Highest proportion of surface losses (37.97%) in European theatre.

MEDITERRANEAN AREAS

By Type

Carriers		2
Cruisers		35
Capital ships		7
Destroyer types		149
destroyer-leaders	*6*	
destroyers	*116*	
escort destroyers	*27*	
Torpedo-boats		61
Escorts		46
frigates, etc.	*3*	
sloops	*14*	
corvettes	*21*	
gunboats	*8*	
Mine warfare		28
minesweepers	*20*	
minelayers	*8*	
Auxiliary AA ships		2
Coast defence ships		2
Total		331

By Country

Royal Navies		127
RAN & RCN	*5*	
US Navy		12
Greece		9
France		20
Morocco	*10*	
Netherlands		1
Poland		1
Italy		114
Germany		47
Yugoslav		1

By Cause

Air attack		131
direct attack	*91*	
air raid	*35*	
ASM	*5*	
Submarine torpedo		56
Surface action		71
gunfire & torpedo	*55*	
MTB torpedo	*13*	
artillery	*3*	
Mine		51
Special forces		6
frogmen, etc.		
Accident		17
foundered	*2*	
stranded	*6*	
collision	*4*	
other: fire, etc.	*5*	

By Year

1939	1
1940	26
1941	77
1942	76
1943	96
1944	45
1945	11

Vital Statistics

22.76% of total losses.

25.50% of all mine losses occurred in this theatre.

27.27% of all losses by stranding occurred here.

35.39% of all RN & Commonwealth losses took place in this theatre.

46.57% of all ships lost in 1943 were lost in the Mediterranean.

E INDIES, S CHINA SEA AND PHILIPPINES

By Type

Carriers		10
Cruisers		28
Capital ships		5
Destroyer types		77
destroyers	*70*	
escort destroyers	*7*	
Torpedo-boats		9
Coast defence ships		2
Escorts		49
frigates, etc.	*34*	
sloops	*3*	
corvettes	*3*	
gunboats	*9*	
Mine warfare		37
fast minecraft – M/S	*3*	
minesweepers	*26*	
minelayers	*8*	
Fast transports		8
Armed merchant cruiser		1
Seaplane tender		1
Total		227

By Country

Royal Navies	20
US Navy	30
France	2
Netherlands	9
Japan	161
Thai	5

By Cause

Air attack		95
'conventional'	*84*	
Kamikaze	*10*	
air raid	*1*	
Submarine torpedo		71
Surface action		45
gunfire & torpedo	*39*	
MTB torpedo	*2*	
artillery	*4*	
Mine		10
Special forces		2
Accident		4
collision	*1*	
stranded	*3*	

By Year

1939	nil
1940	nil
1941	14
1942	38
1943	5
1944	119
1945	51

Vital Statistics

15.61% of total losses.

16.93% of losses to air attack occurred in this theatre.

21.28% of all carrier losses occurred in this theatre.

25.45% of all cruiser losses occured in this theatre.

INDIAN OCEAN

By Type

Carriers	1
Cruisers	3
Destroyers	8
Torpedo-boat	1
Escorts	6
Minesweepers	1
Armed merchant cruisers	5
Total	25

By Country

Royal Navies		12
RN	*8*	
RAN	*3*	
RIN	*1*	
USN		1
France		2
Germany		2
Italy		5
Japan		1
Iran		2

By Cause

Air attack		13
direct attack	*12*	
air raid	*1*	
Submarine torpedo		1
Surface action		7
gunfire & torpedo	*7*	
Mine		1
Accident		3
collision	*1*	
stranded	*1*	
other: fire, etc.	*1*	

By Year

1940	3
1941	9
1942	12
1943	1

Vital Statistic

1.72% of WWII losses.

SW PACIFIC

By Type

Carriers		8
Cruisers		16
Capital ships		2
Destroyer types		68
destroyers	*66*	
escort destroyers	*2*	
Mine warfare		6
minesweepers	*2*	
minelayers	*4*	
Destroyer transports		4
Armed merchant cruiser		1
Total		105

By Country

RAN	2
US Navy	38
Japan	65

By Cause

Air attack		38
direct attack	*38*	
Submarine torpedo		11
Surface action		46
gunfire & torpedo	*45*	
MTB torpedo	*1*	
Mine		5
Accident		5
collision	*2*	
stranded	*3*	

By Year

1942	53
1943	47
1944	5
1945	nil

Vital Statistics

7.22% of total losses.

17.50% of all surface action losses occurred in this theatre.

Highest proportion of surface action losses (43.80%) in any theatre.

Lowest proportion of losses to mine (4.76%) in any major theatre.

JAPANESE EMPIRE

By Type

Carriers		7
Cruisers		5
Capital ships		6
Destroyer types		48
destroyers	*38*	
escort destroyers	*10*	
Torpedo-boats		3
Coast defence ships		1
Escorts		50
frigates, etc.	*47*	
gunboats	*3*	
Mine warfare		30
fast minecraft – M/S	*4*	
minesweepers	*15*	
fast minecraft – ML	*2*	
minelayers	*9*	
Fast transports		12
Armed merchant cruiser		1
Total		163

By Country

RN	1
US Navy	39
Japan	122
Germany	1

By Cause

Air attack		94
direct attack	*60*	
Kamikaze	*34*	
Submarine torpedo		46
Surface action		2
gunfire & torpedo	*2*	
Mine		15
Accident		3
stranded	*1*	
other: fire, etc.	*2*	
Not known		3

By Year

1941	1
1942	2
1943	8
1944	26
1945	126

Vital Statistics

11.21% of total losses.

74.60% of all losses in this theatre resulted from air attack – some 16.8% of the overall air attack losses.

75.55% of losses to suicide attack occurred in this theatre.

30.35% of Japanese losses to all causes occurred here.

PACIFIC OCEAN AREAS

By Type

Carriers		11
Cruisers		7
Capital ships		5
Destroyer types		32
destroyers	*26*	
escort destroyers	*6*	
Torpedo-boats		1
Escorts		5
frigates, etc.	*5*	
Mine warfare		9
fast minecraft – M/S	*2*	
minesweepers	*2*	
fast minecraft – ML	*2*	
minelayers	*3*	
Fast transports		5
Armed merchant cruisers		3
Total		78

By Country

US Navy	24
Japan	53
Germany	1

By Cause

Air attack		34
direct attack	*33*	
Kamikaze	*1*	
Submarine torpedo		28
Surface action		6
gunfire & torpedo	*4*	
artillery	*2*	
Mine		3
Accident		7
collision	*2*	
foundered	*3*	
stranded	*1*	
other: fire, etc.	*1*	

By Year

1941	13
1942	11
1943	7
1944	43
1945	4

Vital Statistics

5.36% of total losses.
23.40% of all aircraft carrier losses occurred in this theatre.

BALTIC AND BLACK SEA

By Type

Capital ships		5
Cruisers		3
Coast defence ship		1
Destroyer types		38
destroyer-leaders	*4*	
destroyers	*34*	
Torpedo-boats		17
Escorts		6
gunboats	*3*	
Mine warfare		55
minesweepers	*53*	
minelayers	*2*	
Auxiliary AA ship		1
Total		126
(20 in Black Sea – All USSR)		

By Country

USSR	61
Poland	2
Germany	58
Finland	1
Denmark	1
Sweden	3

By Cause

Air attack		49
direct attack	*31*	
air raid	*18*	
Submarine torpedo		3
Surface action		8
gunfire & torpedo	*1*	
MTB torpedo	*6*	
artillery	*1*	
Mine		54
Accident		10
collision	*2*	
foundered	*3*	
stranded	*2*	
other: fire, etc.	*3*	
Not known		2

By Year

1939	4
1940	nil
1941	45
1942	16
1943	6
1944	27
1945	28

Vital Statistics

8.66% of total losses.
39% of losses in this theatre resulted from air attack.
Mine losses in this theatre constitute 19.6% of the war total.

WARSHIPS SCUTTLED, CAPTURED AND INTERNED

Scuttled		155
Captured		78
Interned		5
Total		238

By Type

Capital ships		4
Cruisers		13
Destroyer types		79
destroyers	*51*	
leaders	*20*	
escort destroyers	*8*	
Torpedo-boats		52
Escorts		49
sloops	*27*	
corvettes	*18*	
gunboats	*4*	
Mine warfare		35
minesweepers	*26*	
minelayers	*9*	
Coast defence ships		3
Miscellaneous		3

By Navy

Royal Navy	3
US Navy	4
Norway	9
Netherlands	6
Greece	1
Yugoslavia	18
USSR	1
France	65
Latvia	1
Lithuania	1
Denmark	4
Italy	77
Germany	48
Japan	nil

By Year

1940	21
1941	27
1942	68
1943	77
1944	18
1945	27

Vital Statistics

9.63% of all ships lost from all causes were scuttled by their own crews.

12.68% of all ships lost of destroyer type were scuttled or captured.

27.40% of all ships lost in 1943 were scuttled, captured or interned.

39.30% of all Italian losses were due to scuttling, capture or internment.

60.75% of all French losses were due to scuttling or capture.

Indexes

Index of Principal Battles and Actions

Index of Ship Names

Throughout this index, the first page reference is to the Chronology of Warship Losses; the second, in *italic*, is to the Summary of Warship Classes and Particulars

Key to Countries

Arg	Argentina	Neth	Netherlands
Cr	Croatia	Nor	Norway
Den	Denmark	Pol	Poland
Fin	Finland	RAN	Australia
Fr	France	RCN	Canada
Ger	Germany	RIN	India
Gre	Greece	RN	United Kingdom
IJN	Japan	Swe	Sweden
It	Italy	Thai	Thailand
Ir-	Iran	USN	United States
Li	Lithuania	USSR	Soviet Union
Lv	Latvia	Yug	Yugoslavia

Key to Ship Types

AAA	Anti-aircraft ship ('auxiliary')
AMC	Armed Merchant Cruiser or merchant raider
AO	Oiler
APD	Fast transport
AV	Seaplane tender
BB	Battleship
BBL	Battlecruiser
BC	Coast defence ship
BM	Monitor
CA	Heavy cruiser
CCB	Pocket battleship
CGC	Coast guard cutter
CL	Light cruiser
CLAA	Anti-aircraft cruiser
CLT	Training cruiser
CORV	Corvette
CV	Fleet aircraft carrier
CVE	Escort carrier
CVS	Seaplane carrier
DD	Destroyer
DDE	Escort destroyer
DE	Destroyer escort
DL	Flotilla leader/destroyer leader
DM	Destroyer-minelayer
DMS	Destroyer-minesweeper
FF	Frigate or escort
ML	Minelayer
M/S	Minesweeper
OCL	Old cruiser
PB	Patrol boat
PG	Gunboat
PR	River gunboat
SLP	Sloop or aviso
TB	Torpedo-boat
